MUST KNOW SAT

Cynthia Knable

Mc Graw Hill

New York Chicago San Francisco Athens London Madrid
Mexico City Milan New Delhi Singapore Sydney Toronto

1 2 3 4 5 6 7 8 9   LCR   26 25 24 23 22 21

ISBN   978-1-264-25854-3
MHID   1-264-25854-2

e-ISBN   978-1-264-25855-0
e-MHID   1-264-25855-0

Interior design by Steve Straus of Think Book Works.
Cover and letter art by Kate Rutter.

McGraw Hill books are available at special quantity discounts to use as premiums and sales promotions or for use in corporate training programs. To contact a representative, please visit the Contact Us pages at www.mhprofessional.com.

Contents

PRACTICE TESTS ANSWER KEYS

Introduction

Welcome to your new SAT book! Let us try to explain why we believe you've made the right choice. This probably isn't your first rodeo with either a textbook or other kind of study guide. You've probably had your fill of books asking you to memorize lots of terms. This book isn't going to do that—although you're welcome to memorize anything you take an interest in. You may also have found that a lot of books jump the gun and make a lot of promises about all the things you'll be able to accomplish by the time you reach the end of a given chapter. In the process, those books can make you feel as though you missed out on the building blocks that you actually need to master those goals.

With *Must Know SAT,* we've taken a different approach. When you start a new chapter, right off the bat you will immediately see one or more **must know** ideas. These are the essential concepts behind what you are going to study, and they will form the foundation of what you will learn throughout the chapter. With these **must know** ideas, you will have what you need to hold it together as you study, and they will be your guide as you make your way through each chapter.

To build on this foundation, you will find easy-to-follow discussions of the topic at hand, and these are accompanied by comprehensive examples that show you how to apply what you're learning to solve typical SAT questions. Each chapter ends with review questions—more than 300 throughout the book—that are designed to instill confidence as you practice your new skills.

This book has other features that will help you on this SAT journey of yours. It has a number of sidebars that will either provide helpful information or just serve as a quick break from your studies. The 𝔹𝕋𝕎 sidebars ("by the way") point out important information, as well as tell you what to be careful about SAT-wise. Every once in a while, an ⊕IRL sidebar ("in real life") will tell you what you're studying has to do with the real world; other IRLs may just be interesting factoids.

In addition, this book is accompanied by a flashcard app that will give you the ability to test yourself at any time. The app includes more than 100 "flashcards" with a review question on one "side" and the answer on the other. You can either work through the flashcards by themselves or use them alongside the book. To find out where to get the app and how to use it, go to "The Flashcard App."

Before you get started, though, let me introduce you to your guide throughout this book. Cynthia Knable has more than 20 years of experience in writing and editing test prep guides (which may sound familiar if you read the back cover). She has a clear idea about what you should get out of an SAT Prep guide and has developed strategies to help you get there. She also has seen the kinds of trouble that students can run into, and she is an experienced hand at solving those difficulties. In this book, she applies that experience both to showing you the most effective way to learn a given concept as well as how to extricate yourself from traps you may have fallen into. She will be a trustworthy guide as you expand your SAT knowledge and develop new skills.

Before we leave you to your author's capable guidance, let us give you one piece of advice. Although we know that saying something "is the worst" is a cliché, if anything about the SAT is the worst, it's formal SAT guides. Let your new teacher introduce you to the **must know** concepts and show you how to apply them confidently to your SAT problems. Mastering SAT questions will give you an invaluable advantage for the rest of your academic career.

Good luck with your studies!

The Editors at McGraw Hill

The Flashcard App

This book features a bonus flashcard app. It will help you test yourself on what you've learned as you make your way through the book (or in and out). It includes 100-plus "flashcards," both "front" and "back." It gives you two options as to how to use it. You can jump right into the app and start from any point that you want. Or you can take advantage of the handy QR codes at the end of each chapter in the book; they will take you directly to the flashcards related to what you're studying at the moment.

To take advantage of this bonus feature, follow these easy steps:

Search for *Must Know* App from
either Google Play or the App Store.

↓

Download the app to your smartphone or tablet.

↓

Once you've got the app,
you can use it in either of two ways.

↙ ↘

Just open the app and you're ready to go.	Use your phone's QR Code reader to scan any of the book's QR codes.
You can start at the beginning, or select any of the chapters listed.	You'll be taken directly to the flashcards that match your chapter of choice.

↘ ↙

Get ready to test your SAT knowledge!

Introducing the SAT® Test

Welcome to McGraw Hill's *Must Know SAT*. Congratulations on choosing a preparation guide from America's leading educational publisher. When your preparation time is tight but you still want a thorough subject review and plenty of practice, this book is your best choice.

This chapter will give you a brief introduction to the SAT. You'll find out:

- The purpose and structure of the SAT

- How to register for the SAT

- How the tests are scored

- Test-taking tips

- How to use this book to prepare yourself

The Purpose and Structure of the SAT

The SAT is a program run by a nonprofit organization called the College Board. The SAT tests you on skills and concepts you have learned in school. Your score on the SAT is one of the factors—along with your high school grades, recommendations, and extracurricular activities—colleges and universities will consider when making an admission decision. The current version of the SAT debuted in the spring of 2016.

Here's what you need to know about the structure of the test:

- There is an Evidence-Based Reading and Writing section and a Math section. You can earn a score between 200 and 800 for each section for a maximum total of 1600.

- Beginning in June of 2021, there will be no Essay portion of the test.

- You may have the option of taking a paper-and-pencil test or taking a computer-based version of the test.

- There is no guessing penalty, so be sure to answer every question. You won't lose anything by guessing, and that's good news.

- There are four answer choices for each multiple-choice question.

- The test lasts for 180 minutes, not including breaks.

The Evidence-Based Reading and Writing Test

The passages on the Evidence-Based Reading and Writing test are drawn not just from literature, but from history and science. You will see charts and graphs in some of these passages. The idea is for you to be able to apply your reasoning skills to the kinds of text you will encounter in college or in your professional life. Why is it called the "Evidence-Based" Reading and Writing test? Because you will be asked over and over to support your answers to questions using evidence from the passages you read. This approach is meant to test your ability, not only to read and comprehend a passage, but to think about it critically. It won't be enough to find the right answer. You will need to show that you understand why a correct answer is correct. Critics of the earlier version of the test sometimes argued that the reading and writing sections were mostly vocabulary tests that you could ace by studying the dictionary. That is no longer the case, but you will definitely encounter some advanced vocabulary in the passages on the test.

The Math Test

On the Math test, you will find multistep problems and advanced math topics. It's not just arithmetic, algebra, and geometry. You will find some trigonometry in there, too. You will also find questions that don't just ask you to solve an equation—you will need to apply your math skills to "real-world" situations in science, social studies, and business environments. The Math test has two sections: one with a calculator and one without.

How to Register for the SAT

The number of people taking the SAT climbs each year. In 2019, over 2.2 million people took the SAT. That's a lot of people, which is good news for test takers because it means there is likely a testing location convenient to you. You may even be able to take the SAT at your school during the school day.

Registering online is pretty straightforward. Just go to:

https://collegereadiness.collegeboard.org/sat/register

Follow the instructions on the website. You will be asked to set up an account. Definitely read through the "Before You Start" section. It tells you what you will need in order to set up an account—including an appropriate photo of yourself for uploading.

You will also pick the time and location of your test. If you want to find out in advance what your options are for testing locations, use this online tool:

https://sat.collegeboard.org/register/test-center-code-search

You can look up test centers by your state and city name. You will also need to provide College Board codes for your high school and any college or university you want your scores sent to. You can look up the codes here:

https://sat.collegeboard.org/register/sat-code-search

When registering online, be prepared to pay the fee using a credit card or PayPal. The fee is $52. If you cannot afford the fee, you can apply for a fee waiver. Guidelines for applying for a fee waiver can be found here:

https://sat.collegeboard.org/register/sat-fee-waivers

You can also ask your school counselor for more information. The College Board website will let you know of any changes that are taking place as well. Check back before your test date to find out any updates on social distancing or other public health guidelines.

Speaking of school counselors, if you want to register for the SAT by mail, your school counselor is the person to see. She can give you the *Student Registration Guide for the SAT and SAT Subject Tests*, which includes the registration form.

If you need to request accommodations, get an early start on registration. You will need to get your request approved by the College Board first, and that process can take several weeks. Forms and further information can be found here:

https://accommodations.collegeboard.org/?navId=gf-ssd

How the Tests Are Scored

Standardized test scoring is something that baffles and annoys most people. You know that at the end of your test, you will have gotten a certain number of questions right, gotten a certain number wrong, and maybe left some blank. You may ask, why can't you just get a score that reflects the percentage of questions you answered correctly, just as you usually do in school? The answer is that the test makers are trying to be fair to you. No two SATs are exactly equal. The people who make the tests try hard to make them equal, but their own analysis of the tests shows that the test some people receive can be either harder or easier than the version other people receive. You can receive a "scaled" score of 200 to 800 on the Math and Evidence-Based Reading and Writing tests. Someone who took a relatively easy test might answer more questions correctly than someone taking a harder test. That means that a direct comparison of their raw scores would be unfair to the person who took the harder test. In order to correct for that, scores are converted to the scale.

Test-Taking Tips

Some of the most basic test-taking strategies for the SAT are ones you have probably heard many times before:

- **Use the process of elimination.** Remember that on multiple-choice questions, the correct answer is right there. If you aren't sure which is the correct answer, use your reasoning skills to try to eliminate answers that you know are wrong. Sometimes you can arrive at the correct answer just by eliminating wrong answers.

- **If you are stumped, guess.** There is no guessing penalty. You have nothing to lose. If you just have no idea what the correct answer is, guess and move on.

- **Don't spend a lot of time wrestling with a tricky question.** Remember that easy multiple-choice questions are worth the same as hard ones. Don't miss your chance to rack up points on the easy questions. Your time is limited.

- **Speaking of time, keep an eye on it.** It will fly by faster than you think, and you need to get to as many questions as you possibly can. If you have five minutes to go and there are questions left to be answered, move quickly and guess on everything.

- **If you think you might be able to figure out a hard question if you have a little more time . . . guess first.** If you have answered every question in one way or another (with correct responses or guesses) and you still have time left, definitely go back and try to get the points on the hard questions. Just don't leave anything blank.

If you have extra time at the end of a section, go back and check your work. If you notice a real error—something you are positive is wrong—definitely fix it, but do *not* start second-guessing your first guesses. If you used process of elimination and made a choice, stick with your choice. You don't want to start erasing answers while time is running out. Besides, your first choice is usually the best choice.

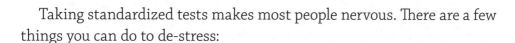

Taking standardized tests makes most people nervous. There are a few things you can do to de-stress:

- **Take practice tests.** There are two full-length tests in this book. Being familiar with the test will help you feel calm because you won't have some surprise question type pop out at you.

- **Make sure you know exactly where your test center is,** how to get there, how long it takes to get there, where to park, and how to get to the room you are supposed to be in. Do a practice run. On the day of the test, leave yourself plenty of time for surprises like bad traffic. If you have to sprint across a parking lot and scramble through a hallway to arrive at the test room in the nick of time, you have definitely started off on the wrong foot.

- **Get a good night's sleep.** Being sleepy will hurt your performance.

- **Eat before you go to the test.** Same as being sleepy. Being hungry will hurt you.

- **Prepare for a room that is way too hot. Or way too cold.** You don't know what you'll get, so dress in layers and bring a sweater even if you are taking the test in June.

- **Be sure to bring your admission ticket, photo ID, two No. 2 pencils with erasers, and an approved calculator.** You may also be required to bring a face-covering if public health requirements suggest it.

How to Use This Book to Prepare Yourself

You are probably reading this book because you want to get ready for the SAT quickly. Just how quickly is up to you. This book is broken into manageable chunks that you can use to go at your own pace. Each chapter begins with the **must know** items for the topics in the chapter. Each topic is followed by an exercise that gives you practice on the topic or skill that has just been covered.

If you are getting ready to take the SAT as a junior or senior in high school, you are probably quite busy with your usual schoolwork. Try to treat your SAT preparation as homework for one extra class. Set aside time for it each day, and be as realistic as you can. Thirty minutes a day is a good goal. If you spend too little time each day preparing, you won't make headway. If you try to cram too much into each study session, you probably won't remember everything you have read.

Take some time to skim through the instructional parts of this book and decide what is reasonable given your schedule and study habits; then write down a specific plan on a calendar. You should finish your SAT preparation shortly before test day (but not the night before, hopefully!). Stick to your goals.

Best of luck on the SAT and beyond!

Reading and Writing

Evidence-Based Reading and Writing

The Evidence-Based Reading and Writing Tests

The Evidence-Based Reading and Writing section of the SAT exam tests your ability to read and understand not only the content of all types of passages, but also their structure and language use. The Reading Test assesses how well you read and comprehend various texts. The Writing and Language Test assesses your ability to revise a wide range of texts so that they follow the rules of Standard English and contain proper grammar, usage, and punctuation.

The Reading Test requires you to answer 52 multiple-choice questions in 65 minutes. The breakdown of questions is up to 10 Words in Context questions, up to 10 Command of Evidence questions, up to 21 Analysis in History/Social Studies questions, and up to 21 Analysis in Science questions.

All questions evaluate your ability to understand reading passages 500 to 750 words in length. One of these passages will be a piece of U.S. or world literature (fiction). The remaining will be informational (nonfiction): two history/social studies passages and two science passages. Four of these passages will be stand-alone pieces, and one will be a paired set of texts you will study together. Graphics such as tables, charts, and graphs will also be included among the passages.

The Evidence-Based Writing section includes 44 multiple-choice questions. You will have 35 minutes to answer these questions. The breakdown of these writing questions is up to 24 Expression of Ideas questions, up to 20 Standard English Conventions questions, up to 8 Words in Context questions, up to 8 Command of Evidence questions, up to 6 Analysis in History/Social Studies questions, and up to 6 Analysis in Science questions.

All writing questions are based on passages 400 to 450 words in length. There are four passages on the Evidence-Based Writing section of the SAT in the following categories: careers, history/social studies, humanities, and science. These passages are all nonfiction: one or two argumentative passages, one or two informational/explanatory passages, and one narrative passage. A set of 11 questions follows each passage, and graphics such as tables, charts, and graphs will also be included among the passages.

Evidence-Based Reading and Writing Review

The following section will give you a thorough overview of each skill tested in the Evidence-Based Reading and Writing sections of the SAT. In each lesson, you will find examples of all the passage types from the exam, accompanied by test-like practice questions.

The correct answers to these questions can be found in the Exercise Answer Keys at the end of this book.

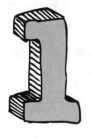

Reading for Information and Ideas

MUST KNOW

- Explicit information is stated clearly in the passage while implicit information is implied.

- Every correct answer is supported by the passage. You should be able to prove every answer you choose.

- While you are reading a passage, look for overall themes and relationships.

- Context clues can help you figure out the meaning of unfamiliar words.

The Evidence-Based Reading section of the SAT exam assesses how well you are able to comprehend different types of writing.

Effective reading comprehension requires the mastery of a number of essential skills. You will be expected to do more than simply recall information on the SAT—the test assesses your ability to determine information and ideas both stated explicitly and merely implied in a text and cite evidence for your conclusions. You will have to identify important ideas and themes and interpret the meanings of words and phrases used in context. You will also have to understand the relationships between ideas in a text and be able to summarize paragraphs or the text as a whole. These skills fall under the heading of "Information and Ideas" and are the most basic reading comprehension skills tested on the SAT.

In this chapter, we will be paying close attention to the information and ideas presented in a text. Some of these pieces of information and ideas are stated explicitly. Some are merely suggested and require you to draw educated conclusions about the messages the writers want to communicate.

BTW

A good strategy for dealing with reading comprehension is to first read the passage through quickly and focus on the main idea, structure of the passage, and the author's tone. Then read the question and go back to the relevant part of the passage to read it more carefully with the question in mind.

Explicit Information

Stating information and ideas explicitly is the simplest and most direct way a writer communicates. Information that is stated explicitly does not require you to figure out what the writer means. All you need to do is pay close attention while reading. Don't you wish that every reading passage was like that? By reading the sentence "The shoe was red," you would know that the color of the shoe is red because the writer stated this information explicitly.

To answer an SAT question about an explicit detail, you will need to **read the passage closely** to identify that information and then match it to an answer choice.

EXAMPLE

▶ Let's look at a question involving explicit meaning. Read this paragraph from a reading passage:

Katherine Mansfield's short story "Prelude" was originally written in 1915 as "The Aloe" and was first published as "Prelude" by Virginia and Leonard Woolf's Hogarth Press in 1918. The impressionistic style of the story and the introspective natures of the characters shattered the traditional short story form. Mansfield foregrounds the family dynamic, deemphasizing the simple plot of a family moving to a new house.

▶ Now let's see the question:

1. "Prelude" was considered a new type of short story when it was published because

▶ Go back to the passage and read the part where it says "Prelude" *shattered the traditional short story form.* Read a line or two before that and a line or two after it to find the answer to the question. The passage says that it was the impressionistic style and the characters' introspective natures that made the story different.

▶ Now we just need to match our answer to one of the answer choices given:

A. the title of the story had changed.

B. the story showed the inner thoughts and feelings of the characters.

C. the story has no plot.

D. it was the first short story published by a female author.

▶ We need an answer choice that says something about impressionism or introspection. The only one that does that is choice B, so it is the best answer.

Reading comprehension questions about explicit details are the easiest questions to answer because the answers are directly stated in the passage and are usually found easily by looking for key words in the question. Proper nouns (the name of a person, place, or thing) are the best key words because they begin with capital letters and those are easy to spot when you scan the passage.

▶ Read this paragraph from the same reading passage:

Mansfield explores how a character's consciousness is invaded by unconscious forces and changed by the vagaries of perception. Each character in the story feels oppressed by the role he or she is required to play: breadwinner, mother, spinster, servant, or obedient child. Mansfield's focus is on the women and girls; for example, Mansfield explores in depth Kezia's relationships with her siblings, her struggle to find an identity she can live with, and the ways she perceives the world.

▶ Here's the question:

2. The author of the passage uses Kezia as an example of

▶ Having that name in the question gives us a great key word to search for in the passage. Go back to the passage and find *Kezia*. The passage says *Mansfield explores in depth Kezia's relationships with her siblings, her struggle to find an identity she can live with, and the ways she perceives the world.*

▶ Since that is the last sentence of the paragraph, just read a line or two before that to be sure you have the answer to the question. The passage says Mansfield focuses on women and girls and gives Kezia as an example.

▶ Let's match our answer to one of these answer choices:

A. someone who cannot live with herself.

B. Mansfield's view that everyone sees the world differently.

C. a girl who does not get along with her family.

D. Mansfield's centering of female characters.

▶ Choice D expresses the idea that the author mentions Kezia as an example of Mansfield's focus on females, so it is the best answer.

Questions involving explicit information are among the easiest types of reading comprehension questions, but they appear less often on the SAT than do questions involving implicit information.

Implicit Information

Unlike explicitly stated information, implicitly stated information calls for a bit of decoding. You will need to locate clues in the passage to draw reasonable inferences and logical conclusions. These questions may ask what the passage infers, implies, or suggests.

EXAMPLE

▶ What can be inferred from this sentence?

Bill embraced me and asked how I've been.

▶ First, the fact that Bill embraced the narrator implies that they may have a close relationship. Notice that I didn't say Bill loves the narrator. Perhaps Bill likes to hug his enemies. All we know is that Bill hugged the narrator, which means they probably have some sort of close relationship.

▶ Second, the fact that Bill asks how the narrator has been indicates they have not seen each other in a while. How long a while? No idea. That's about all we can infer.

Drawing a logical conclusion requires you to think outside the text a little. However, there will always be a reason for you to draw that conclusion. The SAT requires you to draw reasonable inferences and logical conclusions based on textual clues.

▶ Read this paragraph from the reading passage about "Prelude":

Mansfield's narrative slides smoothly from conscious to unconscious to express this tense duality and she frequently uses the image of glass to symbolize the two worlds in which her characters exist. In "Prelude," Mansfield often has her characters look out of windows or into mirrors. The focus shifts from the subject to the object of view and creates a glass barrier between them. This glass barrier acts as a lens, magnifying the distance between the public self and the private self, the conscious and the unconscious.

▶ Here's the question:

3. The passage suggests that glass symbolizes

▶ Let's try to answer the question, using information in the passage, before we even look at the answer choices.

▶ What does the passage say about glass? It says she uses glass to symbolize *the two worlds in which her characters exist*. It shifts focus *from the subject to the object of view*. It magnifies *the distance between the public self and the private self, the conscious and the unconscious*. That sounds like glass symbolizes the two roles people play (public versus private or internal versus external).

For an implicit information question, you need to find the *best* answer. More than one answer may seem logical or reasonable, but only one will be the best answer. That answer will have textual evidence to support it.

EXAMPLE

▶ Let's put it all together. Here is the paragraph and question, this time with answer choices.

Mansfield's narrative slides smoothly from conscious to unconscious to express this tense duality and she frequently uses the image of glass to symbolize the two worlds in which her characters exist. In "Prelude," Mansfield often has her characters look out of windows or into mirrors. The focus shifts from the subject to the object of view and creates a glass barrier between them. This glass barrier acts as a lens, magnifying the distance between the public self and the private self, the conscious and the unconscious.

▶ 3. The passage suggests that glass symbolizes

    A. that people have more than one side.

    B. the clarity with which a person can view herself.

    C. the barrier between rich and poor.

    D. that no one is ever totally alone.

▶ In the example before this one, we concluded that glass symbolizes the two roles people play. That's answer choice A. Don't get tripped up by the other choices. Any of them are possible if you use your imagination, but that's not what we are asked to do. We need textual evidence for our answer, and we could underline several phrases in that paragraph that support answer choice A.

BTW

Watch out for answer choices that use the exact language that the passage used. Those are often traps. Sometimes an answer will be in the passage, but not at all relevant to the question. Sometimes, as is the case here with answer choice C, the first part of the answer choice is a direct quote from the passage, but then the rest of the answer choice is all wrong.

Implicit information questions are quite popular on the SAT, so be sure you are confident in your ability to infer and draw conclusions, while supporting your ideas with evidence from the text.

Using Analogical Reasoning

Analogical reasoning questions entail connecting information in a passage with a new, analogous situation. *Analogous* means similar, so an analogical reasoning question may ask you to make a reasonable connection between two situations that on the surface seem quite different. You will have to think about whether they are similar in some way.

EXAMPLE

▶ Let's say you are reading a passage about a girl who really wants a pet. She finds a lost dog wandering around her neighborhood and must decide what to do with the dog.

▶ You read another passage about a child who went to a store with his mother and found a $20 bill on the floor of an aisle with no other people present.

▶ Although a dog and a $20 bill are very unlike things, the decision to keep what is found or locate the rightful owner is very similar.

Analogical reasoning questions may ask you about similarities between two paired passages or they may ask you to match a single passage with a scenario in the answer choices. If so, watch out for answers that are about the same topic as the passage. If the passage is about fruit, the correct answer probably isn't about fruit. The correct answer may be about shoes. The point here is to find a connection between things that seem different. You will probably see only one of these single-passage questions on your SAT, but being able to make connections is a valuable skill for other question types too.

Citing Textual Evidence

Citing textual evidence involves finding details in a passage to support claims about its ideas. This evidence may include descriptions, examples, and facts.

> ▶ A question may claim that a character in a passage is kind and ask you to support this claim by citing an example of the character's kindness in the passage. Maybe the author describes her as understanding and supportive. Perhaps the character helps someone who is in trouble, or says to a friend, "I would be happy to lend a sympathetic ear while you tell me all your troubles." Such details would be good textual evidence that the character is a kind person.

Textual evidence questions are quite common on the SAT and many of them are paired with implicit information questions. The first question asks you to infer something and then the second question asks you to cite evidence for your inference in the passage.

> ▶ Let's use a longer excerpt from the "Prelude" passage and pair one of our previous example questions with a textual evidence question.
>
> *Mansfield's narrative slides smoothly from conscious to unconscious to express this tense duality and she frequently uses the image of glass to symbolize the two worlds in which her characters exist. In "Prelude," Mansfield often has her characters look out of windows or into mirrors.*
> 5 *The focus shifts from the subject to the object of view and creates a glass barrier between them. This glass barrier acts as a lens, magnifying the distance between the public self and the private self, the conscious and the unconscious. Mansfield explores how a character's consciousness is*

invaded by unconscious forces and changed by the vagaries of perception.
10 *Each character in the story feels oppressed by the role he or she is*
required to play: breadwinner, mother, spinster, servant, or obedient
child.

3. The passage suggests that glass symbolizes

   A. that people have more than one side.

   B. the clarity with which a person can view herself.

   C. the barrier between rich and poor.

   D. that no one is ever totally alone.

4. Which choice provides the best evidence for the answer to the previous question?

   A. lines 1–3 "Mansfield's...exist"

   B. line 3 "In...mirrors"

   C. lines 3–4 "The...them"

   D. lines 7–9 "Each...child"

▶ We previously answered question 3 and chose A. Question 4 asks where we found evidence of that answer.

▶ We highlighted several phrases when we originally answered question 3. Let's see where in the passage we found them:

■ *the two worlds in which her characters exist* was in line 2

■ *from the subject to the object of view* was in line 4

■ *the distance between the public self and the private self, the conscious and the unconscious* was in lines 5–6

▶ The only match we find in the answer choices is choice A: *Mansfield's narrative slides smoothly from conscious to unconscious to express this tense duality and she frequently uses the image of glass to symbolize the two worlds in which her characters exist.* Choice A is the best answer.

When you answer a textual evidence question, be sure that you can literally put your finger on the point in the passage that says whatever it is you are asked about. If you can't do that, you're choosing the wrong answer.

Determining Central Ideas and Themes

Central ideas and **themes** are very similar, but they are not exactly the same. The theme of a passage is more like the overall topic or lesson, while a central idea is a main idea or thesis. In fact, you may see these terms used interchangeably on the test. Think of theme and central idea like this: Ask yourself what topic the passage is about. That's the theme. Then ask yourself what point the passage is making about that topic. That's the central idea. Central idea questions are more common on the SAT than are theme questions.

EXAMPLE

▶ Here are a few examples of themes:

- The theme of a passage about a boy who learns to do long division may be education.
- The theme of a paragraph about cell division may be growth.
- The themes of *The Emancipation Proclamation* are freedom and equality.

The central idea of a passage is its most important point. You've probably been asked many times to find the **main idea** of a passage. Central ideas are the same thing, though on the SAT you may be asked about both the main idea of the whole passage and the main idea of certain paragraphs.

EXAMPLE

Here are central ideas for the passages described in the last example:

■ The central idea of a passage about a boy who learns to do long division may be that education should be the most important focus for children.

■ The central idea of a paragraph about cell division may be that there are two ways cells divide.

■ The central idea of *The Emancipation Proclamation* is that people held as slaves in the Confederate states are now free.

Let's see how theme and central idea questions might look for an excerpt from the "Prelude" passage.

EXAMPLE

Mansfield's narrative slides smoothly from conscious to unconscious to express this tense duality and she frequently uses the image of glass to symbolize the two worlds in which her characters exist. In "Prelude," Mansfield often has her characters look out of windows or into mirrors.

5 *The focus shifts from the subject to the object of view and creates a glass barrier between them. This glass barrier acts as a lens, magnifying the distance between the public self and the private self, the conscious and the unconscious. Mansfield explores how a character's consciousness is invaded by unconscious forces and changed by the vagaries of perception.*

10 *Each character in the story feels oppressed by the role he or she is required to play: breadwinner, mother, spinster, servant, or obedient child.*

▶ 5. What is the central idea expressed by this paragraph?

A. No one is truly happy with the role they are forced to play in society.

B. People often hide their true feelings, even from those close to them.

C. The way in which people present themselves may be different from the way they feel inside.

D. People are sometimes unaware of their true motives.

▸ This paragraph is the one about how Mansfield uses glass to symbolize the dual nature of her characters' public lives versus their inner, private lives. Read the answer choices carefully. Look for what we already said this paragraph was about and don't be distracted by anything else. You could probably justify any of them if you try hard enough, so don't do that. That's why it is so important to answer the question in your own words before you look at the answer choices.

▸ Choice C is very close to our answer, while the others go further than what is presented in the passage.

▸ 6. What theme does Mansfield explore in "Prelude"?

A. Honesty

B. Politeness

C. Insanity

D. Duality

▸ Do you see how this question is different from the first one? This is the topic, in one word. What's it all about? Duality.

> **BTW**
> *Watch out for answer choices that use extreme language. Those are rarely the best answer. Answer choice A in question 5 says "no one is truly happy." Really? No one? Not a single person in the entire world? That's a pretty extreme statement and it's easy to argue with it, so it is not likely to be the credited answer.*

Determining central ideas and themes questions usually require decoding, because writers rarely state their ideas and themes explicitly. For example, instead of ending a story by stating "Better late than never," a writer will more likely illustrate this theme with a character who wants something to happen and waits patiently until it does.

Summarizing

When you summarize, you boil down the most important details and ideas in a passage to a relatively brief statement. A good summary addresses the passage as a whole, eliminating unnecessary details. Summarizing questions may require you to identify the best summary of an entire passage, a single paragraph, or key idea in the passage. A summary of a story about a farmer probably will not include details about what the farmer was wearing unless those articles of clothing are integral to the overall story.

Consider these questions:

- Who are the most important people or characters in the passage?

- What are the most important things they do?

- What are the passage's essential ideas?

▶ Let's look at an excerpt from "Nasty Women" by Isabella Matthews.

In the seventeenth century, a woman was obliged to obey her husband, and all legal and public affairs were under his control. A woman's domain was the home, although, when necessary, widows operated businesses. Women were barred from the professions and from
5 *public life. They could not serve in government or hold religious office, and they were invisible so far as art or literature was concerned.*
Colonial America provided two famous exceptions to this rule: Anne Hutchinson and Anne Bradstreet. Anne Hutchinson of Rhode Island became an active and controversial Protestant preacher in the

10 *1630s and continued to preach publicly until her death in 1643. Anne Bradstreet of Massachusetts had a book of her poems published in London in 1650. She is generally considered to be the first important American poet.*

1. Which of the following provides the best summary of the passage?

   A. Women had few rights or public roles in the seventeenth century, except for widows.

   B. Anne Bradstreet and Anne Hutchinson did not conform to traditional women's roles in the seventeenth century.

   C. Anne Bradstreet and Anne Hutchinson were condemned for their attempts to break out of the traditional roles for women in the seventeenth century.

   D. Colonial American women had more rights than did other women of the same time period in Europe.

Before you look at the answer choices, summarize the passage yourself. The first paragraph is about traditional roles for women in the seventeenth century. The second paragraph is about two exceptions: Anne Bradstreet and Anne Hutchinson. We can summarize the passage by combining those topics: Anne Bradstreet and Anne Hutchinson were exceptions to the traditional roles for women in the seventeenth century. Now, when we look at the answer choices, it is easy to see that choice B is the closest to our summary and is the best answer.

 IRL Summarizing is a really important skill that you will use throughout your life. Friends may ask you what that new movie is about. Your boss may ask you to present an overview of your research on a topic. Both of those require you to summarize a lot of content into just a few sentences.

Understanding Relationships

Certain common relations link the individuals, events, and ideas in a passage. Such basic relationships include:

- **Cause and effect:** One action makes another occur.

- **Comparison and contrast:** One thing is different from another or the same as another.

- **Problem and solution:** One thing is a problem and the other solves it.

- **Sequential order:** One thing comes before or after another.

EXAMPLE

▶ Let's look at a paragraph from the excerpt in the last example.

> *Colonial America provided two famous exceptions to this rule: Anne Hutchinson and Anne Bradstreet. Anne Hutchinson of Rhode Island became an active and controversial Protestant preacher in the 1630s and continued to preach publicly until her death in 1643. Anne*
> 5 *Bradstreet of Massachusetts had a book of her poems published in London in 1650. She is generally considered to be the first important American poet.*

▶ 2. Anne Bradstreet and Anne Hutchinson both

  A. were smarter than the men leading their society.

  B. submitted their ideas to the public.

  C. were disliked for their boldness.

  D. were famous for most of their adult lives.

▶ Here we are asked what the two Annes have in common. Let's go back to the passage and see what we know about each of them.

▶ Hutchinson:

- ■ from Rhode Island
- ■ active Protestant preacher
- ■ controversial
- ■ preached publicly for 13 years
- ■ died 1643

▶ Bradstreet

- ■ from Massachusetts
- ■ poet
- ■ published book of poetry in London 1650
- ■ considered to be the first important American poet

▶ What do they have in common?

- ■ from New England
- ■ lived around the same time
- ■ spoke/wrote in public

▶ Let's look at the answer choices and see what we've got. There is no textual evidence for either choice A or choice D, so eliminate them. Choice B is one of our points in common, so keep it. Choice C might be true of Hutchinson, but there is no evidence that it was true of Bradstreet. Eliminate C and choose B.

Other common relationships include how individuals, events, and ideas copy, contradict, confirm, correct, and cancel each other. A passage may include one or more of these kinds of relationships, which you will have to identify on the SAT.

Interpreting Words and Phrases in Context

You will have to interpret the meanings of words and phrases on the SAT. These will not necessarily be unfamiliar words and phrases, so studying lists of new vocabulary is not the best way to prepare for the questions. Interpreting words and phrases in context questions actually test your ability to define words and phrases based on *how* writers use them.

A single word can have a number of meanings. *Green* most often refers to a secondary color. However, *green* can also be used to mean "naïve," or it may be used to mean "new." In recent years, the word *green* has become a common term for "environmentally friendly," as in an individual, item, or process that causes little or no damage to the natural environment. You can decipher which definition of *green* a writer intends to use based on how that writer uses the word in the context of a passage or sentence.

EXAMPLE

▶ Paolo was so green he did not realize he would have to bring a notebook with him on his first day of school.

▶ As used in this sentence, *green* most nearly means

A. the color of grass.

B. naïve.

C. new.

D. environmentally friendly.

▶ The best way to figure out how *green* is used in the context of this particular sentence is to substitute each answer choice for *green* in the sentence. The only choices that make any sense in place of *green* are B, naïve, and C, new. However, "naïve" is a much more specific substitute for *green* than "new" is, so the best answer choice is B.

These vocabulary questions are more about interpreting meaning than they are about simply knowing the definition of a word. You must determine the context in which the word is used.

EXERCISES

EXERCISE 1–1

Directions: Read the passage, then choose the best answer to each of the questions that follow.

Excerpt from *Gulliver's Travels*
by Jonathan Swift

My father had a small estate in Nottinghamshire; I was the third of five sons. He sent me to Emmanuel College in Cambridge at fourteen years old, where I resided three years, and applied myself close to my studies; but the charge of maintaining me, although I had a very scanty
5 allowance, being too great for a narrow fortune, I was bound apprentice to Mr. James Bates, an eminent surgeon in London, with whom I continued four years; and my father now and then sending me small sums of money, I laid them out in learning navigation, and other parts of the mathematics useful to those who intend to travel, as I always
10 believed it would be, some time or other, my fortune to do. When I left Mr. Bates, I went down to my father, where, by the assistance of him, and my uncle John and some other relations, I got forty pounds, and a promise of thirty pounds a year, to maintain me at Leyden. There I studied physic two years and seven months, knowing it would be useful
15 in long voyages.

Soon after my return from Leyden, I was recommended by my good master, Mr. Bates, to be surgeon to the "Swallow," Captain Abraham Pannell, commander; with whom I continued three years and a half, making a voyage or two into the Levant, and some other parts. When
20 I came back I resolved to settle in London; to which Mr. Bates, my master, encouraged me, and by him I was recommended to several patients. I took part of a small house in the Old Jewry; and, being advised to alter my condition, I married Mrs. Mary Burton, second

daughter to Mr. Edmund Burton, hosier in Newgate Street, with whom I
25 received four hundred pounds for a portion.

1. How many younger brothers does the narrator have?
    A. One
    B. Two
    C. Three
    D. Four

2. Who is the narrator's master?
    A. Mr. Bates
    B. Captain Abraham Pannell
    C. Mrs. Mary Burton
    D. Mr. Edmund Burton

EXERCISE 1–2

Directions: Read the passage, then choose the best answer to each of the
questions that follow.

Excerpt from *House of Mirth*
by Edith Wharton

Selden paused in surprise. In the afternoon rush of the Grand Central
Station his eyes had been refreshed by the sight of Miss Lily Bart.
    It was a Monday in early September, and he was returning to his
work from a hurried dip into the country; but what was Miss Bart doing
5 in town at that season? If she had appeared to be catching a train, he
might have inferred that he had come on her in the act of transition
between one and another of the country-houses which disputed her
presence after the close of the Newport season; but her desultory air
perplexed him. She stood apart from the crowd, letting it drift by her

10   to the platform or the street, and wearing an air of irresolution which might, as he surmised, be the mask of a very definite purpose. It struck him at once that she was waiting for some one, but he hardly knew why the idea arrested him. There was nothing new about Lily Bart, yet he could never see her without a faint movement of interest: it

15   was characteristic of her that she always roused speculation, that her simplest acts seemed the result of far-reaching intentions.

An impulse of curiosity made him turn out of his direct line to the door, and stroll past her. He knew that if she did not wish to be seen she would contrive to elude him; and it amused him to think of putting her

20   skill to the test.

"Mr. Selden—what good luck!"

She came forward smiling, eager almost, in her resolve to intercept him. One or two persons, in brushing past them, lingered to look; for Miss Bart was a figure to arrest even the suburban traveller rushing to

25   his last train.

Selden had never seen her more radiant. Her vivid head, relieved against the dull tints of the crowd, made her more conspicuous than in a ball-room, and under her dark hat and veil she regained the girlish smoothness, the purity of tint, that she was beginning to lose after

30   eleven years of late hours and indefatigable dancing. Was it really eleven years, Selden found himself wondering, and had she indeed reached the nine-and-twentieth birthday with which her rivals credited her?

"What luck!" she repeated. "How nice of you to come to my rescue!"

1. What is the most likely reason Selden wants Miss Bart to notice him?

    A. She owes him money.

    B. She looks lonesome.

    C. He is attracted to her.

    D. He is too shy to introduce himself.

2. Which line from the passage provides the best evidence for the answer to the previous question?
    A. "An impulse of curiosity made him turn out of his direct line to the door, and stroll past her."
    B. "If she had appeared to be catching a train, he might have inferred that he had come on her in the act of transition . . ."
    C. "She came forward smiling, eager almost, in her resolve to intercept him."
    D. "His eyes had been refreshed by the sight of Miss Lily Bart."

3. The passage strongly suggests that Miss Bart
    A. knew Selden would be at the station.
    B. was not waiting for a specific person.
    C. always visited town in September.
    D. had once been married to Selden.

EXERCISE 1–3

Directions: Read the passage, then choose the best answer to each of the questions that follow.

Excerpt from "The Eyes Have It"
by Philip K. Dick

It was quite by accident I discovered this incredible invasion of Earth by lifeforms from another planet. As yet, I haven't done anything about it; I can't think of anything to do. I wrote to the Government, and they sent back a pamphlet on the repair and maintenance of frame houses.
5 Anyhow, the whole thing is known; I'm not the first to discover it. Maybe it's even under control.

I was sitting in my easy-chair, idly turning the pages of a paperbacked book someone had left on the bus, when I came across the reference that first put me on the trail. For a moment I didn't respond.

10   It took some time for the full import to sink in. After I'd comprehended, it seemed odd I hadn't noticed it right away.

The reference was clearly to a nonhuman species of incredible properties, not indigenous to Earth. A species, I hasten to point out, customarily masquerading as ordinary human beings. Their disguise,
15   however, became transparent in the face of the following observations by the author. It was at once obvious the author knew everything. Knew everything—and was taking it in his stride. The line (and I tremble remembering it even now) read:

. . . his eyes slowly roved about the room.

20   Vague chills assailed me. I tried to picture the eyes. Did they roll like dimes? The passage indicated not; they seemed to move through the air, not over the surface. Rather rapidly, apparently. No one in the story was surprised. That's what tipped me off. No sign of amazement at such an outrageous thing. Later the matter was amplified.

25   . . . his eyes moved from person to person.

There it was in a nutshell. The eyes had clearly come apart from the rest of him and were on their own. My heart pounded and my breath choked in my windpipe. I had stumbled on an accidental mention of a totally unfamiliar race. Obviously non-Terrestrial. Yet, to the characters
30   in the book, it was perfectly natural—which suggested they belonged to the same species.

And the author? A slow suspicion burned in my mind. The author was taking it rather *too easily* in his stride. Evidently, he felt this was quite a usual thing. He made absolutely no attempt to conceal this
35   knowledge.

1. The narrator of this passage is most like a person who is
    A. visiting a new city for the first time.
    B. unsure of how to interpret a story.
    C. frightened of being robbed.
    D. unreasonably wary of strangers.

2. This passage might impart a valuable lesson to someone who is
    A. untrustworthy.
    B. over imaginative.
    C. deeply prejudiced.
    D. unpatriotic.

EXERCISE 1–4

Directions: Read the passage, then choose the best answer to each of the questions that follow.

Excerpt from "The Talking Bird, The Singing Tree, and The Golden Water"
from The Arabian Nights

There was an emperor of Persia named Kosrouschah, who, when he first came to his crown, in order to obtain a knowledge of affairs, took great pleasure in night excursions, attended by a trusty minister. He often walked in disguise through the city, and met with many adventures,
5   one of the most remarkable of which happened to him upon his first ramble, which was not long after his accession to the throne of his father.

    After the ceremonies of his father's funeral rites and his own inauguration were over, the new sultan, as well from inclination as
10   from duty, went out one evening attended by his grand vizier, disguised like himself, to observe what was transacting in the city. As he was passing through a street in that part of the town inhabited only by the meaner sort, he heard some people talking very loud; and going close to the house whence the noise proceeded, and looking through a crack in
15   the door, perceived a light, and three sisters sitting on a sofa, conversing together after supper. By what the eldest said he presently understood the subject of their conversation was wishes: "for," said she, "since we

are talking about wishes, mine shall be to have the sultan's baker for
my husband, for then I shall eat my fill of that bread, which by way of
20   excellence is called the sultan's; let us see if your tastes are as good as
mine." "For my part," replied the second sister, "I wish I was wife to the
sultan's chief cook, for then I should eat of the most excellent dishes;
and as I am persuaded that the sultan's bread is common in the palace,
I should not want any of that; therefore you see," addressing herself
25   to her eldest sister, "that I have a better taste than you." The youngest
sister, who was very beautiful, and had more charms and wit than the
two elder, spoke in her turn: "For my part, sisters," said she, "I shall not
limit my desires to such trifles, but take a higher flight; and since we
are upon wishing, I wish to be the emperor's queen-consort. I would
30   make him father of a prince, whose hair should be gold on one side of
his head, and silver on the other; when he cried, the tears from his eyes
should be pearls; and when he smiled, his vermilion lips should look
like a rosebud fresh-blown."

The three sisters' wishes, particularly that of the youngest, seemed so
35   singular to the sultan, that he resolved to gratify them in their desires;
but without communicating his design to his grand vizier, he charged
him only to take notice of the house, and bring the three sisters before
him the following day.

The grand vizier, in executing the emperor's orders, would but
40   just give the sisters time to dress themselves to appear before his
majesty, without telling them the reason. He brought them to the
palace, and presented them to the emperor, who said to them, "Do you
remember the wishes you expressed last night, when you were all in
so pleasant a mood? Speak the truth; I must know what they were." At
45   these unexpected words of the emperor, the three sisters were much
confounded. They cast down their eyes and blushed, and the colour
which rose in the cheeks of the youngest quite captivated the emperor's
heart. Modesty, and fear lest they might have offended by their

conversation, kept them silent. The emperor, perceiving their confusion,
50 said to encourage them, "Fear nothing, I did not send for you to distress
you; and since I see that without my intending it, this is the effect of the
question I asked, as I know the wish of each, I will relieve you from your
fears. You," added he, "who wished to be my wife, shall have your desire
this day; and you," continued he, addressing himself to the two elder
55 sisters, "shall also be married to my chief baker and cook."

1. It can be inferred from the passage that the youngest sister was
    A. the one with the most taste.
    B. the least intelligent.
    C. the most intelligent.
    D. the kindest.

2. Which line from the passage provides the best evidence for the answer to
    the previous question?
    A. "For my part," replied the second sister, "I wish I was wife to the
        sultan's chief cook . . . "
    B. "The youngest sister, who was very beautiful, and had more
        charms and wit than the two elder . . . "
    C. "For my part, sisters," said she, "I shall not limit my desires to
        such trifles, but take a higher flight . . . "
    D. "The three sisters' wishes, particularly that of the youngest,
        seemed so singular to the sultan, that he resolved to gratify them
        in their desires . . . "

3. When the sultan first speaks to the sisters, it can be inferred that
    A. the sisters were concerned about the sultan knowing their wishes.
    B. the sultan was angry with the sisters.
    C. the sisters were afraid that the sultan might kill them.
    D. the sultan wanted to embarrass the two older sisters.

4. Which line from the passage provides the best evidence for the answer to the previous question?

    A. "... looking through a crack in the door, perceived a light, and three sisters sitting on a sofa, conversing together after supper."

    B. "Do you remember the wishes you expressed last night, when you were all in so pleasant a mood?"

    C. "... you," continued he, addressing himself to the two elder sisters, "shall also be married to my chief baker and cook."

    D. "They cast down their eyes and blushed, and the colour which rose in the cheeks of the youngest quite captivated the emperor's heart."

EXERCISE 1–5

Directions: Read the passage, then choose the best answer to each of the questions that follow.

Excerpt from *Ivanhoe*
by Sir Walter Scott

    Such being our chief scene, the date of our story refers to a period towards the end of the reign of Richard I, when his return from his long captivity had become an event rather wished than hoped for by his despairing subjects, who were in the meantime subjected to every
5 species of subordinate oppression. The nobles, whose power had become exorbitant during the reign of Stephen, and whom the prudence of Henry the Second had scarce reduced to some degree of subjection to the crown, had now resumed their ancient license in its utmost extent; despising the feeble interference of the English Council of State,
10 fortifying their castles, increasing the number of their dependants, reducing all around them to a state of vassalage, and striving by every means in their power, to place themselves each at the head of such

forces as might enable him to make a figure in the national convulsions which appeared to be impending.

15 The situation of the inferior gentry, or Franklins, as they were called, who, by the law and spirit of the English constitution, were entitled to hold themselves independent of feudal tyranny, became now unusually precarious. If, as was most generally the case, they placed themselves under the protection of any of the petty kings in their vicinity, accepted 20 of feudal offices in his household, or bound themselves by mutual treaties of alliance and protection, to support him in his enterprises, they might indeed purchase temporary repose; but it must be with the sacrifice of that independence which was so dear to every English bosom, and at the certain hazard of being involved as a party in 25 whatever rash expedition the ambition of their protector might lead him to undertake. On the other hand, such and so multiplied were the means of vexation and oppression possessed by the great Barons, that they never wanted the pretext, and seldom the will, to harass and pursue, even to the very edge of destruction, any of their less powerful 30 neighbours, who attempted to separate themselves from their authority, and to trust for their protection, during the dangers of the times, to their own inoffensive conduct, and to the laws of the land.

1. Which of the following is a theme of the passage?
    A. The abuse of power
    B. The benevolence of royalty
    C. The futility of war
    D. The complexity of politics

2. What is the main idea of the first paragraph?
    A. The peasants revolted against the monarchy.
    B. The gentry fought amongst themselves, which allowed the nobles to strengthen their positions.
    C. The return of Richard I reunited the kingdom and ushered in a period of prosperity.
    D. The nobles sought to consolidate their power and gather armies.

EXERCISE 1–6

Directions: Read the passage, then choose the best answer to each of the questions that follow.

Excerpt from *Buried Cities*
by Jennie Hall

So a living city was buried in a few hours. Wooded hills and green fields lay covered under great ash heaps. Ever since that terrible eruption Vesuvius has been restless. Sometimes she has been quiet for a hundred years or more and men have almost forgotten that she ever thundered
5   and spouted and buried cities. But all at once she would move again. She would shoot steam and ashes into the sky. At night fire would leap out of her top. A few times she sent out dust and lava and destroyed houses and fields. A man who lived five hundred years after Pompeii was destroyed described Vesuvius as she was in his time. He said:
10   "This mountain is steep and thick with woods below. Above, it is very craggy and wild. At the top is a deep cave. It seems to reach the bottom of the mountain. If you peep in you can see fire. But this ordinarily keeps in and does not trouble the people. But sometimes the mountain bellows like an ox. Soon after it casts out huge masses
15   of cinders. If these catch a man, he hath no way to save his life. If they fall upon houses, the roofs are crushed by the weight. If the wind blow stiff, the ashes rise out of sight and are carried to far countries. But this bellowing comes only every hundred years or thereabout. And the air around the mountain is pure. None is more healthy. Physicians send
20   thither sick men to get well."

The ashes that had covered Pompeii changed to rich soil. Green vines and shrubs and trees sprang up and covered it, and flowers made it gay. Therefore people said to themselves:

"After all, she is a good old mountain. There will never be another
25   eruption while we are alive."

So villages grew up around her feet. Farmers came and built little houses and planted crops and were happy working the fertile soil. They did not dream that they were living above a buried city, that the roots of their vines sucked water from an old Roman house, that buried statues
30 lay gazing up toward them as they worked.

1. Which of the following is the most reasonable summary of the passage?
    A. A man who survived a devastating volcano eruption continued to speak about the experience for the rest of his life.
    B. Mount Vesuvius is steep, craggy, and thickly wooded, and at times it makes bellowing sounds that remind many people of an ox's growling.
    C. Even though a volcano once erupted and buried a city and has remained volatile, the people who live near the volcano do not fear it.
    D. Some people do not learn their lessons and continue to put themselves in dangerous situations when there is no sensible reason to do so.

2. Which of the following is the most reasonable summary of the first paragraph?
    A. A volcano erupted and buried a city, covering the hills and fields in the surrounding area with ash.
    B. After a volcano erupted and buried a city, it continued to expel material, which occasionally caused destruction.
    C. The dust and lava a volcano expels can be devastating enough to destroy houses and fields.
    D. The eruption of a volcano can be so severe that it can destroy an entire city no matter how advanced that city may seem.

EXERCISE 1–7

Directions: Read the passage, then choose the best answer to each of the questions that follow.

Excerpt from *On the Origin of Species* by Charles Darwin

It is supposed by some naturalists that the more immediate cause of the instinct of the cuckoo is that she lays her eggs, not daily, but at intervals of two or three days; so that, if she were to make her own nest and sit on her own eggs, those first laid would have to be left for some time
5   unincubated or there would be eggs and young birds of different ages in the same nest. If this were the case the process of laying and hatching might be inconveniently long, more especially as she migrates at a very early period; and the first hatched young would probably have to be fed by the male alone. But the American cuckoo is in this predicament, for
10   she makes her own nest and has eggs and young successively hatched, all at the same time. It has been both asserted and denied that the American cuckoo occasionally lays her eggs in other birds' nests; but I have lately heard from Dr. Merrill, of Iowa, that he once found in Illinois a young cuckoo, together with a young jay in the nest of a blue
15   jay (Garrulus cristatus); and as both were nearly full feathered, there could be no mistake in their identification. I could also give several instances of various birds which have been known occasionally to lay their eggs in other birds' nests. Now let us suppose that the ancient progenitor of our European cuckoo had the habits of the American
20   cuckoo, and that she occasionally laid an egg in another bird's nest. If the old bird profited by this occasional habit through being enabled to emigrate earlier or through any other cause; or if the young were made more vigorous by advantage being taken of the mistaken instinct of another species than when reared by their own mother, encumbered as
25   she could hardly fail to be by having eggs and young of different ages at the same time, then the old birds or the fostered young would gain

an advantage. And analogy would lead us to believe that the young thus
reared would be apt to follow by inheritance the occasional and aberrant
habit of their mother, and in their turn would be apt to lay their eggs in
30 other birds' nests, and thus be more successful in rearing their young. By
a continued process of this nature, I believe that the strange instinct of
our cuckoo has been generated. It has, also recently been ascertained on
sufficient evidence, by Adolf Muller, that the cuckoo occasionally lays
her eggs on the bare ground, sits on them and feeds her young. This rare
35 event is probably a case of reversion to the long-lost, aboriginal instinct
of nidification.

1. Based on the passage, which choice best describes the relationship
   between the naturalists mentioned in the first sentence of the passage
   and Dr. Merrill's research?
       A. Dr. Merrill's research builds on the naturalists' assumption.
       B. Dr. Merrill's research contradicts the naturalists' assumption.
       C. Dr. Merrill's research confirms the naturalists' assumption.
       D. Dr. Merrill's research causes the naturalists' assumption.

2. Based on the passage, which choice best describes the relationship
   between the mother cuckoo and the mother blue jay Dr. Merrill
   described?
       A. The mother cuckoo and the mother blue jay helped each other.
       B. The mother cuckoo disregarded the mother blue jay.
       C. The mother cuckoo took advantage of the mother blue jay.
       D. The mother cuckoo provided a service for the mother blue jay.

3. Based on the passage, which choice best describes the relationship between the mother cuckoo's aberrant behavior and her young's behavior?

    A. The young cuckoo copies its mother's aberrant behavior.
    B. The young cuckoo corrects its mother's aberrant behavior.
    C. The young cuckoo develops upon its mother's aberrant behavior.
    D. The young cuckoo cancels its mother's aberrant behavior.

EXERCISE 1–8

Directions: Read the passage, then choose the best answer to each of the questions that follow.

Excerpt from *Illustrated History of Furniture* by Frederick Litchfield

In the chapter on "Renaissance" the great Art revival in England has been noticed; in the Elizabethan oak work of chimney pieces, panelling, and furniture, are to be found varying forms of the free classic style which the Renaissance had brought about. These fluctuating changes
5 in <u>fashion</u> continued in England from the time of Elizabeth until the middle of the eighteenth century, when, as will be shewn presently, a distinct alteration in the design of furniture took place.

    The domestic habits of Englishmen were getting more established. We have seen how religious persecution during preceding reigns, at
10 the time of the Reformation, had encouraged private domestic life of families, in the smaller rooms and apart from the gossiping retainer, who might at any time bring destruction upon the household by giving information about items of conversation he had overheard. There is a <u>passage</u> in one of Sir Henry Wootton's letters, written in 1600, which
15 shews that this home life was now becoming a settled characteristic of his countrymen.

"Every man's <u>proper</u> mansion house and home, being the theatre of his hospitality, the seate of his selfe fruition, the comfortable part of his own life, the noblest of his son's inheritance, a kind of private
20 princedom, nay the possession thereof an epitome of the whole world, may well deserve by these attributes, according to the degree of the master, to be delightfully adorned."

Sir Henry Wootton was ambassador in Venice in 1604, and is said to have been the author of the well-known definition of an ambassador's
25 calling, namely, "an honest man sent abroad to lie for his country's good." This offended the piety of James I, and caused him for some time to be in disgrace. He also published some 20 years later "Elements of Architecture," and being an antiquarian and <u>man of taste</u>, sent home many specimens of the famous Italian wood carving.

1. As used in paragraph 1, *fashion* most nearly means
    A. construct.
    B. demeanor.
    C. attitude.
    D. style.

2. As used in paragraph 2, *passage* most nearly means
    A. movement.
    B. avenue.
    C. section.
    D. approach.

3. As used in paragraph 3, *proper* most nearly means
    A. appropriate.
    B. accurate.
    C. pertinent.
    D. rightful.

4. As used in paragraph 4, *man of taste* most nearly means
   A. person who savors excellent food.
   B. person who appreciates fine artistry.
   C. person who does not overindulge.
   D. person who values enjoyment above all else.

Answers are on page 548.

Reading for Rhetoric

MUST ⚡ KNOW

⚡ An author's point of view is expressed mainly by word choice and choice of details or examples.

⚡ An author's purpose is the reason why he or she writes the text. Common purposes include: to inform, to entertain, and to persuade.

⚡ A persuasive text includes a claim and evidence to support that claim. Evidence may include facts, statistics, expert testimony, and anecdotes. The logic of the claim should follow from the evidence.

Rhetoric is the ability to use words in a variety of ways for persuasive purposes. The SAT tests numerous rhetorical skills. You will have to analyze why an author uses particular words and structures a passage in a certain way. You examine how the author's point of view affects a text's message and identify the overall purpose of a text. You will also analyze the author's arguments, assessing the effectiveness of claims, counterclaims, reasoning, and evidence.

Analyzing Word Choice

Writes choose their words carefully to shape the meaning and tone of a piece of writing. Certain words help the reader understand information or feel particular emotions.

Think about the word *house*. Taken on its own, it may only conjure an image of a very generic structure. However, the addition of a couple of descriptive words could make that image much clearer.

Word Choice	Effect
The *grand* house.	Dramatic
The *zany* house.	Humorous
The *shadow-cloaked* house.	Spooky
The *secret-filled* house.	Mysterious
The *warm and welcoming* house.	Soothing

Writers use words and phrases in other ways to establish tone and convey meaning. Commonly used phrases have built-in meanings.

EXAMPLE

> The sentence "As if that weren't enough, he was also wearing pants that were two sizes too big for him," contains the common phrase "As if that weren't enough," which implies absurdity.

Writers may also make comparisons for the sake of meaning and tone.

> The comparison "The cat was like a car that had run out of gas" indicates that the cat was exhausted, since cars cannot move without gas.

Analyzing Text Structure

The way a writer organizes a piece of writing is its structure. Text structure is not merely an organizational feature. It is also integral to conveying ideas. Analyzing the structure of a text will help you understand it better.

Analyzing Overall Text Structure

There are a number of common methods for structuring a piece of writing. These methods include:

Cyclical Structure

A text that begins with a particular idea or event and moves through a series of progressions before returning to the original idea or event.

> I had fallen into a routine, getting out of bed at 7 a.m. every morning before padding downstairs to eat breakfast. After that I'd shower, shave, dress, and wander off to work. Following eight difficult hours, I'd get back in my car to head home, eat dinner, and watch a little TV before drifting back to bed at 10 p.m.
>
> This passage begins and ends in the same place (bed), which indicates its cyclical structure.

Descriptive Structure

A text that consists almost entirely of description to help the reader understand how something looks, feels, sounds, behaves, etc.

EXAMPLE

▶ The property located at 1218 Sycamore Avenue is a newly constructed split-level home with two bedrooms, three bathrooms, an eat-in kitchen, living room, dining room, and a large backyard ideal for completing with a swimming pool.

▶ This descriptive text helps you to picture the property at 1218 Sycamore Avenue by describing its condition (it is new), the number of its rooms, and the size of its kitchen and backyard.

Compare-Contrast Structure

A text that examines the similarities and differences between two or more ideas, individuals, situations, or events. This structure can be accomplished in two different ways:

BTW

Here are some words and phrases that may indicate a text that utilizes compare-contrast structure: also, both, but, similarly, in contrast, on the other hand, however, by the same token, as well as

- **Block structure** discusses one topic entirely before moving on to the other topic, to which it is being compared or contrasted.

- **Point-by-point structure** alternates between various aspects of both topics.

EXAMPLE

▶ The Beatles recorded the majority of their first album, *Please Please Me*, in a matter of hours using nothing more than guitars, bass, drums, piano, and their voices. However, their seventh album, *Sgt. Pepper's Lonely Hearts Club Band*, took several months to record and utilized a wide variety of instruments in addition to the core arrangement of guitars, bass, drums, and vocals. For their breakthrough record, the Beatles brought various horns, orchestral strings, Indian instruments, keyboards, and experimental tape effects into the mix.

In that example, the writer's use of the transitional word *however* between the two topics (*Please Please Me* and *Sgt. Pepper's Lonely Hearts Club Band*) is a clue that this passage employs compare-contrast structure. The writer is contrasting two very different albums by the same band. The fact that one topic is discussed in full before the introduction of the second topic indicates block structure. Here is how the passage might read in point-by-point structure:

EXAMPLE

▶ The Beatles recorded the majority of their first album, *Please Please Me*, in a matter of hours. However, their seventh album, *Sgt. Pepper's Lonely Hearts Club Band*, took several months to record. While *Please Please Me* featured nothing more than guitars, bass, drums, piano, and the Beatles' voices, *Sgt. Pepper's* utilized a wide variety of instruments in addition to the core arrangement of guitars, bass, drums, and vocals. For their breakthrough record, the Beatles brought various horns, orchestral strings, Indian instruments, keyboards, and experimental tape effects into the mix.

In that example, we can recognize the point-by-point structure because the writer first discusses the length of each of the albums (point 1), then the types of instruments used on each album (point 2).

BTW

Here are some words and phrases that may indicate a text that utilizes cause-effect structure: so, therefore, since, as a consequence, as a result, consequently, caused, affected, because, due to, therefore

Cause-Effect Structure

A text that introduces an idea or event and explains the effects that it brought into existence.

▶ Johannes Gutenberg's invention of a mechanical movable type printing press completely revolutionized publishing. Publications could now be printed faster, more cheaply, and more easily. Consequently, not only did reading material become easier to obtain and less expensive, but ideas and information could be spread throughout the world more effectively.

The writer's use of the word *consequently* between the two ideas (*Guttenberg's invention and the greater availability* and *the influence of reading materials*) indicates this text's cause-effect structure.

Problem-Solution Structure

A text that introduces a particular problem or set of problems before explaining the solution to that problem.

BTW

Here are some words and phrases that may indicate a text that utilizes problem-solution structure: the question is, that is why, the problem is, to solve this, one answer is, the solution is, effect, hopefully

▶ Knowing what one should and should not recycle sometimes takes more than simply looking for a number inside of a triangle. While plastic containers are marked 1 or 2 to indicate they are fine to recycle, paper is not as clearly identified. For example, people regularly toss used pizza cartons into their recycling bins regardless of the condition of those cartons. Little do they know that an exceptionally greasy carton should not be recycled because it contaminates the paper recycled from it. That is why one should thoroughly study their town's recycling guidelines before assuming an item does or does not belong in a recycling bin. These guidelines are usually available readily online.

This passage introduces the problem of figuring out what should and should not be recycled. The solution is to read the guidelines, and the writer signals this solution with the telltale phrase "That is why."

Sequence Structure

A text structured in order of when the events take place or according to steps in a procedure.

EXAMPLE

▶ After collecting your ingredients, it is time to begin preparing your omelet. Before getting to your eggs, you must prepare the omelet's contents. Chop the peppers and onions finely. Grate the cheese. Now you should begin preheating your pan over a medium flame. Then you are ready to tackle those eggs. Crack them into a bowl and add salt and pepper to taste. Whip the eggs until their whites and yolks are well blended. Drop a pat of butter into the pan. When it is completely melted, drag it around with a spatula until the pan is well coated.

▶ You are now ready to pour your eggs into the pan. Once they begin to solidify, sprinkle the cheese, peppers, and onions over the center. Fold the eggs over the mixture and allow them to solidify completely. A perfect omelet should only be slightly browned. Finally, serve with a sprig of parsley and enjoy!

This sequentially structured passage uses a number of signal words— after, now, then, finally—to indicate the various steps in the procedure of cooking an omelet.

Analyzing Part-Whole Relationships

Texts consist of numerous smaller parts. The basic building blocks of any text are its sentences, which contain various details, examples, and information. They may also include quotations or parenthetical statements:

- **Examples:** parts of a whole separated and described to make a statement about the character of the whole

▶ The New York Yankees produced some of the finest players in the history of baseball, such as Reggie Jackson, Mickey Mantle, and Babe Ruth.

- **Quotation:** a section of text consisting of words someone other than the principal writer said or wrote

▶ "Quotations add different perspectives and evidence to back up statements," said one English teacher.

- **Parenthetical details:** relevant additional details set off with parentheses because they do not fit in with the flow of the text (These are asides, much like the text you're reading right now.)

These are just a few examples of the smaller components a text may include. No matter what they may be, they all have an effect on the text as a whole. The writer may include them to illustrate a point, draw attention to an idea, make a comparison, or support a claim.

Sentences may also be grouped into paragraphs, and these paragraphs may be grouped into sections with specific headings:

- **Paragraph:** an individual segment of a written work that deals with a general idea or topic, usually consisting of three or more sentences

- **Section:** a paragraph or group of paragraphs that deal with a specific topic gathered under a heading

EXAMPLE

▶ **Excerpt from *The Radio Amateur's Hand Book***
by Frederick Collins

Kinds of Transmitters.—There are two general types of transmitters used for sending out wireless messages and these are: (1) *wireless telegraph* transmitters, and (2) *wireless telephone* transmitters. Telegraph transmitters may use either: (*a*) a *jump-*
5   *spark*, (*b*) an *electric arc*, or (*c*) *a vacuum tube* apparatus for sending out dot and dash messages, while telephone transmitters may use either, (*a*) an *electric arc*, or (*b*) a *vacuum tube* for sending out vocal and musical sounds. Amateurs generally use a *jump-spark* for sending wireless telegraph messages and the *vacuum tube* for
10   sending wireless telephone messages.

The Spark Gap Wireless Telegraph Transmitter.—The simplest kind of a wireless telegraph transmitter consists of: (1) a *source of direct or alternating current*, (2) a *telegraph key*, (3) a *spark-coil* or a *transformer*, (4) a *spark gap*, (5) an *adjustable condenser* and
15   (6) an *oscillation transformer*. Where *dry cells* or a *storage battery* must be used to supply the current for energizing the transmitter a spark-coil can be employed and these may be had in various sizes from a little fellow which gives 1/4-inch spark up to a larger one which gives a 6-inch spark. Where more energy is needed it is
20   better practice to use a transformer and this can be worked on an alternating current of 110 volts, or if only a 110 volt direct current is available then an *electrolytic interrupter* must be used to make and break the current.

Analyzing Point of View

The stance a writer takes when writing a text is her point of view. This stance comprises the writer's attitude and opinion about the topic she is discussing. It can be determined from the language the writer uses, as well as the details the writer chooses to include or omit from the text. By expressing her point of view, the writer may be trying to persuade the reader to agree with an opinion. A writer may take the position of:

Advocate: someone who speaks in support of an idea, person, or cause

EXAMPLE

▶ **An advocate might write:** I think everyone should join a fitness club; it's the ideal way to stay in prime physical shape.

Conservator: someone who wants to protect or preserve an idea or way of life

EXAMPLE

▶ **A conservator might write:** Tearing down woodlands to build shopping malls and parking lots is destroying our city's landscape.

Critic: someone who speaks against an idea, person, or cause

EXAMPLE

▶ **A critic might write:** Children are wasting their time watching television when they could be reading or playing outdoors.

Idealist: someone who romanticizes an idea

▶ **An idealist might write:** The 1980s was a better time to grow up than any other period in history.

Mentor: someone who is guiding, teaching, or counseling a student

▶ **A mentor might write:** You will encounter many hurdles as you progress through life, but you should always try your best to overcome each one.

Observer: someone who makes impartial notes and observations

▶ **An observer might write:** The Empire State Building stands 1,250 feet high over Midtown Manhattan.

Reporter: an impartial chronicler of current events

▶ **A reporter might write:** The president gave his State of the Union address last night and discussed such topics as the economy and national security.

Scholar: an expert on a particular topic

▶ **A scholar might write:** The chain pickerel's relatively light coloring and the unique pattern reminiscent of chains on its skin distinguish it from the northern pike.

Analyzing Purpose

Writers create texts for different purposes. A writer might write a piece to entertain, inform, or persuade. By analyzing a text's language, tone, and information, you should be able to decipher its purpose. Consider whether or not the writer is trying to convince you of something. Such a text was likely written to persuade. If a writer merely imparts information without including his opinions about the topic, the piece was probably written to inform. If a text is more concerned with amusing the reader than conveying facts or opinions, it was written to entertain.

EXAMPLE

▶ **Excerpt from** *Manners, Customs, and Dress During the Middle Ages and During the Renaissance Period*
by Paul Lacroix

From the reign of Philip Augustus, a remarkable change seems to have taken place in the private life of kings, princes, and nobles. Although his domains and revenues had always been on the increase, this monarch never displayed, in ordinary
5   circumstances at least, much magnificence. The accounts of his private expenses for the years 1202 and 1203 have been preserved, which enable us to discover some curious details bearing witness to the extreme simplicity of the court at that period. The household of the King or royal family was still very
10   small: one chancellor, one chaplain, a squire, a butler, a few Knights of the Temple, and some sergeants-at-arms were the only officers of the palace. The king and princes of his household only changed apparel three times during the year.

Author's purpose: to inform readers about the behavior and customs of royalty during the reign of Philip Augustus.

Since a passage meant to inform and a passage meant to persuade both rely on conveying information, look at word choice carefully to see the difference between them.

> ▶ **Excerpt from *California Romantic and Resourceful***
> *by John F. Davis*
>
> It is indefensible that in the face of incidents of our history such as these Californians should be ignorant of the lives and experiences of those who preceded them on this coast. The history of their experiences is a part of the history of the nation, and the
> 5 record of the achievement of the empire-builders of this coast is one that inspires civic pride and a reverence for their memories. Why should the story remain practically unknown? Why should every little unimportant detail of the petty incidents of Queen Anne's War, and King Philip's War, and Braddock's campaign be
> 10 crammed into the heads of children who until lately never heard the name of Portolá?
>
> **Author's purpose:** to persuade the reader that California's history is more important to Californians than any well-known historical event that occurred elsewhere.

Analyzing Arguments

A persuasive text makes an argument for or against something. An argument includes a claim and evidence. The claim is the position the writer is arguing (example: Holidays are fun.). Evidence supports that claim (example: Most people do not have to work on holidays, so they can spend them doing the things they enjoy.). Without the evidence, the claim would not be very persuasive. An argument might also contain a counterclaim, which is an argument against a stated claim (example: However, some people actually have to work on holidays, so they aren't fun for everyone.).

Analyzing Claims and Counterclaims

A persuasive text does not have much purpose without claims. They are the backbones of any effective argument. Sometimes an author will state her claims explicitly. Sometimes these claims are only implied, yet can be understood by comprehending textual evidence.

 IRL On the SAT, you will have to identify the claims explicitly stated and implied in persuasive texts and determine counterclaims using textual evidence. You can practice this skill by examining editorials in newspapers or online.

EXAMPLE

Having a free sample of a song available for download on a popular digital music website is one of the most effective kinds of publicity a musical artist can use. The benefits of offering a sample include not only higher sales of the song but may also include fees paid by the website to the artist.

1. Which of the following can be most properly inferred from the author's argument above?

 A. The number of people for whom the sample produces a desire to purchase the song is larger than the number of people for whom the sample proves sufficient as a substitute for the whole song.

 B. The effectiveness of having a sample of a song available on a digital music website is proportional to the overall popularity of that website.

 C. A musical artist can generate as much income from sample download fees for a song as from sales of the entire song.

 D. Songs that do not get played on radio stations get sampled more than songs that do get played on the radio.

E. Since the financial advantage of having sample downloads benefits the musical artist, many digital music websites do not offer sample downloads.

▶ First, find the argument's claim. The argument concludes that providing free samples leads to higher sales. For this to be true, there must be more people buying the song than simply listening to the sample. The best answer is A.

Analzying Reasoning

Simply making an argument is not enough to compose an effect persuasive text. The reasoning behind the argument must be sound. On the SAT, you will have to both recognize the implicit reasoning of arguments and assess the soundness of arguments. The key to assessing the reasoning of an argument is to locate mistakes in that reasoning. Such mistakes are known as logical fallacies. Here are some to look out for in the persuasive texts on the SAT:

- **Ad hominem:** attacking someone personally, rather than criticizing their position on an issue

EXAMPLE

▶ **An ad hominem attack looks like this:** No one would listen to you. You have terrible taste in music.

- **Circular reasoning:** when the claim of an argument is essentially identical to its conclusion

EXAMPLE

▶ **Circular reasoning looks like this:** You have no idea what you're talking about because you don't make any sense.

- **Fallacy of composition:** assuming that what is true of a part is also true of the whole

EXAMPLE
▶ **A composition fallacy looks like this:** Los Angeles is a very fast-moving city, so California must be a fast-moving state.

- **Hasty generalization:** jumping to a conclusion with very little evidence

EXAMPLE
▶ **A hasty generalization looks like this:** I once spoke to a New Yorker, so I know that New Yorkers are very intelligent.

- **Incomplete comparison:** a statement that masquerades as a comparison but actually fails to make a comparison between two things

EXAMPLE
▶ **An incomplete comparison looks like this:** This book is better.

- **Post hoc ergo propter hoc:** confusing sequential order with cause and effect

EXAMPLE
▶ **A post hoc fallacy looks like this:** It rained after I heard the thunder; therefore, thunder causes rain.

- **Slippery slope:** the assumption that one action will naturally lead to another

EXAMPLE

> **A slippery slop fallacy looks like this:** If we start giving away free potato chips with lunch, we'll eventually have to give away the entire lunch for free.

IRL You can see slippery slope fallacies often in the speeches of politicians. At a rally in Vermont on October 21, 2015, Donald Trump said, "You know what's going to happen. They're [Ford] going to build a plant [in Mexico] and illegals are going to drive those cars right over the border. Then they'll probably end up stealing the car and that'll be the end of it." Here, the speaker implies that if Ford builds a plant in Mexico, it will somehow lead to car theft and illegal immigration.

Analyzing Evidence

A strong argument requires strong evidence. Even a well-reasoned argument means little without relevant supporting evidence to prove it. The four essential types of evidence are:

- **Factual evidence:** proven statement

EXAMPLE

> **Factual evidence looks like this:** The *Jazz Singer* is the first feature-length Hollywood movie to contain audible spoken dialogue.

- **Statistical evidence:** data collected through studies

EXAMPLE

> **Statistical evidence looks like this:** As of 2013, 83.8 percent of American households had home computers.

- **Testimonial evidence:** the opinions of authorities

> **Testimonial evidence looks like this:** Professional skier Bob Johnson says that Snow Inc. makes the best skis on the market.

- **Anecdotal evidence:** personal observations

> **Anecdotal evidence looks like this:** I went to Paris on vacation, so I can confirm that you do not need to speak French to enjoy the city.

To analyze any kind of evidence, you must determine its quality. Does the evidence make sense? Is it relevant to the given claim? Does it support the claim on its own or is additional support needed? Is the source of the evidence trustworthy?

EXERCISES

EXERCISE 2–1

Directions: Read the passage, then choose the best answer to each of the questions that follow.

Excerpt from *Elevator Systems of the Eiffel Tower 1889*
by Robert M. Vogel

Preliminary studies for a 300-meter tower were made with the
1889 fair immediately in mind. With an assurance born of positive
knowledge, Eiffel in June of 1886 approached the Exposition
commissioners with the project. There can be no doubt that only

5   the singular respect with which Eiffel was regarded not only by his
profession but by the entire nation motivated the Commission to
approve a plan which, in the hands of a figure of less stature, would
have been considered grossly impractical.
  Between this time and commencement of the Tower's construction

10 at the end of January 1887, there arose one of the most persistently
annoying of the numerous difficulties, both structural and social,
which confronted Eiffel as the project advanced. In the wake of the
initial enthusiasm—on the part of the fair's Commission inspired by
the desire to create a monument to French technological achievement,

15 and on the part of the majority of Frenchmen by the stirring of their
imagination at the magnitude of the structure—there grew a rising
movement of disfavor. The nucleus was, not surprisingly, formed
mainly of the intelligentsia, but objections were made by prominent
Frenchmen in all walks of life. The most interesting point to be noted in

20 a retrospection of this often violent opposition was that, although the
Tower's every aspect was attacked, there was remarkably little criticism
of its structural feasibility, either by the engineering profession or,
as seems traditionally to be the case with bold and unprecedented

undertakings, by large numbers of the technically uninformed laity.
25 True, there was an undercurrent of what might be characterized as
unease by many property owners in the structure's shadow, but the
most obstinate element of resistance was that which deplored the
Tower as a mechanistic intrusion upon the architectural and natural
beauties of Paris. This resistance voiced its fury in a flood of special
30 newspaper editions, petitions, and manifestos signed by such lights of
the fine and literary arts as De Maupassant, Gounod, Dumas *fils*, and
others. The eloquence of one article, which appeared in several Paris
papers in February 1887, was typical:

   We protest in the name of French taste and the national art culture
35 against the erection of a staggering Tower, like a gigantic kitchen
chimney dominating Paris, eclipsing by its barbarous mass Notre
Dame, the Sainte- Chapelle, the tower of St. Jacques, the Dôme des
Invalides, the Arc de Triomphe, humiliating these monuments by an act
of madness.

1. The main rhetorical effect of the use of the word *annoying* in paragraph
   2 ("the most persistently annoying of the numerous difficulties") is to
   A. imply that everyone with an opinion about the tower was foolish.
   B. clarify that there were no legitimate criticisms of the tower.
   C. convey the negative effect the tower was having on Parisian
      society.
   D. criticize critics of the tower and suggest support for Eiffel.

2. The main rhetorical effect of the phrase "not surprisingly" in paragraph 2
   ("The nucleus was, not surprisingly, formed mainly of the intelligentsia")
   is to
   A. indicate the power of the intelligentsia.
   B. imply that the intelligentsia complained often.
   C. convey how Parisians felt about the intelligentsia.
   D. propose that the intelligentsia's criticisms were invalid.

3. The main rhetorical effect of comparing the tower to "a gigantic kitchen chimney" in the article quoted at the end of the passage is to

    A. prove that the tower has a functional purpose.

    B. suggest that the tower would be an eyesore.

    C. predict people would mistake the tower for a chimney.

    D. propose Eiffel should consider redesigning the tower.

EXERCISE 2–2

Directions: Read the passages, then choose the best answer to each of the questions that follow.

Excerpt from *Curiosities of Science: Past and Present* by *John Timbs*

CAN THE CAT SEE IN THE DARK?

No, in all probability, says the reader; but the opposite popular belief is supported by eminent naturalists.

Buffon says: "The eyes of the cat shine in the dark somewhat like
5 diamonds, which throw out during the night the light with which they were in a manner impregnated during the day."

Valmont de Bamare says: "The pupil of the cat is during the night still deeply imbued with the light of the day;" and again, "the eyes of the cat are during the night so imbued with light that they then appear
10 very shining and luminous."

Spallanzani says: "The eyes of cats, polecats, and several other animals, shine in the dark like two small tapers;" and he adds that this light is phosphoric.

Treviranus says: "The eyes of the cat *shine where no rays of light*
15 *penetrate*; and the light must in many, if not in all, cases proceed from the eye itself."

1. The author structured this passage primarily to
    A. ask a question about cats and provide answers to it.
    B. describe a problem about cats and offer a solution.
    C. state an opinion about cats before cycling forward.
    D. describe a specific aspect of cats in clinical detail.

Excerpt from *A Short History of the World*
by H. G. Wells

The first overseas settlements of the Dutch and Northern Atlantic Europeans were not for colonization but for trade and mining. The Spaniards were first in the field; they claimed dominion over the whole of this new world of America. Very soon however the Portuguese
5 asked for a share. The Pope— it was one of the last acts of Rome as mistress of the world—divided the new continent between these two first-comers, giving Portugal Brazil and everything else east of a line 370 leagues west of the Cape Verde islands, and all the rest to Spain (1494). The Portuguese at this time were also pushing overseas
10 enterprise southward and eastward. In 1497 Vasco da Gama had sailed from Lisbon round the Cape to Zanzibar and then to Calicut in India. In 1515 there were Portuguese ships in Java and the Moluccas, and the Portuguese were setting up and fortifying trading stations round and about the coasts of the Indian Ocean. Mozambique, Goa, and two
15 smaller possessions in India, Macao in China and a part of Timor are to this day Portuguese possessions.

2. The author structured this passage primarily to
    A. compare the achievements of the Spaniards to those of the Portuguese.
    B. show the long-term effects of the Pope's division of the new continent.
    C. briefly describe a sequence of significant historical events.
    D. show how events build on each other before returning to the initial event.

Excerpt from *The Art of Public Speaking*
by Dale Carnegie and J. Berg Esenwein

How would you cure a horse that is afraid of cars—graze him
in a back-woods lot where he would never see steam-engines or
automobiles, or drive or pasture him where he would frequently see
the machines?

5   Apply horse-sense to ridding yourself of self-consciousness and
fear: face an audience as frequently as you can, and you will soon stop
shying. You can never attain freedom from stage-fright by reading a
treatise. A book may give you excellent suggestions on how best to
conduct yourself in the water, but sooner or later you must get wet,
10 perhaps even strangle and be "half scared to death."

3. The author structured this passage primarily to
    A. compare horses to people who suffer from stage fright.
    B. describe how stage fright affects the people who suffer from it.
    C. provide sequential steps for overcoming stage fright.
    D. establish the problem of stage fright before suggesting a solution
       to it.

Excerpt from *All About Coffee*
by William H. Ukers, M.A.

We are indebted to three great French travelers for much
valuable knowledge about coffee; and these gallant gentlemen
first fired the imagination of the French people in regard to the
beverage that was destined to play so important a part in the
5 French revolution. They are Tavernier (1605–89), Thévenot
(1633–67), and Bernier (1625–88).
    Then there is Jean La Roque (1661–1745), who made a famous
"Voyage to Arabia the Happy" (*Voyage de l'Arabie Heureuse*) in 1708–
13 and to whose father, P. de la Roque, is due the honor of having
10 brought the first coffee into France in 1644. Also, there is Antoine

Galland (1646–1715), the French Orientalist, first translator of the *Arabian Nights* and antiquary to the king, who, in 1699, published an analysis and translation from the Arabic of the Abd-al-Kâdir manuscript (1587), giving the first authentic account of the origin
15 of coffee.

Probably the earliest reference to coffee in France is to be found in the simple statement that Onorio Belli (Bellus), the Italian botanist and author, in 1596 sent to Charles de l'Écluse (1526–1609), a French physician, botanist and traveler, "seeds used by the Egyptians to make a
20 liquid they call *cave*."

4. The author refers to Tavernier, Thévenot, and Bernier primarily to
    A. compare the achievements of each man to the others.
    B. credit three people who spread information about coffee.
    C. provide examples of important travelers in French history.
    D. illustrate how coffee came to be appreciated in France.

5. The author included the quote at the end of the passage primarily to
    A. defer to the authority of the quote's author.
    B. discuss the specific language of the quote.
    C. question the position of the quote's author.
    D. ensure the reader does not misunderstand a message.

EXERCISE 2–3

Directions: Read the passages, then choose the best answer to each of the questions that follow.

Excerpt from *The History of the Decline and Fall of the Roman Empire*
by Edward Gibbon

In the second century of the Christian Aera, the empire of Rome comprehended the fairest part of the earth, and the most civilized

portion of mankind. The frontiers of that extensive monarchy were guarded by ancient renown and disciplined valor. The gentle but
5 powerful influence of laws and manners had gradually cemented the union of the provinces. Their peaceful inhabitants enjoyed and abused the advantages of wealth and luxury. The image of a free constitution was preserved with decent reverence: the Roman senate appeared to possess the sovereign authority, and devolved on the emperors all the
10 executive powers of government. During a happy period of more than fourscore years, the public administration was conducted by the virtue and abilities of Nerva, Trajan, Hadrian, and the two Antonines. It is the design of this, and of the two succeeding chapters, to describe the prosperous condition of their empire; and after wards, from the death
15 of Marcus Antoninus, to deduce the most important circumstances of its decline and fall; a revolution which will ever be remembered, and is still felt by the nations of the earth.

1. The stance the author takes in the passage is best described as that of
    A. an advocate who describes an example that must be followed.
    B. an observer who refuses to express a specific opinion.
    C. a scholar intent on disproving preconceived notions.
    D. an idealist who romanticizes a historical period.

Excerpt from *Captain Cook's Journal. First Voyage*
by James Cook

Wednesday, 4th. First part, genteel breeze and Clear; latter, fresh gales, with heavy squalls of wind and rain, which brought us under our courses and main topsails close reefed. Soon after noon saw the appearance of Land to the Eastward, and being in the Latitude of
5 Peypes Island, as it is lay'd down in some Charts, imagined it might be it.* (*Pepys' Island, placed on charts, from a report by Captain Cowley in 1683, about 230 miles north of Falkland Islands, and long

imagined to exist. It was eventually recognised, after the discovery of Cowley's manuscript Journal, that Cowley had sighted the Falklands.)

10 Bore down to be Certain, and at 1/2 past 2 p.m. discovered our Mistake, and hauld the Wind again. At 6 sounded, and had 72 fathoms black sand and mud. Variation 19 degrees 45 minutes East. Wind West- North-West to South-West by South; course South 30 degrees East; distance 76 miles; latitude 48 degrees 28 minutes South,

15 longitude 60 degrees 51 minutes West.

2. The stance the author takes in the passage is best described as that of

    A. a reporter cataloguing details impartially.

    B. a mentor guiding pupils through a series of steps.

    C. a coordinator making sense of two opposing viewpoints.

    D. a conservator preserving important historical events.

EXERCISE 2–4

Directions: Read the passages, then choose the best answer to each of the questions that follow.

Excerpt from *A History of the Peloponnesian War* by Thucydides

Thucydides, an Athenian, wrote the history of the war between the Peloponnesians and the Athenians, beginning at the moment that it broke out, and believing that it would be a great war and more worthy of relation than any that had preceded it. This belief was not without

5 its grounds. The preparations of both the combatants were in every department in the last state of perfection; and he could see the rest of the Hellenic race taking sides in the quarrel; those who delayed doing so at once having it in contemplation. Indeed this was the greatest movement yet known in history, not only of the Hellenes, but of a large

10 part of the barbarian world—I had almost said of mankind. For though
the events of remote antiquity, and even those that more immediately
preceded the war, could not from lapse of time be clearly ascertained,
yet the evidences which an inquiry carried as far back as was practicable
leads me to trust, all point to the conclusion that there was nothing on
15 a great scale, either in war or in other matters.

1. The primary purpose of this passage is to
- A. describe the circumstances of how an author wrote a text.
- B. prove an author's decision to write a text was misguided.
- C. explain an author's reason for writing a text.
- D. imply an author made careless mistakes.

Excerpt from *The Elements of Style*
by William Strunk, Jr.

Enclose parenthetic expressions between commas.

The best way to see a country, unless you are pressed for time, is to travel on foot.

This rule is difficult to apply; it is frequently hard to decide
5 whether a single word, such as *however*, or a brief phrase, is or is not parenthetic. If the interruption to the flow of the sentence is but slight, the writer may safely omit the commas. But whether the interruption be slight or considerable, he must never insert one comma and omit the other.

2. The primary purpose of this passage is to
- A. expose the inherent flaws of a system.
- B. prove there are exceptions to every rule.
- C. suggest one way to accomplish a task.
- D. explain the correct way to do something.

Excerpt from *The Outline of Science, Vol. 1*
by J. Arthur Thomson

There is abundant evidence of a widened and deepened interest in modern science. How could it be otherwise when we think of the magnitude and the eventfulness of recent advances?

But the interest of the general public would be even greater than it
5 is if the makers of new knowledge were more willing to expound their discoveries in ways that could be "understanded of the people." No one objects very much to technicalities in a game or on board a yacht, and they are clearly necessary for terse and precise scientific description. It is certain, however, that they can be reduced to a minimum without
10 sacrificing accuracy, when the object in view is to explain "the gist of the matter." So this Outline of Science is meant for the general reader, who lacks both time and opportunity for special study, and yet would take an intelligent interest in the progress of science which is making the world always new.

3. The primary purpose of this passage is to
   A. criticize a common educational method.
   B. explain the difficulties of science education.
   C. suggest an effective way to educate.
   D. prove people can understand difficult concepts.

EXERCISE 2–5

Directions: Read the passages, then choose the best answer to each of the questions that follow.

Excerpt from "How to Tell a Story"
by Mark Twain

I do not claim that I can tell a story as it ought to be told. I only claim to know how a story ought to be told, for I have been almost daily in the company of the most expert story-tellers for many years.

There are several kinds of stories, but only one difficult
kind—the humorous. I will talk mainly about that one. The
humorous story is American, the comic story is English, the witty
story is French. The humorous story depends for its effect upon the
manner of the telling; the comic story and the witty story upon the
matter.

The humorous story may be spun out to great length, and
may wander around as much as it pleases, and arrive nowhere
in particular; but the comic and witty stories must be brief and
end with a point. The humorous story bubbles gently along, the
others burst.

The humorous story is strictly a work of art—high and delicate art—
and only an artist can tell it; but no art is necessary in telling the comic
and the witty story; anybody can do it. The art of telling a humorous
story—understand, I mean by word of mouth, not print—was created
in America, and has remained at home.

1. What is the author's central claim?
    A. Each kind of story must be told differently.
    B. Humorous stories should never be too long.
    C. Anyone can tell a humorous story well.
    D. There is a specific way to tell a humorous story.

2. Which line from the passage provides the best support for the answer to
   the previous question?
    A. "The humorous story depends for its effect upon the manner of
       the telling..."
    B. "I do not claim that I can tell a story as it ought to be told."
    C. "The humorous story is American, the comic story is English, the
       witty story is French."
    D. "...no art is necessary in telling the comic and the witty story..."

Excerpt from *The Analysis of the Mind*
by Bertrand Russell

Few things are more firmly established in popular philosophy than the distinction between mind and matter. Those who are not professional metaphysicians are willing to confess that they do not know what mind actually is, or how matter is constituted; but
5 they remain convinced that there is an impassable gulf between the two, and that both belong to what actually exists in the world. Philosophers, on the other hand, have maintained often that matter is a mere fiction imagined by mind, and sometimes that mind is a mere property of a certain kind of matter. Those who maintain that
10 mind is the reality and matter an evil dream are called "idealists"—a word which has a different meaning in philosophy from that which it bears in ordinary life. Those who argue that matter is the reality and mind a mere property of protoplasm are called "materialist." They have been rare among philosophers, but common, at certain periods,
15 among men of science. Idealists, materialists, and ordinary mortals have been in agreement on one point: that they knew sufficiently what they meant by the words "mind" and "matter" to be able to conduct their debate intelligently. Yet it was just in this point, as to which they were at one, that they seem to me to have been all alike
20 in error.

The stuff of which the world of our experience is composed is, in my belief, neither mind nor matter, but something more primitive than either. Both mind and matter seem to be composite, and the stuff of which they are compounded lies in a sense between the two, in a sense
25 above them both, like a common ancestor.

3. Which line from the text provides the best counterclaim to the idea that mind and matter are firmly established in popular philosophy?

   A. "Few things are more firmly established in popular philosophy than the distinction between mind and matter."

   B. "Those who argue that matter is the reality and mind a mere property of protoplasm are called 'materialists.'"

   C. "Yet it was just in this point, as to which they were at one, that they seem to me to have been all alike in error."

   D. "The stuff of which the world of our experience is composed is, in my belief, neither mind nor matter, but something more primitive than either."

EXERCISE 2–6

Directions: Read the passages, then choose the best answer to each of the questions that follow.

Excerpt from *A Guide to Health*
by Mahatma Gandhi

The most important portion of the body is the stomach. If the stomach ceases to work even for a single moment, the whole body would collapse. The work of the stomach is to digest the food, and so to provide nourishment to the body. Its relation to the body is the same as that of the steam engine to the Railway train.

1. The author most likely compares the stomach to a steam engine to

   A. prove that the body functions just as a machine does.

   B. refute arguments that the heart is the most important organ.

   C. illustrate how it is the organ that powers the body.

   D. reiterate that a body would collapse without its stomach.

Excerpt from *Making Life Worth While*
by Douglas Fairbanks

Holding down a seat in the rocking chair fleet out on the shady piazza is most certainly not making the most out of life.

We all remember the line—"If wishes were fishes we'd have some fried." That is the answer to those who rock and dream, and hope for
5 something to *turn up* instead of *turning up* something on their own account.

Of course, there is a time for everything, even the stealthy, creeping rocking chair—and that's about bedtime. In the estimation of an eminent neurologist there is no crime against nature in the home
10 that cannot be traced to this monstrous thief of time, which, while apparently screeching and groaning under its load, is, in reality, shouting with joy at the job it is putting up on its occupant.

Taking the most out of life is the proper label for this old squeaker— breeder of idle contentment, day-dreams, inertia. Like everything else
15 that saps the energy from mind and body, it counts its victims by the score, and throws them up on the sands of time.

2. The passage most strongly suggests that contentment
   A. is the enemy of achievement.
   B. plays an important role in mental health.
   C. can be painful to experience.
   D. is not the same thing as relaxation.

3. Which line from the passage provides the best support for the answer to the previous question?
   A. "...this monstrous thief of time..."
   B. "...hope for something to *turn up* instead of *turning up* something on their own account."
   C. "...saps the energy from mind and body..."
   D. "...there is a time for everything, even the stealthy, creeping rocking chair..."

EXERCISE 2–7

Directions: Read the passages, then choose the best answer to each of the questions that follow.

Excerpt from *Dream Psychology*
by Sigmund Freud

Three tendencies can be observed in the estimation of dreams. Many philosophers have given currency to one of these tendencies, one which at the same time preserves something of the dream's former over-valuation. The foundation of dream life is for them a peculiar state of
5 phychical activity, which they even celebrate as elevation to some higher state. Schubert, for instance, claims: "The dream is the liberation of the spirit from the pressure of external nature, a detachment of the soul from the fetters of matter." Not all go so far as this, but many maintain that dreams have their origin in real spiritual excitations, and are the
10 outward manifestations of spiritual powers whose free movements have been hampered during the day ("Dream Phantasies," Scherner, Volkelt). A large number of observers acknowledge that dream life is capable of extraordinary achievements—at any rate, in certain fields ("Memory").

1. The author supports the claim that dream life is "a peculiar state of psychical activity" in this passage by
    A. providing the results of an experiment.
    B. quoting a source who supports the claim.
    C. describing the claim in great detail.
    D. listing all the people who support this claim.

Excerpt from *English Synonyms and Antonyms*
by James C. Fernald, L.H.D.

In our own day, when so many are eager to write, and confident that they can write, and when the press is sending forth by the ton that which is called literature, but which somehow lacks the imprint of immortality, it is of the first importance to revive the study

5 of synonyms as a distinct branch of rhetorical culture. Prevalent errors need at times to be noted and corrected, but the teaching of pure English speech is the best defense against all that is inferior, unsuitable, or repulsive. The most effective condemnation of an objectionable word or phrase is that it is not found in scholarly works,

10 and a student who has once learned the rich stores of vigorous, beautiful, exact, and expressive words that make up our noble language, is by that very fact put beyond the reach of all temptation to linguistic corruption.

Special instruction in the use of synonyms is necessary, for the

15 reason that few students possess the analytical power and habit of mind required to hold a succession of separate definitions in thought at once, compare them with each other, and determine just where and how they part company; and the persons least able to do this are the very ones most in the need of the information. The distinctions between words

20 similar in meaning are often so fine and elusive as to tax the ingenuity of the accomplished scholar; yet when clearly apprehended they are as important for the purposes of language as the minute differences between similar substances are for the purposes of chemistry. Often definition itself is best secured by the comparison of kindred terms and

25 the pointing out where each differs from the other. We perceive more clearly and remember better what each word is, by perceiving where each divides from the another of kindred meaning; just as we see and remember better the situation and contour of adjacent countries, by considering them as boundaries of each other, rather than by an exact

30 statement of the latitude and longitude of each as a separate portion of the earth's surface.

2. Which claim does the author fail to support?
    A. The press labels writing "literature" too easily.
    B. Special instruction about synonyms is necessary.
    C. Objectionable words or phrases can be eliminated.
    D. Understanding the distinction between similar words is important.

3. What is the central claim of the second paragraph?
    A. Teaching English better produces better literature.
    B. The press does not understand good writing.
    C. The distinction between synonyms is important.
    D. Good writers should use many synonyms.

Answers are on page 549.

3 Reading for Synthesis

MUST ⚡ KNOW

⚡ For a pair of related passages, focus on subtle differences in point of view and focus.

⚡ Analyze graphic elements (charts, graphs, etc.) carefully to see how they relate to the reading passage. Be sure to read all the labels provided.

The SAT tests your ability to connect information across more than one source. Synthesis questions require you to relate information, ideas, and rhetorical techniques between two passages or a passage and a graphic, such as a table, chart, or graph.

Analyzing Multiple Texts

Everything you learned in the previous two chapters can be applied to synthesis questions. These questions require you to read two passages and examine how they are similar or different in terms of their information, ideas, and rhetorical properties.

In the Reading section of the SAT, you will see one set of paired passages, introduced by a common blurb. The pair will have 10–12 questions. There will be a few questions about the first passage alone, then a few questions about the second passage alone, and then a few questions about both passages together.

The questions that relate to both passages are called synthesis questions, and they are among the hardest questions in the reading section because they require you to have read and understood two passages well enough to compare them and contrast often subtle differences between the two passages.

The best strategy for approaching the paired passages is:

1. Save the paired passages for last since synthesis questions are probably the most difficult.

2. Read Passage 1 and then answer all the questions about Passage 1 alone.

3. Read Passage 2 and then answer all the questions about Passage 2 alone.

4. Review what you know about each passage and contrast the passages in your own words.

5. Answer the synthesis questions. By now, you probably know enough about the passages to be able to answer the synthesis questions correctly.

The questions that relate to each individual passage are the same as any other reading passage questions, so they are no more difficult than any other reading comprehension questions. Work them in the same way you would any others. The synthesis questions, however, require a bit more effort.

The two passages may share a particular topic, idea, or structure, but they will never be exactly the same. One writer's point of view may differ from the other's point of view. One writer may be critical of her topic, while the other writer approves of his.

BTW

If you run out of time, at least you answered the easier questions first. This maximizes your points!

EXAMPLE

▶ 1. Social media fools users into believing they are engaging with others when they are really just exchanging superficial sound bites while avoiding genuine human contact.

▶ 2. Social media has revolutionized the way we communicate, putting every member of online communities in touch with other people from all over the world.

▶ Both of these statements address the same topic—social media—yet each conveys a very different opinion of this topic. The first excerpt is quite negative, while the second excerpt is positive.

The ability to recognize distinctions between passages is integral to mastering synthesis questions. First, identify the focus of each passage and see if they differ in any way. Then, identify each author's point of view and see if they differ in any way. The synthesis questions focus on identifying how the ideas in the two passages are connected and comparing and contrasting the claims made.

IRL You can practice comparing and contrasting by reading two accounts of the same event, or by asking two people to describe the same item.

Analyzing Quantitative Information

Graphic elements are frequently used with math questions. On the SAT, they are applied to social studies, history, and science texts, too. These graphic elements illustrate quantitative information. Quantitative information is anything that can be measured numerically, such as size, weight, time, population, proportion, cost, temperature, and score. The graphic elements conveying such quantitative data include:

Charts: graphic elements that use bars, pie slices, or lines to represent data. Be sure to read the graph title, axis titles, and data labels. Look for any trends in the graph, such as increases, decreases, largest value, and smallest value.

EXAMPLE

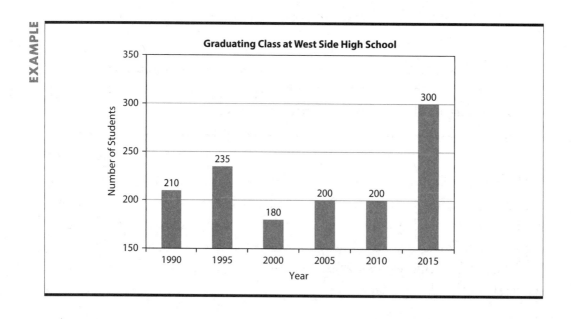

Tables: graphic elements that organize data in columns or rows with headings. Be sure to read the table's title, row headings, and column headings.

EXAMPLE

Major Developments in the Film Industry

Year	Development
1890	Founding of first motion picture companies
1895	First short film shown in cinemas
1906	First feature-length film enters production
1927	First film with synchronized sound is released
1930	Silent films are no longer produced in the United States

Graphs: graphic elements that use points connected by lines to represent data. Be sure to read the graph title, axis titles, and data labels. Look for any trends in the graph, such as increases, decreases, largest value, and smallest value.

EXAMPLE

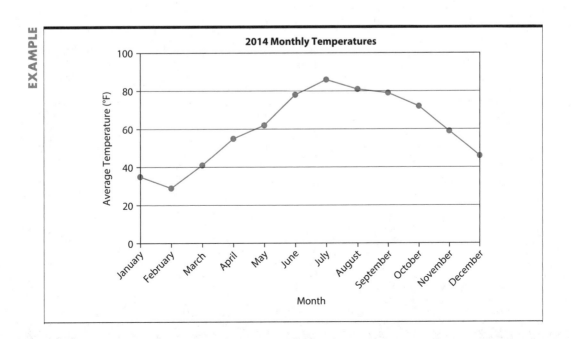

On the SAT, graphic elements are paired with informational reading passages. Your job is to use information from a passage in concert with information from its accompanying graphic element to answer questions. The graphic element will illustrate information in the passage, making that information clearer and easier to understand. All you have to do is read the passage and its graphic element carefully to answer the questions that follow. These questions will be similar to others you learned about earlier in this book. They may require you to make inferences, identify details, or locate supporting information.

BTW

If you want to review charts and graphs, see Chapter 10: Statistics.

EXERCISES

EXERCISE 3-1

Directions: Read the passages, then choose the best answer to each of the questions that follow.

> Passage 1 is an excerpt from *Memoirs of Napoleon Bonaparte*, written by his private secretary, Louis Antoine Fauvelet de Bourrienne, and published in 1831. Passage 2 is an excerpt adapted from *The Journals of Lewis and Clark*, written by Meriwether Lewis and published in 1814.

Passage 1

On the morning of the 30th of March, while the battle before the walls of Paris was at its height, Bonaparte was still at Troyes. He quitted that town at ten o'clock, accompanied only by Bertrand, Caulaincourt, two aides de camp, and two orderly officers. He was not more than
5   two hours in traveling the first ten leagues, and he and his slender escort performed the journey without changing horses, and without even alighting. They arrived at Sens at one o'clock in the afternoon. Everything was in such confusion that it was impossible to prepare a suitable mode of conveyance for the Emperor. He was therefore obliged
10   to content himself with a wretched cariole, and in this equipage, about four in the morning, he reached Froidmanteau, about four leagues from Paris. It was there that the Emperor received from General Belliard, who arrived at the head of a column of artillery, the first intelligence of the battle of Paris. He heard the news with an air of composure,
15   which was probably affected to avoid discouraging those about him. He walked for about a quarter of an hour on the high road, and it was after that promenade that he sent Caulaincourt to Paris. Napoleon afterwards went to the house of the postmaster, where he ordered his maps to be brought to him, and, according to custom, marked the

20   different positions of the enemy's troops with pine, the heads of which
     were touched with wax of different colours. After this description of
     work, which Napoleon did every day, or sometimes several times a day,
     he repaired to Fontainebleau, where he arrived at six in the morning.
     He did not order the great apartments of the castle to be opened, but
25   went up to his favourite little apartment, where he shut himself up, and
     remained alone during the whole of the 31st of March.

Passage 2

     August 8th 1804 we had seen but a few aquatic fouls of any kind on
     the river since we commenced our journey up the Missouri, a few
     geese accompanied by their young, the wood duck which is common
     to every part of this country & cranes of several kinds which will be
5   described in their respective places—this day after we had passed the
     river Sioux as called by Mr. MacKay (or as is more properly called the
     stone river,) I saw a great number of feathers floating down the river
     those feathers had a very extraordinary appearance as they appeared
     in such quantities as to cover pretty generally sixty or seventy yards
10   of the breadth of the river. For three miles after I saw those feathers
     continuing to run in that manner, we did not perceive from whence
     they came, at length we were surprised by the appearance of a flock
     of pelicans at rest on a large sand bar attached to a small Island the
     number of which would if estimated appear almost in credible; they
15   appeared to cover several acres of ground, and were no doubt engaged in
     procuring their ordinary food; which is fish, on our approach they flew
     and left behind them several small fish of about eight inches in length,
     none of which I had seen before—the pelican rested again on a sand
     bar above the Island which we called after them from the number we
20   saw on it. We now approached them within about three hundred yards
     before they flew; I then fired at random among the flock with my rifle
     and brought one down; the description of this bird is as follows.

Habits

They are a bird of clime remain on the coast of Florida and the
25 borders of the Gulf of Mexico & even the lower portion of the
Mississippi during the winter and in the Spring (see for date my
thermometrical observations at the river Dubois.) visit this country and
that farther north for the purpose of raising their young—this duty
seems now to have been accomplished from the appearance of a young
30 pelican which was killed by one of our men this morning, and they
are now in large flocks on their return to their winter quarters. They
lay usually two eggs only and choose for a nest a couple of logs of drift
wood near the water's edge and with out any other preparation but the
threat formed by the proximity of those two logs which form a trough
35 they set and hatch their young which after nurture with fish their
common food.

1. What can be inferred from the description of Napoleon's journey from
Troyes to Froidmanteau in Passage 1?

    A. Napoleon never traveled without a large entourage.
    B. Napoleon did not want to go to Paris.
    C. Napoleon did not care about his men.
    D. Napoleon was in a hurry.

2. In Passage 2, what surprised Lewis the most about the pelicans?

    A. Learning that they only lay two eggs at a time
    B. The large number of pelicans
    C. Seeing them abandon the fish they were eating when the men
approached
    D. The fact that they fly north to raise their offspring

3. Which line from Passage 2 provides the best evidence for the answer to the previous question?
    A. "They lay usually two eggs only and choose for a nest a couple of logs of drift wood near the water's edge and with out any other preparation..."
    B. "...we did not perceive from whence they came..."
    C. "...on our approach they flew and left behind them several small fish..."
    D. "...on a large sand bar attached to a small Island the number of which would if estimated appear almost in credible..."

4. In what way is Napoleon Bonaparte most like Meriwether Lewis?
    A. They both share a keen interest in nature.
    B. They both devise tactics masterfully.
    C. They both pay close attention to details.
    D. They both understand European geography very well.

5. Which of the following is a theme of both passages?
    A. Long journeys present difficulties.
    B. Work often requires great dedication.
    C. Waging war rarely has any benefits.
    D. History tends to repeat itself.

6. The primary purpose of both passages is to
    A. record important historical events.
    B. celebrate fierce military leaders.
    C. educate about the natural world.
    D. prove that memories can be unreliable.

7. The stance the authors take in both passages is best described as that of
     A. passionate defenders.
     B. impartial observers.
     C. awestruck fanatics.
     D. disgruntled critics.

Passage 1 is an excerpt from *Soap-Making Manual* by E. G. Thomssen, PhD.
Passage 2 is an excerpt from *Lace: Its Origin and History* by
Samuel L. Goldenberg.

Passage 1

Soap is ordinarily thought of as the common cleansing agent well
known to everyone. In a general and strictly chemical sense this term
is applied to the salts of the non-volatile fatty acids. These salts are not
only those formed by the alkali metals, sodium and potassium, but also
5 those formed by the heavy metals and alkaline earths. Thus we have the
insoluble soaps of lime and magnesia formed when we attempt to wash
in "hard water"; again aluminum soaps are used extensively in polishing
materials and to thicken lubricating oils; ammonia or "benzine" soaps
are employed among the dry cleaners. Commonly, however, when we
10 speak of soap we limit it to the sodium or potassium salt of a higher
fatty acid.
    It is very generally known that soap is made by combining a fat
or oil with a water solution of sodium hydroxide (caustic soda lye), or
potassium hydroxide (caustic potash). Sodium soaps are always harder
15 than potassium soaps, provided the same fat or oil is used in both cases.
    The detergent properties of soap are due to the fact that it acts as
an alkali regulator, that is, when water comes into contact with soap,
it undergoes what is called hydrolytic dissociation. This means that
it is broken down by water into other substances. Just what these
20 substances are is subject to controversy, though it is presumed caustic
alkali and the acid alkali salt of the fatty acids are formed.

Passage 2

The instrument that is responsible for lace is the needle, but the
earliest forms of lace were not the woven fabric that we know to-day,
but rather cutwork, which, as far as we have any authentic records,
was first practiced by the nuns in the convents of central and southern
5 Europe. This work was sometimes characterized as nun's work, and
was designed almost exclusively for altar decorations and the robes of
prelates, though it was also regarded as the insignia of rank and station.
Some of the specimens of this work, still preserved in museums, show
that the early workers possessed a skill in the art never excelled. Of
10 course, with the progress of time, designs have become more ornate and
intricate, but many of the old patterns still survive, and doubtless will
continue to survive, till the end of recorded time.
   The desire to elaborate the edges of plain fabrics, whether of linen
or heavier material, was an entirely natural impulse to get away from
15 the harsh simplicity of the times. To this desire must be ascribed the
beginning of the mammoth lace industry of to-day.

8. The author of Passage 1 would most likely agree that
   A. we have more to learn about the action of soaps.
   B. benzine soaps have less cleaning power than do lye soaps.
   C. people should not use lye-based soaps to wash their hands.
   D. salts are formed only by alkalis.

9. Which of the following lines from Passage 2 expresses an opinion?
   A. The earliest forms of lace were not the woven fabric.
   B. This work was sometimes characterized as nun's work.
   C. Early workers possessed a skill in the art never excelled.
   D. Many of the old patterns still survive.

10. Both passages mention materials such as lye and linen primarily to
    A. provide some background information on their topics.
    B. teach the reader the meanings of unfamiliar terms.
    C. explain to the reader how to perform a craft.
    D. indicate the essential components of their topics.

11. Both authors structured their passages primarily to
    A. compare one kind of material to another.
    B. provide sequential steps for creating something.
    C. explain some basic information about materials.
    D. illustrate how particular materials came into being.

12. Soap and lace share the common trait that they
    A. can be created in different ways.
    B. are no longer commonly used.
    C. require special tools to make them.
    D. have important functional purposes.

13. The stance the authors take in both passages is best described as that of
    A. advocates.
    B. educators.
    C. idealists.
    D. coordinators.

EXERCISE 3–2

Directions: Read the passages, then choose the best answer to each of the questions that follow.

Excerpt from *The Outline of Science, Vol. 1*
by J. Arthur Thomson

The *Cambrian* period was the time of the establishment of the chief stocks of backboneless animals such as sponges, jellyfishes, worms, sea-cucumbers, lamp-shells, trilobites, crustaceans, and molluscs. There is something very eloquent in the broad fact that the peopling of the seas had definitely begun some thirty million years ago, for Professor H. F. Osborn points out that in the Cambrian period there was already a colonisation of the shore of the sea, the open sea, and the deep waters.

The *Ordovician* period was marked by abundant representation of the once very successful class of Trilobites—jointed-footed, antenna-bearing, segmented marine animals, with numerous appendages and a covering of chitin. They died away entirely with the end of the Palæozoic era. Also very notable was the abundance of predatory cuttlefishes, the bullies of the ancient seas. But it was in this period that the first backboned animals made their appearance—an epoch-making step in evolution. In other words, true fishes were evolved—destined in the course of ages to replace the cuttlefishes (which are mere molluscs) in dominating the seas.

RECENT TIMES		Human civilisation
CENOZOIC ERA	PLEISTOCENE OR GLACIAL TIME	Last great Ice Age.
	MIOCENE AND PLIOCENE TIMES	Emergence of Man.
	EOCENE AND OLIGOCENE TIMES	Rise of higher mammals.
MESOZOIC ERA	CRETACEOUS PERIOD	Rise of primitive mammals, flowering plants, and higher insects.
	JURASSIC PERIOD	Rise of birds and flying reptiles.
	TRIASSIC PERIOD	Rise of dinosaur reptiles.

PALÆOZOIC ERA	PERMIAN PERIOD	Rise of reptiles.
	CARBONIFEROUS PERIOD	Rise of insects.
	DEVONIAN PERIOD	First amphibians.
	SILURIAN PERIOD	Land animals began.
	ORDOVICIAN PERIOD	First fishes.
	CAMBRIAN PERIOD	Peopling of the sea.
PROTEROZOIC AGES	Many of the backboneless stocks began.	
ARCHÆOZOIC AGES	Living creatures began to be upon the earth.	
FORMATIVE TIMES	Making of continents and ocean-basins.	
	Beginnings of atmosphere and hydrosphere.	
	Cooling of the earth.	
	Establishment of the solar system.	

1. Which claim does information in the passage and the table support?
    A. Lamp-shells and trilobites lived in the seas.
    B. Sea-cucumbers first appeared in the Formative times.
    C. Dinosaurs were the first creatures with jointed feet.
    D. The earliest forms of birds did not have backbones.

2. It can be reasonably inferred from the passage and the table that
    A. humans lived during the Ordovician period.
    B. trilobites did not exist during the Cenozoic era.
    C. trilobites may have been killed off by glaciers.
    D. dinosaurs existed before cuttlefish.

3. Which claim does information in the passage and the table support?
    A. Sponges, jellyfishes, and worms evolved backbones.
    B. Sponges, jellyfishes, and worms are currently extinct.
    C. Sponges, jellyfishes, and worms emerged as the earth cooled.
    D. Sponges, jellyfishes, and worms were not the first creatures.

4. It can be reasonably inferred from the passage and the table that the author
   A. does not consider jellyfish to be true fishes.
   B. believes crustaceans were the first dinosaurs.
   C. does not believe in an evolutionary link between fish and mammals.
   D. considers the Palæozoic era to be the defining era of Earth's history.

Excerpt Adapted from *Boy Scouts Handbook, The First Edition*
Road-side Cribbage

This is a game we often play in the train, to pass the time pleasantly.

Sometimes one party takes the right side of the road, with the windows there, and the other the left. Sometimes all players sit on the same side.

The game is, whoever is first to see certain things agreed on scores so many points.

Thus:

Animals	Points
A crow or a cow	1
A cat	2
A hawk	3
An owl	4
A sheep	5
A goat	6
A horse	7

The winner is the one who first gets twenty-five . . . points . . .

When afoot, one naturally takes other things for points, as certain trees, flowers, etc.

5. It can be reasonably inferred from the passage and the chart that someone who sees

    A. a crow is more likely to win the game than someone who sees a cow.

    B. an owl is less likely to win the game than someone who sees a hawk.

    C. a goat is more likely to win the game than someone who sees a cat.

    D. a sheep is less likely to win the game than someone who sees a raccoon.

6. Which claim does information in the passage and the chart support?

    A. It is impossible to see perching crows during a train ride.

    B. Cats understand that train tracks are dangerous areas.

    C. Sheep are generally faster on their feet than goats are.

    D. It is relatively rare to see a horse during a train ride.

7. Which claim does information in the passage and the chart support?

    A. The first person to see three horses will win a game of Road-side Cribbage.

    B. The first person to see five sheep will win a game of Road-side Cribbage.

    C. The first person to see seven hawks will win a game of Road-side Cribbage.

    D. The first person to see nine cats will win a game of Road-side Cribbage.

Answers are on page 551.

4 Writing: Standard English Conventions

MUST ⚡ KNOW

⚡ A sentence is constructed of clauses. A complete sentence must have at least one independent clause (a subject and a verb), express a complete thought, begin with a capital letter, and end with a punctuation mark.

⚡ Avoid shifts in verb tense, mood, and voice. Use active voice when possible.

⚡ Items in a list or comparison should use parallel forms.

⚡ Pronouns must agree in number, person, case, and gender. It must be clear which noun a pronoun replaces.

⚡ Modifiers should be near the words they modify. Adjectives modify nouns and pronouns. Adverbs modify verbs, adjectives, and other adverbs.

When constructing sentences, we must follow Standard English conventions. These are the rules for composing grammatically correct writing. This chapter focuses on the Standard English conventions you will need to know on the SAT. These rules will help you to master:

- Structure: the basic formats for constructing sentences

- Usage: the ways parts of speech and sentences are used

- Punctuation: the symbols that separate sentence parts and end sentences

Punctuation

Punctuation marks are symbols that indicate divisions of ideas in a sentence and the end of a sentence. Different marks are used for different purposes.

Punctuation may seem like a strange place to start this chapter, but punctuation is a part of every single sentence. The rest of the chapter will be easier to understand if you already know what each punctuation mark does and when and why to use each one.

End Punctuation

Let's start with a topic you are already familiar with—end punctuation. You know that every sentence ends with a punctuation mark: a period, a question mark, or an exclamation mark. Each of these three end-of-sentence punctuation marks has its own purpose.

A **period** (.) ends a basic declarative or imperative statement.

I planted these flowers.

An **exclamation point** (!) ends a sentence that expresses excitement, a dire warning, extreme anger, or extreme passion.

BTW

A sentence might also end with closing quotation marks (") after the end punctuation if the sentence ends with a quote. In such a case, a period, exclamation mark, or question mark must still be used immediately before the closing quotation marks. For example: Omar said, "This is my car."

EXAMPLE

> Watch where you're going—you almost stepped on the flowers I planted!

A **question mark** (?) ends a sentence that asks a question.

EXAMPLE

> Do you like the flowers I planted?

Commas

Some people never use commas, and some people throw commas around like sprinkles on a cupcake. Stop it. Many people think you should put a comma wherever you would pause in a sentence read aloud. Also stop it. There are actual rules about when to use a comma and you should learn them not only for the SAT, but also for use in your own writing. You'll be writing a lot of essays in college, and your professors will definitely care where you put commas.

There are seven basic reasons to use a comma.

1. Use commas to separate items in a list. Yes, you should put a comma before the *and*.

EXAMPLE

> Bob wears *a helmet, gloves, and a jacket* when he rides his motorcycle.

2. Use a comma to join two **independent clauses** with a **coordinating conjunction**. An independent clause can stand alone as a sentence. The coordinating conjunctions are: *for, and, nor, but, or, yet,* and *so* (FANBOYS).

▶ *Elba Dean writes short essays,* but *they are good.*

▶ *Jack asked me to marry him,* and *he gave me a huge diamond ring!*

▶ The phrases in italics are independent clauses because they can stand alone as sentences.

▶ *DO NOT use a comma to join an independent clause to a **dependent clause**. A dependent clause cannot stand alone as a sentence.

▶ **Incorrect:** Elba Dean writes short essays, but *makes good grades.*

Makes good grades is a dependent clause that cannot stand alone. It does not need to be set off by a comma.

▶ **Correct:** Jack asked me to marry him and *gave me a huge diamond ring!*

The phrase in italics is a dependent clause because it cannot stand alone as a sentence. No comma is needed.

---

3. To set off parenthetical information (bonus info).

▶ Zane, *who works in the Student Center,* was born in China.

▶ Nicholle may study abroad in Auckland, *New Zealand,* next year.

---

4. To set off an introductory phrase.

EXAMPLE

> *While baking her cake,* Lori studied for her final exam.

5. To separate coordinate adjectives (when you could separate them with "and").

EXAMPLE

> Sergio is a *talented, experienced* baseball player.

6. To set off a quote.

EXAMPLES

> *"Please help me,"* said Nick, *"I didn't study for the quiz!"*

> *DO NOT use a comma for an **embedded quote**. An embedded quote is a quote that is integrated into your own sentence.

> Kalee says that the teacher wants to *"ruin her."*

7. To set off phrases that show contrast.

EXAMPLE

> I am talking about *cars, not trucks.*

Apostrophes

We use apostrophes (') to show possession. Let's look at how apostrophes are used to form singular possessives, plural possessives, and compound possessives.

To form the possessive of a singular word, put the apostrophe before the *s*. Do this even if the word already ends in an *s*.

EXAMPLES

- That is *Andy's* dog.
- Trash in the neighborhood is *everyone's* problem.
- Let's go over to the *Sites's* house.

To form the possessive of a plural word, put the apostrophe after the *s*.

EXAMPLE

- Boys are not allowed in the *girls'* locker room.

For plural words that don't end in *s*, put the apostrophe before the possessive *s*.

EXAMPLES

- The teacher gathered the *children's* art projects.
- The *men's* room is on the left and the *women's* room is on the right.

To form the possessive of a compound word or phrase, put the apostrophe after the last part of the compound.

EXAMPLES

- My *sister-in-law's* car was demolished.
- *Marisa and John's* baby will be born in April.

Some possessive pronouns do not require an apostrophe and an added *s*.

Incorrect	Correct
His' desk is next to mine's.	His desk is next to mine.
It's tires are flat.	Its tires are flat.
Those cups are their's.	Those cups are theirs.
Who's book is this?	Whose book is this?

We also use an apostrophe to form contractions. In this case, the apostrophe goes in place of the letter omitted to form the contraction.

EXAMPLES

▶ Amee *doesn't* want to go to the party.

▶ Disco was popular in the *'70s*.

 IRL   People often confuse *its* and *it's*. The possessive form is *its*. *It's* is a contraction and means *it is* or *it has*.

An apostrophe is also used to form some plurals. This is true for all lowercase letters, as well as for the capital letters A, I, J, and P.

EXAMPLES

▶ When Preston was in graduate school, he earned only *A's*.

Do **not** use apostrophes for dates or abbreviations.

▶ Carolyn was born in the *1960s*.

▶ I have twelve *DVDs* of zombie movies.

Semicolons

Semicolons confuse a lot of people and are often used incorrectly. They have two functions. First, a semicolon can be used to separate two related independent clauses, with or without a **transitional expression**. Transitional expressions such as *however*, *for example*, and *therefore* link ideas. To see whether a semicolon is appropriate to separate clauses, check to see whether a period could be substituted for the semicolon. If so, the semicolon is appropriate.

EXAMPLES

▶ Britt ate an entire pizza; he can't still be hungry.

▶ Britt ate an entire pizza; however, he is still hungry.

Semicolons are also used to separate items in a list that already has commas. This helps avoid confusion.

EXAMPLES

▶ Kathy traveled to Houston, TX; Chicago, IL; and New York, NY.

▶ My grandma called me, my sister, and my mom on Thursday; my dad, my uncle, and my aunt on Friday; and a whole bunch of my cousins on Saturday.

Colons

A colon introduces a list that is given after an independent clause.

EXAMPLE

▶ You only need three ingredients to make shortbread cookies: *flour, sugar, and butter.*

A colon introduces a long quotation.

▶ *In an interview with Katie Couric, Supreme Court Justice Ruth Bader Ginsburg said:*

You can't have it all, all at once. Who—man or woman—has it all, all at once? Over my lifespan I think I have had it all. But in different periods of time things were rough. And if you have a caring life partner, you help the other person when that person needs it. I had a life partner who thought my work was as important as his, and I think that made all the difference for me.

A colon explains something. This is done with an **appositive** after an independent clause. An appositive renames or identifies something.

▶ There is only one thing left to do: *take a nap.*

There are a few more specific uses for a colon.

- A colon is used after a salutation in a business letter.

- A colon separates a title from its subtitle.

- A colon separates hour from minutes in an expression of exact time.

- A colon separates amounts in a ratio.

- A colon separates chapter and verse.

▶ *Dear Governor:* There are too many school days...

▶ The book I have to read for class is titled *Walking Dead: College Students in Finals Week.*

▶ I will meet you at *3:45.*

▶ The ratio of students to teachers at my school is *18:1.*

▶ Have you read Luke *2:14?*

Hyphens

Use a hyphen to form compound words, especially compound adjective modifiers that come before nouns.

EXAMPLE

▶ My *sister-in-law* Brie is a *fourteen-year-old* fashion model.

Use a hyphen to create compounds.

EXAMPLE

▶ Adam and David wanted to ride the *merry-go-round.*

Use a hyphen to write out numbers from 21 to 99 and to write out fractions.

EXAMPLE

▶ *One-fourth* of the *twenty-six* employees called in sick.

Use a hyphen to add certain prefixes to words. The prefixes *self-, all-,* and *ex-* nearly always require a hyphen.

EXAMPLE

▶ Henri's *ex-wife* spoke fluent French.

Parentheses and Em Dashes

Like commas, parentheses and em dashes can be used to set off extra details in sentences. Each type of punctuation is used for a slightly different purpose.

Commas separate details that are relevant to the sentence.

EXAMPLE

▶ This book, *which McCormick Jones wrote*, is not very interesting.

Em dashes separate information that is more relevant to the sentence and deserving of attention than information in commas would be.

EXAMPLE

▶ This book—*an alleged thriller that is full of talk and precious little action*—is not very interesting.

Parentheses separate details that are fairly unnecessary to the sentence.

EXAMPLE

▶ This book *(a New York Times bestseller)* is not very interesting.

Sentence Structure

Now that we have all that pesky punctuation out of the way, let's discuss the ways sentences are formed.

Parts of Speech

Each word in a sentence serves a different function and can be sorted into categories called parts of speech.

Part of Speech	Function	Examples	Example Sentences
Noun	a person, place, thing, or idea	mother, Paris, phone, love	This is my **mother.** She was born in **Paris.**
Pronoun	replaces a noun	I, you, she, it, they, me, ours, who, some	I left **my** book at Ann's house; **she** is bringing **it** to **me.**
Verb	action or state of being	(to) be, have, do, go, like	Austin **is** the capital of Texas. I **like** broccoli.
Adjective	describes a noun or pronoun	big, bad, yellow, funny	My **yellow** purse is **big.** I like **funny** movies.
Adverb	describes a verb, adjective, or adverb	quickly, well, very, really	He talks **quickly.** When he is **very** excited, he talks **really** quickly.
Preposition	links a noun to another word	to, by, after, on, but	Get the book **on** the table **before** you leave.
Conjunction	joins words or clauses	and, but, when, for, nor, or, yet, so, since,	I need time **and** money. You are late, **but** I forgive you.
Determiner	introduces a noun	a, the, this, those, many	**A** dog ran into **the** street.
Interjection	a short exclamation	Oh! Wow! Well	**Well,** I think it's fine.

▶ Identify the part of speech for each of the underlined words.

Hey, do you have a spatula and a very small spoon?

Valerie asked Kai to carry the large bucket of popcorn into the movie theater.

> In the first sentence, *Hey* is an interjection, *you* is a pronoun, *a* is a determiner, *and* is a conjunction, and *very* is an adverb that modifies the adjective *small*. In the second sentence, *Valerie* is a noun, *to carry* is a verb, *into* is a preposition, and *movie* is an adjective.

You may also be familiar with the terms **subject** and **predicate**. These are not parts of speech, but functions within the sentence. The subject of a sentence, usually a noun, performs the action. The predicate is a verb or verb phrase that describes the action.

Independent and Dependent Clauses

A sentence is constructed of clauses. A **clause** is a group of words that contains a subject and a verb. This is different from a **phrase**, which is a group of words that does not contain both a subject and verb.

An independent clause contains a subject and verb and expresses a complete idea. However, a sentence may contain more than one clause. It may include dependent clauses (also called **subordinate clauses**), which do not express complete ideas when separated from their accompanying independent clauses.

EXAMPLES

> **Independent clause:** Chris left the house.

This clause contains a subject, the noun *Chris*, and a predicate, the verb *left*. It expresses a complete thought.

> **Dependent clause:** While I was sleeping.

This clause contains a subject, the pronoun *I*, and a predicate, the verb phrase *was sleeping*. However, it is not a complete thought. The word *while* makes this a dependent clause because now a reader will want to know what happened while the writer was sleeping. The sentence is incomplete.

Subordination and Coordination

Subordination and coordination are two ways to connect ideas in a sentence. Their use depends on how those ideas relate to each other. If one idea is more important than the other, the less important idea should be subordinated by using a dependent clause. Coordination is used when the ideas are of equal importance.

Subordination

Subordination uses a relative pronoun (who, whom, which, whoever, whomever, whichever, that) or subordinating conjunction (after, although, as, before, if, than, unless, until, while, etc.) to show that one idea in a sentence is more important than the other. Depending on their placement in a sentence, some subordinate clauses need to be set off with commas.

EXAMPLES

> *As I thought about nothing in particular,* I heard a crash in the other room.

> The man *who lives next door to me* is moving to California next week.

> The book, *which I found on the train,* is actually very interesting.

> In these examples, the subordinated clauses are in italics.

Coordination

Coordination uses coordinating conjunctions (*for, and, nor, but, or, yet,* and *so*) or punctuation to connect ideas of equal importance. You can also use a semicolon to connect ideas of equal importance in a single sentence.

EXAMPLES

> *I like you,* and *you like me.*

> *Kaveri is doing the laundry; Ron is cleaning the garage.*

> *Elena likes trucks,* but *she doesn't like cars.*

> In these examples, the coordinated independent clauses are in italics. Notice that each of them could stand alone as a sentence.

Types of Sentences

Writers form grammatically correct sentences by structuring independent and dependent clauses correctly. We can build sentences by combining clauses. There are four essential sentence structures: simple, compound, complex, and compound-complex. On the SAT, you will revise sentences to follow those four sentence structures.

A **simple sentence** consists of a single independent clause.

EXAMPLES

> I love music.

> The teacher spoke loudly.

> There is one way to succeed in life.

> My sister vacationed in Thailand.

A **compound sentence** consists of two or more independent clauses. The independent clauses can be joined together by a comma and a coordinating conjunction (*for*, *and*, *nor*, *but*, *or*, *yet*, and *so*), by a semicolon, by a colon, or by an em dash.

EXAMPLES

> I love music, and I listen to it often.

> The teacher spoke loudly; it hurt my ears.

> There is one way to succeed in life: help others.

> My sister vacationed in Thailand—she did not take me with her.

A **complex sentence** consists of at least one independent clause and at least one dependent clause.

▶ I listen to music *after doing my homework.*

▶ *When the teacher spoke loudly* it hurt my ears.

▶ There is one way to succeed in life: *by helping others.*

▶ *Although my sister vacationed in Thailand,* she did not take me with her.

The dependent clauses are in italics. Notice that they cannot stand alone.

A **compound-complex sentence** consists of two or more independent clauses and one or more dependent clauses.

▶ *I listen to music* after doing my homework, and *I listen to it often.*

▶ *The teacher spoke loudly*; when she spoke *it hurt my ears.*

▶ *There is one way to succeed in life: help others* whenever you can.

▶ *My sister vacationed in Thailand—she did not take me with her* although she should have.

Here, the independent clauses are in italics. Notice that each of them can stand alone.

Run-on Sentences

When clauses are joined incorrectly, the result may be a run-on sentence. Knowing when to begin or end a sentence is key to expressing clear and focused ideas. There are two types of run-on sentences: fused sentences and comma splices.

A **fused sentence** is two independent clauses joined with no punctuation or conjunction at all.

EXAMPLE

▶ **Incorrect:** The man ran the stop sign he didn't even look at it.

This is a fused sentence. It has two independent clauses just jammed together.

A **comma splice** is two independent clauses joined with only a comma (no coordinating conjunction).

EXAMPLE

▶ **Incorrect:** The man ran the stop sign, he didn't even look at it.

This is a comma splice. It has two independent clauses joined with only a comma.

There are four ways to fix run-on sentences:

- Use a comma and a coordinating conjunction.

- Use a semicolon.

- Break the clauses into separate sentences.

- Rewrite the sentence, usually by subordinating one of the clauses.

EXAMPLES

▶ Each of these versions is correct.

- The man ran the stop sign, and he didn't even look at it.

- The man ran the stop sign; he didn't even look at it.

- The man ran the stop sign. He didn't even look at it.

- The man didn't even look at the stop sign as he ran it.

Sentence Fragments

A sentence fragment is a group of words that is punctuated like a sentence but is not actually a sentence because it lacks a subject or a predicate or does not express a complete thought.

EXAMPLES

Each of the following examples is a sentence fragment.

▶ **Incorrect:** As we walked down the street.

This is a dependent clause that has a subject and predicate but does not express a complete thought.

▶ **Incorrect:** Some income tax rules that did not apply to first-time home buyers.

This fragment is just a really long subject phrase. There is no verb to go with the simple subject *rules*.

▶ **Incorrect:** And then she smiled.

You can't start a sentence with a coordinating conjunction. They are used to connect words and clauses.

▶ **Incorrect:** Running into the living room after dinner.

This fragment lacks a subject. Who was running?

To fix a sentence fragment, you can either add the missing subject or predicate or combine a dependent clause fragment with an independent clause to make a complex sentence.

EXAMPLES

Let's fix each of the previous fragment examples.

▶ **Correct:** As we walked down the street, I held his hand.

Here I added an independent clause to the dependent clause.

▶ **Correct:** I took advantage of some income tax rules that did not apply to first-time home buyers.

Here I added a subject (*I*) and a predicate (*took*) and made the fragment into the object of the sentence.

▶ **Correct:** Her father said he was proud of her, and then she smiled.

Here I added another independent clause and connected by adding a comma to the coordinating conjunction *and*.

▶ **Correct:** The children were running into the living room after dinner.

Here I added a subject, *the children*, and I added the helping verb *were* to complete the predicate.

 IRL If you read a lot, you probably notice that writers sometimes use sentence fragments for dramatic effect.

She walked all day. And then she walked some more.

That's fine, but on the SAT we must use Standard English conventions. Remember, coordinating conjunctions connect—so don't start a sentence with one.

Parallel Construction

When a sentence lists several items or compares items, each item should be similar grammatically. This is known as parallel structure. Mixing different parts of speech and types of phrases and clauses in a single list or comparison violates parallel structure.

Lists

When a sentence lists several items, each item should be similar grammatically. This is true when the items in the list are one-word items, such as:

> I *walked*, *skipped*, and *jumped* through the park.

This is also true when the items in the list are longer phrases, such as:

> For the camping trip, I packed *some warm turtleneck sweaters*, *some comfortable hiking boots*, and *some thick wool socks*.

Notice that those phrases are structured in the exact same way: the word *some*, then two adjectives, then the type of clothing.

EXAMPLE

▶ **1.** We went sailing, surfing, and to the skateboard park over the summer.

    A. NO CHANGE

    B. We went to go sailing, surfing, and to the skateboard park over the summer.

    C. We went sailing, surfed, and skateboarded over the summer.

    D. We went sailing, surfing, and skateboarding over the summer.

In the original sentence, *sailing* and *surfing* are similar, but *to the skateboard park* is different. We need to change that. Choice B is still inconsistent. In choice C, *surfed* and *skateboarded* are similar, but *sailing* is different. In choice D, all three activities are in the same grammatical form: *sailing*, *surfing*, and *skateboarding*.

Comparisons

Another form of parallel construction is comparisons. If two items in a sentence are being compared, each item should be similar grammatically. You can compare two verbs or two nouns, but you should not compare a noun and a verb.

▶ **Incorrect:** I like to surf more than sailing.

To surf is a verb and *sailing* is a **gerund** (a verb form used as a noun). We need to change that.

▶ **Correct:** I like to surf more than to sail.

or

▶ **Correct:** I like surfing more than sailing.

Both of these sentences compare activities using the same grammatical form.

In addition, a comparison between two things needs to follow logic. Check for three different qualities when assessing the logic of a comparison:

Clarity: Precisely used words do not result in an ambiguous comparison.

EXAMPLE

> **Incorrect:** We scored fewer points than the other team.

The two things being compared are unclear in this sentence.

> **Correct:** We scored fewer points than the other team scored.

Completeness: Both things being compared are included in the sentence.

EXAMPLE

> **Incorrect:** This brand of cereal is better.

This sentence is incomplete because it does not indicate what this brand of cereal is better than.

> **Correct:** This brand of cereal is better than the other brand.

Consistency: The two things being compared share some similar quality.

EXAMPLE

> **Incorrect:** The van traveled farther than the pickup truck.

This sentence compares a distance to a vehicle.

> **Correct:** The van traveled farther than the pickup truck did.

Nouns and Verbs

Now that we understand how sentences are constructed and punctuated, let's look at some of the major sentence components and how they are tested on the SAT. For nouns, we need to be concerned with agreement. For verbs, we need to be concerned with subject-verb agreement, verb tense, mood, and voice.

Noun Agreement

When a sentence uses a noun to describe its subject, the subject noun and the modifying noun need to agree in terms of number and gender.

EXAMPLES

▶ **Correct:** Gil grew from a small boy into a man.

The subject of this sentence is *Gil*. He was a boy and grew up to be a man. Both *boy* and *man* are masculine nouns, so all the nouns in this sentence are in agreement.

▶ **Incorrect:** My brothers and sisters grew up to be a doctor.

The subject of this sentence is the plural *brothers and sisters*. The noun that describes what they grew up to be, *doctor*, is singular. The nouns in this sentence are not in agreement.

▶ **Correct:** My brothers and sisters all grew up to be doctors.

Subject-Verb Agreement

Complete sentences contain at least one subject and one verb. The number of a subject and its verb must be in agreement. A singular verb, which may end with the letter s, describes the action a singular noun takes. A plural verb, which may not end with the letter s, describes the action a plural noun takes.

EXAMPLES

▶ **Singular:** The tree grows.

▶ **Plural:** The trees grow.

Subject-verb agreement may sound pretty straightforward, but it can be a bit more complicated. Prepositional phrases between the subject and verb can distract you and confuse you. Isolate the simple subject and verb to see if they match.

BTW

Since verbs do not form their plurals by adding an s as nouns do, it may be hard to remember the correct verb form. In order to determine which verb is singular and which one is plural, think of which verb you would use with he or she and which verb you would use with they.

EXAMPLE

▶ **Incorrect:** The horses near that big red barn that belongs to my new neighbor is breaking out.

In this sentence there are eleven words in between the subject and the verb! By the time you reach the singular verb, you have probably forgotten what the subject was. There is a singular noun right before the singular verb, so the sentence might sound fine, but the subject is plural and needs a plural verb.

▶ **Correct:** The *horses* near that big red barn that belongs to my new neighbor *are* breaking out.

A **compound subject** is a subject with two parts. If the two parts of the subject are joined by *and*, the compound subject is plural and requires a plural verb.

EXAMPLE

▶ **Correct:** The tree and the grass grow.

If the two parts of a compound subject are joined by *or* or *nor*, the verb is determined by the part of the subject that is physically closer to the verb.

> **Correct:** My brother or my *parents are* picking me up after school.

> **Also correct:** My parents or my *brother is* picking me up after school.

If that second one sounds weird to you, you are not alone. It is, however, correct.

Subject-verb agreement can also be tricky if the subject is a **collective noun**. Collective nouns describe a group as a single entity (e.g., the jury, the committee, the audience). Collective nouns are singular.

> **Correct:** An audience of angry people is a dangerous thing.

The subject is *audience*, which is a collective noun, so the verb needs to be the singular *is*. Yes, *people* is plural, but that isn't the subject—it's part of a prepositional phrase describing the subject.

Even more tricky are **indefinite pronouns**. Indefinite pronouns do not refer to a specific person or thing (e.g., anyone, each, nobody, someone, everyone, etc.). Indefinite pronouns are almost always singular.

> **Correct:** Each of the kids enjoys eating cookies.

The subject is *each*, which is singular and requires the singular verb *enjoys*. *Of the kids* is a prepositional phrase describing the subject.

Of course, English has a lot of exceptions. A few indefinite pronouns (all, some, any, none) as well as fractions and percentages may be either singular or plural depending on the entire subject phrase.

> **Correct:** Some of the students believe in ghosts. Some of the class believes in ghosts.

In both sentences, the subject is *some*, but that indefinite pronoun can be either singular or plural. For the first sentence, *some of the students* requires a plural verb because *students* is plural. For the second sentence, *some of the class* requires a singular verb because *class* is singular.

Verb Tense

Verb **tense** indicates when something is happening. You are probably comfortable with the simple present, past, and future tenses.

> Let's look at the verb **to jump.**

> **Simple present tense:** *I like to jump on the trampoline.*

This indicates an action that happens regularly or all the time.

> **Simple past tense:** *I jumped on the trampoline.*

This indicates an action that has already taken place.

> **Simple future tense:** *I will jump on the trampoline.*

This indicates an action that will take place in the future.

The SAT is mainly concerned with consistency. Do not shift tenses without a good reason to do so. Look at the context of the sentence to see what tense you should use. Look at other verbs in the sentence for clues too.

Mood

Mood indicates the "attitude" of the verb. Verbs have five kinds of moods: indicative, interrogative, imperative, conditional, and subjunctive. Mood is not a common topic on the SAT, so a basic familiarity with mood should be sufficient.

The **indicative** mood states facts.

EXAMPLES

▸ There are twelve books on the shelf.

▸ Whales are mammals.

The **interrogative** mood asks a question.

EXAMPLES

▸ Are you going to the gym?

▸ Can I help you carry your bags?

The **imperative** mood is for direct commands.

EXAMPLES

▸ Go to the gym.

▸ Don't forget your backpack.

The **conditional** mood makes a statement that depends on a particular circumstance. These are commonly known as *if/then* statements.

> ▶ I will go to the gym if you come with me.
>
> ▶ If you pay me, I will mow your lawn.

The **subjunctive** mood expresses hypothetical situations and states orders and requests. Subjunctive mood is not used as much in English as it is in many other languages.

> ▶ If I were rich, I would move to a tropical island.
>
> ▶ The teacher suggests that you finish your exam.

Voice

Voice expresses whether the subject of the sentence is performing an action (**active voice**) or is having an action performed on him/her/it (**passive voice**). The active voice is always a stronger way to express ideas than is the passive voice.

> ▶ **Passive voice**: The baseball team was coached by me.
>
> ▶ **Active voice**: I coached the baseball team.

Pronouns

A pronoun replaces a more specific noun and, in some cases, another pronoun. Some sentences on the SAT have to be revised because of errors in pronoun agreement, case, or clarity.

Pronoun Agreement

An antecedent is a noun or pronoun to which a pronoun refers. The antecedent and its referring pronoun need to agree. This means they have to be alike in terms of number and gender.

Number refers to whether the antecedent is singular or plural.

Singular pronouns: pronouns that refer to a single person or thing

> *I, me, my, mine, you, he, she, it, anyone, someone, somebody, himself, herself, that,* etc.

EXAMPLES

Plural pronouns: pronouns that refer to more than one person or thing

> *us, they, ours, them, their, we, those,* etc.

EXAMPLES

If a sentence shifts between singular and plural pronouns, check it carefully for errors.

▶ **Incorrect:** Somebody called, but I have no idea who they were.

This sentence contains an error in number. There is a shift from the singular pronoun *Somebody* to the plural pronoun *they*. This is inappropriate because these words refer to the same person.

▶ **Correct:** Somebody called, but I have no idea who she was.

Gender is rarely tested on the SAT. Gender simply refers to choosing the correct pronoun to match the antecedent. While it is becoming more common for a single person to use *they/them* pronouns, on the SAT you should only use *they* and *them* to refer to a group of more than one person.

▶ **Incorrect:** Marietta is a girl who knows where he is going in life.

The pronoun in this sentence should refer to the antecedent *Marietta*, and the sentence makes it clear that Marietta is a girl. Therefore, the feminine pronoun *she* should be used.

▶ **Correct:** Marietta is a girl who knows where she is going in life.

Pronouns must also agree in person. Person refers to who is speaking or being spoken about.

First person refers to the person who is speaking or a group that includes the speaker. For example: *I, me, my, mine, myself, we, us, our, ours,* and *ourselves* are first-person pronouns.

EXAMPLES

▶ *I* am going home.

▶ The teacher gave the test to *us*.

▶ *My* book is sitting on *our* table.

Second person refers to the person being addressed. For example: *you, your, yours, yourself,* and *yourselves* are second-person pronouns.

EXAMPLES

▶ Did *you* bring *your* ticket?

▶ That cup is *yours*.

▶ Don't be so hard on *yourself!*

Third person refers to a person or group of people being spoken about. For example: *he, him, his, himself, she, her, hers, herself, it, its, itself, they, them, their, theirs,* and *themselves* are third-person pronouns.

EXAMPLES

▶ *She* lives in *their* building.

▶ The cat found *itself* in a precarious position, balanced on *its* front paws.

▶ *They* gave *him* two chances to redeem *himself*.

A sentence should not shift between different pronoun forms inappropriately.

EXAMPLE

Incorrect: If you don't wear warm clothes on a cold day, someone might get sick.

This sentence contains an error in person. The first clause is written in the second person, using the pronoun *you*. The second clause is written in the third person, using the pronoun *someone*.

Correct: If you don't wear warm clothes on a cold day, you might get sick.

Pronoun Case

Pronoun case form shows a word's function in a sentence. Replace a noun in a certain case with a pronoun of the same case.

Subjective Pronouns	Objective Pronouns	Possessive Pronouns
I	me	my
you	you	your
he/she/it	him/her/it	his/hers/its
we	us	our
they	them	their

Subjective case pronouns replace the subject of a sentence or clause.

EXAMPLES

Correct: Alex ran home quickly because *he* was late for dinner.

The pronoun replaces the subject of the sentence (*Alex*), so it should be the subjective case pronoun *he*.

Correct: Maria denied that the writer of the note was *she*.

Does the second sentence sound weird? Think of it this way: Who denied writing the note? Maria denied that she wrote the note. *Maria* is the subject of the sentence, so we need the subjective case pronoun *she*.

Objective case pronouns replace objects.

EXAMPLES

▶ **Correct:** The children were not very tall, so reaching the top shelf was difficult for *them*.

The pronoun replaces *the children* as the object of the preposition *for*, so we need the objective case pronoun *them*.

▶ **Correct:** The kids were chasing Angus and *her*.

The pronoun replaces a direct object, so we need the objective case pronoun *her*.

▶ **Correct:** Dad gave Trisha and *me* a ten-minute head start.

The pronoun replaces an indirect object, so we need the objective case pronoun *me*.

BTW

Compound subjects and objects can be tricky. Ignore the other half of the compound to simplify. Instead of Trisha and me, just think about me. Who did Dad give the head start to? He gave it to me.

Possessive case pronouns replace possessive nouns. Use the possessive case to show ownership.

EXAMPLE

▶ Dad said, "Back off—that's *my* waffle."

We also use the possessive case to modify a gerund. A gerund is a verb form that functions as a noun.

EXAMPLE

▶ **Incorrect:** The chances of *you* becoming the president are decreasing.

In this sentence, the pronoun describes the process of *becoming the president*, which is a gerund. We need a possessive pronoun.

▶ **Correct:** The chances of *your* becoming the president are decreasing.

Comparisons using pronouns can be confusing. Which sentence below is correct?

Dad likes waffles more than I.

or

Dad likes waffles more than me.

Actually, it depends on your meaning. To see which you want, add the missing part of the sentence:

Dad likes waffles more than I like waffles.

or

Dad likes waffles more than he likes me.

You probably mean the first one! In that case, use the subjective pronoun *I*, even if it sounds weird.

You may remember from our discussion of colons that an appositive defines something or renames it. You may want to use a pronoun in the appositive, so be careful to choose the correct pronoun case.

EXAMPLES

▶ **Correct:** Two of the group, *she* and Jacques, picked up the trash.

Remember, you can simplify compound subjects and objects to help you. Leave Jacques out of it. Who picked up the trash? *She* did.

> **Correct:** The trash was picked up by two people: Jacques and *her*.

Here, the pronoun is replacing the object of the preposition *by*. Again, leave Jacques out of it. The trash was picked up *by her*.

Who and *whoever* are subject pronouns and should be used to replace subjects. Try substituting *she* for *who* and *whoever*.

> **Correct:** *Who* did Kevin say brought the cookies? (*She* brought the cookies.)

> **Correct:** *Whoever* baked the cookies did a great job. (*She* baked them.)

Whom and *whomever* are object pronouns and should be used to replace objects. *Whom* and *whomever* may sound weird to a native American English speaker. Try substituting *her* for *whom* and *whomever*.

> **Correct:** To *whom* did Kendra give the letter? (Kendra gave it to *her*.)

> **Correct:** Where is the photo of the nurse *whom* Dad met? (Dad met *her*.)

> **Correct:** Mom will take home *whomever* needs a ride. (Mom will take *her* home.)

Pronoun Clarity

Ideas need to be expressed carefully so that pronouns clearly refer to particular antecedents. Antecedent-pronoun relationships may be unclear in poorly constructed sentences.

EXAMPLE

▶ **Incorrect:** Alshad looked for his pen and his notebook, and eventually he found *it*.

This sentence contains an unclear antecedent-pronoun relationship. There are two antecedents (pen and notebook), but the pronoun *it* is singular. Does *it* refer to the pen or the notebook? Which item did Alshad find?

Here are some clearer ways to express this idea:

▶ **Correct:** Alshad looked for his pen and his notebook, and eventually he found his pen.

or

Alshad looked for his pen and his notebook, and eventually he found his notebook.

or

Alshad looked for his pen and his notebook, and eventually he found them.

Modifiers

Modifiers are words and phrases that describe other words. Adjectives and adverbs are modifiers. Adjectives describe nouns and pronouns. Adverbs describe verbs, adjectives, other adverbs, as well as adverbial phrases, verb phrases, and adjective phrases.

▶ **Correct:** The *brown* cow chewed its cud *slowly*.

Brown is an adjective that modifies the noun *cow*. *Slowly* is an adverb that modifies the verb phrase *chewed its cud*.

Be careful not to confuse adverbs and adjectives. Many people have trouble remembering when to use *good* and *well*. *Good* is always an adjective.

▶ **Correct:** *It's a Wonderful Life* is a *good* movie to watch during the holidays.

Here, *good* is an adjective that modifies the noun *movie*.

Well is an adverb, except when referring to health. In that case, well functions as an adjective and modifies a noun or pronoun.

▶ **Correct:** Lynda did *well* the first time she tried skiing.

Here, *well* is an adverb that modifies the verb *tried*.

▶ **Incorrect:** Alex did not feel *good* after that spider bite.

Since we are talking about health, we need to use *well*.

▶ **Correct:** Alex did not feel *well* after that spider bite.

There are three common mistakes that affect modifiers. A **misplaced modifier** is a modifier that is not placed next to the word it modifies. This sometimes confuses the meaning of the sentence.

▶ **Incorrect:** The driver transported the passengers to the concert hall in a taxi.

According to this sentence, the concert hall is in a taxi. The phrase *in a taxi* needs to modify *transported the passengers*.

▶ **Correct:** The driver transported the passengers in a taxi to the concert hall.

A **dangling modifier** is a modifier without a word in the sentence to modify.

▶ **Incorrect:** Sailing down the Mississippi River, the French Market was seen.

Who is sailing down the river? It wasn't the French Market!

▶ **Correct:** As I was sailing down the Mississippi River, I saw the French Market.

A **squinting modifier** is a modifier that is unclear because it could modify either a word before it or a word after it.

▶ **Incorrect:** Eating your food quickly causes stomachaches.

The adverb *quickly* is in the middle, so we can't tell whether it is meant to modify *Eating your food* or *causes stomachaches*. What is happening quickly? Does eating quickly give you a stomachache or are you quickly getting a stomachache anytime you eat food? Probably eating too quickly is what gives you the stomachache.

▶ **Correct:** Quickly eating your food can cause stomachaches.

Commonly Confused Words

The SAT will test your ability to use correctly some frequently confused words and phrases. It is important to familiarize yourself with some of them.

Homophones

Homophones are words that sound the same but have different meanings and spellings. Frequently confused homophones include:

This word . . .	is frequently confused with . . .
accept (to agree to do)	except (apart from)
advice (a recommendation)	advise (to recommend)
affect (to change)	effect (a result)
brake (a mechanism for stopping)	break (to crack or a crack)
coarse (rough)	course (an educational class)
draw (to illustrate)	drawer (a storage compartment)
elicit (to bring forth)	illicit (illegal)
fourth (number four in a sequence)	forth (forward)
illusion (a visual trick)	allusion (a reference)
its (the possessive form of *it*)	it's (a contraction of *it is* or *it has*)
loose (not secured)	lose (to misplace or drop)
pole (a long cylinder of metal or wood)	poll (a sampling of data)
principal (main)	principle (a rule or code)
stationary (still)	stationery (writing paper)
their (the possessive form of *they*)	there (at a particular place) and they're (a contraction of *they are*)
your (the possessive form of *you*)	you're (a contraction of *you are*)

▶ **Incorrect:** Wu picked up the briefcase by it's handle.

It's is a contraction of the words *it is*, so that is incorrect here. We need the possessive form of *it*, which is *its*.

▶ **Correct:** Wu picked up the briefcase by its handle.

Conventional Expressions

Conventional expressions are commonly used phrases. Some conventional expressions are used so often that mistakes in their meanings or wordings may accidentally fall into common use. On the SAT, you will be expected to use expressions correctly, avoiding these common mistakes.

You cannot be expected to remember every single common mistake in conventional expressions, but some of the most common are:

Incorrect Expression	Correct Expression
baited breath	bated breath
bold-faced lie	bald-faced lie
besides the point	beside the point
chock it up to	chalk it up to
could of	could have
different than	different from
expresso	espresso
extract revenge	exact revenge
for all intensive purposes	for all intents and purposes
hone in	home in
I could care less	I couldn't care less
in parenthesis	in parentheses

nip it in the butt	nip it in the bud
now and days	nowadays
on accident	by accident
one in the same	one and the same
peaked my interest	piqued my interest
should of	should have
statue of limitations	statute of limitations
take for granite	take for granted
tongue-and-cheek	tongue-in-cheek
tow the line	toe the line
wet your appetite	whet your appetite

EXAMPLE

▶ **Incorrect:** Your hair is really different than your mother's.

The correct expression is *different from.*

▶ **Correct:** Your hair is really different from your mother's.

EXERCISES

EXERCISE 4–1

Directions: Read each sentence, then choose the best revision.

1. Erlene has a question she would like to ask you?
    A. NO CHANGE
    B. Erlene has a question she would like to ask you,
    C. Erlene has a question she would like to ask you.
    D. Erlene has a question she would like to ask you

2. Irene asked, "Can you tell me the way to Fifth Avenue"
    A. NO CHANGE
    B. Irene asked, "Can you tell me the way to Fifth Avenue!"
    C. Irene asked, "Can you tell me the way to Fifth Avenue"?
    D. Irene asked, "Can you tell me the way to Fifth Avenue?"

3. This pen which is out of ink is useless.
    A. NO CHANGE
    B. This pen, which is out of ink is useless.
    C. This pen which is out of ink, is useless.
    D. This pen, which is out of ink, is useless.

4. Rhonda bought a dress, matching shoes and a necklace.
    A. NO CHANGE
    B. Rhonda bought, a dress, matching shoes, and a necklace.
    C. Rhonda bought a dress matching shoes and a necklace.
    D. Rhonda bought a dress, matching shoes, and a necklace.

5. Somebody's package was left in my mailbox.
    A. NO CHANGE
    B. Somebodies' package was left in my mailbox.
    C. Somebodys package was left in my mailbox.
    D. Somebodys' package was left in my mailbox.

6. The construction workers performed a hard days work.
    A. NO CHANGE
    B. The construction workers performed a hard day' work.
    C. The construction workers performed a hard day's work.
    D. The construction workers performed a hard days' work.

7. Cassie did not watch the debate so she has no idea which candidate she will choose.
    A. NO CHANGE
    B. Cassie did not watch the debate; she has no idea which candidate she will choose.
    C. Cassie did not watch the debate, she has no idea which candidate she will choose.
    D. Cassie did not watch the debate she has no idea which candidate she will choose.

8. I really enjoy three particular movie genres: science-fiction films, which deal with outer space and the future; Westerns, which are set in the American frontier; and romantic comedies, which find the humor in romantic relationships.
    A. NO CHANGE
    B. I really enjoy three particular movie genres: science-fiction films, which deal with outer space and the future, Westerns, which are set in the American frontier and romantic comedies, which find the humor in romantic relationships.

C. I really enjoy three particular movie genres: science-fiction films, which deal with outer space and the future, Westerns, which are set in the American frontier, and romantic comedies, which find the humor in romantic relationships.

D. I really enjoy three particular movie genres: science-fiction films which deal with outer space and the future, Westerns which are set in the American frontier, and romantic comedies which find the humor in romantic relationships.

9. Be sure to pack the following items in your suitcase: warm outerwear, two, sweaters, ski goggles, and ointment.

A. NO CHANGE

B. Be sure to pack the following items in your suitcase warm outerwear, two sweaters, ski goggles, and ointment.

C. Be sure to pack the following items in your suitcase: warm outerwear, two sweaters ski goggles, and ointment.

D. Be sure to pack the following items in your suitcase: warm outerwear, two sweaters, ski goggles, and ointment.

10. I sprinkle fertilizer on the garden, every time I plant something new.

A. NO CHANGE

B. I sprinkle fertilizer on the garden—every time I plant something new.

C. I sprinkle fertilizer on the garden; every time I plant something new.

D. I sprinkle fertilizer on the garden every time I plant something new.

11. The teacher asked us to read "chapter 3" for tomorrow's assignment.
    A. NO CHANGE
    B. The teacher asked us to read chapter 3 for tomorrow's assignment.
    C. The teacher asked us to read chapter 3 for tomorrow's assignment!!!
    D. The teacher, asked us to read chapter 3 for tomorrow's assignment.

12. The primary colors red, blue, yellow, can be combined to make secondary colors, green, orange, purple.
    A. NO CHANGE
    B. The primary colors (red, blue, yellow) can be combined to make secondary colors—green, orange, purple.
    C. The primary colors (red, blue, and yellow) can be combined to make secondary colors (green, orange, and purple).
    D. The primary colors "red, blue, yellow" can be combined to make secondary colors "green, orange, purple."

EXERCISE 4–2

Directions: Read each sentence, then choose the best revision.

1. Because I am going to help you move you are such a good friend.
    A. NO CHANGE
    B. Because you are such a good friend, because I am going to help you move.
    C. You are such a good friend, because I am going to help you move.
    D. I am going to help you move because you are such a good friend.

2. It started raining, but we had to cancel the picnic.

    A. NO CHANGE

    B. It started raining, after we had to cancel the picnic.

    C. It started raining, so we had to cancel the picnic.

    D. It started raining, we had to cancel the picnic.

3. Because no one asked for my opinion.

    A. NO CHANGE

    B. Because no one asked me for my opinion.

    C. Because no one asked for my opinion at any time.

    D. I said nothing because no one asked for my opinion.

4. This is my favorite kind of sandwich because it contains tomatoes and I love tomatoes.

    A. NO CHANGE

    B. This is my favorite kind of sandwich it contains tomatoes and I love tomatoes.

    C. This is my favorite kind of sandwich because it contains tomatoes I love tomatoes.

    D. This is my favorite kind of sandwich because it contains tomatoes and I love.

5. The movie begins at 8:30 make sure you're there by 8:00.

    A. NO CHANGE

    B. The movie begins at 8:30, make sure you're there by 8:00.

    C. The movie begins at 8:30. Make sure you're there by 8:00.

    D. The movie begins at 8:30 making sure you're there by 8:00.

6. He decided to go along with the group even though he disagreed.

    A. NO CHANGE

    B. Decided to go along with the group even though he disagreed.

    C. Deciding to go along with the group even though he disagreed.

    D. To decide to go along with the group even though he disagreed.

EXERCISE 4–3

Directions: Read each sentence, then choose the best revision.

1. Today I am going to the gym, meeting a friend for lunch, and then to the bookstore.
   A. NO CHANGE
   B. Today I am going to the gym, meeting a friend for lunch, and going to the bookstore.
   C. Today I am going to the gym, meeting a friend for lunch, and to the bookstore.
   D. Today I am going to the gym, meeting a friend for lunch, and the bookstore.

2. The toddler has just started to say basic words, eat with a spoon, and drink from a cup.
   A. NO CHANGE
   B. The toddler has just started to say basic words, eat with a spoon, and is drinking from a cup.
   C. The toddler has just started to say basic words, eats with a spoon, and drink from a cup.
   D. The toddler has just started saying basic words, eating with a spoon, and will drink from a cup.

3. The birds I saw in the park were more colorful than in that tree.
   A. NO CHANGE
   B. The birds I saw in the park were more colorful than the ones in that tree.
   C. The birds I saw in the park were more colorful in that tree.
   D. The birds I saw in the park were more colorful.

4. Walking in the park is more interesting than going to a movie.

    A. NO CHANGE

    B. Walking in the park is more interesting than we go to a movie.

    C. Walking in the park is more interesting than to go to a movie.

    D. To walk in the park is more interesting than going to a movie.

EXERCISE 4–4

Directions: Read each sentence, then choose the best revision.

1. The students study in the library after school.

    A. NO CHANGE

    B. The students studies in the library after school.

    C. The students studying in the library after school.

    D. The student study in the library after school.

2. The team of football players were accompanied by their coach.

    A. NO CHANGE

    B. The team of football players accompanied by their coach.

    C. The team of football players are accompanied by their coach.

    D. The team of football players was accompanied by the coach.

3. Either Aaron or his parents has a pet.

    A. NO CHANGE

    B. Either Aaron or his parents are having a pet.

    C. Either Aaron or his parents have a pet.

    D. Either Aaron or his parents having a pet.

4. Tomorrow the sun will be setting at 7 p.m.

    A. NO CHANGE

    B. Tomorrow the sun set at 7 p.m.

    C. Tomorrow the sun had set at 7 p.m.

    D. Tomorrow the sun is set at 7 p.m.

5. The tomato and mozzarella sandwich was eaten by me.

    A. NO CHANGE

    B. I ate the tomato and mozzarella sandwich.

    C. The tomato and mozzarella sandwich was ate by me.

    D. I eaten the tomato and mozzarella sandwich.

6. The puppies will become a large hound someday.

    A. NO CHANGE

    B. The puppy will become a large hound someday.

    C. The puppy will become a large hounds someday.

    D. The puppies will become a large hounds someday.

EXERCISE 4–5

Directions: Read each sentence, then choose the best revision.

1. We will all write my phone numbers in the book.

    A. NO CHANGE

    B. We will all write our phone numbers in the book.

    C. We will all write his phone numbers in the book.

    D. We will all write her phone numbers in the book.

2. Every person with an opinion should make his voice heard.

   A. NO CHANGE

   B. Every person with an opinion should make their voice heard.

   C. People with an opinion should make his voice heard.

   D. Every person with an opinion should make their voices heard.

3. The tree dropped their leaves in the autumn.

   A. NO CHANGE

   B. The tree dropped that leaves in the autumn.

   C. The tree dropped its leaves in the autumn.

   D. The trees dropped its leaves in the autumn.

4. The government must decide how much risk they can handle.

   A. NO CHANGE

   B. The government must decide how much risk he or she can handle.

   C. The government must decide how much risk it can handle.

   D. The government must decide how much risk them can handle.

5. Mom asked Alexia and me to explain why we were late.

   A. NO CHANGE

   B. Mom asked Alexia and me to explain why us was late.

   C. Mom asked Alexia and I to explain why we were late.

   D. Mom asked Alexia and myself to explain why we were late.

6. Everyone except you and myself went to the party.

   A. NO CHANGE

   B. Everyone except yours and mine went to the party.

   C. Everyone except you and me went to the party.

   D. Everyone except you and I went to the party.

7. Sarah and Sadie were going to that university, but she transferred to another school last month.
    A. NO CHANGE
    B. Sarah and Sadie were going to that university, then she transferred to another school last month.
    C. Sarah and Sadie were going to that university, and it transferred to another school last month.
    D. Sarah and Sadie were going to that university, but Sadie transferred to another school last month.

8. The lightbulb and the fuse blew out, so you will need to replace it.
    A. NO CHANGE
    B. The lightbulb and the fuse blew out, so you will need to replace us.
    C. The lightbulb and the fuse blew out, so you will need to replace them.
    D. The lightbulb and the fuse blew out, so you will need to replace this.

EXERCISE 4–6

Directions: Read each sentence, then choose the best revision.

1. Ginger was talking loud on the phone to Jake.
    A. NO CHANGE
    B. Ginger talking loudly on the phone to Jake.
    C. Ginger was talking loudly on the phone to Jake.
    D. Ginger was loud talking on the phone to Jake.

2. Sydney ran quickly to the bathroom because he wasn't feeling well.
   A. NO CHANGE
   B. Sydney ran quick to the bathroom because he wasn't feeling good.
   C. Sydney ran quick to the bathroom because he wasn't feeling well.
   D. Sydney ran quickly to the bathroom because he wasn't feeling good.

3. The deer concerned a predator was near, ran into the woods.
   A. NO CHANGE
   B. Concerned a predator was near, ran into the woods.
   C. Concerned a predator was near, ran the deer into the woods.
   D. Concerned a predator was near, the deer ran into the woods.

4. The waiter handed the bill to the diners on a silver platter.
   A. NO CHANGE
   B. The waiter handed the bill on a silver platter to the diners.
   C. On a silver platter, the waiter handed the bill to the diners.
   D. The waiter, on a silver platter, handed the bill to the diners.

EXERCISE 4–7

Directions: Read each sentence, then choose the best revision.

1. I like every flavor of jelly bean except for lemon.
   A. NO CHANGE
   B. I like every flavor of jelly bean accept for lemon.
   C. I like every flavor of jelly bean exempt for lemon.
   D. I like every flavor of jelly bean expect for lemon.

2. The poet made an illusion to a famous Shakespearean sonnet.
   A. NO CHANGE
   B. The poet made an allusion to a famous Shakespearean sonnet.
   C. The poet made an attribution to a famous Shakespearean sonnet.
   D. The poet made a disillusion to a famous Shakespearean sonnet.

3. When my car came back from the body shop, it's front fender looked like new again.

    A. NO CHANGE

    B. When my car came back from the body shop, it is front fender looked like new again.

    C. When my car came back from the body shop, its front fender looked like new again.

    D. When my car came back from the body shop, it front fender looked like new again.

4. I'm going to have to buy some groceries if their coming to dinner on Friday night.

    A. NO CHANGE

    B. I'm going to have to buy some groceries if they're coming to dinner on Friday night.

    C. I'm going to have to buy some groceries if there coming to dinner on Friday night.

    D. I'm going to have to buy some groceries if their' coming to dinner on Friday night.

5. I should of seen you standing there.

    A. NO CHANGE

    B. I should a seen you standing there.

    C. I should seen you standing there.

    D. I should have seen you standing there.

Answers are on page 552.

5 Writing: Expression of Ideas

MUST ⚡ KNOW

⚡ A writer's claim (main idea) must be supported with relevant, precise, and concise details.

⚡ Paragraphs should follow a logical sequence, begin with a topic sentence, and include only relevant details.

⚡ Transition words and phrases should be used to introduce, to conclude, and to move from one topic to another.

⚡ Writing style, tone, and syntax should be chosen based on the writer's rhetorical purpose.

Strong language skills are necessary to write as effectively as possible. On the SAT, you will read nonfictional passages and ensure their ideas, claims, counterclaims, and topic sentences are written and organized clearly and effectively. You will ensure that the focus of passages remains on track and that style and tone remain consistent. You will also correct any mistakes in the sequence of words and ideas and revise introductions, conclusions, and translations that are not placed correctly.

The SAT also tests your ability to recognize and correct errors in grammar, usage, and punctuation. This means you will need a strong understanding of how subjects, verbs, pronouns, other parts of speech, and punctuation function in grammatically correct sentences. You will make sure writers use words and expressions correctly and make comparisons that are clear and logical. To do so you will either select the best revision of a piece of writing from a series of choices or you will opt to leave writing that requires no revision as it is by selecting NO CHANGE.

In this chapter, we will review how texts are developed and organized and how to use language effectively.

Development of Text

The following skills all involve revising text for rhetorical purposes. On the SAT, you will be expected to edit central ideas, claims, counterclaims, topic sentences, details, facts, statistics, and graphic elements to construct effective pieces of writing.

Proposition

The proposition is the main idea or claim of a text. A strong proposition has a central (main) idea, a topic sentence, and may include counterclaims:

▶ **Central idea:** the point a rhetorical text argues for or against

example: Wintertime is unpleasant.

▶ **Topic sentence:** the statement containing the central idea

example: With its harsh snows, winds, and temperatures, winter is by far the most difficult time of the year.

▶ **Counterclaims:** claims that argue against the central idea

example: However, wintertime activities such as skiing, snowboarding, and snowman building can be great fun.

Support

Writers support their main claims with clearly stated facts, statistics, examples, and details:

▶ **Claim:** the main idea

example: Dinosaur National Monument is a highly educational vacation destination.

▶ **Facts:** proven statements

example: President Woodrow Wilson approved the establishment of the Dinosaur National Monument in 1915.

▶ **Statistics:** quantitative data

example: Clams belonging to the *Unio* genus are the most common fossils in Dinosaur National Monument.

> **Examples:** specific examples of aspects of the claim

example: At Dinosaur National Monument, visitors can learn about both paleontology and geology.

> **Details:** general descriptions

example: Dinosaur National Monument is located on the northern edge of the Colorado Plateau.

On the SAT, you will be expected to choose the claims that are most strongly supported by facts, statistics, examples, and details.

EXAMPLE

> In the nineteenth century, the United States vastly increased the amount of territory it occupied. <u>The Louisiana Purchase, in 1803, doubled the size of the United States.</u>

> 1. Which choice provides the best supporting example for the main idea of the paragraph?

   A. NO CHANGE

   B. In 1803, France sold the Louisiana Territory to the United States.

   C. The United States was interested in westward expansion.

   D. John O'Sullivan is credited with coining the term "Manifest Destiny" to describe American expansion.

> The main idea is that the United States greatly increased its territory in the 1800s. We are asked to provide a supporting example of this. The underlined sentence does that, so the best answer is NO CHANGE. Choice B is very similar, but it focuses on France selling the territory rather than the United States acquiring it. Neither choice C nor choice D provides a specific example of increasing territory. The best answer is A.

Focus

When supporting a claim with facts, statistics, and details, it is crucial to ensure they are relevant to that claim. Supporting information that veers off topic should be deleted or substituted with facts, statistics, and details that maintain their focus.

 IRL Focus presents a problem in speech as well as in writing. Don't you hate it when someone tells you a story and keeps inserting irrelevant information? If I am telling you an exciting story about the football game I won, you don't care how many fish I caught last weekend.

Some focus questions ask you about possible additions to the text. You will need to decide whether to include the new sentence and why.

EXAMPLE

In the late eighteenth century the Atlantic slave trade reached its peak. European nations such as Britain, France, and Spain were enslaving tens of thousands of Africans per year and transporting them to their colonies to labor in horrible conditions.

1. The author is considering adding this sentence to the end of this section:

African and native peoples struggled for their very survival and the slavers struggled for the right to dominate the land as well as the people who worked it.

Should the author include that sentence in that location?

    A. Yes, because it shows the struggle of slaves in the colonies.

    B. Yes, because it expands the previous statements to include native peoples.

C. No, because it is not directly relevant to the previous statements that focus on the extent of slavery.

D. No, because it changes the focus from African slaves to both African and native peoples.

Our first job is to decide if the sentence should be included. Is it directly relevant? No. That eliminates choices A and B. Why is it not directly relevant? The first two sentences focus on the huge number of people enslaved. That makes choice C the best answer.

Quantitative Information

Some passages on the SAT contain graphic elements that convey quantitative information. As stated earlier, quantitative information is measurable: units of time, statistics, temperature, weight, size, population—anything with a number value. Sentences that refer to quantitative information in graphic elements must relay that information accurately. Any sentences that do not must be revised for accuracy.

EXAMPLE

Planet	Day Length	Distance from Sun	Year (in Earth days)
Mercury	4222.6 hours	35,980,000 miles	88 days
Venus	2802 hours	67,240,000 miles	224.7 days
Earth	24 hours	92,900,000 miles	365.2 days
Mars	24.7 hours	141,600,000 miles	687 days
Jupiter	9.9 hours	483,800,000 miles	4331 days
Saturn	10.7 hours	890,700,000 miles	10,747 days
Uranus	17.2 hours	1,787,000,000 miles	30,589 days
Neptune	16 hours	2,798,000,000 miles	59,800 days

A year is determined by how long it takes for a planet to complete its orbit around the sun.

1. Which choice completes the sentence with accurate data based on the table?

   A. NO CHANGE

   B. and the majority of planets in our solar system take longer to make that journey than ours does.

   C. and no planet makes that journey with greater velocity than the outermost planet, Neptune.

   D. and though Pluto is no longer officially considered to be a planet, it takes 247.7 Earth years to orbit the sun.

What does the data in the table show? The day lengths decrease as we move down the table, while the distance from the sun and the year (in Earth days) increase. The statement presents a fact, but it does not make a claim. We probably should add something. Let's look at the answer choices. Choice B makes sense. Earth is third on the list, with five planets after it, so we could certainly say that the majority of planets take longer to orbit the sun. Keep B. Choice C brings up velocity, which is not mentioned in the table or the statement, so eliminate C. Choice D is also irrelevant because the table only includes planets. We might be sad that Pluto is no longer a planet, but that's no reason to include it. The best choice is B.

Organization

A strong piece of writing is well organized. The basic organizational structure of a text is:

- Introduction: the paragraph that establishes the claim or main idea

- Body: the paragraphs that support that claim

- Conclusion: the final paragraph, which summarizes the findings of the other paragraphs

Each individual paragraph should also be well organized. Ideas should lead into each other logically and be linked by transitional words and phrases.

Logical Sequence

Even the most relevant information should not be randomly assembled in a passage. Organization is key to presenting that information effectively. Topic sentences should lead into supporting details. General ideas should lead into more specific ones. The sequence of ideas can also be improved by building toward a climax. Phrases and sentences that do not follow logically from the preceding ideas should be moved to where they make the most sense.

EXAMPLE

▶ Few animals live longer than giant tortoises. A tortoise discovered in Tonga was 188 when it died in 1965. These creatures live for an average of 100 years.

The second sentence of this example is not placed logically. The ideas in a paragraph should get increasingly specific, yet the sentence about the 188-year-old tortoise is more specific than the general one about how these creatures live for an average of 100 years. It's also anticlimactic, since a 188-year lifespan is much more impressive than a 100-year lifespan.

This is a better revision of the example:

▶ Few animals live longer than giant tortoises. These creatures live for an average of 100 years. A tortoise discovered in Tonga was 188 when it died in 1965.

Introductions, Conclusions, and Transitions

Strong introductions, conclusions, and transitions are crucial elements of effectively organized writing. They ensure that a text begins and ends logically, and that the ideas in between flow into each other logically.

The key to composing strong introductions, conclusions, and transitions is to use logical transitional words, phrases, and sentences.

Transitional words and phrases may indicate:

BTW

When you are writing essays in school, be sure to use some of these transition words and phrases in your own writing. They will help your essay flow smoothly.

■ **An addition**

EXAMPLES

▶ **Here are some examples of transitional words and phrases that show additions:** also, furthermore, moreover, in addition, additionally, secondly

■ **The passage of time**

EXAMPLES

▶ **Here are some examples of transitional words and phrases that show passage of time:** next, later, meanwhile, afterward, subsequently

■ **Illustrations and examples**

EXAMPLES

▶ **Here are some examples of transitional words and phrases that show examples:** to illustrate, for example, for instance, to demonstrate, specifically

■ **Cause**

EXAMPLES

▶ **Here are some examples of transitional words and phrases that indicate causality:** because, since

■ **Effect**

EXAMPLES

▶ **Here are some examples of transitional words and phrases that show effects:** therefore, consequently, as a result

■ **Comparison**

EXAMPLES

▶ **Here are some examples of transitional words and phrases that indicate a comparison:** similarly, comparatively, in comparison, in similar fashion, likewise

■ **Contrast**

EXAMPLES

▶ **Here are some examples of transitional words and phrases that indicate contrast:** however, nevertheless, yet, notwithstanding, at the same time, in contrast, on the contrary

■ **Clarification**

EXAMPLES

▶ **Here are some examples of transitional words and phrases that signal a clarification:** in other words, that is to say, to put it another way

■ **Conclusion**

EXAMPLES

▶ **Here are some examples of transitional words and phrases that signal a conclusion:** in conclusion, ultimately, to summarize, to conclude, in short, to sum up

Transitional sentences may begin with these kinds of transitional words and phrases. However, introductory sentences are more likely to simply establish the main topic or claim of a text.

EXAMPLE

▶ A good introductory sentence for a passage about the history of electric locomotives is "For nearly 180 years, electric locomotives have been transporting people and goods across great distances."

On the SAT you will revise introductions, conclusions, and transitions to organize texts effectively.

Effective Language Use

An effective rhetorical text displays a confident grasp of language. The writer chooses her words carefully to ensure the text does not ramble, lose focus, or fail to make grammatical sense. The following skills are essential for using language effectively in rhetorical texts.

Precision

Rhetorical texts are persuasive at heart, and an effective way to be persuasive is to make it clear you know what you're talking about. A good way to achieve this is to use precise language.

> Please turn off the thing.
>
> This is not a very effective way to persuade someone to perform an action. The person being directed may not have any idea what the "thing" in question is. A more effective direction would be "Please turn off the television." *Television* is a precise word that refers to a specific object. *Thing* is vague and can refer to any number of objects.

Imprecise language may not necessarily be as vague as in the previous example. Some words may have meanings very similar to that of the most precise word but not be quite right. For example, a power saw is a kind of machine, so it is not incorrect to refer to it as a "machine." However, there are many different kinds of machines. A table saw is very different from a car or a dishwasher, which are both kinds of machines too. A much more precise way to describe a table saw is "power tool." On the SAT, you may encounter questions with more than one answer choice that is not necessarily incorrect. However, there will always be one choice that is most precise and, therefore, is the best choice.

Concision

An effective rhetorical text holds the reader's interest. The writer does not waste space with words that aren't necessary to the idea being expressed. Concise writing also avoids unnecessary repetition and rambling structures that do not express ideas as succinctly as possible. Concision is an important factor in clear, focused writing.

EXAMPLE

▶ Pulping is the process that results in the creation or formation of paper. One kind of pulping is chemical pulping, and this involves submitting wood chips to high pressures and treating them with a chemical solution that dissolves the wood's lignin. Lignin is the organic substance that holds the wood's fibers together.

This is not the most concise way to express the paragraph's ideas. There are rambling sentence structures (the first and second sentences). There are unnecessary words (the first sentence unnecessarily uses both *creation* and *formation*, which essentially share the same meaning). There is unnecessary repetition (in the second sentence, the reader can figure out that chemical pulping is a kind of pulping without the phrase "One kind of pulping." The word *lignin* does not need to be used in both the second and third sentences.

Here is a more concise way to express the ideas in the example paragraph:

> Paper is created through a process called pulping. Chemical pulping involves submitting wood chips to high pressures and treating them with a chemical solution that dissolves the wood's lignin, which is the organic substance that holds its fibers together.

Style and Tone

A writer uses different styles and tones to suit the particular purpose of a rhetorical text.

Style is the way a writer chooses words for a particular audience. He may use words formally to reach academic readers or informally to appeal to the general public.

EXAMPLES

> **Formal tone:** The African bush elephant is the largest living land mammal.

> **Informal tone:** Land animals just don't get any bigger than the African bush elephant!

Tone refers to the writer's attitude. A text's tone may be objective or subjective, logical or emotional, serious or humorous. Tone should also suit the particular topic and intended audience of a text. A humorous tone may be inappropriate for an article decrying the horrors of war, just as a logical tone may not suit an article about the joy of falling in love.

Shifting one's style and tone in a single text can be distracting. A writer who does so may lose the reader's interest or even his own credibility. On the SAT, you will revise sentences for the sake of consistent style and tone.

Syntax

Syntax is the way a writer structures sentences. A writer's use reflects different rhetorical purposes. Technically, a fragment is a grammatically incorrect way to compose a sentence, yet a writer may choose to use fragments to achieve a terse and forceful effect (example: There is no way I'd ever vote for that candidate. *No way*.). However, on the SAT you need to focus on grammatical correctness.

On the SAT, you will revise sentences for the sake of effective syntax. These questions may require you to combine sentences, correct grammatical errors, and improve logical transitions and clarity.

EXAMPLE

▶ 1. Since Jenna had to pick up her dog from the groomer after work and I made dinner.

    A. NO CHANGE

    B. Because Jenna had to pick up her dog from the groomer after work.

    C. Because Jenna had to pick up her dog from the groomer after work and I am making dinner.

    D. Since Jenna had to pick up her dog from the groomer after work, I made dinner.

▶ The original sentence is a fragment. Choices B and C are also sentence fragments. Choice D completes the thought properly and is the best answer.

EXERCISES

EXERCISE 5-1

Directions: Read the paragraphs, then choose the best answer to each of the questions that follow.

[1] Once considered a threat to musicians because of the illegal trading of copyrighted recordings online, digital files and online distribution may ultimately prove to be the salvation of musicians currently receiving less support from traditional music labels than ever before. [2] Digital recording with home computers has eliminated the need for expensive recording studios. [3] Digital distribution through websites, social media sites, and blogs allows music artists to reach a global audience without cost and without having to sign a potentially unfavorable contract. [4] How do artists distinguish themselves in an online environment overcrowded with competing artists?

1. Which choice is the most effective topic sentence for this paragraph?
   A. MP3s used to be the most common digital music files, but now music listeners can choose from FLAC, AIFF, and ATRAC Lossless files.
   B. Many personal computers now include digital recording programs as part of their basic packages.
   C. Digital music files and the ease of uploading them to the Internet has altered the music business drastically.
   D. There once was a time when musicians had to go to studios and record on expensive tape.

2. Which choice is the most effective revision of sentence 4?
   A. NO CHANGE
   B. Most important of all: How do artists distinguish themselves in an online environment overcrowded with competing artists?
   C. Artists also have to distinguish themselves in an online environment overcrowded with competing artists.
   D. However, a significant problem lingers: How do artists distinguish themselves in an online environment overcrowded with competing artists?

[1] When examining nineteenth-century Scandinavian literature written by female authors, one must consider not only the genres in which women wrote, but *why* those genres were chosen. [2] In some cases, the choice was perhaps more a political one than an aesthetic one. [3] Naturalistic narratives were a mode of writing that women could use without excessive opposition. [4] They chose naturalistic narrative as a vehicle through which to discuss cultural and social inequalities and enter the debate on women's rights.

3. Which choice provides the best support for sentence 3?
   A. They emphasize the diversity of voices and attempt to avoid generalization.
   B. Modern feminists are still grappling with many of the same issues that the first feminist writers did.
   C. Many female authors used pseudonyms.
   D. The choice of modes of writing deemed acceptable to the male establishment allowed female writers to more freely explore feminist topics.

4. The writer wants to include a quotation to support sentence 4. Which choice best accomplishes that goal?

   A. Amalie Skram's writes in her novel *Knut Tandberg*, "Therefore she simply could not be fulfilled in the children, as she knew people expected a mother should."

   B. In Illa Christensen's novel *"Idling Away the Days"—and Working Days*, she writes, "Francois did not work, he aestheticised, and to his mind *that* was the worthiest pastime for a human being."

   C. For example, the main character in Amalie Skram's novel *Lucie* "fell motionless and burst into tears, reached out towards her weeping image in the mirror."

   D. For example, the main character in Illa Christensen's novel *"Idling Away the Days"—and Working Days* "stayed sitting thus, without weeping, without thinking, merely with the feeling of having been deposited, arbitrarily, both in life and at this very moment."

Directions: Read each sentence, then choose the best answer to each of the questions that follow.

On August 27, 1908, Lyndon Johnson was born in Stonewall, Texas, currently the second most populous U.S. state, to Samuel Ealy Johnson, Jr., and Rebekah Baines Johnson.

5. Which is the least relevant detail in this statement?

   A. On August 27, 1908
   B. Lyndon Johnson was born in Stonewall, Texas
   C. currently the second most populous U.S. state
   D. to Samuel Ealy Johnson, Jr., and Rebekah Baines Johnson

Certain compounds biodegrade faster than others. A paper towel breaks down in as little as two weeks. A cardboard box can take two months to disintegrate.

6. The author is considering adding this sentence to the end of this section:

Tin cans, however, can take as many as 100 years to break down.

Should the author include that sentence?
   A. Yes, because it gives another example of the increasing breakdown time.
   B. Yes, because it shows the importance of recycling.
   C. No, because it is not directly relevant to the previous statements.
   D. No, because it contradicts the first sentence.

According to the National Center for Education Statistics, individuals who had earned their bachelor's degrees were more likely to find employment than those who had not in the years 2000 through 2013.

7. Which additional detail would be most relevant to this statement?
   A. About 55 percent of college students are female.
   B. The National Center for Education Statistics is based in Washington, D.C.
   C. As of 2007, about 18,423,000 adult males in the United States had bachelor's degrees.
   D. The individuals in this study are between the ages of 20 and 64.

Directions: Examine each graphic element and read each sentence, then choose the best answer to each of the questions that follow.

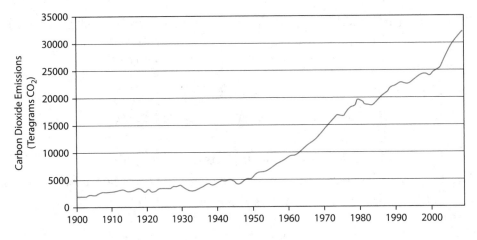

Since 1900 there has been a major upswing in the level of fossil fuel–created carbon emissions throughout the world

8. Which choice completes the sentence with accurate data based on the graph?
    A. NO CHANGE
    B. with only fleeting periods of decrease throughout the years.
    C. however, there is no reason to believe this upswing will continue.
    D. yet the cause of this upswing continues to be a source of debate.

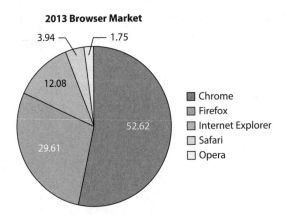

By a great margin, no web browser was more widely used in 2013 than Chrome.

9. Which choice completes the sentence with accurate data based on the chart?

    A. NO CHANGE

    B. a statistic that may or may not have changed since the previous statistics were compiled and reported in 2012.

    C. with the second most popular browser, Firefox, finding favor with little more than half the number of Chrome users.

    D. however, 17.20 percent of Internet users browsed with Internet Explorer in the previous year according to another chart.

EXERCISE 5–2

Directions: Read the paragraphs, then choose the best answer to each of the questions that follow.

[1] After its publication in *New Monthly Magazine*, "The Vampyre" inspired a stage play that became a sensation. [2] In the summer of 1816, 18-year-old Mary Godwin traveled to Geneva, Switzerland, for a holiday with her stepsister Clair Clairmont, boyfriend poet Percy Shelley, poet Lord Byron, and Byron's assistant John Polidori. [3] While it is well known that Godwin composed one of the essential works of fantastical fiction, *Frankenstein*, during this trip, it is less well known that Polidori too made literary history in Geneva. [4] There he began work on a short story titled "The Vampyre," the first major modern tale about that particular fictional creature. [5] The play *Le Vampire* set off the nineteenth-century fascination with creatures of the night that would culminate with Bram Stoker's publication of *Dracula* before the end of the century.

1. For the sake of the cohesion of this paragraph, sentence 1 should be placed
   A. where it is now.
   B. before sentence 3.
   C. after sentence 4.
   D. after sentence 5.

2. For the sake of the cohesion of this paragraph, sentence 5 should be placed
   A. where it is now.
   B. before sentence 2.
   C. after sentence 2.
   D. before sentence 4.

[1] The Internet began to come into common use in the 1990s and flourished in the first decade of the twenty-first century. [2] Today it is the main mode of commerce and communication. [3] The Internet is hardly a recently developed technology. [4] In fact, its birth can be traced back to the 1960s, when the U.S. Department of Defense commissioned the development of a system called the ARPANET (Advanced Research Projects Agency Network), a network that served as a sort of early version of today's Internet. [5] In 1981, academic institutions obtained their own version of the ARPANET called the CSNET (Computer Science Network). [6] NSFNET (the National Science Foundation Network), a system for the National Science Foundation, followed in 1985; commercial Internet service providers began offering the technology to private citizens across the globe.

3. Which revision of sentence 1 most effectively introduces the paragraph?

    A. NO CHANGE

    B. The Internet began to come into common use in the 1990s.

    C. The Internet flourished in the first decade of the twenty-first century.

    D. People everywhere use the Internet; they used it in the nineties and they really use it a lot more today.

4. Which of the following is the most effective revision of sentence 3?

    A. NO CHANGE

    B. So, the Internet is hardly a recently developed technology.

    C. However, the Internet is hardly a recently developed technology.

    D. Therefore, the Internet is hardly a recently developed technology.

5. Which of the following is the most effective revision of sentence 6?

    A. NO CHANGE

    B. NSFNET (the National Science Foundation Network), a system for the National Science Foundation, followed in 1985, not long before commercial Internet service providers began offering the technology to private citizens across the globe.

    C. And finally NSFNET (the National Science Foundation Network), a system for the National Science Foundation, followed in 1985; commercial Internet service providers began offering the technology to private citizens across the globe.

    D. In conclusion, NSFNET (the National Science Foundation Network), a system for the National Science Foundation, followed in 1985; commercial Internet service providers began offering the technology to private citizens across the globe.

EXERCISE 5–3

Directions: Read each sentence, then choose the most effective revision of the sentence.

1. Physics and biology are my two favorite things to study in school.
   A. NO CHANGE
   B. Physics and biology are my two favorite subjects to study in school.
   C. Physics and biology are my two favorite topics to study in school.
   D. Physics and biology are my two favorite ideas to study in school.

2. To replace your car's oil filter you must first loosen it using a filter wrench to turn it.
   A. NO CHANGE
   B. To replace your car's oil filter you must first loosen it using a filter wrench to turn it well.
   C. To replace your car's oil filter you must first loosen it using a filter wrench to turn it counterclockwise.
   D. To replace your car's oil filter you must first loosen it using a filter wrench to spin it.

3. Scientists once believed there were two distinct dinosaurs called the Brontosaurus and the Apatosaurus, but the realization that these creatures were, in fact, one and the same caused one of the names to fall out of official use.

   A. NO CHANGE
   B. Scientists once believed there were two distinct dinosaurs called the Brontosaurus and the Apatosaurus, but the realization that these creatures were, in fact, one and the same caused one of the names to stop being used.
   C. Scientists once believed there were two distinct dinosaurs called the Brontosaurus and the Apatosaurus, but the realization that these creatures were, in fact, one and the same caused a name to not be used anymore officially.
   D. Scientists once believed there were two distinct dinosaurs called the Brontosaurus and the Apatosaurus, but the realization that these creatures were, in fact, one and the same caused the designation *Brontosaurus* to fall out of official use.

4. It is expected that a new company manager will be taking over the company within the next two months.

   A. NO CHANGE
   B. It is expected that a new manager will be taking over the company at the company in the next two months.
   C. A new manager will be taking over the company within the next two months at the company.
   D. A new manager is expected to take over the company within the next two months.

5. The artist took a photograph of Albert and used it to paint a perfect likeness of him.
   A. NO CHANGE
   B. The artist painted a perfect likeness of Albert using a photograph she had taken of Albert.
   C. The artist took a photograph of Albert and used that photograph to paint a perfect likeness of him.
   D. The artist photographed Albert and then used that photograph to paint a perfect likeness of him.

6. In the near future, people who have suffered severe burns may use cultured skin cells on a biodegradable bandage to increase the rate of healing someday.
   A. NO CHANGE
   B. In the near future, people who have suffered severe burns may one day use cultured skin cells on a biodegradable bandage to increase the rate of healing someday.
   C. In the near future, people who have suffered severe burns may use cultured skin cells on a biodegradable bandage to increase the rate of healing.
   D. In the near future, people who have suffered severe burns may one day use cultured skin cells on a biodegradable bandage to increase the rate of healing someday.

7. There's no reason to perform the unnecessary task of idling your car to warm it up on a cold day.
   A. NO CHANGE
   B. There's no reason to idle your car to warm it up on a cold day.
   C. There's no reason to unnecessarily idle your car to warm it up on a cold day.
   D. The unnecessary task of idling your car to warm it up on a cold day is pointless.

8. If a person who seems to be suffering a sudden cardiac arrest has no pulse or is not breathing, a medic should use an automated external defibrillator on him immediately.

    A. NO CHANGE
    B. If a person who seems to be suffering a sudden cardiac arrest has no pulse or is not breathing, a medic should zap the person with an automated external defibrillator immediately.
    C. If a guy who seems to be suffering a sudden cardiac arrest has no pulse or is not breathing, a medic should use an automated external defibrillator on him immediately.
    D. If a person who seems to be suffering a sudden cardiac arrest has no pulse or is not breathing, a medic should use an automated external defibrillator on him with absolute lightning speed.

9. Parochial school students are expected to follow a strict dress code, wearing school uniforms during class hours and OK'd athletic ones during physical education sessions.

    A. NO CHANGE
    B. Parochial school students are expected to follow a strict dress code, wearing school uniforms during class hours and approved athletic ones during physical education sessions.
    C. Parochial school students are expected to follow a strict dress code, wearing school uniforms during class hours and OK'd athletic uniforms during physical education sessions.
    D. Parochial school students are expected to follow a strict dress code, wearing school uniforms during class hours and OK'd athletic gear during physical education sessions.

10. Our natural environment continues to be destroyed for the sake of profit, and it is necessary to improve environmental protection standards.
    A. NO CHANGE
    B. Our natural environment continues to be destroyed for the sake of profit; it is necessary to improve environmental protection standards.
    C. Our natural environment continues to be destroyed for the sake of profit, and therefore it is necessary to improve environmental protection standards.
    D. Our natural environment continues to be destroyed for the sake of profit, and let's improve environmental protection standards.

11. As more people choose to view entertainment on the Internet, cable television companies will either have to adapt to the new online environment or go out of business.
    A. NO CHANGE
    B. As more people choose to view entertainment on the Internet, cable television companies adapt to the new online environment, or go out of business.
    C. Cable television companies adapt to the new online environment or go out of business, and more people choose to view entertainment on the Internet.
    D. Either adapting to the new online environment or going out of business, cable television companies see more people choose to view entertainment on the Internet.

12. Henry Wadsworth Longfellow was a member of the informal Fireside Poets group in the nineteenth century. Other Fireside Poets included William Cullen Bryant, John Greenleaf Whittier, James Russell Lowell, and Oliver Wendell Holmes, Sr.

   A. NO CHANGE
   B. Henry Wadsworth Longfellow was a member of the Fireside Poets group in the nineteenth century, and so were William Cullen Bryant, John Greenleaf Whittier, James Russell Lowell, and Oliver Wendell Holmes, Sr.
   C. Henry Wadsworth Longfellow, as well as William Cullen Bryant, John Greenleaf Whittier, James Russell Lowell, and Oliver Wendell Holmes, Sr., were members of the Fireside Poets group in the nineteenth century.
   D. Henry Wadsworth Longfellow, William Cullen Bryant, John Greenleaf Whittier, James Russell Lowell, and Oliver Wendell Holmes, Sr., were members of the Fireside Poets group in the nineteenth century.

Answers are on page 554.

Mathematics

The Math Test

The Math section of the SAT exam tests your mastery of math skills and concepts such as linear equations, functions, ratios, percents, and proportions. You will also see some plane geometry questions. The SAT tests your ability to analyze data and use reasoning skills to solve "real-world" problems. You will see data sets and scenarios drawn from science, social studies, business, and other fields. You can expect some problems that require a multistep process to arrive at the correct answer. There will be 46 multiple-choice questions, each with four answer choices, and 12 grid-in questions.

There are two parts of the Math Test: Math Test—Calculator and Math Test—No Calculator. The "no calculator" section is worth one-third of your score. You will have 80 minutes to complete the Math Test—55 minutes for the Calculator portion and 25 minutes for the No Calculator portion.

At the start of each section of the Math Test, there will be a "Reference Section" that includes common geometrical formulas and facts, including:

- Area and circumference of a circle

- Area of a rectangle

- Area of a triangle

- The Pythagorean Theorem

- Special right triangle pattern formulas

- Volume of a rectangular solid, cylinder, sphere, cone, and pyramid

- The following facts: (1) the number of degrees of arc in a circle is 360, (2) the number of radians of arc in a circle is 2π, and (3) the sum of the measure of degrees in a triangle is 180.

Math Review

The following section will give you a thorough overview of each skill tested in the Math section of the SAT. In each lesson, you will get the chance to practice your skills on test-like practice questions.

The correct answers to these questions can be found in the Exercise Answer Key at the end of this book.

Working with Expressions

MUST KNOW

 The rules of exponents include:

- $x^m x^n = x^{m+n}$

- $\dfrac{x^m}{x^n} = x^{m-n}$

- $(x^m)^n = x^{m \times n}$

- $\dfrac{1}{x^n} = x^{-n}$ for non-zero values of x and n

- $x^0 = 1$

 When working with polynomials, always simplify by combining like terms.

 Use FOIL to help you remember the order in which to multiply binomial terms: first terms, outside terms, inside terms, last terms.

 When performing operations on rational expressions, find common denominators, then cancel out common factors to simplify.

lgebraic expressions like $3x + 2y$ and $-\dfrac{x^2}{2} + 4$ involve variables and constants, but no equal sign. On the SAT, you will need to be confident in working with expressions and using common algebraic rules and techniques to simplify them and rewrite them. In this chapter, we will review some of the rules you will need to be familiar with when it comes time to take the SAT.

Exponents

As you may recall from basic mathematics, exponents represent how many times to multiply a quantity by itself. $4^2 = 4 \times 4 = 16$ and $2^3 = 2 \times 2 \times 2 = 8$. In 4^2, we call the 4 the base and the 2 the exponent. For terms like x, it is understood that the exponent is 1.

On the SAT, you won't be working with exponents in this simple form. Instead, you will work, most often, with exponents and variables. Often, this will be through simplifying expressions.

The Rules of Exponents

Algebraic expressions with exponents can be simplified using the rules of exponents, which are stated below, using number m and n:

$$x^m \, x^n = x^{m+n}$$
$$\frac{x^m}{x^n} = x^{m-n}$$
$$(x^m)^n = x^{m \times n}$$

Remember that the first and second rules can only be applied if the two terms have the same base.

EXAMPLE

▶ Simplify the expression.

$$\frac{2a^2b^7}{4ab^5}$$

▶ This expression is simplified by applying the rules of exponents to any terms with the same base and by cancelling common factors in the numerator and denominator.

$$\frac{\cancel{2}^1 a^2 b^7}{\cancel{4}^2 ab^5} = \frac{a^2 b^7}{2ab^5}$$
$$= \frac{a^{2-1}b^{7-5}}{2}$$
$$= \frac{a^1 b^2}{2}$$
$$= \frac{ab^2}{2}$$

One shortcut to a problem like the last example is to think of yourself as cancelling like terms. Instead of subtracting as we did in the example (direct application of the rules), we could write:

$$\frac{\cancel{2}^1 a^2 b^7}{\cancel{4}^2 ab^5} = \frac{a^{\cancel{2}1} b^{\cancel{7}2}}{2 \cancel{a} \cancel{b}^{\cancel{5}}}$$
$$= \frac{ab^2}{2}$$

The a in the denominator cancelled with one of the a's in the numerator and all 5 of the b's being multiplied in the denominator cancelled with 5 of those in the numerator, leaving only 2.

Let's try this method in the next example.

▶ Simplify the expression.

$$\frac{14x^4x^2}{x^8y}$$

$$\frac{14x^4x^2}{x^8y} = \frac{14x^{4+2}}{x^8y}$$

$$= \frac{14x^6}{x^8y}$$

$$= \frac{14x^{\cancel{6}}}{x^{\cancel{8}2}y}$$

$$= \frac{14}{x^2y}$$

▶ Notice in the first step that we added the exponents because the x^4 and x^2 are multiplied.

Negative Exponents and an Exponent of Zero

If you applied the rules of exponents directly to the last example, you would have had the following result:

$$\frac{14x^4x^2}{x^8y} = \frac{14x^{4+2}}{x^8y}$$

$$= \frac{14x^6}{x^8y}$$

$$= \frac{14x^{6-8}}{y}$$

$$= \frac{14x^{-2}}{y}$$

This isn't quite simplified yet due to the negative exponent, but how do you fix this? The general rule is as follows:

$$\text{For nonzero values of } x \text{ and } n \ \frac{1}{x^n} = x^{-n}.$$

This means that something like y^{-5} can be written as $\frac{1}{y^5}$, but what if the negative exponent is already in a fraction, as it is above? The trick here is to move it to the other part of the fraction and change the sign.

$$\frac{14x^{-2}}{y} = \frac{14}{x^2 y}$$

This works even if the negative exponent is in the denominator.

$$\frac{2x}{5y^{-3}} = \frac{2xy^3}{5}$$

EXAMPLE

▶ Simplify the expression.

$$\frac{(-3x^2 y^{-2})^2}{x^{-3} y}$$

▶ There is a lot going on with this example. Just remember that anytime you are going to simplify an expression like this and there is an exponent on the outside of the parentheses, take care of that first. Since the operation within the parentheses is multiplication, the exponent on the outside can distribute to each term.

$$\frac{(-3x^2y^{-2})^2}{x^{-3}y} = \frac{(-3)^2(x^2)^2(y^{-2})^2}{x^{-3}y}$$

$$= \frac{9x^4y^{-4}}{x^{-3}y}$$

$$= \frac{9x^4x^3}{yy^4}$$

$$= \frac{9x^{4+3}}{y^{1+4}}$$

$$= \frac{9x^7}{y^5}$$

Finally, when working with exponents, you may encounter exponents of zero. It is important to remember that any value with a zero exponent is 1.

That is, $x^0 = 1$, $134^0 = 1$, and $\left(\frac{x^52y}{z}\right)^0 = 1$.

Rational Exponents and Roots

You are probably familiar with the square root, represented by the symbol $\sqrt{\ }$. On the SAT, you may be asked to simplify expressions involving roots such as the square root or the cube root ($\sqrt[3]{\ }$). Roots like this can also be viewed as exponents using the property shown below.

$$\text{For } n > 1, \ x^{\frac{1}{n}} = \sqrt[n]{x}.$$

 IRL   Exponents are used often in many fields such as architecture, finance, biology, and construction—just to name a few. For example, to calculate compound interest on a loan, we use the formula $P\left(1 + \frac{r}{n}\right)^{nt}$ where P is the principle amount, r is the interest rate, n is the number of periods compounded, and t is the time.

According to this property, if n isn't shown in the root symbol, it is understood to be the square root. Using exponents, $\sqrt{x} = x^{\frac{1}{2}}$. Negative exponents still hold the same meaning, so an expression like $x^{-\frac{1}{3}}$ can be written as $\dfrac{1}{x^{\frac{1}{3}}}$ or $\dfrac{1}{\sqrt[3]{x}}$.

To simplify a root, we should first try to rewrite anything under the root as a product involving perfect squares. Numerically, a perfect square is a number with a whole-number square root. For example, $4 = 2 \times 2$, so 4 is a perfect square. We can write $\sqrt{4a}$ as $2\sqrt{a}$.

EXAMPLE

▶ Simplify the expression.

$$\sqrt{20x^6}$$

▶ Since $20 = 4 \times 5$, we can use that to simplify this expression.

▶ Further, we can use the fact that $\sqrt{x} = x^{\frac{1}{2}}$ to say that $\sqrt{x^6} = x^3$ since $6 \times \dfrac{1}{2} = 3$.

▶ Let's put these steps together.

$$\sqrt{20x^6} = \sqrt{4 \times 5 \times x^6}$$
$$= 2x^3\sqrt{5}$$

▶ This expression is now completely simplified because we took the square root of any factors that were perfect squares.

Remember that a square root is just another way of writing an exponent, so you can evaluate the root of a fraction over the numerator and denominator separately. $\sqrt{\dfrac{25}{4}} = \dfrac{\sqrt{25}}{\sqrt{4}} = \dfrac{5}{2}$

▶ Simplify the expression.

$$\sqrt{\dfrac{8x^7}{x^2y}}$$

▶ First, simplify any expression within the root. Then, break the expression down and take out any perfect squares.

$$\sqrt{\dfrac{8x^7}{x^2y}} = \sqrt{\dfrac{8x^5}{y}}$$

$$= \sqrt{\dfrac{2 \times 4 \times x^4 x}{y}}$$

$$= 2x^2\sqrt{\dfrac{2x}{y}}$$

If you are working with a cube root, look for perfect cubes instead of perfect squares. You can simplify them in the same way. $\sqrt[3]{8} = \sqrt[3]{2 \times 2 \times 2} = 2$

▶ Simplify the expression.

$$\sqrt[3]{-8x^4y^6}$$

$$\sqrt[3]{-8x^4y^6} = \sqrt[3]{-2^3x^3xy^6}$$

$$= -2xy^2\sqrt[3]{x}$$

Remember that a negative exponent is the same as the reciprocal of the corresponding positive exponent: $x^{-n} = \dfrac{1}{x^n}$

EXAMPLE

▶ Simplify the expression, writing the final result using radicals.

$$\left(\frac{x^5 y^8}{2xy} \right)^{-\frac{1}{2}}$$

▶ Remember to simplify within the parentheses first. After this, the negative exponent can be handled by writing the reciprocal of the expression within the parentheses.

$$\left(\frac{x^5 y^8}{2xy} \right)^{-\frac{1}{2}} = \left(\frac{x^4 y^7}{2} \right)^{-\frac{1}{2}}$$

$$= \left(\frac{2}{x^4 y^7} \right)^{\frac{1}{2}}$$

$$= \left(\frac{2}{x^4 y^6 y} \right)^{\frac{1}{2}}$$

$$= \frac{1}{x^2 y^3} \left(\frac{2}{y} \right)^{\frac{1}{2}}$$

$$= \frac{1}{x^2 y^3} \sqrt{\frac{2}{y}}$$

On the SAT, a problem like this would likely have you find an equivalent expression from a choice of several. Recognizing what to do with the negative exponent is an important step in getting the final answer.

Polynomials

Polynomials are algebraic expressions that consist of terms that are either added to or subtracted from each other. These terms are either constants or a variable taken to a power such as $2x^2$ or $-3x^5$. When working with polynomials, the number in front of the variable (2 or -3 here) is called a coefficient. Some examples of polynomials are shown below:

$$-3x^2 + 2x + 1$$

$$x + 5$$

$$2x^6 + x^5 - x^3 + 2$$

Adding and Subtracting Polynomials

Adding and subtracting polynomials is really just about collecting like terms. The one thing to be careful about is distributing the negative while subtracting.

EXAMPLES

▶ Find the sum.

$$(x^2 - 3x + 1) + (4x^2 - 5x + 10)$$

$$(x^2 - 3x + 1) + (4x^2 - 5x + 10) = x^2 - 3x + 1 + 4x^2 - 5x + 10$$
$$= 5x^2 - 8x + 11$$

▶ Find the difference.

$$(-2x^3 + 4x^2 + x - 3) - (x^3 + 5x^2 + 2)$$

▶ Distribute the negative across the second polynomial and then simplify.

$$(-2x^3 + 4x^2 + x - 3) - (x^3 + 5x^2 + 2)$$
$$= -2x^3 + 4x^2 + x - 3 - x^3 - 5x^2 - 2$$
$$= -3x^3 - x^2 + x - 5$$

Multiplying Binomials

Binomials are polynomials with exactly two terms. Multiplying these follows a special procedure known as FOIL. Let's use $x + 1$ and $x - 3$ as an example of how this works.

EXAMPLE

▶ Find the product.

$$(x + 1)(x - 3)$$

- First—multiply the first two terms.

  $$x \times x = x^2$$

- Outer—multiply the outer two terms.

  $$-3 \times x = -3x$$

- Inner—multiply the inner two terms.

  $$1 \times x = x$$

- Last—multiply the last two terms.

  $$1 \times -3 = -3$$

▶ Putting it all together,

$$(x + 1)(x - 3) = x^2 - 3x + x - 3$$
$$= x^2 - 2x - 3$$

 IRL The mnemonic FOIL helps us remember how to multiply binomials. FOIL stands for First, Outside, Inside, Last. We multiply the first terms of the two binomials first, then the outside terms, then the inside terms, then the last terms.

Usually, you won't write each step out as a separate step, but instead will use the steps to write out the terms, and then simplify.

EXAMPLE

▶ Find the product.

$$(2x + 5)(3x - 4)$$

▶ Since this is the product of two binomials, apply FOIL.

$$(2x + 5)(3x - 4) = 2x \times 3x - 4 \times 2x + 5 \times 3x + 5 \times -4$$
$$= 6x^2 - 8x + 15x - 20$$
$$= 6x^2 + 7x - 20$$

You can apply FOIL to terms that include exponents and roots as well. Go slowly and write everything down. It's easy to become confused if you try to do it all in your head.

EXAMPLE

▶ Find the product.
$$(x^2 - 8)(x^2 - 1)$$

▶ Even though these binomials include terms to the second power, you can still apply FOIL.

$$(x^2 - 8)(x^2 - 1)$$
$$= x^2 \times x^2 - 1 \times x^2 - 8 \times x^2 + -8 \times -1$$
$$= x^4 - x^2 - 8x^2 + 8$$
$$= x^4 - 9x^2 + 8$$

BTW

You may find questions on the SAT that ask you to simplify an expression such as $(x - 5)^2$. This expression is not equal to $(x^2 - 25)$! Instead, you must use FOIL to simplify it as $(x - 5)^2 = (x - 5)(x - 5) = x^2 - 10x + 25$.

Multiplying General Polynomials

For polynomials with more than two terms, we will need a different approach. We will take each term in the first polynomial and distribute it across the second. We just need to be sure that we are very careful and don't miss any terms in the process.

EXAMPLE

▶ Find the product.

$$(x + 4)(x^2 - 4x + 1)$$

▶ We will distribute the x across each term and then distribute the 4 across each term. Finally, we will simplify.

$$(x + 4)(x^2 - 4x + 1)$$
$$= x \times x^2 + x \times -4x + x \times 1 + 4 \times x^2 + 4 \times -4x +$$
$$= x^3 - 4x^2 + x + 4x^2 - 16x + 4$$
$$= x^3 - 15x + 4$$

While this method can be used to multiply even larger polynomials, you aren't likely to see that on the SAT. Many of the problems will instead focus on you finding an equivalent expression given a product such as those seen above.

Dividing Polynomials

The easiest case of dividing polynomials is when the polynomial being divided has more terms than and shares factors with the polynomial dividing it. When this happens, we can just write the polynomials as a rational expression (studied in the next section) and then cancel terms.

▶ Divide.

$$(x^3 + 4x^2 - x) \div (2x)$$

▶ This division problem can be written as $\dfrac{x^3 + 4x^2 - x}{2x}$. Now we can factor the numerator and then cancel common factors.

$$\frac{x^3 + 4x^2 - x}{2x} = \frac{\cancel{x}(x^2 + 4x - 1)}{2\cancel{x}}$$

$$= \frac{x^2 + 4x - 1}{2}$$

$$= \frac{x^2}{2} + \frac{4x}{2} - \frac{1}{2}$$

$$= \frac{1}{2}x^2 + 2x - \frac{1}{2}$$

Notice that in the last step of that example we wrote the polynomial as separate terms. This was possible because there was only one term in the denominator. We could break up the fraction over this term. This can only be done when there is a single term like 2 or 4 or $4x$.

▶ Divide.

$$(x^2 - 4) \div (x - 2)$$

▶ Once again, we will write the problem as a fraction and then cancel common factors.

$$(x^2 - 4) \div (x - 2) = \frac{x^2 - 4}{x - 2}$$

$$= \frac{\cancel{(x - 2)}(x + 2)}{\cancel{x - 2}}$$

$$= x + 2$$

When common factors can't be cancelled, we must find the quotient using long division. This process is best understood using an example.

▶ Divide.

$$(2x^3 - 5x^2 + x - 1) \div (2x + 1)$$

▶ The setup of the problem is just like long division with numbers.

$$2x + 1 \overline{) 2x^3 - 5x^2 + x - 1}$$

▶ To perform the division, we will always be looking at the terms with x. As a first step, we will ask, "What do I have to multiply $2x$ by to get $2x^3$?". The answer is x^2. We write this at the top and then multiply to get the next line.

$$
\begin{array}{r}
x^2 \\
2x+1 \overline{) 2x^3 - 5x^2 + x - 1} \\
2x^3 + x^2
\end{array}
$$

▶ Now we will subtract—remember to distribute the negative!

$$
\begin{array}{r}
x^2 \\
2x+1 \overline{) 2x^3 - 5x^2 + x - 1} \\
\underline{-(2x^3 + x^2)} \\
0 - 6x^2
\end{array}
$$

▶ Bring down the x and then continue the process.

$$
\begin{array}{r}
x^2 - 3x + 2 \\
2x+1 \overline{) 2x^3 - 5x^2 + x - 1} \\
\underline{-(2x^3 + x^2)} \\
-6x^2 + x \\
\underline{-(-6x^2 - 3x)} \\
4x - 1 \\
\underline{-(4x + 2)} \\
-3
\end{array}
$$

> To write the final answer, take the result up top and then add the remainder divided by the divisor $2x + 1$.
>
> $$(2x^3 - 5x^2 + x - 1) \div (2x + 1) = x^2 - 3x + 2 + \frac{-3}{2x + 1}$$

Well, that was a lot of work, wasn't it? Take a breath. Stretch. Since that was a little complicated, let's look at one more example to be sure you've got it.

EXAMPLE

> Divide.
>
> $$(x^4 - 3x^3 + x^2 + x + 1) \div (x - 2)$$
>
> Using long division:

$$
\begin{array}{r}
x^3 - x^2 - x - 1 \\
x - 2 \overline{\smash{\big)}\, x^4 - 3x^3 + x^2 + x + 1} \\
\underline{-(x^4 - 2x^3)} \\
-x^3 + x^2 \\
\underline{-(-x^3 + 2x^2)} \\
-x^2 + x \\
\underline{-(-x^2 + 2x)} \\
-x + 1 \\
\underline{-(-x + 2)} \\
-1
\end{array}
$$

> Thus, the answer is $x^3 - x^2 - x - 1 + \dfrac{-1}{x - 2}$.

Rational Expressions

A rational expression is a fraction where either the numerator or denominator (or both) is a polynomial. Operations with rational expressions require a bit more work than polynomials, but if you can translate your skills of working with fractions in general, you will see that the same rules apply to rational expressions.

Adding and Subtracting Rational Expressions

When adding or subtracting two fractions, like $\frac{1}{3}$ and $\frac{1}{2}$, you know that you must have a common denominator. In this case, that common denominator would be 6, and if you write each fraction with this denominator, you can just add (or subtract) across the top.

This same idea applies to rational expressions. If you want to add $\frac{1}{x}$ and $\frac{1}{3x}$, you will need to find a common denominator. A common denominator can always be found by multiplying the two denominators (here that would be $3x^2$), but if the two denominators share a factor (in this case, they both share the factor x), then you can save yourself some work by using a simpler term. Let's look at this one a little more closely.

EXAMPLE

▶ Find the sum.

$$\frac{1}{x} + \frac{1}{3x}$$

▶ As noted above, one possible common denominator is $x \times 3x = 3x^2$. However, both denominators share a factor of x. The only difference is that the second denominator also has a factor of 3. Therefore, if we rewrite the first fraction with a denominator of $3x$, then we will be all set!

▶ To do this, we will multiply the top and the bottom of the fraction by 3. It is important to always multiply the top and the bottom by the same value so that the fraction we get is equivalent to the original.

$$\frac{1}{x} + \frac{1}{3x} = \frac{3}{3}\left(\frac{1}{x}\right) + \frac{1}{3x}$$

$$= \frac{3}{3x} + \frac{1}{3x}$$

$$= \frac{4}{3x}$$

Now let's try a problem involving subtraction. Follow the same procedure of finding a common denominator. Don't forget to distribute the negative to each term you are subtracting. Seriously, don't forget.

EXAMPLE

▶ Find the difference.

$$\frac{x}{x-5} - \frac{3x}{x+1}$$

▶ This time, the two denominators do not share any factors, so the common denominator we will use will be their product: $(x-5)(x+1)$. To write the rational expressions with this denominator, we will multiply the top and bottom of each fraction by the missing factor.

BTW

The final form of the answer will depend on the question being asked on the SAT. You may need to multiply the terms in the denominator or factor the numerator (as we did in this example).

$$\frac{x}{x-5} - \frac{3x}{x+1} = \frac{x+1}{x+1}\left(\frac{x}{x-5}\right) - \frac{x-5}{x-5}\left(\frac{3x}{x+1}\right)$$

$$= \frac{x^2+x}{(x+1)(x-5)} - \frac{3x^2-15x}{(x+1)(x-5)}$$

$$= \frac{-2x^2+16x}{(x+1)(x-5)}$$

$$= \frac{2x(-x+8)}{(x+1)(x-5)}$$

There are two things to note about this problem. First, the negative must distribute to all of the terms when you are subtracting, just like when you worked with polynomials.

Second, you will need to make sure your final answer is simplified completely. That means that any factors shared by the numerator and the denominator have been cancelled.

EXAMPLE

▶ Find the difference.

$$\frac{x+2}{x^2+4x+3} - \frac{x-1}{x^2-2x-3}$$

▶ At first, it looks like we will have to multiply the two denominators to get a common denominator. By factoring, you can see that they actually share some factors.

$$x^2+4x+3 = (x+1)(x+3)$$

$$x^2-2x-3 = (x+1)(x-3)$$

▶ Thus, the common denominator would be $(x+1)(x+3)(x-3)$. We need to multiply each fraction (the numerator and denominator) by the missing factor. When a denominator is this complicated, wait to multiply it out until you have simplified the numerator, as some factors may cancel.

$$\frac{x+2}{x^2+4x+3} - \frac{x-1}{x^2-2x-3}$$

$$= \frac{x+2}{(x+1)(x+3)} - \frac{x-1}{(x+1)(x-3)}$$

$$= \frac{(x-3)}{(x-3)}\left(\frac{x+2}{(x+1)(x+3)}\right) - \frac{(x+3)}{(x+3)}\left(\frac{x-1}{(x+1)(x-3)}\right)$$

$$= \frac{x^2-x-6}{(x-3)(x+1)(x+3)} - \frac{x^2+2x-3}{(x+3)(x+1)(x-3)}$$

$$= \frac{x^2-x-6-(x^2+2x-3)}{(x-3)(x+1)(x+3)}$$

$$= \frac{-3x-3}{(x-3)(x+1)(x+3)}$$

$$= \frac{-3\cancel{(x+1)}}{(x-3)\cancel{(x+1)}(x+3)}$$

$$= \frac{-3}{(x-3)(x+3)}$$

$$= \frac{-3}{x^2-9}$$

▶ Again, either $\frac{-3}{(x-3)(x+3)}$ or $\frac{-3}{x^2-9}$ could be the final answer depending on the choices given on an SAT question.

Notice that if we had multiplied the denominator out first, we might have never noticed that the common factor $x+1$ could be cancelled out. Situations like these are common on the SAT, as questions are written to reward recognizing the structure of expressions.

Multiplying Rational Expressions

Multiplying two rational expressions doesn't require you to be concerned about like denominators as multiplication is straight across (numerator times numerator and denominator times denominator). Instead, it will be important to notice common factors in order to save yourself work in simplifying at the end.

EXAMPLE

▶ Find the product.

$$\left(\frac{1}{x+5}\right)\left(\frac{x^2}{x-3}\right)$$

▶ This is a very straightforward product, so we can multiply straight across.

$$\left(\frac{1}{x+5}\right)\left(\frac{x^2}{x-3}\right) = \frac{x^2}{(x+5)(x-3)}$$

$$= \frac{x^2}{x^2+2x-15}$$

▶ Here, there were no common factors to cancel and so it really was about multiplying the polynomials that make up the individual rational expressions.

In other cases, it may be possible to cancel common factors before even multiplying. This idea is called *cross cancelling*. Using this technique, you cancel out any common factors in the numerators or denominators of either of the expressions.

EXAMPLE

▶ Find the product.

$$\left(\frac{x+4}{x^2-1}\right)\left(\frac{x+1}{x^2+3x-4}\right)$$

▶ Both denominators here are factorable. Before multiplying, we will factor these denominators and then cancel any common factors.

$$\left(\frac{x+4}{x^2-1}\right)\left(\frac{x+1}{x^2+3x-4}\right) = \left(\frac{\cancel{x+4}}{(x-1)\cancel{(x+1)}}\right)\left(\frac{\cancel{x+1}}{(x-1)\cancel{(x+4)}}\right)$$

$$= \left(\frac{1}{x-1}\right)\left(\frac{1}{x-1}\right)$$

$$= \frac{1}{(x-1)(x-1)}$$

$$= \frac{1}{(x-1)^2}$$

$$= \frac{1}{x^2-2x+1}$$

As with addition and subtraction, the correct answer in a multiple-choice question could be $\frac{1}{(x-1)^2}$ or $\frac{1}{x^2-2x+1}$, so make sure you are comfortable with both forms!

As you saw, cross cancelling can make the multiplication much simpler. Notice that when you cancel the numerator or denominator completely, as we did above, a 1 remains. A common mistake is to treat this as zero.

Dividing Rational Expressions

Dividing rational expressions is very similar to multiplication in that you don't need to worry about a common denominator and you should pay close attention to factors that can be cancelled. The general idea behind division of rational expressions is "flip and multiply." In other words, every division problem is actually a multiplication problem!

EXAMPLE

▶ Divide.

$$\frac{x^2}{x-5} \div \frac{x^3 + 5x^2}{x+2}$$

▶ First, write the division problem as a multiplication problem using the rule "flip and multiply." This means you keep the first fraction the same, flip the second, and then multiply.

$$\frac{x^2}{x-5} \div \frac{x^3 + 5x^2}{x+2} = \frac{x^2}{x-5} \times \frac{x+2}{x^3 + 5x^2}$$

▶ Now you can treat this as a multiplication problem. Be sure to watch for factors that can be cancelled!

$$\frac{x^2}{x-5} \div \frac{x^3 + 5x^2}{x+2} = \frac{x^2}{x-5} \times \frac{x+2}{x^3 + 5x^2}$$

$$= \frac{\cancel{x^2}}{x-5} \times \frac{x+2}{\cancel{x^2}(x+5)}$$

$$= \frac{1}{x-5} \times \frac{x+2}{x+5}$$

$$= \frac{x+2}{(x-5)(x+5)}$$

$$= \frac{x+2}{x^2 - 25}$$

Don't forget that you can use FOIL—even in reverse! Factoring $x^2 - 4$ gives us $(x - 2)(x + 2)$. Factoring trinomials and perfect square binomials may allow us to cancel out like terms that we didn't notice at first.

EXAMPLE

▶ Divide.

$$\frac{x^2 - x - 20}{x^2 + 1} \div \frac{x^2 - 16}{x^2 - 1} = \frac{x^2 - x - 20}{x^2 + 1} \times \frac{x^2 - 1}{x^2 - 16}$$

$$= \frac{\cancel{(x+4)}(x-5)}{x^2 + 1} \times \frac{x^2 - 1}{\cancel{(x+4)}(x-4)}$$

$$= \frac{(x-5)(x^2 - 1)}{(x^2 + 1)(x-4)}$$

$$= \frac{x^3 - 5x^2 - x + 5}{x^3 - 4x^2 + x - 4}$$

IRL Polynomials are typically written with the largest exponent first, but you may find the terms of a polynomial in any order—don't let that confuse you. $21 - 4x^2 + 3x$ is the same thing as $-4x^2 + 3x + 21$.

EXERCISES

EXERCISE 6–1

Simplify each of the following expressions.

1. $(2xy)^3(xy)^5$

2. $\dfrac{8mn}{4m^2}$

3. $\dfrac{-x^5y^{-1}}{x^2}$

4. $\dfrac{(x^2y^{-3})^{-1}}{8}$

5. $\dfrac{3x^{-2}y^2x}{x^3}$

EXERCISE 6–2

For exercises 1–3, simplify the expression completely.

1. $\sqrt{64x^{10}y^2}$

2. $\sqrt[3]{54x^7y^8}$

3. $\sqrt{\dfrac{6x^5xy}{16y^2}}$

For exercises 4 and 5, simplify the expression and write the final answer using radicals.

4. $(16x^5y^2z)^{-\frac{1}{3}}$

5. $\left(\dfrac{24x^2}{xy}\right)^{\frac{1}{2}}$

EXERCISE 6-3

Find the sum or difference.

1. $(x^2 + x - 5) + (-x + 1)$

2. $(x^4 + x^2 - 5x + 1) - (3x^4 - 2x + 8)$

3. $(5x^3 + x - 1) + (-x^3 - 2x^2 + x + 1)$

4. $(3x^2 + 5x - 6) - (x^2 - 9x + 4)$

5. $(x^5 + x^4 + x^2 - 2) - (x^3 + x^2 + 4)$

EXERCISE 6-4

Find and simplify each of the following products.

1. $(x + 9)(x - 2)$

2. $(3x - 6)(x - 5)$

3. $\left(\dfrac{1}{2}x + 4\right)\left(\dfrac{1}{2}x - 3\right)$

4. $(5x^2 + 1)(-2x^2 + 4)$

5. $(3x^2 - x)(x^2 + x)$

EXERCISE 6-5

Find the products.

1. $(x - 5)(2x^2 + x - 2)$

2. $(3x + 2)(x^2 + x + 1)$

EXERCISE 6-6

Divide.

1. $(4x^4 - 3x^2 + x) \div (3x)$

2. $(-2x^3 + 6x^2 - 8x) \div (4x)$

3. $(6x^2 - 5x + 1) \div (2x - 1)$

4. $(2x^2 - x + 2) \div (2x + 1)$

5. $(4x^3 - x^2 + x - 1) \div (x - 1)$

EXERCISE 6-7

Find the sum or difference as indicated.

1. $\dfrac{2}{x^2} - \dfrac{3}{x^4}$

2. $\dfrac{x+3}{x-1} - \dfrac{x-5}{x+4}$

3. $\dfrac{x^2+1}{x} - \dfrac{x^2}{x+1}$

4. $\dfrac{2x-1}{x^2+4x+4} - \dfrac{3x-1}{x^2-x-6}$

5. $\dfrac{x}{x^2-4} + \dfrac{3x}{x-2}$

EXERCISE 6-8

Find the product.

1. $\left(\dfrac{x}{x+2}\right)\left(\dfrac{4}{x^2-3x}\right)$

2. $\left(\dfrac{x-3}{x}\right)\left(\dfrac{5x}{x+3}\right)$

3. $\left(\dfrac{2x^2 - 3x + 1}{x + 1}\right)\left(\dfrac{x^2 - 4x - 5}{2x^2 + 9x - 5}\right)$

4. $\left(\dfrac{x - 5}{3}\right)\left(\dfrac{9x}{x^2 - 25}\right)$

5. $\left(\dfrac{4x + 4}{x}\right)\left(\dfrac{5x^2 + x}{x + 1}\right)$

EXERCISE 6–9

Divide.

1. $\dfrac{1}{x^2 - 4} \div \dfrac{x + 2}{x - 2}$

2. $\dfrac{x^2 + 6x + 9}{x^2} \div \dfrac{2x^2 + 6x}{x + 2}$

3. $\dfrac{x^3 - 9x}{x + 5} \div \dfrac{x}{x^2 - 25}$

4. $\dfrac{3x}{4} \div \dfrac{5x}{8}$

5. $\dfrac{7}{x^2 + 5x - 6} \div \dfrac{9}{2x^2 - x - 1}$

Answers are on page 556.

Flashcard App

7 Solving Equations and Inequalities

MUST ⚡ KNOW

 Whatever you do to one side of an equation or inequality, you must do to the other side. If you multiply or divide an inequality by a negative number, flip the direction of the inequality sign.

 There are three ways to solve systems of equations:
1. substitution: solve one equation for one variable and then use the result in the other equation
2. elimination: manipulate the equations in such a way as to make one variable drop out when the equations are added or subtracted
3. graphing: graph both equations; the intersection of the lines is the solution

 There are three ways to solve quadratic equations:
1. by using the square root rule: if $x^2 = c$, then $x = \pm\sqrt{c}$
2. by factoring, using the zero product rule: if $AB = 0$, then either $A = 0$ or $B = 0$
3. by using the quadratic formula: $x = \dfrac{-b \pm \sqrt{b^2 - 4ac}}{2a}$

he problems on the SAT require you to know how to solve a wide variety of equations and inequalities. In this chapter, we will review each type of equation you will need to know and the best techniques you can apply to find the right answer.

Linear Equations

Linear equations are those where the variable (or in some cases, variables) doesn't have an exponent and isn't in the denominator of a fraction. Some examples of these types of equations are shown below.

$$3x + 2 = 1$$

$$-x + y = 14$$

$$\frac{x}{4} + \frac{1}{2} = -1$$

As you can see, some linear equations include only one variable, while others may include two or more variables. We will look at each of these individually, but the approaches to solving them are very similar.

Solving Linear Equations in One Variable

For a linear equation in one variable, *solving* means finding the value of the variable that makes the equation true. This can be done by "undoing" any of the math that has been applied to the variable. Let's use an example to see this process.

EXAMPLE

▶ Solve $2x + 1 = 16$.

▶ In this equation, the x has been multiplied by 2 and then had 1 added to it. To "undo" this, we will subtract 1 and then divide by 2. Just remember, anything you do to one side of the equation must be done to both sides!

$$2x + 1 = 16$$
$$2x + 1 - 1 = 16 - 1$$
$$2x = 15$$
$$\frac{2x}{2} = \frac{15}{2}$$
$$x = \frac{15}{2}$$

In some cases, the variable will be on both sides of the equation. When this happens, you will use the same techniques to bring the variables to the same side of the equation.

EXAMPLE

▶ Solve $-5w + 1 = w - 4$.

▶ Since w is on the right-hand side, we can subtract it from both sides to bring it to the left.

$$-5w + 1 = w - 4$$
$$-5w + 1 - w = w - 4 - w$$
$$-6w + 1 = -4$$
$$-6w + 1 - 1 = -4 - 1$$
$$-6w = -5$$
$$\frac{-6w}{-6} = \frac{-5}{-6}$$
$$w = \frac{-5}{-6}$$
$$= \frac{5}{6}$$

You may be thinking right now, "What if a fraction is multiplying the variable?" The same rules apply to those types of equations, but there are a couple of nice shortcuts that can be used.

EXAMPLE

▶ Solve $\dfrac{2}{3}x + 5 = 1$.

▶ To solve this equation, we can follow the same process and subtract 5 from both sides and then divide by $\dfrac{2}{3}$. Since dividing by a fraction is the same as multiplying by its reciprocal, we can just multiply both sides by $\dfrac{3}{2}$ instead.

$$\frac{2}{3}x + 5 = 1$$

$$\frac{2}{3}x + 5 - 5 = 1 - 5$$

$$\frac{2}{3}x = -4$$

$$\frac{3}{2}\left(\frac{2}{3}x\right) = \frac{3}{2}(-4)$$

$$x = \frac{-12}{2}$$

$$= -6$$

Sometimes the arithmetic will be complicated by all of the fractions. A trick that you can use for equations that contain a lot of fractions is called "clearing the fractions." This is done by multiplying both sides of the equation by the product of the denominators. This will cause the fractions to cancel out, making the numbers easier to work with.

EXAMPLE

Solve $\dfrac{4}{3}a + \dfrac{1}{2} = \dfrac{1}{2}a + 2.$

As in the previous example, it is possible to apply the exact same steps to solve for a in this equation, but it will be a lot simpler if we clear the fractions. As the first step, we will multiply both sides by 6.

$$\frac{4}{3}a + \frac{1}{2} = \frac{1}{2}a + 2$$

$$6\left(\frac{4}{3}a + \frac{1}{2}\right) = 6\left(\frac{1}{2}a + 2\right)$$

$$\frac{24}{3}a + \frac{6}{2} = \frac{6}{2}a + 12$$

$$8a + 3 = 3a + 12$$

$$5a + 3 = 12$$

$$5a = 9$$

$$a = 9/5$$

Let's take a closer look at one of the steps in that last example.

$$6\left(\frac{4}{3}a + \frac{1}{2}\right) = 6\left(\frac{1}{2}a + 2\right)$$

In this step, we multiplied *every term* within the parentheses by 6 to get $\dfrac{24}{3}a + \dfrac{6}{2} = \dfrac{6}{2}a + 12$. This is required by the distributive property and should be done every time you have a number multiplying terms inside of parentheses. If this comes up in an equation, make sure to simplify like this before going through the usual steps.

EXAMPLE

▶ Solve $2(x + 1) = x - 3$.

$$2(x + 1) = x - 3$$
$$2x + 2 = x - 3$$
$$2x + 2 - x = x - 3 - x$$
$$x + 2 = -3$$
$$x + 2 - 2 = -3 - 2$$
$$x = -5$$

Linear Equations with Infinitely Many or No Solutions

In some cases, a linear equation represents a statement that is always or never true. Recognizing when this is the case is a skill commonly tested on the SAT.

EXAMPLE

▶ Solve $-3x + 1 = -3(2 + x)$.

▶ To solve this equation, we would first distribute the negative three on the right-hand side.

$$-3x + 1 = -6 - 3x$$

▶ Notice that the terms with the x on both sides are exactly the same. To see why this matters, let's add $3x$ to both sides.

$$-3x + 1 + 3x = -6 - 3x + 3x$$
$$1 = -6$$

▶ After combining like terms, the terms involving x all cancel, leaving just the untrue statement $1 = -6$.

Anytime you are solving an equation and end up with a statement that is never true, then you can say that there is no solution to the equation. This means that no matter what value you pick for x, the equation can never be made to be a correct statement. You may also encounter equations that are always true no matter what variables are used.

EXAMPLE

Solve $\dfrac{1}{3}x - 5 = \dfrac{2}{3}x - \left(\dfrac{1}{3}x + 5\right)$

Let's approach this equation as we usually would by simplifying the right-hand side.

$$\frac{1}{3}x - 5 = \frac{2}{3}x - \left(\frac{1}{3}x + 5\right)$$

$$\frac{1}{3}x - 5 = \frac{2}{3}x - \frac{1}{3}x - 5$$

$$\frac{1}{3}x - 5 = \frac{1}{3}x - 5$$

Notice that we have ended up with identical right- and left-hand sides. If we now subtract $\dfrac{1}{3}x$ from both sides, then we get the following.

$$\frac{1}{3}x - 5 = \frac{1}{3}x - 5$$

$$\frac{1}{3}x - 5 - \frac{1}{3}x = \frac{1}{3}x - 5 - \frac{1}{3}x$$

$$-5 = -5$$

The statement $-5 = -5$ is always true.

If you are solving an equation and you end up with a statement like this, then there are infinitely many solutions. This means that no matter which value of x you choose, the original equation will be a correct statement.

These two special cases of solving equations are often tested on the SAT by having you find a coefficient that makes the equation have either no solution or infinitely many solutions. Let's see how we might approach these using a couple of examples.

▶ Find the value of a such that $ax - 8 = 2(1 - x)$ has no solution.

▶ Your first step to a problem like this should be to simplify (if needed). On the right-hand side of the equation, we can apply the distributive property.

$$ax - 8 = 2(1 - x)$$
$$ax - 8 = 2 - 2x$$

▶ On each individual side of the equation, there are no like terms to combine. We can now think about how this equation may lead to one without any solutions. Recall that if you end up with a statement that is never true, then the equation has no solution. To get to that statement, all the x terms must cancel out.

▶ This happens if the coefficient is the same on both sides. In other words, if $a = -2$, then when we add $2x$ to both sides, we would be left with the statement $-8 = 2$. Thus, $a = -2$.

Let's try one with infinitely many solutions. To do that, we will need to simplify the equation in such a way that it leaves a statement of equality.

▶ Find the value of a such that $2x - ax + 1 = 4x + 1$ has infinitely many solutions.

▶ There are no parentheses to handle here, so we can look directly at the structure of the equation. The constant 1 appears on both sides, so if we can get the same coefficient of x on the left as on the right, then they will cancel, leaving the statement $1 = 1$. This would mean the equation has infinitely many solutions.

▶ On the right, the coefficient on x is 4. On the left, when we combine like terms, the coefficient of x will be $2 - a$. We need $2 - a = 4$. Solving this equation for a:

$$2 - a = 4$$
$$2 - a - 2 = 4 - 2$$
$$-a = 2$$
$$a = -2$$

▶ Thus, if $a = -2$, then the equation will have infinitely many solutions.

Solving Linear Equations in Two or More Variables

Linear equations can have two or more variables, and sometimes on the SAT you will be asked to solve for one of the variables in the equation. For example, if you are asked to "solve for y in terms of x," then your answer will be of the form $y =$ some expression involving x. In other words, you want to get y by itself on one side of the equation.

EXAMPLE

▶ Solve the equation $-2y + x = 4 + y$ for y.

▶ When solving any linear equation, the same steps apply: undo the operations and bring the variable of interest to one side. In this equation, we will need to subtract x from both sides and subtract y from both sides (along with other steps). Note that the order of these two steps isn't important.

$$-2y + x = 4 + y$$
$$-2y + x - x = 4 + y - x$$
$$-2y = 4 + y - x$$
$$-2y - y = 4 + y - x - y$$
$$-3y = 4 - x$$
$$\frac{-3y}{-3} = \frac{4 - x}{-3}$$
$$y = -\frac{4 - x}{3}$$

Let's try one with more complicated steps. Here, we will have to deal with fractions and use the distributive property.

▶ Solve the equation $-p + q = \dfrac{1}{3}(p + 2q)$ for p.

▶ Remember to simplify using the distributive property first!

$$-p + q = \frac{1}{3}(p + 2q)$$

$$-p + q = \frac{1}{3}p + \frac{2}{3}q$$

$$-p + q - q = \frac{1}{3}p + \frac{2}{3}q - q$$

$$-p = \frac{1}{3}p - \frac{1}{3}q$$

$$-p - \frac{1}{3}p = \frac{1}{3}p - \frac{1}{3}q - \frac{1}{3}p$$

$$-\frac{4}{3}p = -\frac{1}{3}q$$

$$-\frac{3}{4}\left(-\frac{4}{3}p\right) = -\frac{3}{4}\left(-\frac{1}{3}q\right)$$

$$p = \frac{1}{4}q$$

$$= \frac{q}{4}$$

You will usually see linear equations with more than two variables on the SAT in the form of formulas. In these types of problems, you are given a formula and asked to solve for a particular variable. Even though there are no numbers in the equation, the same steps will still apply.

EXAMPLE

▶ The volume of a triangular prism is found using the formula $V = \frac{1}{2}wh\ell$, where w is width of the triangular base, h is its height, and ℓ is the length of the prism. Rewrite this formula so that it shows the width in terms of the other variables.

▶ Since we want to show the width in terms of the other variables, we need to solve for w.

$$V = \frac{1}{2}wh\ell$$
$$2V = wh\ell$$
$$\frac{2V}{h\ell} = \frac{wh\ell}{h\ell}$$
$$\frac{2V}{h\ell} = w$$

▶ Note that even though w is on the right, it is the same as writing $w = \frac{2V}{h\ell}$.

Solving Linear Inequalities with One Variable

Equations get their name from the equal sign used between the two pieces, so, as you might imagine, an inequality would mean the two sides are not necessarily equal. With inequalities, the symbols $<$ and $>$ indicate that one side is greater than the other, while the symbols $\leq$ and $\geq$ indicate that one side is equal to OR greater than the other. Even though a new symbol is used, the rules used for solving linear equations still apply.

▶ Solve $3x - 9 \geq x + 2$.

$$3x - 9 \geq x + 2$$
$$3x - 9 - x \geq x + 2 - x$$
$$2x - 9 \geq 2$$
$$2x - 9 + 9 \geq 2 + 9$$
$$2x \geq 11$$
$$\frac{2x}{2} \geq \frac{11}{2}$$
$$x \geq \frac{11}{2}$$

▶ This means that any value of x that is greater than or equal to $\frac{11}{2}$ will make the original inequality true. Thus, the least possible value of x is $\frac{11}{2}$. In some SAT questions, you might be given an inequality like this and then be asked something like "If x is a whole number, what is the minimum value of x?" Since $\frac{11}{2} = 5.5$ is the least possible value of x in general, if we knew x were a whole number, then the minimum, or least possible, value would be 6.

There is one important new rule to keep in mind when solving inequalities. If you divide or multiply both sides by a negative number, you must flip the inequality sign.

▶ Solve $4(x - 1) < 6x + 10$.

▶ When solving this, in the last step we end up needing to divide by a negative number. Notice that the sign of the inequality is flipped when we do this.

$$4(x - 1) < 6x + 10$$
$$4x - 4 < 6x + 10$$
$$4x - 4 - 6x < 6x + 10 - 6x$$
$$-2x - 4 < 10$$
$$-2x - 4 + 4 < 10 + 4$$
$$-2x < 14$$
$$\frac{-2x}{-2} > \frac{14}{-2}$$
$$x > -7$$

Applications of Linear Equations and Inequalities

Many problems on the SAT are application problems where you will write a linear equation or inequality to represent a given situation and then either solve it for a numerical answer or write one of the variables in terms of the other (if there are multiple variables). The next few examples will walk you through some of the best approaches to these types of problems.

Let's start with a question that simply asks us to write an equation.

EXAMPLE

▶ So far this year, Randy has run 184 miles. Suppose that from now on, he plans to run 20 miles each week. Write an equation that can be used to find the number of weeks, w, until he has run a total of 500 miles.

▶ From reading this problem, we can see that we need some equation of the form "SOMETHING = 500." The SOMETHING would be the total number of miles run, but that depends on the number of weeks. Since Randy will run 20 miles each week, that means after w weeks he will have run $20w$ miles. Further, since he has already run 184 miles, the total amount he would have run for the year would be $20w + 184$. This gives us the equation $20w + 184 = 500$.

Now, let's look at a question for which we must write an equation and then solve it for one variable in terms of the other.

▶ The value of a variable x is 10 units greater than twice the value of a variable y. What is the value of y in terms of x?

▶ This is a very abstract problem because it doesn't involve a real-life situation, but we can still write an equation to relate x and y and then solve it for y to answer the question. The first part of the statement "x is . . ." tells us to start with "$x =$." From here, we are told that it is "10 units greater than twice the value of y." This means if we take y, multiply it by 2, and then add 10, we will have the value of x.

$$x = 2y + 10$$

▶ Now we can solve for y.

$$x = 2y + 10$$
$$x - 10 = 2y$$
$$\frac{x - 10}{2} = y$$

Let's try an inequality. We will still have to write the inequality before we solve it. Be careful to choose the correct inequality sign.

▶ A marketing team is given a budget of $1,580 to complete a photography project. The photographer charges $50 an hour, and supplies are estimated to be $830. What is the maximum number of hours that the committee can utilize the services of the photographer?

▶ Since the idea of a budget is that you don't exceed it, the team must spend at most $1,580. In other words: total spent ≤ 1580. The total spent would depend on the number of hours, so let this be represented by h. Using the description from the problem, $50h$ would be the cost of hiring the photographer for h hours. Considering the cost of supplies, the total spent would then be $50h + 830$, so $50h + 830 \leq 1580$.

▶ Solving this inequality:

$$50h + 830 \leq 1580$$
$$50h \leq 750$$
$$h \leq 15$$

▶ Thus, the committee can hire the photographer for a maximum of 15 hours.

Sometimes, the specifics of the problem require estimation or rounding. Let's look at an inequality like that.

EXAMPLE

▶ Eric's new diet requires that he eat at least 150 grams of protein each day. He has determined that from his usual daily diet, he already eats 80 grams, and he plans to eat protein bars to make up the difference. If each protein bar has 12 grams of protein, then what is the minimum number he will need to eat in order to meet or exceed his new diet's requirements? Assume he will only consume whole bars.

▶ The requirement of eating at least 150 grams of protein each day can be thought of mathematically as daily protein ≥ 150. The amount he eats each day depends on the number of protein bars, so call that p. Since each protein bar adds 12 grams to his total, p protein bars would add $12p$. Now, including the protein he already eats, we can write $12p + 80 \geq 150$.

▶ Solving for p:

$$12p + 80 \geq 150$$
$$12p \geq 70$$
$$p \geq \frac{70}{12} \approx 5.833$$

▶ He must eat at least 5.8 bars, but since he will only consume whole bars, that means he must eat at least 6 as 5 would not be enough (because the minimum is 5.8).

IRL As you can see from these examples, we solve equations and inequalities frequently in our daily lives, even if we don't think of them that way. For example, I may ask myself *Can I see a 2-hour movie and still make it home in time for curfew?* or *If I have $50 and movie tickets cost $8 each, how many friends can I bring with me?*

Solving Systems of Linear Equations

A system of equations can be thought of as a group of equations where one set of values for all the variables makes all of the equations true simultaneously. On the SAT, you will mostly see systems of two linear equations with two unknowns, such as x and y. That means, if there is a solution, there is one set of values for x and y that makes both equations true.

There are two common methods of solving a system of equations: substitution and elimination.

Solving Systems of Linear Equations Using Substitution

With the substitution method, you will solve for one variable and then substitute the result into the other equation. This method is best applied when the coefficient of one of the variables is 1.

EXAMPLE

▶ Solve the system of equations.

$$-2x + 3y = -11$$
$$x + 5y = -1$$

▶ In the second equation, the coefficient of x is 1. Therefore, we will solve for x in that equation.

$$x + 5y = -1$$
$$x = -1 - 5y$$

▶ Now we will substitute this in place of x in the first equation.

$$-2x + 3y = -11$$
$$-2(-1 - 5y) + 3y = -11$$

▶ Solving this equation will give us the value of y.

$$-2(-1 - 5y) + 3y = -11$$
$$2 + 10y + 3y = -11$$
$$2 + 13y = -11$$
$$13y = -13$$
$$y = -1$$

▶ Now we can use this value in either of the original equations to solve for x. If we use the first equation, then we have:

$$-2x + 3y = -11$$
$$-2x + 3(-1) = -11$$
$$-2x - 3 = -11$$
$$-2x = -8$$
$$x = 4$$

▶ This gives us the solution $x = 4$ and $y = -1$.

BTW

Note that this solution can also be written as (4, −1). When written this way, the x-value is always first and the y-value is always second. We will see later that this corresponds to the point where the two graphs intersect in the xy-plane.

Solving Systems of Linear Equations Using Elimination

The idea of the elimination method is to eliminate one of the variables so that the result is a regular linear equation in one variable. After solving this, we can use the result to find the value of the other variable. You can see this method applied in the next example.

EXAMPLE

▶ Solve the system of equations.

$$4x + 5y = -8$$
$$-3x + 2y = 6$$

▶ It doesn't matter which variable you choose to eliminate first, so we will use x. To eliminate x, we will multiply the first equation by 3 and the second equation by 4.

$$\begin{array}{l} 3(4x + 5y = -8) \\ 4(-3x + 2y = 6) \end{array} \Rightarrow \begin{array}{l} 12x + 15y = -24 \\ -12x + 8y = 24 \end{array}$$

▶ This results in the opposite coefficients, so that when we add the two equations, only y remains.

$$\begin{array}{r} 12x + 15y = -24 \\ -12x + 8y = 24 \\ \hline 23y = 0 \\ y = 0 \end{array}$$

▶ Now we can use this value in one of the original equations. Using the first equation:

$$4x + 5y = -8$$
$$4x + 5(0) = -8$$
$$4x = -8$$
$$x = -2$$

▶ Thus, the solution is $x = -2$ and $y = 0$, or (–2, 0).

BTW

We can also solve systems of linear equations by graphing. The intersection of the two lines is the solution. If you are comfortable using your graphing calculator, this may be a good way to solve systems of equations.

When applying this method, you will always choose values to multiply each equation by so that when the equations are added, one of the variables is eliminated. Again, the variable you choose to eliminate doesn't matter although one may be more or less work than the other.

Systems of Equations with Infinitely Many or No Solutions

As with individual linear equations, it is possible that a system of equations has either infinitely many solutions or no solution. In fact, you will look for the exact same thing to determine whether one of these is the case.

When solving a system of equations:

- If you end up with a statement that is always true, then the system has infinitely many solutions.

- If you end up with a statement that is never true, then the system has no solution.

EXAMPLE

▶ Solve the system of equations.

$$-x + 2y = -8$$
$$5x - 10y = -15$$

▶ Using the elimination method, we can eliminate the x by multiplying the first equation by 5 and then adding the equations.

$$-5x + 10y = -40$$
$$\underline{5x - 10y = -15}$$
$$0 = -55$$

▶ All of the variables cancelled out, leaving the untrue statement "$0 = -55$." This means that the system has no solution.

Here is an example of a system that has infinitely many solutions.

▶ Solve the system of equations.

$$3x + 9y = 3$$
$$x + 3y = 1$$

▶ Multiplying the second equation by –3 and adding:

$$3x + 9y = 3$$
$$-3x - 9y = -3$$
$$0 = 0$$

▶ This time, everything cancelled out, and we get the statement $0 = 0$, which is always true. Therefore, this system of equations has infinitely many solutions.

There are some similarities between the last two examples that you can use to figure out some types of SAT problems. In the first example, we were given the following system of equations.

$$-x + 2y = -8$$
$$5x - 10y = -15$$

Looking at just the left-hand sides of both equations:

$$-5(-x + 2y) = 5x - 10y$$

In other words, they are multiples of each other. However, multiplying –8 by –5 does not give –15, so the system has no solution.

The equations for the second example were:

$$3x + 9y = 3$$
$$x + 3y = 1$$

Notice that if you divide the first equation by 3, you get the second equation. In other words, the entire equation (left- and right-hand side) is a multiple of the other. This is why we ended up with infinitely many solutions. Keep this in mind when you work with problems like those shown in the next two examples. First, let's look at a system with no solutions.

Find the value of a such that the system of equations has no solution.

$$5x + 3y = 1$$
$$ax + 6y = 4$$

Look at the coefficients of y, 3 and 6. Consider that 2 times $3y$ will give you $6y$. This should be the same for the coefficients of x. In other words, $a = 2(5) = 10$. This gives the following system of equations:

$$5x + 3y = 1$$
$$10x + 6y = 4$$

Now the left-hand sides are multiples, but $2(1)$ is not 4, so there is no solution. Thus, the correct answer is $a = 10$.

Now let's try a system that has infinitely many solutions.

Find the value of a such that the system of equations has infinitely many solutions.

$$-4x + 2y = 5$$
$$2x - y = a$$

Remember that for there to be infinitely many solutions, the two equations must be multiples of each other. We should figure out what constant we would multiply $-4x + 2y$ by to get $2x - y$. Then we can multiply this constant and 5 to get a.

Looking closely, you can see that $-\dfrac{1}{2}(-4x + 2y) = 2x - y$.

Therefore, $a = -\dfrac{1}{2}(5) = -\dfrac{5}{2}$.

Solving Quadratic Equations

Quadratic equations are equations that can be written in the form $ax^2 + bx + c = 0$, where a, b, and c are numbers and a is nonzero. There are several different methods used to solve these types of equations, and on the SAT it will be assumed that you are familiar with all of them. We will look at each method individually.

Solving Quadratic Equations Using the Square Root Rule

The square root rule states that if $x^2 = c$, then $x = \pm\sqrt{c}$. For example, if $x^2 = 4$, then $x = \pm\sqrt{4} = \pm2$. The solutions are $x = -2$ and $x = 2$. As you can see in the examples below, this rule can be applied even when the equation isn't quite this simple.

▶ Solve $9x^2 = 5$.

▶ The goal when using the square root rule is to first get the equation in the form $x^2 = c$. Here, that means that we should divide both sides by 9 before applying the rule.

$$9x^2 = 5$$
$$\frac{9x^2}{9} = \frac{5}{9}$$
$$x^2 = \frac{5}{9}$$
$$x = \pm\sqrt{\frac{5}{9}}$$
$$= \pm\frac{\sqrt{5}}{3}$$

▶ Thus, the two solutions are $x = -\dfrac{\sqrt{5}}{3}$ and $x = \dfrac{\sqrt{5}}{3}$.

The SAT sometimes asks not just for x or y, but for some other relationship involving the variable. Be sure to read the question carefully to avoid choosing a partial answer.

EXAMPLE

▶ If $\dfrac{x^2}{4} + 1 = 6$, what is the value of $2x$?

▶ Again, isolate the x^2 and then apply the square root rule.

$$\frac{x^2}{4} + 1 = 6$$

$$\frac{x^2}{4} + 1 - 1 = 6 - 1$$

$$\frac{x^2}{4} = 5$$

$$4\left(\frac{x^2}{4}\right) = 4(5)$$

$$x^2 = 20$$

$$x = \pm\sqrt{20}$$

$$= \pm 2\sqrt{5}$$

▶ This shows that the two solutions are $x = -2\sqrt{5}$ and $x = 2\sqrt{5}$.

▶ Since the question asks for the value of $2x$, we need to multiply each solution by 2. $(2)(-2\sqrt{5}) = -4\sqrt{5}$ and $(2)(2\sqrt{5}) = 4\sqrt{5}$.

Using the square root rule doesn't always require us to have the single term x squared—we just need *something* that is squared.

 IRL We use quadratic equations when we calculate area, profit for a business, speed and velocity of an object, and many other things.

EXAMPLE

▶ Solve $3(x-2)^2 = 27$.

▶ This equation looks different from the previous two, but the square root rule can still be used. Instead of isolating just an x^2 term, we will want to isolate the term $(x-2)^2$.

$$3(x-2)^2 = 27$$
$$\frac{3(x-2)^2}{3} = \frac{27}{3}$$
$$(x-2)^2 = 9$$
$$x-2 = \pm\sqrt{9}$$
$$x-2 = \pm 3$$
$$x-2+2 = \pm 3 + 2$$
$$x = \pm 3 + 2$$

▶ The two solutions are $3 + 2 = 5$ and $-3 + 2 = -1$.

Solving Quadratic Equations by Factoring

In mathematics, a rule called the *zero product rule* states that if $AB = 0$, then either $A = 0$ or $B = 0$. As you will see in the next examples, this rule can be applied to solve quadratic equations.

EXAMPLE

▶ Solve $x^2 + 2x = 15$.

▶ First, we will write the equation so that all terms are on one side. After this, we will factor the left-hand side.

$$x^2 + 2x = 15$$
$$x^2 + 2x - 15 = 0$$
$$(x+5)(x-3) = 0$$

▶ Applying the zero product rule:

$$x + 5 = 0$$
$$x = -5$$

or

$$x - 3 = 0$$
$$x = 3$$

▶ Thus, the solutions are −5, 3.

On the SAT, the solutions to this equation may be called the *roots* or *zeros* of $x^2 + 2x - 15$. A quadratic equation can have 0, 1, or 2 real roots.

EXAMPLE

▶ Solve $6x^2 - x - 1 = 0$.

▶ In this case, all the terms are already on one side of the equation, so we can factor and then apply the zero product rule. Remember that you must have all of the terms on one side of the equation before you do this.

$$6x^2 - x - 1 = 0$$
$$(2x - 1)(3x + 1) = 0$$

$$2x - 1 = 0$$
$$2x = 1$$
$$x = \frac{1}{2}$$

or

$$3x + 1 = 0$$
$$3x = -1$$
$$x = -\frac{1}{3}$$

▶ The solutions to this equation are $-\dfrac{1}{3}, \dfrac{1}{2}$.

Solving Quadratic Equations Using the Quadratic Formula

The last two methods, the square root rule and factoring, only apply to some quadratic equations. One method that can be used to solve *any* quadratic equation is the quadratic formula. For a quadratic equation $ax^2 + bx + c = 0$, the formula gives the solutions as:

$$x = \frac{-b \pm \sqrt{b^2 - 4ac}}{2a}$$

To apply this formula, you must first make sure all the terms of the equation are on the same side of the equation and then identify the values of a, b, and c. After that, it is all arithmetic!

EXAMPLE

▶ Solve $3x^2 - x - 1 = 0$.

▶ As all the terms are on one side of the equation, we can go ahead and identify the values needed for the quadratic formula. In this equation, $a = 3$, $b = -1$, and $c = -1$.

$$x = \frac{-b \pm \sqrt{b^2 - 4ac}}{2a}$$

$$= \frac{-(-1) \pm \sqrt{(-1)^2 - 4(3)(-1)}}{2(3)}$$

$$= \frac{1 \pm \sqrt{1 + 12}}{6}$$

$$= \frac{1 \pm \sqrt{13}}{6}$$

▶ Thus, the two solutions are $\dfrac{1 + \sqrt{13}}{6}$ and $\dfrac{1 - \sqrt{13}}{6}$.

In the example above, the final answer couldn't be simplified any further. However, you will often need to do some simplification.

▶ Solve $x^2 - 6x = -1$.

▶ First, the –1 needs to be moved to the left-hand side of the equation.

$$x^2 - 6x = -1$$
$$x^2 - 6x + 1 = -1 + 1$$
$$x^2 - 6x + 1 = 0$$

▶ Now we can see that $a = 1$, $b = -6$, and $c = 1$.

$$x = \frac{-b \pm \sqrt{b^2 - 4ac}}{2a}$$

$$= \frac{-(-6) \pm \sqrt{(-6)^2 - 4(1)(1)}}{2(1)}$$

$$= \frac{6 \pm \sqrt{36 - 4}}{2}$$

$$= \frac{6 \pm \sqrt{32}}{2}$$

$$= \frac{6 \pm \sqrt{16 \times 2}}{2}$$

$$= \frac{6 \pm 4\sqrt{2}}{2}$$

$$= 3 \pm 2\sqrt{2}$$

BTW

A quadratic equation always has two solutions: two distinct real solutions, a double real solution, or two imaginary solutions.

▶ The solutions are $3 + 2\sqrt{2}$ and $3 - 2\sqrt{2}$.

Other Types of Equations Common to the SAT

While there are many types of equations across mathematics, linear and quadratic equations are the types you will most often see on the SAT. However, there are two other types of equations that may come up, which we will now review.

Equations with Radicals

In Chapter 6, we learned how to work with radicals such as the square root and the cube root. Here, we will learn how to solve equations involving these symbols. These types of equations introduce a new complication in the form of *extraneous solutions*. This means that through the process of solving the equation, we may introduce a value that looks like a solution but isn't. For this reason, we will always be checking our answers by plugging them back into the original equation.

EXAMPLE

▶ Solve $\sqrt{5x + 4} = x + 2$.

▶ Squaring both sides of the equation will remove the radical sign, but be very careful when squaring the right-hand side. $(x + 2)^2 \neq x^2 + 4$. Instead, we will need to use FOIL to simplify this part of the equation.

$$\sqrt{5x + 4} = x + 2$$
$$(\sqrt{5x + 4})^2 = (x + 2)^2$$
$$5x + 4 = x^2 + 4x + 4$$
$$5x - 5x + 4 - 4 = x^2 + 4x - 5x + 4 - 4$$
$$0 = x^2 - x$$
$$0 = x(x - 1)$$

▶ Applying the zero product rule gives us solutions $x = 0$ and $x = 1$. Now, we must check the solutions to see if any are extraneous.

▶ For $x = 0$:

$$\sqrt{5x + 4} = x + 2$$
$$\sqrt{5(0) + 4} = 0 + 2$$
$$\sqrt{4} = 2$$

▶ This is a true statement, so 0 is a solution.

▶ For $x = 1$:

$$\sqrt{5x + 4} = x + 2$$
$$\sqrt{5(1) + 4} = 1 + 2$$
$$\sqrt{9} = 3$$

▶ This is also a true statement, so 1 is also a solution.

Not all equations with radicals will have the radical isolated on one side of the equation. Before you can square both sides of the equation, you may need to take an extra step or two to isolate the radical.

EXAMPLE

▶ Solve $x + \sqrt{2x + 1} = 7$.

▶ Before squaring both sides, isolate the radical.

$$x + \sqrt{2x + 1} = 7$$
$$x + \sqrt{2x + 1} - x = 7 - x$$
$$\sqrt{2x + 1} = 7 - x$$
$$(\sqrt{2x + 1})^2 = (7 - x)^2$$
$$2x + 1 = 49 - 14x + x^2$$
$$0 = x^2 - 16x + 48$$
$$0 = (x - 4)(x - 12)$$

▶ By the zero product rule, the solutions are $x = 4$ and $x = 12$. Don't stop there! We need to check to see whether either of these solutions is extraneous.

▶ For $x = 4$:

$$x + \sqrt{2x + 1} = 7$$
$$4 + \sqrt{2(4) + 1} = 7$$
$$4 + \sqrt{9} = 7$$
$$4 + 3 = 7$$

▶ This is a true statement, so 4 is a solution to the original equation.

▶ For $x = 12$:

$$x + \sqrt{2x + 1} = 7$$
$$12 + \sqrt{2(12) + 1} = 7$$
$$12 + \sqrt{25} = 7$$
$$12 + 5 = 7$$
$$17 = 7$$

▶ This is a false statement, so 12 is *not* a solution to the original equation.

▶ Since the second solution was extraneous, we say this equation has only one solution: $x = 4$.

Equations with other types of radicals, such as cube roots, can be solved in a similar way.

EXAMPLE

▶ Solve $\sqrt[3]{x - 5} = 3$.

▶ In this example, we have a cube root isolated on the left-hand side of the equation. Therefore, we can cube both sides of the equation to help us find the solution.

$$\sqrt[3]{x - 5} = 3$$
$$(\sqrt[3]{x - 5})^3 = 3^3$$
$$x - 5 = 27$$
$$x = 32$$

BTW

Equations with radicals usually have simple integer solutions. It may be easier to just plug in the answer choices to see which one works!

▶ Plugging this value back into the original equation shows that this is a good solution.

Rational Equations

Rational equations are equations that involve rational expressions such as $\dfrac{1}{x-1}$ or $\dfrac{x}{x+2}$. While there are different ways to approach one of these equations, we will focus on the general shortcut of *clearing fractions*. As with radical equations, as a last step, we will need to check for extraneous solutions.

EXAMPLE

▶ Solve $\dfrac{4}{x+2} + \dfrac{1}{x-1} = 2$.

▶ For any equation, multiplying both sides by the same value will not change the solution or solutions. Therefore, we can clear fractions by multiplying both sides of the equation by a common denominator for the fractions on the left. This will simplify things so that we can apply techniques from earlier in the chapter.

$$((x+2)(x-1))\left(\frac{4}{x+2} + \frac{1}{x-1}\right) = ((x+2)(x-1))2$$

$$\frac{4(\cancel{(x+2)}(x-1))}{\cancel{x+2}} + \frac{((x+2)\cancel{(x-1)})}{\cancel{x-1}} = 2(x^2 + x - 2)$$

$$4(x-1) + (x+2) = 2x^2 + 2x - 4$$

$$4x - 4 + x + 2 = 2x^2 + 2x - 4$$

$$5x - 2 = 2x^2 + 2x - 4$$

$$0 = 2x^2 - 3x - 2$$

$$0 = (2x+1)(x-2)$$

▶ The zero product rule gives the solutions as $x = -\dfrac{1}{2}$ and $x = 2$, but we need to check each of these answers.

▶ For $x = -\dfrac{1}{2}$:

$$\frac{4}{x+2} + \frac{1}{x-1} = 2$$

$$\frac{4}{-\dfrac{1}{2}+2} + \frac{1}{-\dfrac{1}{2}-1} = 2$$

$$\frac{4}{\dfrac{3}{2}} + \frac{1}{-\dfrac{3}{2}} = 2$$

$$\frac{8}{3} - \frac{2}{3} = 2$$

$$\frac{6}{3} = 2$$

▶ This is a true statement, so $x = -\dfrac{1}{2}$ is a solution to the original equation.

▶ For $x = 2$:

$$\frac{4}{x+2} + \frac{1}{x-1} = 2$$

$$\frac{4}{2+2} + \frac{1}{2-1} = 2$$

$$\frac{4}{4} + \frac{1}{1} = 2$$

$$1 + 1 = 2$$

▶ This is also a true statement, so $x = 2$ is a solution to the original equation.

▶ This equation has two solutions: $x = -\dfrac{1}{2}$ and $x = 2$.

These types of questions can be difficult and require many steps. Let's try one more to be sure you've got it.

EXAMPLE

▶ Solve $\dfrac{1}{4x} + \dfrac{1}{2x} = \dfrac{x-2}{3x+5}$.

▶ Since $4x$ and $2x$ share a factor of $2x$, a common denominator here is $4x(3x+5)$.

$$\frac{1}{4x} + \frac{1}{2x} = \frac{x-2}{3x+5}$$

$$(4x(3x+5))\left(\frac{1}{4x} + \frac{1}{2x}\right) = 4x(3x+5)\left(\frac{x-2}{3x+5}\right)$$

$$\frac{\cancel{4x}(3x+5)}{\cancel{4x}} + \frac{\overset{2}{\cancel{4x}}(3x+5)}{\cancel{2x}} = \frac{4x\,\cancel{(3x+5)}(x-2)}{\cancel{3x+5}}$$

$$(3x+5) + 2(3x+5) = 4x(x-2)$$

$$3x + 5 + 6x + 10 = 4x^2 - 8x$$

$$9x + 15 = 4x^2 - 8x$$

$$0 = 4x^2 - 17x - 15$$

$$0 = (4x+3)(x-5)$$

▶ Using the zero product rule, $x = -\dfrac{3}{4}$ or $x = 5$.

▶ Remember that you always must check your solutions for this type of equation.

▶ For $x = -\dfrac{3}{4}$:

$$\frac{1}{4x} + \frac{1}{2x} = \frac{x-2}{3x+5}$$

$$\frac{1}{4\left(-\dfrac{3}{4}\right)} + \frac{1}{2\left(-\dfrac{3}{4}\right)} = \frac{\left(-\dfrac{3}{4}\right) - 2}{3\left(-\dfrac{3}{4}\right) + 5}$$

$$\frac{1}{-3} + \frac{1}{-\dfrac{3}{2}} = \frac{-\dfrac{11}{4}}{-\dfrac{9}{4} + 5}$$

$$-\frac{1}{3} - \frac{2}{3} = \frac{-\dfrac{11}{4}}{\dfrac{11}{4}}$$

$$-1 = -1$$

▶ This is a true statement, so $x = -\dfrac{3}{4}$ is a solution.

▶ For $x = 5$:

$$\frac{1}{4x} + \frac{1}{2x} = \frac{x-2}{3x+5}$$

$$\frac{1}{4(5)} + \frac{1}{2(5)} = \frac{5-2}{3(5)+5}$$

$$\frac{1}{20} + \frac{1}{10} = \frac{3}{20}$$

$$\frac{1}{20} + \frac{2}{20} = \frac{3}{20}$$

▶ This is also a true statement, so $x = 5$ is a solution as well.

▶ Thus, the original equation has two solutions: $x = -\dfrac{3}{4}$ and $x = 5$.

EXERCISES

EXERCISE 7–1

Solve each equation.

1. $-8x + 3 = 1$

2. $\dfrac{1}{5} + x = \dfrac{2}{3}x$

3. $\dfrac{1}{2}(6x + 2) = 4x$

4. $7(x - 1) = -3(x + 1)$

5. $\dfrac{x}{3} + \dfrac{x}{4} = \dfrac{x}{2} + 3$ (Hint: $\dfrac{x}{3}$ is the same as $\dfrac{1}{3}x$)

EXERCISE 7–2

For exercises 1–3, determine whether the equations have no solution or infinitely many solutions.

1. $-(-x - 1) = x + 1$

2. $3x + 5x - 10 = -2x + 10x - 4$

3. $2(2x - 3) = 4(x + 6)$

4. Find the value of a such that the following equation has no solution.

$$a(x + 4) = -2x + 1$$

5. Find the value of a such that the following equation has infinitely many solutions.

$$5x - ax + 3 = x + 3$$

EXERCISE 7–3

For exercises 1–3, solve the equation for the indicated variable.

1. $\dfrac{m}{2} + \dfrac{n}{4} = 1, m$

2. $-x + a = 3a + 3, a$

3. $2x + 2y = 9, y$

4. The volume of a rectangular prism is found using the formula $V = \ell w h$, where ℓ is the length, w is the width of the rectangular base, and h is its height. Write this formula so that it shows the height in terms of the other variables.

5. The area of a triangle is found using the formula $A = \dfrac{1}{2}bh$, where b is the base and h is the height. Find b in terms of A and h.

EXERCISE 7–4

Solve each of the following inequalities.

1. $x + 2 > -x + 8$

2. $\dfrac{x+1}{4} \le 5 + 2x$ (Hint: Clear fractions first.)

3. $\dfrac{1}{2}x + \dfrac{2}{5} > 1$

4. $3(2x + 1) \ge 2(x - 4)$

5. $\dfrac{3}{8}x < -\dfrac{1}{2}x + \dfrac{1}{2}$

EXERCISE 7–5

1. Three times the value of a variable m is 2 less than four times the value of a variable n. What is the value of n in terms of m?

2. Each weekday a customer service department handles at least 350 calls. Suppose each call takes an average of 8 minutes. Write an inequality that describes the minimum number of minutes, m, spent on calls each day.

3. Carson's goal is to read 25 books over the summer. Suppose that each book is an average of 320 pages and that Carson can read x pages each hour. If h is the number of hours he will spend reading, write an equation that shows the value of h in terms of x.

4. A shipment contains 40 bags of rice and 18 bags of flour, and it weighs 1,500 pounds. If each bag of flour weighs 50 pounds, then how much does each bag of rice weigh?

5. An investor instructs his financial advisor that at least twice as much money should be invested in bonds as is invested in stocks at any given time. If s represents the amount invested in stocks and b represents the amount invested in bonds, then write an inequality that shows the maximum amount that can be invested in stocks in terms of b.

EXERCISE 7–6

Solve the following systems of equations.

1.
$$2x - y = -3$$
$$6x - 2y = -5$$

2.
$$\frac{1}{2}x - y = -2$$
$$x + 2y = 4$$

3. $3x + 4y = 19$
   $7x + 5y = 14$

4. $-2x + 4y = 12$
   $\dfrac{3}{2}x - \dfrac{1}{2}y = 1$

5. $\dfrac{1}{4}x + y = 0$
   $-x + 3y = \dfrac{7}{4}$

EXERCISE 7–7

For exercises 1–3, determine whether the system of equations has infinitely many solutions or no solution.

1. $\dfrac{1}{2}x - 3y = 8$
   $2x - 12y = 1$

2. $-3x - y = 1$
   $6x + 2y = -2$

3. $8x - 4y = -10$
   $12x - 6y = -15$

4. Determine the value of a such that the system of equations has no solution.
   $8x + 2y = 4$
   $x - ay = 5$

5. Determine the value of a such that the system of equations has infinitely many solutions.
   $4x + 10y = 7$
   $6x + 15y = a$

EXERCISE 7–8

Solve each equation for x. Simplify your answer completely.

1. $x^2 = 45$

2. $-x^2 + 1 = 0$

3. $\dfrac{1}{2}x^2 = \dfrac{1}{4}$

4. $\dfrac{(x-1)^2}{2} - \dfrac{1}{2} = 1$

5. $-2(x+5)^2 + 8 = 0$

EXERCISE 7–9

Solve each of the following equations by factoring.

1. $x^2 + x = 2$

2. $x^2 = -9x - 20$

3. $x^2 - 6x + 9 = 0$

4. $2x^2 - x - 36 = 0$

5. $9x^2 + 15x + 4 = 0$

EXERCISE 7–10

Solve the equations using the quadratic formula.

1. $x^2 = 2x + 17$

2. $x^2 - 6x + 7 = 0$

3. $9x^2 - 12x = 1$

4. $2x^2 - 2x - 1 = 0$

5. $x^2 - 10x - 7 = 0$

EXERCISE 7–11

Solve the following equations.

1. $\sqrt{x-6} = 12$

2. $\sqrt{x+4} + 8 = x$

3. $0 = x + \sqrt{2x+3}$

4. $\sqrt[3]{5x-1} + 2 = 0$

5. $\sqrt[3]{2x} = \dfrac{1}{4}$

EXERCISE 7–12

Solve each of the following equations.

1. $\dfrac{1}{x} - \dfrac{3}{4} = 3$

2. $\dfrac{2x}{x^2-1} + \dfrac{1}{x-1} = \dfrac{7}{x+1}$

3. $\dfrac{x-1}{2} = \dfrac{x+5}{3}$

4. $\dfrac{1}{2x} - \dfrac{1}{x} = -1$

5. $\dfrac{1}{3x+1} + \dfrac{2}{3x+4} = \dfrac{3}{x+3}$

Flashcard App

Answers are on page 559.

 **Functions and Graphs**

⚡ A function is like a set of directions. Any input, x, results in a certain output, y, which we show as $f(x)$. Those inputs and outputs can be graphed as points (x, y).

⚡ A linear function can be written as $y = mx + b$, where m is the slope and b is the y-intercept.

⚡ A quadratic function forms a parabola and has the form $y = ax^2 + bx + c$, where a, b, and c are constants and $a \neq 0$.

⚡ The graph of any function can be moved through transformations such as reflection, which creates a mirror image across an axis; translation, which moves a function up, down, left, or right; and stretching or compressing.

F unctions, their properties, and graphs are used throughout advanced mathematics to represent real-life phenomena. On the SAT, you will need to be able to evaluate functions and be familiar with the properties of graphs arising from linear and quadratic equations. Finally, you will need to understand the connection between graphs, equations, and the zeros of polynomials. In this chapter, we will review each of these ideas in depth so that you are prepared for any question you might come across on test day.

Evaluating Functions

A function is a special rule that assigns exactly one output for any input. The notation $f(x)$ is often used, where x represents the input and the value of $f(x)$ represents the corresponding output. To evaluate a function means to find its value for a specific input.

▶ Find $f(-1)$ when $f(x) = -3x + x^3$.

▶ To find $f(-1)$, let $x = -1$. Make sure you replace every instance of x with the input value of -1.

$$f(-1) = -3(-1) + (-1)^3$$
$$= 3 - 1$$
$$= 2$$

▶ Find $f(2)$ when $f(x) = \dfrac{x+4}{x-3} + 2$.

▶ Let $x = 2$.

$$f(2) = \frac{2+4}{2-3} + 2$$
$$= \frac{6}{-1} + 2$$
$$= -6 + 2$$
$$= -4$$

It is more common for questions to ask for the for the value of $f(x)$ when x equals a certain value, but you may also be asked to find which value of x makes a function equal to a certain value.

EXAMPLE

▶ If the value of the function $f(x) = \dfrac{1}{3}x - 4$ equals -5, what is the value of x?

▶ This is not that different from the previous examples. If we know $f(x) = \dfrac{1}{3}x - 4$ and $f(x) = -5$, then we can say that $-5 = \dfrac{1}{3}x - 4$ and solve the equation for x.

$$-5 = \frac{1}{3}x - 4$$

$$-1 = \frac{1}{3}x$$

$$-3 = x$$

Functions can also be evaluated for inputs that are algebraic expressions. With these types of problems, the same idea applies: let all instances of x represent the input.

EXAMPLE

▶ Find $f(x + 2)$ for $f(x) = x^2 + x$.

▶ Remember, replace every instance of x in the function rule with the input $x + 2$.

$$f(x + 2) = (x + 2)^2 + (x + 2)$$
$$= x^2 + 4x + 4 + x + 2$$
$$= x^2 + 5x + 6$$

Graphing Functions

The graph of a function is a visual representation of all the input/output pairs for the function. On the xy-plane, the point (x, y) represents the value $y = f(x)$ for the input value x. The graphs of certain types of functions share some specific properties that are important to understand if you want to do well on the SAT.

Graphs of Linear Functions

A linear function is any function that can be written in the form $y = f(x) = mx + b$. The graph of a linear function is a line that passes through the y-axis at the point $(0, b)$ (called the y-intercept) and has slope (a way to measure the "steepness" of the line) m. The greater the slope, the "steeper" the line. Further, since the graph is a line, it will only cross through the x-axis at one point (called the x-intercept).

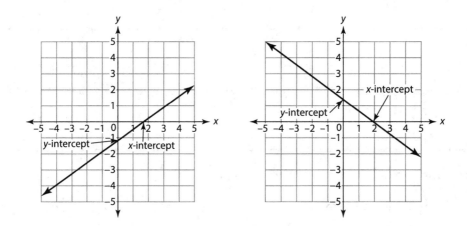

As you can see in the graphs above, a line with positive slope rises from left to right while a line with negative slope falls from left to right. A horizontal (flat) line has a slope of 0 and a vertical line has a slope that is "undefined."

What is the slope of the line defined by $-2y + 3x = 8$?

If the line is written in the form $y = mx + b$, then the slope is the value of m. Thus, we can solve for y to find the slope.

$$-2y + 3x = 8$$
$$-2y + 3x - 3x = 8 - 3x$$
$$-2y = 8 - 3x$$
$$\frac{-2y}{-2} = \frac{8}{-2} - \frac{3x}{-2}$$
$$y = -4 + \frac{3}{2}x$$

The slope is $\frac{3}{2}$.

From the equation of a line, we can also determine the x-intercept and y-intercept of the line. All we need to do to find the x-intercept is set y equal to zero. To find the y-intercept, we set x equal to zero.

Find the x- and y-intercepts of the line defined by the function $f(x) = -2x + 4$.

The value of the y-intercept of any function is found by letting $x = 0$.

$$f(0) = -2(0) + 4$$
$$= 4$$

Thus, the y-intercept is 4. This means that the graph of this function crosses the y-axis at the point $(0, 4)$.

The value of the x-intercept is found by letting $f(x) = y = 0$ and solving for x.

$$0 = -2x + 4$$
$$-4 = -2x$$
$$\frac{-4}{-2} = \frac{-2x}{-2}$$
$$2 = x$$

▶ Thus, the x-intercept is 2. This means that the graph of this function crosses the x-axis at the point (2, 0).

While SAT questions won't directly ask you to graph a linear function, being able to graph one may be useful to you. The SAT may ask you to identify the graph of a linear function given the equation or a description. If you are able to directly graph a linear equation, then these questions won't be too difficult.

One quick method for graphing linear functions is to use the intercepts. Since we know the graph is a line, we can simply plot these intercepts and then "connect the dots." For example, the graph of the function we just worked with, $f(x) = -2x + 4$, is shown below.

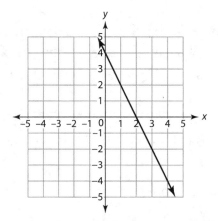

Notice that the graph passes through the two points that we found in the example.

Considering the properties we have reviewed for linear functions, how could you find the equation that represents a given line? Let's consider this as part of an example.

EXAMPLE

▶ Find the equation of the line represented in the graph below.

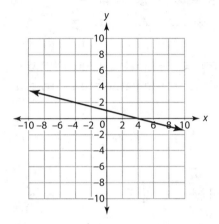

▶ Remember that the general form of a linear function is $y = f(x) = mx + b$, where m is the slope and b is the y-intercept. One way to think about the slope is as "rise over run" or "the change in y over the change in x." This is represented by the formula

$$m = \frac{y_2 - y_1}{x_2 - x_1}$$

where (x_1, y_1) and (x_2, y_2) are two points along the line.

▶ Looking at this graph, we can see that the function has a y-intercept at 1 and an x-intercept at 4. This means that the graph passes through the points (0, 1) and (4, 0). Letting $(x_1, y_1) = (4, 0)$ and $(x_2, y_2) = (0, 1)$, and using the slope formula:

$$m = \frac{y_2 - y_1}{x_2 - x_1} = \frac{1 - 0}{0 - 4} = \frac{1}{-4} = -\frac{1}{4}$$

▶ Putting this information together with the y-intercept, this graph is the graph of the function $y = f(x) = mx + b = -\frac{1}{4}x + 1$ or simply $y = -\frac{1}{4}x + 1$.

Graphs of Quadratic Functions

Quadratic functions are functions of the form $y = f(x) = ax^2 + bx + c$, where a, b, and c are constants such that $a \neq 0$. The graph of a quadratic function is called a *parabola*, and these graphs either open up (and thus the function reaches a minimum value but no maximum) or open down (where the function reaches a maximum value but no minimum). This is illustrated below.

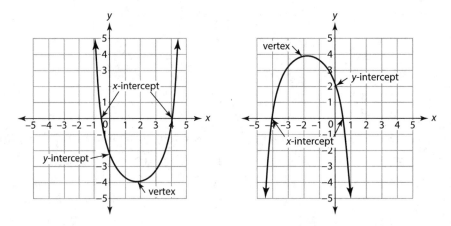

Notice that for a parabola opening up, the graph is falling from left to right until it gets to the vertex and then it is rising from left to right. Mathematically, we would say that the function is *decreasing* for values of x on the left-hand side of the vertex and *increasing* for values of x on the right-hand side of the vertex. The opposite is true for parabolas opening down. The function is increasing for values of x on the left-hand side of the vertex and decreasing for values of x on the right-hand side of the vertex.

EXAMPLE

▶ The minimum value of a quadratic function $f(x) = x^2 - 2x + 5$ occurs when $x = 1$. If this function were graphed, what would be the coordinates of its vertex?

▶ Here, we are told that the minimum occurs at $x = 1$. This means that the x-coordinate of the vertex is 1. Finding $f(1)$ will give the y-coordinate.

$$f(1) = 1^2 - 2(1) + 5$$
$$= 1 - 2 + 5$$
$$= 4$$

▶ Thus, the vertex is located at (1, 4).

BTW

Many SAT questions will indirectly test your knowledge by seeing if you can connect algebraic ideas about functions with properties of their graphs. This question is asking for the point (x, y) that defines the vertex. We know that the vertex will be either the minimum or maximum value of a quadratic function.

Earlier, we found the x- and y-intercepts for a line. You may also be asked to find the x- and y-intercepts for a function. Sometimes, it may be as easy as it was for a line.

EXAMPLE

▶ Find the y-intercept of the function $y = -3x^2 + 4x - 1$.

▶ Recall that the y-intercept is found by letting $x = 0$.

$$y = -3(0)^2 + 4(0) - 1$$
$$= -1$$

▶ Thus, the y-intercept is -1. This means that the graph of the function crosses the y-axis at the point (0, −1).

All we needed to do there was set $x = 0$ and solve for y. At other times, it may be more difficult to find the x- and y-intercepts and you may need the quadratic formula:

$$x = \frac{-b \pm \sqrt{b^2 - 4ac}}{2a}$$

EXAMPLE

▶ Find any x-intercept(s) of the function $f(x) = x^2 + x - 4$.

▶ The x-intercepts of any function are found by letting $y = f(x) = 0$. This means that we need to solve the equation $x^2 + x - 4 = 0$. This function doesn't appear to be factorable, so we will use the quadratic formula.

$$x = \frac{-b \pm \sqrt{b^2 - 4ac}}{2a}$$

$$= \frac{-1 \pm \sqrt{1^2 - 4(1)(-4)}}{2(1)}$$

$$= \frac{-1 \pm \sqrt{1 + 16}}{2}$$

$$= \frac{-1 \pm \sqrt{17}}{2}$$

▶ This expression can't be simplified any further, so the function has two x-intercepts: $\dfrac{-1 + \sqrt{17}}{2}$ and $\dfrac{-1 - \sqrt{17}}{2}$. That is, the graph crosses the x-axis at the points $\left(\dfrac{-1 + \sqrt{17}}{2},\ 0 \right)$ and $\left(\dfrac{-1 - \sqrt{17}}{2},\ 0 \right)$.

It is also possible for a quadratic function to either cross the x-axis at no points or cross the x-axis at exactly one point. Let's take a look at each of these two cases.

EXAMPLE

▶ Find any x-intercept(s) of the function $f(x) = x^2 - 3x + 5$.

▶ Set this function equal to zero and solve.

$$x^2 - 3x + 5 = 0$$

$$x = \frac{-b \pm \sqrt{b^2 - 4ac}}{2a}$$

$$= \frac{-(-3) \pm \sqrt{(-3)^2 - 4(1)(5)}}{2(1)}$$

$$= \frac{3 \pm \sqrt{9 - 20}}{2}$$

$$= \frac{3 \pm \sqrt{-11}}{2}$$

▶ The square root of a negative number is not a real number, and since this expression involves $\sqrt{-11}$, this equation has no real solution. Therefore, the graph does not cross the x-axis at any point and there are no x-intercepts. The graph of this function is shown below.

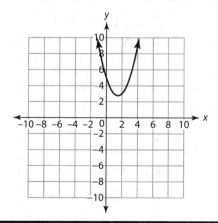

Now let's look at an example of a function with only one x-intercept.

EXAMPLE

▶ Find any x-intercepts of the function $y = x^2 - 6x + 9$.

▶ Setting this function equal to zero, we see that it is factorable.

$$x^2 - 6x + 9 = 0$$
$$(x - 3)(x - 3) = 0$$
$$(x - 3)^2 = 0$$
$$x = 3$$

▶ This equation has only one solution, however, so the function has only one x-intercept: 3. This is shown on the graph below.

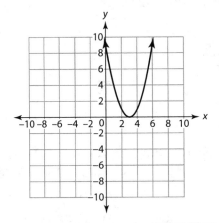

Linear Factors and Zeros of Polynomials

In the preceding two sections, you saw that the x-intercept of a graph is the point (or the points) where the graph crosses the x-axis. You also saw that this can be found by letting the function $f(x) = 0$. For this reason, these values are often called *zeros* of the function $f(x)$.

When working with polynomial functions, including quadratic functions, these zeros correspond to linear factors. Specifically, if $f(c) = 0$, then $(x - c)$

is a factor of the polynomial. Combine this with the fact that any nth degree polynomial (a polynomial whose largest exponent is n) has at most n roots, and you are able to describe a lot of properties of the graph of any given polynomial.

▶ A polynomial function has zeros –1, 1, and 2. If the function can be written as $(x - k)(x^2 - x - 2)$, then what is the value of k?

▶ The second factor of the polynomial, $x^2 - x - 2$, can itself be factored as $(x + 1)(x - 2)$. Using the zero product rule, this means that the polynomial has zeros –1, 2, and k. Using the information from the problem, it must be that $k = 1$.

On the SAT, you will find that there is no "one way" that these types of questions are written. Instead, you should make sure that you understand the connection between x-intercepts, zeros, and linear factors completely so that you can be prepared for any way the questions might be posed.

▶ The graph of the polynomial $p(x) = x^5 + 5x^4 - 10x^3 - 20x^2 + 24x$ crosses the x-axis at the points $(-6, 0)$, $(-2, 0)$, $(0, 0)$, $(1, 0)$, and $(2, 0)$. Factor this polynomial completely.

▶ This is a fifth degree polynomial, so it has at most five real zeros. The problem has given us five zeros, so each of these must correspond to a linear factor of the polynomial. Remember that $x - c$ is a linear factor if c is a zero.

▶ Using each point:

- Intercept at $(-6, 0)$, so $(x - (-6)) = (x + 6)$ is a linear factor.
- Intercept at $(-2, 0)$, so $(x - (-2)) = (x + 2)$ is a linear factor.

- Intercept at (0, 0), so $(x - (0)) = (x)$ is a linear factor.
- Intercept at (1, 0), so $(x - (1)) = (x - 1)$ is a linear factor.
- Intercept at (2, 0), so $(x - (2)) = (x - 2)$ is a linear factor.
- This means that we can factor $p(x)$ as follows.

$$p(x) = x^5 + 5x^4 - 10x^3 - 20x^2 + 24x$$
$$= x(x + 6)(x + 2)(x - 1)(x - 2)$$

Transformations of Graphs

The graph of any function can be moved or stretched using a mathematical *transformation*. There are several different types of transformations, and in this section, you will see how to determine the type of transformation based on either a verbal description or formula.

Reflections

Reflections across the x- or y-axis treat the axis like a mirror with the graph being flipped either upside down or left/right.

Given the graph of a function $f(x)$:

- The graph of $-f(x)$ is the reflection of the graph across the x-axis.
  - When the graph of a function is reflected across the x-axis, each point (x, y) becomes the point $(x, -y)$. Points along the x-axis do not change.

- The graph of $f(-x)$ is the reflection of the graph across the y-axis.
  - When the graph of a function is reflected across the y-axis, each point (x, y) becomes the point $(-x, y)$. Points along the y-axis do not change.

EXAMPLE

▶ Given the function $f(x)$ graphed below, sketch the graph of $-f(x)$ and $f(-x)$.

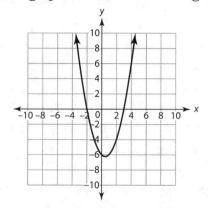

▶ The graph of $-f(x)$ is the reflection of this graph across the x-axis. This is shown below.

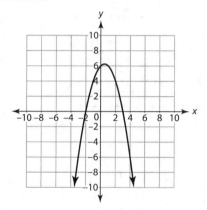

BTW

Notice that the points along the x-axis, the x-intercepts, did not change.

▶ The graph of $f(-x)$ is the reflection of the original graph across the y-axis, as shown below.

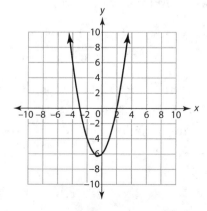

▶ Notice here that the y-intercept didn't change, but the location of the x-intercepts were flipped. That is because the entire graph was flipped across the y-axis.

Usually on the SAT, you won't be selecting the graph of a transformed function. Instead, you will be describing how the transformation affected basic properties of the function such as intercepts, where the function is decreasing or increasing, or maximum values.

▶ Consider the function $f(x) = x^2 + 2x - 3$. What is the least zero of the function $f(-x)$?

▶ The function $f(x) = x^2 + 2x - 3$ can be written as $f(x) = x^2 + 2x - 3 = (x + 3)(x - 1)$ and so has zeros -3 and 1. The function $f(-x)$ is a reflection of this function across the y-axis, so the zeros will be at 3 and -1. Thus, the least zero will be -1.

Translations

Moving the graph of a function left, right, up, or down is called a *translation*. Translations can be described in words (such as "the graph of the function is moved two units up and three units to the left") or mathematically, as shown below.

Given the graph of a function $f(x)$:

- The graph of the function $f(x) + c$ is a translation up or down c units— up if c is positive and down if c is negative.

- The graph of the function $f(x + c)$ is a translation left or right c units—left if c is positive and right if c is negative. Note that this is the opposite of what you might expect!

Given the graph of the function below, sketch the graph of $f(x) + 1$, $f(x) - 1$, $f(x + 1)$, and $f(x - 1)$.

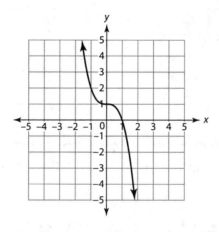

Let's look at the graphs from the last example all next to each other so that it is easy to compare the graphs. Now you can see how the graph has been translated in various directions.

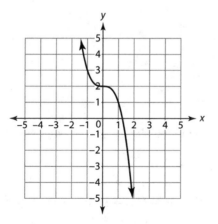

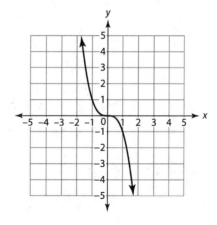

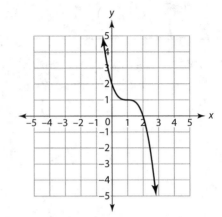

▶ The graph of the function $f(x) = y = \dfrac{1}{2}x + 4$ is shifted up 3 units and to the left 2 units. What is the y-intercept of the resulting graph?

▶ If the graph of a function $f(x)$ is shifted up 3 units and to the left 2 units, then the resulting function is $f(x + 2) + 3$. Using the equation for the function $f(x)$:

$$f(x + 2) + 3 = \frac{1}{2}(x + 2) + 4 + 3$$

$$= \frac{1}{2}x + 1 + 7$$

$$= \frac{1}{2}x + 8$$

▶ This is of the form $y = mx + b$, so the y-intercept is 8.

Stretching and Compressing

You should be familiar with one last set of transformations: those that stretch or compress the graph of a function. This can be done either horizontally or vertically with each being represented in a different way mathematically.

Given the graph of a function $f(x)$:

■ The graph of the function $f(cx)$, is a horizontal stretch when $0 < c < 1$ and a horizontal compression when $c > 1$.

■ The graph of $cf(x)$ is a vertical stretch when $c > 1$ and a vertical compression when $0 < c < 1$.

▶ Given the graph of a function $f(x)$ below, sketch the graph of $f(2x)$, $f\left(\dfrac{1}{2}x\right)$, $2f(x)$, and $\dfrac{1}{2}f(x)$.

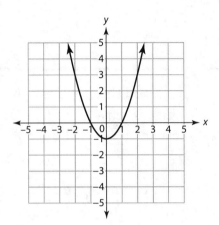

Once again, let's look at the graphs from the previous example side-by-side so that we can truly compare their properties.

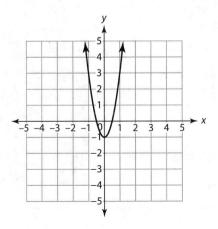

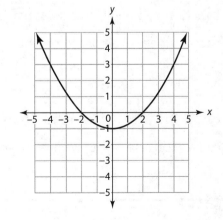

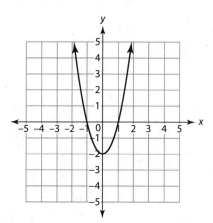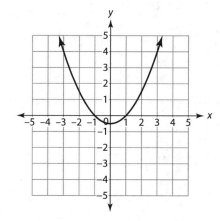

▶ Suppose that the point (x, y) lies on the graph of a function $f(x)$. Suppose that the graph of this function is horizontally stretched by a factor of 3. Give an example of a point that lies on the transformed graph.

▶ A horizontal stretch by a factor of 3 means that the x-coordinate of each point is multiplied by 3. Thus, the point $(3x, y)$ will lie on the graph, which will be the graph of $f\left(\dfrac{1}{3}x\right)$.

▶ You may think, given the function notation, that the point should be $\left(\dfrac{1}{3}x, y\right)$, but this is incorrect. While plugging $\dfrac{1}{3}x$ into the original function will give you the transformed function, the y-value will be based on this new input. If the y-value stays the same, then the x-value will actually be three times as great and thus the point $(3x, y)$ will actually lie on the graph of $f\left(\dfrac{1}{3}x\right)$. This causes the stretching we see, as you have to have a greater x-value to get the same y-value.

BTW

This is certainly confusing, but your best bet is to remember that when dealing with horizontal compressions or stretches, the behavior is the opposite of what you might expect.

Equations, Systems of Equations, and Graphs

We can connect the idea of a solution to an equation, or a solution to a system of equations, to graphs through considering intersection points. For example, suppose you were solving the equation $3 = 2x - 1$.

Instead of applying the usual algebra techniques, let's consider the graph of $y = 3$ and the graph of $y = 2x - 1$, shown below.

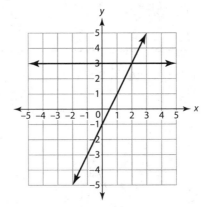

These two lines intersect at the point $(2, 3)$. The x-coordinate here is 2, so the solution to the equation above is 2. This concept can be applied to any two functions $f(x)$ and $g(x)$.

EXAMPLE

▶ The graph below shows the functions $f(x)$ and $g(x)$. How many solutions are there to the equation $f(x) = g(x)$?

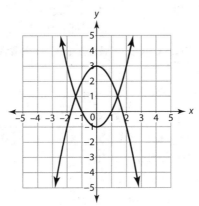

▶ Notice that the graphs of the two functions intersect at two
points. This means that there are two solutions to the equation
$f(x) = g(x)$.

Applying this to systems of equations, the solution to a system of two
linear equations with two unknowns (x, y) is the point where the two lines
intersect.

▶ What is the solution to the system of equations graphed below?

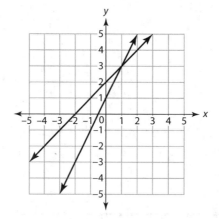

▶ The two lines intersect at the point $(1, 3)$. Thus, the solution is $x = 1$ and
$y = 3$.

Systems of Linear Inequalities and Graphs

When we studied how to solve linear inequalities, we applied almost
identical rules as those we applied to linear equations, but we have not
discussed systems of inequalities before now. Why is that? Well, solving a
system of inequalities algebraically requires techniques that are well outside
the scope of what you would need to know for the SAT. Instead, these are
best approached using a graphical technique.

The steps we will apply are:

1. Solve each inequality for y.

2. Graph the line represented as if the inequality were an equation.

3. Shade the region above or below the line (depending on the direction of the inequality).

The region where the shading overlaps is the solution set to the system of inequalities. This means that any point within this shaded region makes all of the inequalities true.

EXAMPLE

▶ Sketch the solution set to the system of inequalities.
$$2x + y \leq 10$$
$$2y - x \leq 16$$

▶ Solving each inequality for y:

$$2x + y \leq 10$$
$$2x + y - 2x \leq 10 - 2x$$
$$y \leq 10 - 2x$$

$$2y - x \leq 16$$
$$2y - x + x \leq 16 + x$$
$$\frac{2y}{2} \leq \frac{16 + x}{2}$$
$$y \leq 8 + \frac{1}{2}x$$

▶ Now we graph the lines $y = 10 - 2x$ and $y = 8 + \frac{1}{2}x$. Solid lines are used since the inequalities include equality. (We would use dashed lines if we had $<$ or $>$ to indicate that the line is not part of the solution set.)

▶ Once the lines are graphed, we will shade below each line since each inequality is $\leq$. The region where the shading overlaps is the solution set.

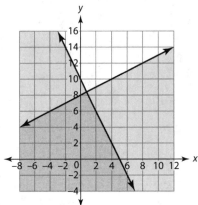

▶ Any point in the region where the shading overlaps represents a solution. You can see that (2, 4) is in this region. Thus, $x = 2, y = 4$ is one solution to this system of inequalities. The point (6, 2) is in a region that was only shaded once. Therefore, $x = 6, y = 2$ is *not* a solution to the system of inequalities. (It satisfies only one of the inequalities and not both.)

Let's try one more example, this time with greater than/less than inequalities. Remember, for those we draw dotted lines rather than solid lines.

EXAMPLE

▶ Sketch the solution set for the system of inequalities.

$$-3y + x < -3$$
$$3y + 2x < 9$$

▶ Solving for y:

$$-3y + x < -3$$
$$-3y + x - x < -3 - x$$
$$\frac{-3y}{-3} > \frac{-3 - x}{-3}$$
$$y > 1 + \frac{1}{3}x$$

$$3y + 2x < 9$$
$$3y + 2x - 2x < 9 - 2x$$
$$\frac{3y}{3} < \frac{9 - 2x}{3}$$
$$y < 3 - \frac{2}{3}x$$

▶ Now we graph the dotted lines $y = 1 + \frac{1}{3}x$ and $y = 3 - \frac{2}{3}x$, shading above $y = 1 + \frac{1}{3}x$ (since the inequality is $>$) and below $y = 3 - \frac{2}{3}x$ (since the inequality is $<$).

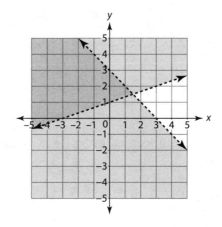

▶ Here, much of the solution set is in the second quadrant. One of the solutions where both x and y are positive is $x = 1$ and $y = 2$.

 IRL Graphing functions is a great way to see how trends change over time. For example, we use graphs like these in economics to show supply and demand, inflation and deflation, and interest rates.

EXERCISES

EXERCISE 8–1

Evaluate each of the following. Simplify your answer completely, when needed.

1. Find $f(0)$ for $f(x) = -2x + 9$.

2. Find $f\left(\dfrac{3}{4}\right)$ for $f(x) = \dfrac{x}{x-5}$.

3. Find $f(2x)$ for $f(x) = 3x^2 - 4x + 2$.

4. Find $f(x-1)$ for $f(x) = \dfrac{x-3}{x+4}$.

5. Find $f\left(\dfrac{x}{2}\right)$ for $f(x) = -x + x^2$.

EXERCISE 8–2

For exercises 1 and 2, find the slope, x-intercept, and y-intercept of the line defined by the given equation.

1. $3x + 5y = -1$

2. $-x + 2y = 3$

3. Write the equation of a linear function that passes through the x-axis at the point $(-1, 0)$ and the y-axis at the point $(0, 3)$.

4. Write the equation of a linear function that has a slope of $-\dfrac{1}{2}$ and passes through the x-axis at the point $(5, 0)$.

5. Find the equation of the function graphed below.

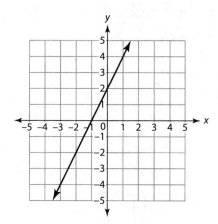

EXERCISE 8–3

1. For values of $x < \dfrac{3}{4}$, the quadratic function $f(x) = 2x^2 - 3x + 3$ is decreasing, while for values of $x > \dfrac{3}{4}$, the function is increasing.

   What is the minimum value of this function?

2. At how many points does the graph of the function $g(x) = 4x^2 - 3x + 1$ cross the x-axis?

3. Find the point at which the graph of $g(x) = 4x^2 - 3x + 1$ crosses the y-axis.

4. Find any x-intercepts of the function $f(x) = 2x^2 + 7x - 4$.

5. A quadratic function has exactly one x-intercept and reaches a maximum value when $x = -2$. What are the coordinates of this function's vertex?

EXERCISE 8–4

1. Using the graph of a polynomial function $g(x)$ below, give one example of a solution to the equation $g(x) = 0$.

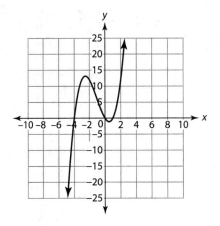

2. A polynomial function $p(x)$ can be written as $p(x) = (x - 5)(2x^3 + x^2 - 3x)$. What is the least zero of this polynomial?

3. The graph of a third degree polynomial crosses the x-axis at the points $(-3, 0)$, $(1, 0)$, and $(3, 0)$. Write an expression that defines the described polynomial.

4. For a quadratic function $f(x)$, $f(-2) = 0$ and $f(3) = 0$. If this function is graphed, then at what point would it cross the y-axis?

5. The following graph is the graph of a third degree polynomial. Write an expression that defines the graphed polynomial.

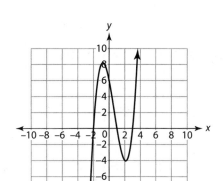

EXERCISE 8–5

1. The graph of a linear function $y = 3x + 1$ is shifted to the left 3 units and then to the right 1 unit. What is the x-intercept of the transformed graph?

2. The zeros of a quadratic function $f(x)$ are -2 and 2. What are the zeros of the function $f\left(\dfrac{1}{2}x\right)$?

3. The minimum value of a quadratic function $f(x)$ is -4. If the function has two real zeros, then how many real zeros does the function $f(x) + 5$ have? What about $f(x + 5)$?

4. The graph of a polynomial function $p(x)$ is increasing for all values of $x < -1$, all values of $0 < x < 1$, and all values of $x > 2$. State all values of x for which the function $p(x - 4)$ is increasing.

5. The graph of the function $f(x) = x^2 - 9$ is reflected across the x-axis and then shifted to the left 4 units. What are the x-intercepts of the transformed function?

EXERCISE 8-6

1. At what point in the xy-plane do the graphs of the functions $f(x) = 1$ and $g(x) = 2x$ intersect?

2. At what points in the xy-plane do the graphs of the functions $f(x) = x^2$ and $g(x) = 2x + 3$ intersect?

3. At what point in the xy-plane do the lines represented by $3x - 2y = 1$ and $4x + 3y = 10$ intersect?

4. A system of two linear equations with two unknowns has no real solution. What can you conclude about the two lines represented by the two equations?

5. The equations that make up a system of equations are graphed below. How many solutions are there to the system?

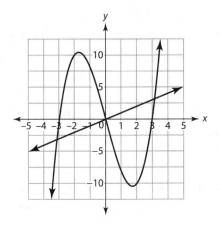

EXERCISE 8–7

Sketch the solution sets for each of the following systems of inequalities.

1. $x + y \leq 3$
   $2x - y \leq 1$

2. $3x + 4y \geq 2$
   $y \leq 5$

3. $x \geq 2$
   $y \leq 3$

4. $2y - x \geq 2$
   $y + x \geq 3$

5. $y - 3x \leq 2$
   $y - 2x \leq 2$

Answers are on page 563.

Ratios, Rates, Proportions, and Percentages

MUST KNOW

⚡ A ratio is used to compare two or more quantities. A ratio can be increased or decreased by using a multiplier.

⚡ A rate is used to compare two quantities with different units. A unit rate is the amount per one unit of a quantity.

⚡ A proportion states that two ratios—usually expressed as fractions—are equal. We use proportions to increase or decrease amounts evenly.

⚡ Percentages show parts per hundred.

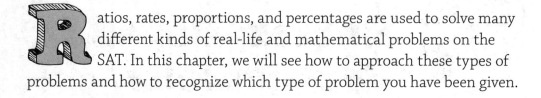

atios, rates, proportions, and percentages are used to solve many different kinds of real-life and mathematical problems on the SAT. In this chapter, we will see how to approach these types of problems and how to recognize which type of problem you have been given.

Ratios

Ratios are used to compare two or more quantities.

> Suppose that in a group there are 6 men and 2 women. Using a ratio, we can write that the ratio of men to women is 6 to 2. This can also be written using a colon, 6:2, or as a fraction $\frac{6}{2}$.

Ratios can be simplified in the same way that fractions can be simplified. Dividing both sides of the ratio 6:2 by 2, we get the equivalent ratio 3:1. Therefore, it would also be correct to say that the ratio of men to women in the previous example is 3:1. This means that there are three times as many men as women.

> There are 5 pennies, 5 quarters, and 4 ten-dollar bills in a purse. In simplest terms, what is the ratio of coins to bills?
>
> There is a total of 10 coins while there are only 4 bills. This is a ratio of 10:4, which in simplest terms is 5:2.

Ratios can be increased or decreased by multiplying the entire ratio by some constant.

EXAMPLE

Laura is making lemonade for a party. Her recipe says it takes 1 part lemon juice, 4 parts water, and ½ part sugar. Laura has lots of lemon juice, but only 3 cups of sugar. How many cups of lemon juice and water will she need to make lemonade with 3 cups of sugar?

BTW
Make sure you always use the same multiplier for the entire ratio. When a value is fixed and does not change, it is called a constant.

First, let's make a chart to help us organize. Here's what we have so far:

	Ratio	Multiplier	Actual
Lemon juice	1		
Water	4		
Sugar	1/2		3 cups

Now, find the multiplier by using the row for sugar. What times ½ equals 3? Six. The multiplier is 6 and the multiplier will be 6 for each row. Now we can fill in the other amounts.

	Ratio	Multiplier	Actual
Lemon juice	1	6	6 cups
Water	4	6	24 cups
Sugar	1/2	6	3 cups

Laura needs 6 cups of lemon juice and 24 cups of water. Hope everyone is thirsty!

Rates

Rates also compare two quantities, but they specifically compare quantities with different units.

▶ Consider a family on a road trip that has driven a total of 315 miles over a period of 6 hours. This would be represented by a rate of $\dfrac{315 \text{ miles}}{6 \text{ hours}}$.

▶ As another example, suppose that every 3 acres of a field require 8 pounds of fertilizer. This could be represented by the rate $\dfrac{8 \text{ pounds}}{3 \text{ acres}}$.

A *unit rate* is a rate where the denominator is one. In everyday language, we use the word *per* to describe unit rates.

▶ If a family drives 315 miles in 6 hours, what is the unit rate in miles per hour?

$$\frac{315 \text{ miles}}{6 \text{ hours}} = \frac{\frac{1}{6} \times 315 \text{ miles}}{\frac{1}{6} \times 6 \text{ hours}} = \frac{52.5 \text{ miles}}{1 \text{ hour}}$$

▶ This means that the family traveled an average of 52.5 miles per hour.

▶ You may also be asked to find an approximate unit rate.

▶ If every 3 acres of a field requires 8 pounds of fertilizer, about how many pounds of fertilizer is required per acre?

$$\frac{8 \text{ pounds}}{3 \text{ acres}} = \frac{\frac{1}{3} \times 8 \text{ pounds}}{\frac{1}{3} \times 3 \text{ acres}} \approx \frac{2.67 \text{ pounds}}{1 \text{ acre}}$$

▶ This means that about (the wiggly equal sign means *approximately*) 2.67 pounds of fertilizer per acre are required.

IRL   Unit rate is very helpful in the grocery store. How do you know which is more expensive: 12 ounces of olive oil for $7.99 or 30 ounces of olive oil for $17.99? You can't compare them directly since they aren't the same size. Many stores now show the unit rate to help customers compare the prices of items of different amounts. You may see a listing on the shelf that shows the price per ounce: $0.67 per ounce for the 12-ounce bottle and $0.60 for the 30-ounce bottle. The unit rate lets you know that the 30-ounce bottle is a better deal.

Proportions

Proportions result from setting two ratios equal to each other and are common in many types of applied math problems and on the SAT. Let's start with a fairly simple problem that can be solved using a proportion. This problem is just like the lemonade example, but we will solve it a different way—with a proportion rather than a chart.

EXAMPLE

▶ A cookie recipe requires that the ratio of sugar to flour be 1:3. Suppose that this recipe is being used to make a large batch of cookies. If 4 pounds of flour are used, then how many pounds of sugar should be used?

▶ The ratio of the sugar to flour must be 1:3 or $\dfrac{1}{3}$. Since we don't know how many pounds of sugar will be used in the large batch, let this be represented by x. We can write the following proportion.

$$\frac{1}{3} = \frac{x}{4}$$

▶ Proportions like this can be solved using a method called *cross multiplication*.

$$\frac{1}{3} = \frac{x}{4}$$

$$1(4) = 3x$$

$$4 = 3x$$

$$\frac{4}{3} = x$$

$$1\frac{1}{3} = x$$

▶ Thus, $\frac{4}{3}$, or equivalently $1\frac{1}{3}$, pounds of sugar should be used.

 IRL Increasing and decreasing ratios is a useful skill. For example, we do this any time we double a recipe or cut a recipe in half.

Proportions are useful for increasing or decreasing all sorts of things. When architects or landscapers make scale models, they use proportions.

EXAMPLE

▶ A 1:800 scale model of a 1,250-foot-tall skyscraper is constructed. To the nearest tenth of an inch, what is the height of the scale model?

▶ Scale models are built so that their measurements follow a set ratio with the measurements of the original figure, building, or location. In the case of a 1:800 scale model, the ratio of the model size to the actual size is 1:800.

▶ If x is the height of the scale model, then we can write the following proportion.

$$\frac{1}{800} = \frac{x}{1{,}250}$$

▶ Solving for x:

$$\frac{1}{800} = \frac{x}{1,250}$$
$$800x = 1,250$$
$$x = \frac{1,250}{800} = \frac{25}{16}$$

▶ The height is therefore $\frac{25}{16} \approx 1.6$ feet. However, the problem asked for the height in inches. Since there are 12 inches in each foot, the height of the model is $\frac{25}{16} \times 12 = 18.75$ inches. To the nearest tenth of an inch, the model is 18.8 inches high.

More complicated problems can be solved by combining some of the skills you have seen so far.

EXAMPLE

▶ Suppose that the ratio of men to women in a group is 1:5. If there are 48 people in the group, then how many are women?

▶ Let x represent the number of men and y represent the number of women. Then we can write the following proportion.

$$\frac{1}{5} = \frac{x}{y}$$

▶ Cross multiplying, this is equivalent to $y = 5x$.

▶ We are also told that the total number of people is 48. This means that the sum $x + y = 48$. Substituting the equation above, $x + 5x = 48$ or $6x = 48$. Dividing, we get $x = 8$. Therefore, $y = 48 - 8 = 40$. There are 40 women in the group.

We can use proportions to help us solve geometry problems too.

▶ The two triangles in the figure below are similar. What is the value of x?

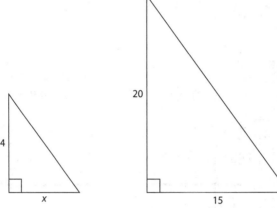

20

4

x

15

Note: Figure not drawn to scale.

▶ In geometry, when two figures are similar, the ratios of corresponding sides are equal. In this example, that means that the following equation is true:

$$\frac{4}{20} = \frac{x}{15}$$

▶ Solving for x by cross multiplying:

$$\frac{4}{20} = \frac{x}{15}$$
$$4(15) = 20x$$
$$60 = 20x$$
$$3 = x$$

▶ Thus, $x = 3$.

Percentages

A percentage, such as 76%, represents a part out of a whole. Specifically, it represents the part *per* 100. Percentages can be written either as fractions or as decimals and, just as with proportions, show up in many applied SAT problems.

Writing Percentages as Decimals and Fractions

Let's use the example of 76%. Since, by definition, any percentage means "part per 100," the percentage can be written as a fraction over 100. Thus, 76% is equivalent to $\frac{76}{100}$. In simplest terms, this would be $\frac{19}{25}$.

Dividing 76 by 100 will give the decimal equivalent. This can be done by simply moving the decimal point that is understood to be at the end of 76 to the left two places. Thus, as a decimal, 76% is written as 0.76.

EXAMPLE

▶ Write 1.2% as a simplified fraction and as a decimal.

▶ Moving the decimal place two places to the left, the equivalent decimal is 0.012.

▶ As a fraction, we can write $\frac{1.2}{100} = \frac{12}{1,000} = \frac{3}{250}$.

BTW

Important: To solve problems involving percentages, you may want to use either the decimal or fraction equivalent form.

Solving Problems with Percentages

Before we solve more complex problems with percentages, let's review how to find percentages in general. To find a certain percent of a number, you probably know to change the percentage to a decimal and then multiply it times the number.

▶ What is 22% of 418?

▶ As a decimal, 22% is 0.22. We will multiply to find the answer to this question.

$$0.22(418) = 91.96$$

▶ Thus, 22% of 418 is 91.96.

The key to solving that problem was recognizing that *of* means to multiply. Now let's see if we can use a similar technique to solve more complex problems.

▶ Suppose that 20% of a constant k is 16. What is the value of k?

▶ Using the idea that *of* means to multiply, we can write the following equation.

$$0.20k = 16$$

▶ Solving for k:

$$0.20k = 16$$
$$\frac{0.20k}{0.20} = \frac{16}{0.20}$$
$$k = 80$$

Sometimes a problem may ask you to increase or decrease a number by a percentage and then again by another percentage. You need to be careful when working problems like these. An increase of 10% and then another increase of 10% does not equal an increase of 20%.

▶ In each of the last two years, the value of a collectible has increased by 12%. If the original value was $50, then to the nearest cent, what is the current value?

▶ The first increase in value was 0.12(50) = $6. The value afterward was $50 + $6 = $56. Then the value increased by 12% again. This time, however, the starting value was $56. As 0.12(56) = $6.72, the value is currently $56 + $6.72 = $62.72.

In problems like this example in which you add a percentage to a total, you can always take the decimal equivalent of the percentage, place a 1 in front of it, and multiply.

▶ Suppose sales tax on an item that costs $6.59 is 8%. The price after tax can be found in two ways: (1) multiply $6.59 by 0.08 and add to the base price *or* (2) multiply $6.59 by 1.08. Either way, you will find that the price of the item with tax is $7.12.

The SAT also will ask *percent change* problems. The general formula for finding this percentage is $\dfrac{\text{increase or decrease}}{\text{original}}$ times 100. The increase or decrease is written as a positive number; that is, always subtract the lesser value from the greater value.

▶ Over the last week, the number of people enrolled in a workshop has increased from 10 to 45. By what percent has enrollment increased?

▶ For this example, the percentage by which the enrollment has increased is:

$$\frac{45 - 10}{10} = \frac{35}{10} = 3.5$$

▶ This is actually the decimal equivalent, so the percentage is $100(3.5) = 350\%$. This may seem like a strange result, but since 35 is larger than 10, it represents more than 100% of 10.

EXERCISES

EXERCISE 9–1

Solve the following ratio problems.

1. In a jar containing only red and green marbles, the ratio of red marbles to green marbles in the jar is 3:5. If there is a total of 16 marbles in the jar, then how many are red?

2. In a group of kittens, there are 2 white kittens and 3 tan kittens. What is the ratio of tan kittens to all kittens?

3. Bethesda Junior High School has 743 students. There are 431 students in seventh grade and the rest of the students are in the eighth grade. What is the ratio of seventh- to eighth-grade students?

4. Jim is making shortbread cookies. The recipe says to use 3 parts flour, 2 parts butter, and 1 part sugar. Jim has plenty of flour and sugar, but only 1 cup of butter. If he uses the entire cup of butter, how much sugar and flour will he need?

5. Two squares are drawn in the *xy*-plane such that the ratio of the side length of the larger square to the side length of the smaller square is 3:2. What is the ratio of the area of the smaller square to the area of the larger square?

EXERCISE 9–2

Solve the following rate problems.

1. At a contest, Bruce ate 11 hot dogs in 5 minutes. How long would it take him to eat 20 hot dogs at the same rate?

2. Suppose that the price of 4 pounds of sugar is $4.99 and that there are about 30 tablespoons in each pound of sugar. To the nearest cent, what is the cost of 5 tablespoons of sugar?

3. A particle travels along a curve in the xy-plane at the rate of 3 units each 18 minutes. How many minutes will it take for the particle to cover a total distance of 45 units?

4. Store A has a bag of 12 apples for $4. Store B has a bag of 20 apples for $9. What is the price per apple at the store that has the better deal?

5. Noah ran a 5-kilometer race in 23.3 minutes. Bella ran a 3-kilometer race in 17.6 minutes. What was the rate for the faster runner in minutes per kilometer?

EXERCISE 9–3

Solve the following proportion problems.

1. Landon needs to make 36 cupcakes. The recipe calls for 2 eggs and makes 24 cupcakes. How many eggs will Landon need to make 36 cupcakes?

2. If Molly lays bricks for 2 hours and uses 68 bricks, how many bricks will she use in 3 hours at the same speed?

3. If 6 inches is 15.24 centimeters, how many centimeters is 8 inches?

4. The triangles in the figure below are similar. Find the value of x.

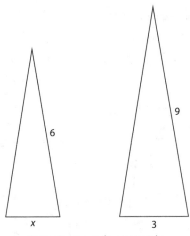

Note: Figure not drawn to scale.

5. A photo measures 4 inches wide and 6 inches long. Vicky is making a scrapbook and wants to increase the photo proportionally to make it 8 eight inches long and put a thin ribbon border around the outside edge. How many inches of ribbon will she need?

EXERCISE 9–4

1. Suppose that 5% of $x + 1$ is $\dfrac{2}{3}$. What is the value of x?

2. After a 5% sales tax is applied, the total for an online order is $15.88. To the nearest cent, what was the total before tax?

3. Last week Ryan ran a total of 21 miles, while this week he ran only 18 miles. By what percentage did his mileage decrease?

4. The value of an investment increases by 6% each year for 3 years. If the initial value is x, then write an expression that represents the value now, in terms of x.

5. If 42% of 180 is k, then what is the value of k?

Answers are on page 567.

10 Statistics

MUST ⚡ KNOW

⚡ The mean of a data set is calculated by adding up the values and then dividing that total by the number of values in the data set.

⚡ The mode of a data set is the most frequently occurring value in the data set.

⚡ The median of a data set is the middle value, or the average of the two middle values.

⚡ The range of a data set is the difference between the largest and smallest value in the set.

⚡ The standard deviation for a data set is a measure of how far from the mean the data is spread. A larger data spread means a larger standard deviation.

tatistics is used to understand data, or information with a context. Statistics is a huge topic and becoming more and more important as technology advances and our ability to collect data increases. Even so, on the SAT, you will only need to understand some of the basic ideas used in everyday data analysis and describing data sets. In this chapter, we will examine measures of center such as mean, median, and mode; measures of variation such as range and standard deviation; and mathematical modeling.

Measures of Center

A measure of center is a way of trying to describe the typical value in a data set. For example, when someone says that the average temperature in a city is about 55 degrees, she is trying to describe the typical value in the data set of temperatures for that city. There are three common ways to describe the center of a data set: mean, median, and mode.

Mean

The mean of a data set is the arithmetic average. This is found by adding all of the values in a data set and then dividing by the number of data values in the set.

$$m = \frac{\text{sum of values}}{\text{number of values}}$$

EXAMPLE

▶ The ages of a random sample of people at a restaurant are 18, 20, 21, 18, 26, 21, 30. What is the mean age of a person in this sample?

$$\text{mean} = \frac{18 + 20 + 21 + 18 + 26 + 21 + 30}{7} = \frac{154}{7} = 22$$

▶ The mean age is 22 years.

One weakness of the mean is that it may be misleading if a data set contains outliers (unusual values) or is skewed (tends to have a long "tail" on one end when graphed). Looking at the example above, 22 does a good job of describing the typical age of someone in that sample.

EXAMPLE

▶ Now suppose that instead, the sample ages were as follows:

18, 20, 21, 18, 26, 21, 85

▶ Comparing this to the original data set, only one value has changed, but the value is now a large outlier. Let's see how the mean changes.

$$\text{mean} = \frac{18 + 20 + 21 + 18 + 26 + 21 + 85}{7} = \frac{209}{7} \approx 29.9$$

▶ Looking at the sample, no one's age is close to 29.9 years. The outlier has "pulled" the mean higher and made it misrepresent the typical value.

A similar situation happens when you are working with *skewed* data sets. You can recognize these data sets in most plots as they will have a tail going off to the right or left.

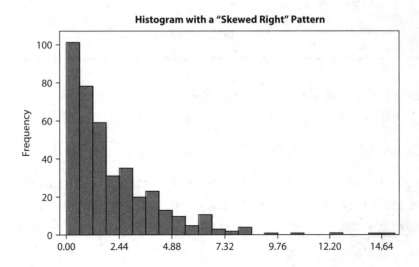

Histogram with a "Skewed Right" Pattern

The large values represented by the tail will "pull" the mean away from the majority of data, leading to a mean that is too great to represent the typical value well. Similarly, if there is a tail to the left, indicating the data is skewed left, then the mean will be pulled by the smaller values and be too small to represent the typical value well. For this reason, the mean is best used to represent data that is symmetric (no tails) and has no outliers.

Median

The median of a data set represents the middle value when the data set is placed in order. In the case of an odd number of data values, this is easy to calculate.

▶ Using the data from the first example in this chapter, find the median age of a person from the sample.

▶ The original sample of ages was 18, 20, 21, 18, 26, 21, 30.

▶ Placing these values in order from smallest to largest:

   18, 18, 20, 21, 21, 26, 30

▶ The middle value is 21; thus, the median age is 21 years.

Notice that if we change the data set by replacing 30 with a much larger outlier value such as 85, the median doesn't change.

   18, 18, 20, 21, 21, 26, 85

The middle value is still 21. A large outlier does not affect the median in the same way it affects the mean. For this reason, the median is a better measure of center in data sets with outliers or with skewed data sets.

When there is an even number of values, things are slightly more complicated (but luckily not by much!).

EXAMPLE

▶ In a different sample of people at the restaurant, the ages were 19, 17, 18, 24. What is the median age for this sample?

▶ Placing these values in order from least to greatest, we get

> 17, 18, 19, 24

▶ There is an even number of values in this data set, so there is no one value that is the middle value. In cases like this, you will use the average of the middle two values.

$$\text{median} = \frac{18 + 19}{2} = 18.5$$

▶ Thus, for this sample, the median age is 18.5 years.

Mode

The mode doesn't come up in many problems and it is a very simple idea, so we can keep our discussion short. For any data set, the mode represents the most commonly occurring value.

EXAMPLE

▶ For the data set { 1, 4, 3, 1, 5, 2, 4, 4}, what is the mode?

▶ All we have to do here is find the most frequently occurring value. The value 4 appears three times, which is more than any other value, so the mode is 4.

Using this definition, it is possible to have no mode if all the values are different. It is also possible to have more than one mode if there is more than one most frequently occurring value.

EXAMPLE

▶ Kim tracked her points per game for the 10 games she played during the basketball season. Her points per game are as follows:

Game 1	Game 2	Game 3	Game 4	Game 5	Game 6	Game 7	Game 8	Game 9	Game 10
7	6	9	7	8	24	7	6	5	6

▶ What is the mode of this data set?

▶ She scored 7 points three times, in games 1, 4, and 7. She also scored 6 points three times, in games 2, 8, and 10. No other value appears more than three times. That means this data set has two modes: 6 and 7. Notice that the outlier value of 24 would make the mean a poor indicator of center. Here, the mode is a better indicator.

IRL Mode can be a really helpful measure of center. If you wanted to find out about salaries at a local company and the boss makes $200,000 while the employees each make $40,000, then the outlier makes the mean pretty skewed. The mode is a much better indicator of the typical salary at that company.

Measures of Variation

Measures of variation are used to understand how different data values are from each other. The larger the difference, the more variable we say the data sets are. For example, the data set 1, 2, 1, 2, 1 has very low variability, while the data set 1, 15, 8, 26 is more variable.

Questions on the SAT will expect you to be familiar with two common ways of measuring variation: range and standard deviation.

Range

The range is the most simple way of measuring the variation of a data set. To find the range, you just subtract the least value in the data set from the greatest value. The idea is that the larger the range, the more variable the data set.

EXAMPLE

▶ Before buying a new computer, Vivian finds the price of a particular model from several different retailers. The prices she finds are as follows:

$399.99, $357.99, $419.99, $367.99

▶ What is the range for this set of data?

Range = $419.99 − $357.99 = $62

Standard Deviation

A more powerful method of determining variability is through the standard deviation. The calculation of the standard deviation can be complex, so typically technology is used to find this value. SAT problems will only expect you to understand the value's general meaning instead of having you find it.

For any data value, define the deviation as the difference between the data value and the mean for the data set. If the mean is 2 and the value is 5, the deviation is 3. The standard deviation can be loosely interpreted as the average deviation from the mean. If the mean of a data set is 10 and the standard deviation is 3, then on average, most values are about 3 away from the mean of 10. The larger the standard deviation, the more variability in the data set.

EXAMPLE

▶ Which of the following data plots has the larger standard deviation?

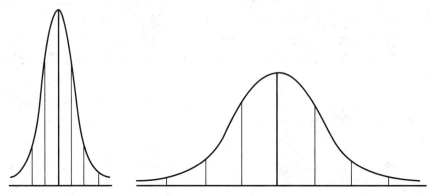

▶ The graph on the left has the data grouped much closer together. This means that the standard deviation is small. The graph on the right has the data much more spread out. This means that the standard deviation is larger than that of the graph of the left.

Like the mean, the standard deviation should really only be interpreted for data sets that are symmetric, meaning that the mean is very close to the median. You often see these data sets shown as a "bell curve," with the data on the left side of the mean closely resembling the data on the right. A given standard deviation loses its helpfulness when the data set is skewed in one way or another. In essence, the standard deviation is no longer "standard."

BTW

You should be careful about comparing standard deviations of two data sets when the means are different. A standard deviation of 2 when the mean is 100 is quite small and means most of the values are really close to the mean. A standard deviation of 2 when the mean is 8 is, of course, much greater relatively speaking.

Scatterplots and Mathematical Modeling Data

In everyday life, we often encounter two variables that "move" together. For instance, generally if people spend more time studying they tend to do better on exams. Patterns like this can be understood using scatterplots and then modeled using linear, exponential, quadratic, or other types of mathematical functions.

Scatterplots

Suppose that we collected data from a group of students, including how much time they had spent studying for a particular exam and their exam scores, with the goal of understanding whether more time spent studying generally leads to better exam scores. In this situation, we are letting studying time be the *predictor*, or independent variable (often denoted x), and the exam scores be the *response*, or dependent variable (often denoted y).

A scatterplot takes this data and plots each individual's studying time and exam score as a point (x, y).

EXAMPLE

▶ Let's use some example data and its corresponding scatterplot to see this.

Time Spent Studying (hours)	4	2	8	10	3	1	11	4	6	9	2	5
Exam Score (100-point scale)	72	70	91	94	71	72	95	68	80	89	78	70

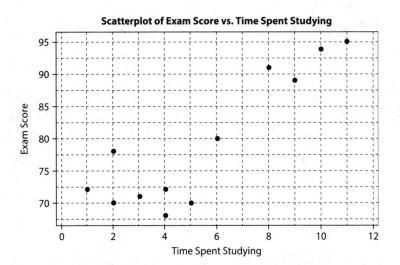

> As you look across from left to right, you see that generally the points rise. This indicates that as more time is spent studying, the exam scores do tend to be higher. Notice that this isn't a perfect pattern but a general pattern.

When reading a scatterplot like this, the idea is to look at the overall pattern. Further, we are looking for several common types of patterns.

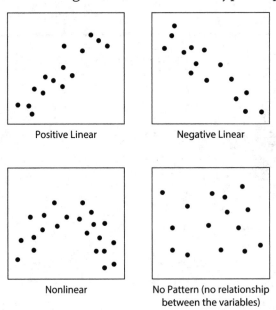

The data set we plotted above follows a positive linear pattern. This means that it can best be modeled with a linear function.

The previous figure shows only one possible type of nonlinear pattern. There are many, and in some cases they follow patterns similar to exponential or quadratic functions. If this is the case, then a function of that type can be used to model the relationship between the variables.

Lines and Curves of Best Fit

The line or curve used to model the relationship between two variables is commonly called the line or curve of best fit. This line or curve can be used for prediction or to better understand the relationship by interpreting the parameters (such as the slope of the line).

The scatterplot below shows the studying time and exam score data along with the line of best fit.

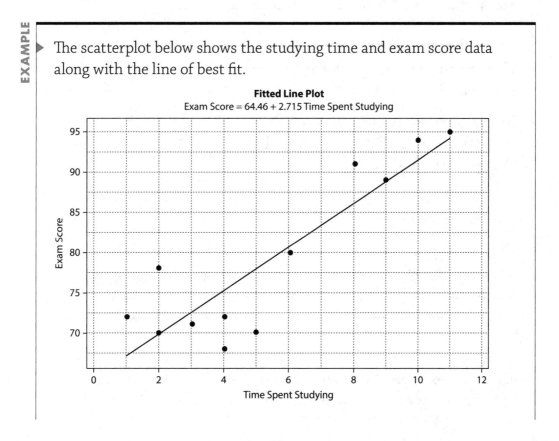

Fitted Line Plot
Exam Score = 64.46 + 2.715 Time Spent Studying

▶ The points represent the *observed* values from our sample, while the values along the line represent the *predicted* values. For example, using the line of best fit, the predicted score for someone who studied 5 hours is about a 77 or 78, as this is approximately the point at which the line is when time is 5 hours.

▶ However, we observed an individual who studied 5 hours and only scored a 70, which is much lower than the predicted value.

▶ At the top of the plot, we also have the equation for the line of best fit: Exam Score $= 64.46 + 2.715 \times$ Time. Using x for the time spent studying and y for the exam score, this is the line $y = 64.46 + 2.715x$.

You may also be asked about the slope of the line of best fit.

▶ Interpret the slope and y-intercept of the line of best fit in this situation.

▶ In general, the slope of any line is the change in y over the change in x. When the slope is written as a decimal, this can be thought of as the change in y for a one-unit increase in x.

▶ The slope 2.715 means that for each additional hour spent studying, the exam score increases by 2.715 points, on average.

▶ The y-intercept of any line represents the value of y when $x = 0$. Here, $x = 0$ means that someone did not study at all, so the y-intercept of 64.46 is the predicted exam score for someone who did not study.

Sometimes the interpretation of the y-intercept is not realistic to the situation. For example, if we were studying the time it takes runners to complete a 5k race as it relates to their age, a value of zero would represent a runner who is 0 years old. We have to pay attention to the real-life situation when we consider this type of interpretation!

For nonlinear models, you won't be asked to directly interpret the data as in the example above, but you may be asked to compare predicted (values on the curve) with observed values (points) or provide a prediction using the formula for the curve of best fit. You might also be asked to determine which type of function is the best fit.

EXAMPLE

▶ The relationship between two variables is being studied. Two models have been suggested, as shown in the plots below. Which model appears to better fit the data?

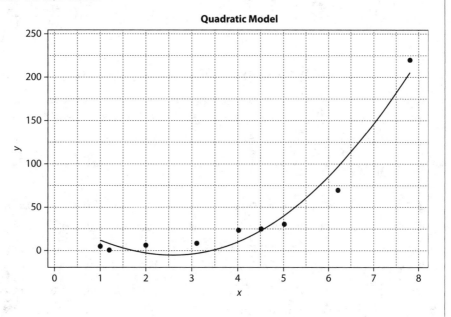

Quadratic Model

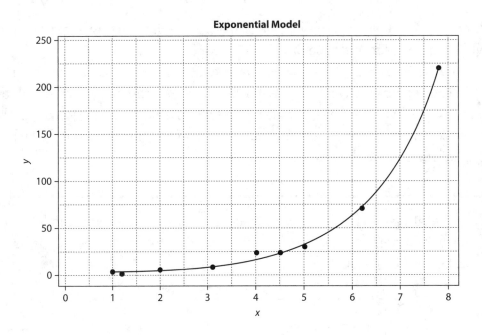

▶ The quadratic model seems to first underestimate values and then overestimate values, while the exponential model seems to be a very good fit, with observed values being very close to the predicted values. Therefore, the exponential model is the better fit.

You can also recognize when an exponential model may be the best to represent a data set because of the rapid and increasing growth of *y* values as *x* values increase. Linear growth is steady and based on the slope. A one-unit increase in *x* will always result in a fixed increase in *y*. With exponential growth, the change in *y* is moderate at first but increasing. In the plot above, for example, when *x* increases from 2 to 3, there is not much of a change in the value of *y*. When *x* increases from 7 to 8, there is a very large change in the value of *y*.

Understanding Populations

In statistics, the idea of taking a sample is so that the larger population can be understood. For this reason, it is important that a sample truly represents the given population. A small number of SAT questions may have you relate sample data or information to the population by determining if sample data applies or using the concept of *margin of error*.

EXAMPLE

▶ A random sample of 340 high school students found that 8% owned their own vehicle. Suppose that the margin of error on this estimate is 2%. Is it reasonably possible that the true percentage of high school students who own their own vehicle is 15%? Explain.

▶ Adding and subtracting the margin of error from the sample estimate gives you a range of possible values for the population percentage. This means that it is reasonable to say that the true percentage is somewhere between 6% and 10%. Therefore, it is unlikely that 15% of all high school students own their own car.

The smaller the margin of error, the better we can estimate the true value. Using a larger sample size is a common way to reduce the margin of error.

When it comes to applying ideas like this to a population, always consider the sample. Samples should be randomly selected from the population so that they best represent it. For example, if we wanted to understand the mean GPA of high school students, it wouldn't make sense to sample only honors students. This would likely cause our estimate to be too high compared to the average of the true population.

EXERCISES

EXERCISE 10–1

1. Find the mean, median, and mode of the data set below.

   64, 61, 60, 58, 50, 52, 54, 60

2. The mean of 1, 5, 10, and x is 5.5. What is the value of x?

3. The average weight of four people is 175 pounds. If one of the people weighs 190 pounds, what is the average weight of the other three people?

   Use the data set below for question 4.

   {15, 9, 23, 8, 42, 6, 35, 8}

4. What would need to be added to the data set to raise the average to 19?

5. If a set of numbers consists of all the prime integers between 10 and 20, what is the median of the set?

EXERCISE 10–2

1. Consider the data set described by the table below.

Range	Number of Values
Less than 100	5
Greater than 100 but less than 200	18
Greater than 200	35

   Within what range is the median value of this data set?

2. The values in a data set can be represented by k, $k + 2$, $k - 3$, and $k + 4$, for a positive constant k. What is the range of this data set?

3. Two classes take the same math test. In the first class, the mean score was 75 with a standard deviation of 8.4, whereas in the second class, the mean was 74 with a standard deviation of 9.7. For which class were the scores more variable? Assume the scores were generally symmetric with no outliers.

EXERCISE 10–3

Use the information below to answer the following questions.

A random sample of people living in two-bedroom condominiums were asked to provide information about their monthly natural gas bill (in dollars). A portion of this data is plotted against the mean high temperature (in degrees F) for the month billed. This is shown below.

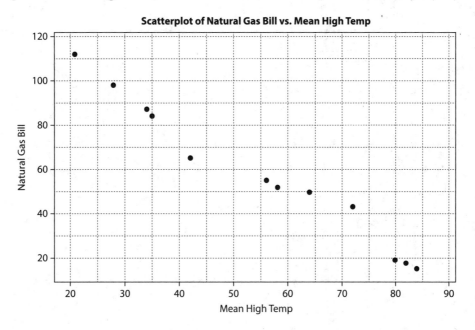

1. Approximately what was the lowest mean high temperature observed in the sample data?

2. Describe the general pattern shown in the scatterplot. What happens as the mean high temperature increases?

3. One month had a mean average high temperature of 80 degrees. What was the bill that corresponded with this value in the sample?

4. How many bills in the sample were less than $20?

5. Explain why the sample only included two-bedroom condominiums. What might be the problem if the data also included larger homes?

EXERCISE 10–4

Use the following information for exercises 1 and 2.

After the discovery of mineral deposits nearby, the population of a town has increased rapidly. The plot below shows the population over the last five years, along with the curve of best fit.

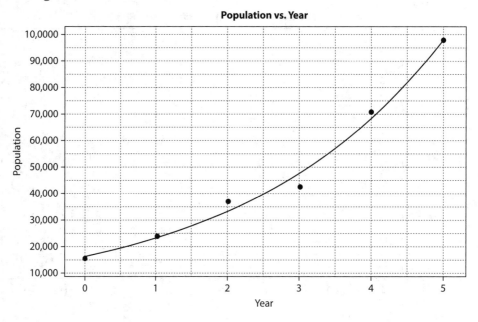

1. For how many observed values does the model's predicted population underestimate the actual population?

2. What is the approximate difference between the predicted population and the observed population in year 3?

Use the following information for exercises 3–5.

Based on a sample of hotel employees, it is found that the total amount received in tips and the total number of customers checking in during an employee's shift have a positive linear relationship, which is best modeled by the equation $y = 2.512x + 0.864$.

3. Interpret the slope of this model in terms of the situation.

4. Interpret the y-intercept of this model in terms of the situation. Does it make sense? Why or why not?

5. Predict the total tips an employee will earn if a total of 5 new customers check in during his shift.

EXERCISE 10–5

1. When 75 people were surveyed about their choice of candidate for the upcoming election, 57% chose candidate A. If the margin of error in the survey is 0.8%, which of the following could be the number of people who chose candidate A?

   A. 38
   B. 40
   C. 42
   D. 44

2. Scientists estimate the population of snow leopards to be 6,000 at a 95% confidence interval with a 6% margin of error. What is the range of the actual population of snow leopards?

Answers are on page 569.

11 Additional Topics

MUST KNOW

 The sum of the interior angles of any triangle is always 180°, and any exterior angle of a triangle is equal to the sum of the opposite interior angles.

 The Pythagorean theorem is $a^2 + b^2 = c^2$, where c is the hypotenuse and a and b are the other two sides of a right triangle.

 We can use the phrase SohCahToa to remember the trigonometric ratios. Sine is opposite over hypotenuse; cosine is adjacent over hypotenuse; and tangent is opposite over adjacent.

 An arc of a circle is a fraction of the circumference, and a sector is a fraction of the area.

 We can find the general equation for a circle by multiplying out the equation as it is written in standard form and then moving all quantities to one side of the equation.

 Any complex number can be written as $a + bi$, where a and b are real numbers and i is the imaginary number $\sqrt{(-1)}$.

handful of questions on the SAT come from what are called "additional topics in mathematics." As you will see, many of these topics come from courses like geometry or trigonometry.

Triangles

There are many possible topics to study when it comes to different types of triangles and related theorems. However, on the SAT, you will only need to know a handful of basic properties, which are reviewed below.

Interior and Exterior Angles

The interior angles of a triangle are those that are formed by the intersection of the edges. In the figure below, the interior angles have measures $x°$, $y°$, and $z°$.

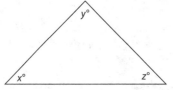

The sum of the interior angles of any triangle is always $180°$.

EXAMPLE

▶ The measures of the interior angles of a triangle are $(2x)°$, $45°$, and $80°$. What is the value of x?

$$2x + 45 + 80 = 180$$
$$2x + 125 = 180$$
$$2x = 55$$
$$x = 27.5$$

An exterior angle is formed when one of the sides of the triangle is extended. In the figure below, an exterior angle is labeled x.

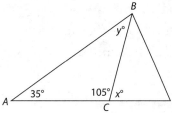

Note: Figure not drawn to scale.

The measure of an exterior angle is always equal to the sum of the two opposite interior angles. Here, the measure of the angle labeled x is equal to $35° + y°$.

EXAMPLE

▶ Find the value of x in the figure below.

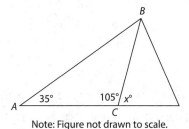

Note: Figure not drawn to scale.

▶ First, let's find the measure of the missing angle in triangle ABC.

$$180° − (35° + 105°) = 40°$$

▶ The angle with measure $x°$ is an exterior angle to triangle ABC. Thus,

$$x = 35 + 40 = 75.$$

BTW

In this example, you may have noticed that the 105° angle and angle x form a line. You know that a line is 180°, so you can also find the measure of angle x by subtracting 180° − 105° = 75°.

Right Triangles

Some properties hold only for right triangles, or those that contain a right angle (an angle measuring 90°). You can recognize a right triangle by the small square marking the right angle.

The Pythagorean Theorem

For any right triangle, the side opposite the right angle is called the hypotenuse, while the other sides are called legs. The hypotenuse is the longest side. Below, the length of the hypotenuse is labeled c.

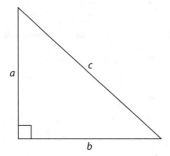

The Pythagorean theorem shows the relationship between the lengths of the legs and the hypotenuse. Note that this applies only to right triangles.

For a right triangle with legs of length a and b and a hypotenuse of length c, $a^2 + b^2 = c^2$.

EXAMPLE

▶ The legs of a right triangle have lengths 7 and x units. If the hypotenuse is 9 units long, then find the value of x.

▶ Using the Pythagorean theorem:

$$7^2 + x^2 = 9^2$$
$$49 + x^2 = 81$$
$$x^2 = 32$$
$$x = \sqrt{32} = 4\sqrt{2}$$

BTW

You may have noticed in that example that the negative square root was not included as a possible value of x. Since lengths must be positive, this solution to the equation is ignored and we keep only the positive value.

Trigonometric Ratios

Given an angle of a right triangle, we can define quantities known as trigonometric ratios. These are based on a pair of lengths of either the hypotenuse, the side opposite the angle (opp), or the side adjacent to the angle (adj).

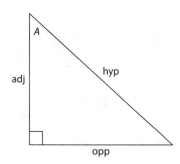

$$\sin A = \frac{\text{opp}}{\text{hyp}} \quad \cos A = \frac{\text{adj}}{\text{hyp}}$$

$$\tan A = \frac{\text{opp}}{\text{adj}} \quad \cot A = \frac{\text{adj}}{\text{opp}}$$

$$\sec A = \frac{\text{hyp}}{\text{adj}} \quad \csc A = \frac{\text{hyp}}{\text{opp}}$$

These may seem like a lot to remember, but there are some tricks to help! First, memorize the phrase SohCahToa. This helps you remember that sine is opp over hyp; cosine is adj over hyp; and tangent is opp over adj.

From there, the following properties hold:

$$\cot A = \frac{1}{\tan A}$$

$$\sec A = \frac{1}{\cos A}$$

$$\csc A = \frac{1}{\sin A}$$

Let's try it out.

EXAMPLE

▶ For angle α below, find the value of each of the trigonometric ratios.

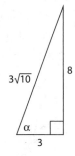

$$\sin\alpha = \frac{\text{opp}}{\text{hyp}} = \frac{8}{3\sqrt{10}} \qquad \cos\alpha = \frac{\text{adj}}{\text{hyp}} = \frac{3}{3\sqrt{10}} = \frac{1}{\sqrt{10}}$$

$$\tan\alpha = \frac{\text{opp}}{\text{adj}} = \frac{8}{3} \qquad \cot\alpha = \frac{\text{adj}}{\text{opp}} = \frac{3}{8}$$

$$\sec\alpha = \frac{\text{hyp}}{\text{adj}} = \frac{3\sqrt{10}}{3} = \sqrt{10} \qquad \csc\alpha = \frac{\text{hyp}}{\text{opp}} = \frac{3\sqrt{10}}{8}$$

General Angles

The definition of the trigonometric ratios can be extended to include angles of any measure in the *xy*-plane. While these angles can be measured in degrees, they are commonly measured in a unit called a radian.

Radians

In advanced mathematics, a common way to measure angles is using radians. Angles can be converted from degrees to radians or from radians to degrees using the ratio $\frac{\pi \text{ rad}}{180°}$.

▶ Convert 52° to radians.

▶ The ratio given above is a conversion factor. This means that it can be used as is or flipped depending on which unit you wish to cancel. In this case, we want to cancel out degrees and be left with radians. That means we should use the form $\dfrac{\pi \text{ rad}}{180°}$.

$$52\cancel{°} \times \left(\frac{\pi \text{ rad}}{180\cancel{°}}\right) = \frac{52\pi}{180} \text{ rad} = \frac{13\pi}{45} \text{ rad}$$

▶ Thus, 52° is equivalent to $\dfrac{13\pi}{45}$ rad.

Now let's convert from radians to degrees.

▶ Convert $\dfrac{5\pi}{4}$ radians to degrees.

▶ This time we want to cancel out radians, so use $\dfrac{180°}{\pi \text{ rad}}$.

$$\frac{5\cancel{\pi}}{4} \cancel{\text{ rad}} \times \left(\frac{180°}{\cancel{\pi} \cancel{\text{ rad}}}\right) = \frac{5 \times 180°}{4} = 225°$$

▶ Thus, $\dfrac{5\pi}{4}$ radians is equivalent to 225°.

Some common angles and their corresponding measures in radians are shown in the table below.

30°	45°	60°	90°	180°	270°	360°
$\dfrac{\pi}{6}$	$\dfrac{\pi}{4}$	$\dfrac{\pi}{3}$	$\dfrac{\pi}{2}$	π	$\dfrac{3\pi}{2}$	2π

It is also useful to know the values of sine, cosine, and tangent for these common angles. These are shown below.

Angle A	Sin A	Cos A	Tan A
$\dfrac{\pi}{6}$	$\dfrac{1}{2}$	$\dfrac{\sqrt{3}}{2}$	$\dfrac{\sqrt{3}}{3}$
$\dfrac{\pi}{4}$	$\dfrac{\sqrt{2}}{2}$	$\dfrac{\sqrt{2}}{2}$	1
$\dfrac{\pi}{3}$	$\dfrac{\sqrt{3}}{2}$	$\dfrac{1}{2}$	$\sqrt{3}$
$\dfrac{\pi}{2}$	1	0	Undefined
π	0	−1	0
$\dfrac{3\pi}{2}$	−1	0	Undefined
2π	0	1	0

If you carefully inspect this table, you will notice an interesting property. For sine and cosine, if two angles A and B are complementary, that is if they add to $\dfrac{\pi}{2}$ rad (or 90°), then the value of $\sin A = \cos B$. This property can also be written as

$$\sin A = \cos\left(\frac{\pi}{2} - A\right)$$
$$\cos A = \sin\left(\frac{\pi}{2} - A\right)$$

EXAMPLE

▶ For an angle β, suppose that $\sin\beta = x + \dfrac{1}{8}$ and $\cos\left(\dfrac{\pi}{2} - \beta\right) = 2x$. What is the value of x?

▶ Using the properties above, it must be that $x + \dfrac{1}{8} = 2x$. Solving for x:

$$x + \frac{1}{8} = 2x$$

$$\frac{1}{8} = x$$

General Angles and Properties of the Trigonometric Functions

In the xy-plane, a *standard* angle is one where the vertex is at the origin and one ray is along the positive x-axis. The angle is formed by moving the other ray counterclockwise, as shown below.

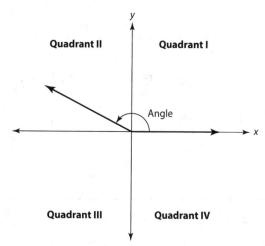

In the picture you can also see the name given to each segment of the xy-plane. The sign of a trigonometric ratio of a given general angle depends on its location. A common way to remember these signs is using the saying "All Students Take Calculus."

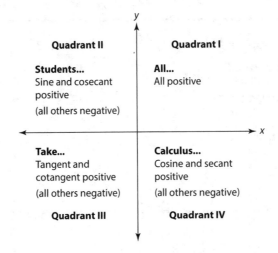

▶ An angle α lies in the xy-plane such that $\dfrac{\pi}{2} < \alpha < \pi$. What is the sign of $\cos\left(\dfrac{\alpha}{3}\right)$?

▶ The angle is in the second quadrant since $\dfrac{\pi}{2} < \alpha < \pi$. Further, if $\dfrac{\pi}{2} < \alpha < \pi$, then $\dfrac{1}{3} \times \dfrac{\pi}{2} < \dfrac{\alpha}{3} < \dfrac{1}{3} \times \pi$. Simplified, that gives the inequality $\dfrac{\pi}{6} < \dfrac{\alpha}{3} < \dfrac{\pi}{3}$. This means that $\dfrac{\alpha}{3}$ is in the first quadrant, so $\cos\left(\dfrac{\alpha}{3}\right)$ is positive.

Circle Theorems

As with triangles, there are a variety of theorems that apply to different properties of circles. In this section, we will review those that are most important to your success on the SAT.

Central Angles and Arc Length

Given a circle centered at the point O, a central angle is formed by the point O and two radii.

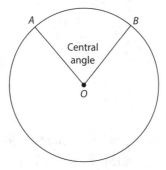

The portion of the circumference between points A and B is called an arc. More specifically, it is the arc intercepted by the central angle. This is often denoted AB. Arcs can be measured by degrees or using units of length. If measured in degrees, the measure of the arc is the same as the measure of the central angle that intercepts it. In the figure below, $m\overset{\frown}{AB} = 80°$.

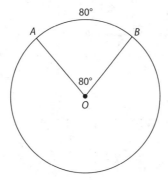

The length of the arc can be found using the following formula:

$$\text{arc length} = \frac{\text{arc measure}}{360°} \times \text{circumference}$$

▶ Find the length of $\overset{\frown}{AB}$ in the figure below.

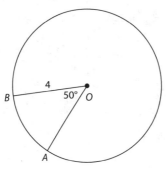

▶ Recall that the arc measure is the same as the measure of the central angle. Further, using the radius of 4, we know that the circumference is $2\pi(4) = 8\pi$. Now, using the formula:

$$\text{arc length} = \frac{\text{arc measure}}{360°} \times \text{circumference}$$

$$= \frac{50°}{360°} \times 8\pi$$

$$= \frac{10}{9}\pi$$

Inscribed Angles

Angles formed by points along a circle's circumference are called *inscribed angles*.

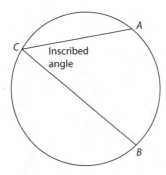

One interesting property of inscribed angles is when you have two different inscribed angles with the same endpoints, as shown below.

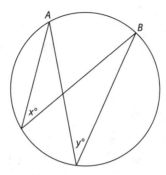

Since the two angles with measures $x°$ and $y°$ have the same endpoints, it must be true that $x = y$. This is true for any inscribed angles that share endpoints.

EXAMPLE

▶ Using the figure above, suppose that $y = 3z - 20$ and $x = 35$. What is the value of z?

▶ Since it must be true that $x = y$, we can write $y = 35$. Using the fact that $y = 3z - 20$:

$$35 = 3z - 20$$
$$55 = 3z$$
$$\frac{55}{3} = z$$

A second property is that the measure of an inscribed angle with endpoints A and B is half the measure of the central angle that intercepts the arc $\overset{\frown}{AB}$.

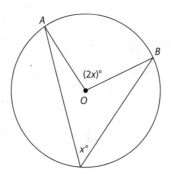

EXAMPLE

▶ Suppose that, for a given circle, $m\overset{\frown}{AB} = (2x + 1)°$ and an inscribed angle with endpoints A and B has measure $(4x)°$. Find the value of x.

▶ Using the property stated above, $2x + 1 = 2(4x)$. Solving for x:

$$2x + 1 = 8x$$
$$1 = 6x$$
$$\frac{1}{6} = x$$

Area of a Sector

Area formulas, like the area of a circle ($A = \pi r^2$) are provided on the SAT. However, you might be asked more advanced questions, like the area of a sector or section of a circle. Sectors are formed by central angles and the arcs they intersect.

BTW

Circle problems are usually done in degrees, so if you are using your calculator to help you on a circle problem, be sure that your calculator is set to degrees rather than radians.

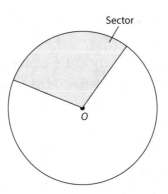

Sector

The area of a sector depends on the central angle that forms it and is found using the formula $A_{\text{sector}} = \dfrac{\text{central angle measure}}{360} \cdot \pi r^2$. Note that the central angle here is measured in degrees.

EXAMPLE

▶ Find the area of a sector of a circle with radius 3 formed by a central angle of 45°.

▶ Using the formula:

$$A_{\text{sector}} = \frac{\text{central angle measure}}{360} \cdot \pi r^2$$

$$= \frac{45}{360} \pi (3)^2$$

$$= \frac{9}{8} \pi \approx 3.53 \text{ square units}$$

▶ The final answer can be expressed either as an exact value $\left(\dfrac{9}{8}\pi\right)$ or a decimal approximation (3.53) and will be in square units since this represents an area.

Circles in the Plane

We have studied how lines in the xy-plane are defined by equations of the form $y = mx + b$ and how $y = ax^2 + bx + c$ defines the graph of a parabola. Similarly, equations for circles in the plane are defined by certain types of equations. In this section, we will see the two forms of the equation of a circle and how to convert between them.

Standard Form of the Equation of a Circle

The equation $(x - h)^2 + (y - k)^2 = r^2$ defines a circle in the xy-plane centered at the point (h, k) with a radius of r. This is known as the *standard form* of an equation of a circle.

EXAMPLE

▶ What are the center and the radius of a circle defined by the equation $(x + 1)^2 + (y - 1)^2 = 9$?

▶ This equation is in standard form, so we can "read" the coordinates needed for the center. Be careful, though: In the first set of parentheses, the 1 is added instead of subtracted. The center is at (h, k) when written as $(x - h)^2 + (y - k)^2 = r^2$, where the numbers are subtracted from x and y.

▶ We can rewrite our equation as $(x - (-1))^2 + (y - 1)^2 = 9$ to see that the center is at $(-1, 1)$.

▶ The number on the right is 9, which is r^2, so $r = \sqrt{9} = 3$. (We only take the positive square root since this is a radius.)

▶ Thus, the circle has a radius of 3 and is centered at the point $(-1, 1)$.

What if the equation you are given does not appear to be in standard form? Check it carefully, because it may just be disguised!

EXAMPLE

▶ What are the center and the radius of a circle defined by the equation $x^2 + y^2 = 8$?

▶ This doesn't quite look like standard form, but it is! This equation can be thought of as:

$$(x - 0)^2 + (y - 0)^2 = 8$$

▶ The center is at the point $(0, 0)$ and the radius is $\sqrt{8} = 2\sqrt{2}$.

General Form of the Equation of a Circle

A second form of the equation of a circle is called the *general form*. This is found by multiplying out the equation as it is written in standard form and then moving all quantities to one side of the equation.

EXAMPLE

▶ A circle in the xy-plane is defined by the equation $(x+1)^2 + (y-1)^2 = 9$. Find the general form of the equation to represent this circle.

▶ Remember to use FOIL when squaring $(x+1)$ and $(y-1)$.

$$(x+1)^2 + (y-1)^2 = 9$$
$$(x+1)(x+1) + (y-1)(y-1) = 9$$
$$x^2 + 2x + 1 + y^2 - 2y + 1 = 9$$
$$x^2 + 2x + y^2 - 2y + 2 = 9$$
$$x^2 + 2x + y^2 - 2y - 7 = 0$$
$$x^2 + y^2 + 2x - 2y - 7 = 0$$

▶ The general form of the equation for this circle is $x^2 + y^2 + 2x - 2y - 7 = 0$.

Going from the general form back to the standard form requires a little more algebra and a series of steps called *completing the square*. This process is shown in the example below.

EXAMPLE

▶ Find the radius of the circle defined by the equation $x^2 + y^2 + 4x - 6y - 3 = 0$.

▶ To find the radius, we will need to write the equation in standard form using the process of completing the square.

▶ First, we will group all the x and y terms and move the constant to the other side of the equation.

$$x^2 + y^2 + 4x - 6y - 3 = 0$$
$$(x^2 + 4x) + (y^2 - 6y) = 3$$

▶ The next step is the tricky one! Here, we will take half of the coefficient of x, square it, and add it to both sides. Then, we will do the same thing with the coefficient of y.

▶ The coefficient of x is 4, so for that we will be adding $\left(\dfrac{4}{2}\right)^2 = 2^2 = 4$ to both sides.

▶ The coefficient of y is -6. For this we will add $\left(\dfrac{-6}{2}\right)^2 = (-3)^2 = 9$ to both sides.

$$(x^2 + 4x + 4) + (y^2 - 6y + 9) = 3 + 4 + 9$$

▶ Notice that we added them within the parentheses on the left. Each of these polynomials inside the parentheses can now be factored.

$$(x^2 + 4x + 4) + (y^2 - 6y + 9) = 3 + 4 + 9$$
$$(x^2 + 4x + 4) + (y^2 - 6y + 9) = 16$$
$$(x + 2)^2 + (y - 3)^2 = 16$$

▶ After factoring, we ended up with the standard form of the equation: $(x + 2)^2 + (y - 3)^2 = 16$. Now we can use this to answer the question.

▶ The radius of the circle is $\sqrt{16} = 4$.

We can use the same process to find the center of a circle.

▶ Find the center of the circle defined by the equation $x^2 + y^2 - 2x - 8y + 15 = 0$.

▶ Again, we will need to write this equation in standard form. Using the same steps as in the last example:

$$x^2 + y^2 - 2x - 8y + 15 = 0$$
$$(x^2 - 2x) + (y^2 - 8y) = -15$$
$$(x^2 - 2x + 1) + (y^2 - 8y + 16) = -15 + 1 + 16$$
$$(x - 1)^2 + (y - 4)^2 = 2$$

▶ Now that the equation is in standard form, we see that the center of the circle is at the point (1, 4).

Complex Numbers

The set of numbers we work with every day with counting and measurements is called real numbers. Another set of numbers, called *complex numbers*, is based on the imaginary unit i, which is defined to be $\sqrt{-1}$. Any complex number can be written as $a + bi$, where a and b are real numbers. When written like this, a is called the real part and bi is called the imaginary part.

Addition and Subtraction

Adding and subtracting complex numbers is very similar to adding and subtracting polynomials. It is all about collecting like terms.

▶ Find the sum.

$$(2 + 4i) + (-3 + i)$$

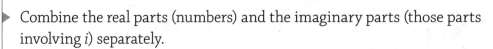

▶ Combine the real parts (numbers) and the imaginary parts (those parts involving i) separately.

$$(2 + 4i) + (-3 + i) = 2 - 3 + 4i + i$$
$$= -1 + 5i$$

We can use the same process to find difference between two complex numbers, but we must remember to distribute the negative sign first.

EXAMPLE

▶ Find the difference.

$$(2 - i) - (6 + 4i)$$

▶ Apply the same technique, but remember to distribute the negative first!

$$(2 - i) - (6 + 4i) = 2 - i - 6 - 4i$$
$$= 2 - 6 - i - 4i$$
$$= -4 - 5i$$

It is possible to add or subtract two complex numbers and end up with just a real number. For example, the sum of $(1 + i)$ and $(1 - i)$ is 2. Don't let an answer like this make you question whether you are correct!

Multiplication and Division

Remember that the imaginary unit i is defined as $\sqrt{-1}$. This means that $i^2 = (\sqrt{-1})^2 = -1$. This fact is used quite a bit when it comes to multiplying complex numbers.

EXAMPLE

▶ Find the product.

$$(3i)(-2i)$$

▶ Since each of these complex numbers consists only of an imaginary part (one term each), you can multiply as usual. Just keep in mind that $i^2 = -1$.

$$(3i)(-2i) = -6i^2$$
$$= -6(-1)$$
$$= 6$$

When complex numbers have two terms, we need to apply FOIL.

EXAMPLE

▶ Find the product.

$$(-1 + 4i)(6 + i) = -1(6) + (-1)(i) + (4i)(6) + (4i)(i)$$
$$= -6 - i + 24i + 4i^2$$
$$= -6 - i + 24i + 4(-1)$$
$$= -6 + 23i - 4$$
$$= -10 + 23i$$

Division of complex numbers is a bit more complex, so we use something called the *complex conjugate* to help us. For any complex number $a + bi$, we can define the *conjugate* as $a - bi$. That is, it is the same as the original with only the sign in the middle changing. Division of complex numbers is done by multiplying both the numerator and denominator by the conjugate.

IRL You might think that unless you are a mathematician, you'll never use this knowledge about complex numbers, but many careers involve working with imaginary and complex numbers. Electrical engineers, software developers, economists, statisticians, and physicists all use them!

▶ Divide.

$$(-2+i) \div (1+i)$$

▶ First, we will write the division as a fraction. Then we will multiply the numerator and the denominator by the conjugate of the denominator.

$$\frac{-2+i}{1+i}\left(\frac{1-i}{1-i}\right)$$

▶ From here, we will apply FOIL and simplify.

$$\frac{-2+i}{1+i}\left(\frac{1-i}{1-i}\right) = \frac{-2+2i+i-i^2}{1-i^2}$$

$$= \frac{-2+2i+i-(-1)}{1-(-1)}$$

$$= \frac{-1+3i}{2}$$

$$= -\frac{1}{2}+\frac{3}{2}i$$

Notice that we write the final answer in the form $a + bi$.

EXERCISES

EXERCISE 11–1

1. The interior angles of a triangle have measures $(x + y)°$, $(4y)°$, and $(3x)°$. If $y = 20$, then what is the value of x?

2. Suppose that the sum of two interior angles of a triangle is 108°. The remaining angle has a measure of $(2x - k)°$. What is the value of x in terms of k?

3. For a triangle ABC, the measure of the largest angle is twice the measure of the next largest, while the measure of the smallest angle is one-third the measure of the largest. To the nearest tenth of a degree, what are the measures of the interior angles of this triangle?

Use the following figure for exercises 4 and 5.

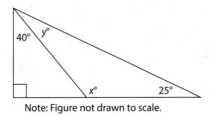

Note: Figure not drawn to scale.

4. What is the value of x?

5. What is the value of y?

EXERCISE 11–2

1. If the legs of a right triangle have lengths 2 and 5, what is the length of the hypotenuse?

2. The legs of a right triangle have lengths x and 3, while the hypotenuse has length 9. What is the value of x?

3. Suppose that the legs of a right triangle have lengths m and n. If the hypotenuse has length 10, find the value of m in terms of n.

4. For the angle x below, find the value of all six trigonometric ratios.

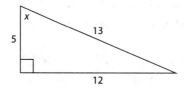

5. In the figure below, $\sin B = \dfrac{3}{5}$. What is the value of $\cos B$?

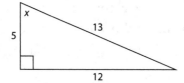

EXERCISE 11–3

1. Convert $320°$ to radians.

2. Convert $\dfrac{\pi}{12}$ rad to degrees.

3. What value of x makes the statement below true?

$$\cos\left(\frac{2\pi}{9}\right) = \sin x$$

4. Given an angle β in the xy-plane where $\dfrac{3\pi}{2} < \beta < 2\pi$, what is the sign of $\tan\left(\dfrac{\beta}{2}\right)$?

5. For an angle A, $\sin A > 0$, but $\cos A < 0$. What values of x and y make the statement $x < A < y$ true?

EXERCISE 11–4

Use the following figure for exercises 1–5. Note that the radius of this circle is 4 units.

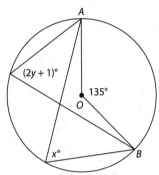

Note: Figure not drawn to scale.

1. Find the length of the minor arc $\overarc{AB}$.

2. Find the area of the sector formed by the central angle 135°.

3. Find the value of x.

4. Find the value of y.

5. Write an expression that shows the value of y in terms of x.

EXERCISE 11–5

1. Find the center and radius of the circle defined by the equation $(x-5)^2 + (y-2)^2 = 18$.

2. Find the center and radius of the circle defined by the equation $x^2 + (y+3)^2 = 10$.

3. Write the equation $(x-2)^2 + (y-4)^2 = 6$ in general form.

4. Find the center and radius of the circle defined by the equation $x^2 + 2x + y^2 + 10y + 18 = 0$.

5. Find the center and radius of the circle defined by the equation $x^2 - 4x + y^2 - 2y + 4 = 0$.

EXERCISE 11–6

Find the sum or difference.

1. $(3 + 2i) + (-1 + 4i)$

2. $(1 - i) + (1 - 3i)$

3. $(4 + 2i) - (3 + 2i)$

4. $(-2 + 5i) - (-1 + 2i)$

5. $(3 + i) - (3 - 6i)$

Divide or multiply, as indicated.

6. $(-2 + i)(-2 - i)$

7. $(4 - 4i)(2 + 6i)$

8. $(6 + 3i) \div (1 - 2i)$

9. $(-3 - i) \div (-1 - i)$

10. $(2 + 2i) \div (-4 + 2i)$

Answers are on page 570.

SAT PRACTICE TESTS

How to Use the Practice Tests

The following practice tests mimic the real exam closely in structure and difficulty. Taking the tests will help you find out where your strengths and weaknesses lie. To get the most out of these tests and the review material in this book, follow this procedure:

1. Take the first practice test before you start reading the review sections in this book.

2. Take the first test in test-like conditions. Find a quiet place, like the library, and make sure you stick to the time limits for each section. Use a watch or timer to alert you when your time is up. Complete the test in one sitting, and mark your answers on the test page. It may be that you do not finish. Note how many questions you did not answer. This will help you design a course of study.

3. Remember: Answer *every* question, even if you do not even have time to read the question. There is no guessing penalty on the revised SAT, so you have nothing to lose by guessing. Your chances of a correct guess are better, of course, if you can eliminate one or two answer options that you know are incorrect.

4. Check your answers and make note of any pattern in your performance. Did you ace the writing section but struggle with analyzing texts? Were the geometry questions easy for you, but polynomials hard?

5. Write down all the areas in which you think you need to improve. Speed? Specific topics? This list will show you where you need to focus most when working through the review chapters in this book.

6. After you finish working through the review sections in this book, take the second test—again under timed, test-like conditions. Check your answers and analyze your performance. You will have improved, but go back and review topics as necessary.

7. This is explicitly written on the actual SAT, but it is worth remembering: When you finish each section of the SAT on test day, you may *not* continue to the next section until you are told to do so. The word "STOP" is at the end of each section in big, bold letters to remind you. So when you are practicing, try following the same procedure. Set a timer. If you finish early, don't just move on. Ask yourself how you would use the extra time on the real day of the test. You should obviously go back and make sure all the questions are answered, using some of the time to wrestle with problems you think you might actually be able to answer instead of just guess on. You should *not* second-guess yourself. Resist at all costs the urge to go back and start reviewing questions you answered confidently the first time. You run the risk of undoing the good work you already accomplished.

The number of questions and time limit for each practice test are given in the chart below:

Practice Test	Number of Questions	Time Limit
Reading	52	65 minutes
Writing	44	35 minutes
Math	58 total: 38 in the Calculator portion and 20 in the No Calculator portion	80 minutes: 55 for the Calculator portion and 25 for the No Calculator portion

Please note: Scores on the SAT range from 200 to 800 for Math and for Evidence-Based Reading and Writing, meaning the lowest score you can get is a 400 and the highest is a 1600. These are scaled scores, meaning they don't reflect a set number of right and wrong answers because each version of the test is different. The test makers try to make each test have the same difficulty level, but this is not possible in practice. So scoring is fair, raw scores (just the number of correct answers) are converted into a standardized score. That way, you aren't penalized if you happen to get a harder version of the test than someone who took it a few months before you. What this means for our practice tests, however, is that we cannot give you a way to convert your raw score into a scaled score. You will have to base your analysis of your performance on your raw score.

SAT Practice Test 1

Practice Test Answer Sheet

Reading Test

1. Ⓐ Ⓑ Ⓒ Ⓓ   14. Ⓐ Ⓑ Ⓒ Ⓓ   27. Ⓐ Ⓑ Ⓒ Ⓓ   40. Ⓐ Ⓑ Ⓒ Ⓓ
2. Ⓐ Ⓑ Ⓒ Ⓓ   15. Ⓐ Ⓑ Ⓒ Ⓓ   28. Ⓐ Ⓑ Ⓒ Ⓓ   41. Ⓐ Ⓑ Ⓒ Ⓓ
3. Ⓐ Ⓑ Ⓒ Ⓓ   16. Ⓐ Ⓑ Ⓒ Ⓓ   29. Ⓐ Ⓑ Ⓒ Ⓓ   42. Ⓐ Ⓑ Ⓒ Ⓓ
4. Ⓐ Ⓑ Ⓒ Ⓓ   17. Ⓐ Ⓑ Ⓒ Ⓓ   30. Ⓐ Ⓑ Ⓒ Ⓓ   43. Ⓐ Ⓑ Ⓒ Ⓓ
5. Ⓐ Ⓑ Ⓒ Ⓓ   18. Ⓐ Ⓑ Ⓒ Ⓓ   31. Ⓐ Ⓑ Ⓒ Ⓓ   44. Ⓐ Ⓑ Ⓒ Ⓓ
6. Ⓐ Ⓑ Ⓒ Ⓓ   19. Ⓐ Ⓑ Ⓒ Ⓓ   32. Ⓐ Ⓑ Ⓒ Ⓓ   45. Ⓐ Ⓑ Ⓒ Ⓓ
7. Ⓐ Ⓑ Ⓒ Ⓓ   20. Ⓐ Ⓑ Ⓒ Ⓓ   33. Ⓐ Ⓑ Ⓒ Ⓓ   46. Ⓐ Ⓑ Ⓒ Ⓓ
8. Ⓐ Ⓑ Ⓒ Ⓓ   21. Ⓐ Ⓑ Ⓒ Ⓓ   34. Ⓐ Ⓑ Ⓒ Ⓓ   47. Ⓐ Ⓑ Ⓒ Ⓓ
9. Ⓐ Ⓑ Ⓒ Ⓓ   22. Ⓐ Ⓑ Ⓒ Ⓓ   35. Ⓐ Ⓑ Ⓒ Ⓓ   48. Ⓐ Ⓑ Ⓒ Ⓓ
10. Ⓐ Ⓑ Ⓒ Ⓓ   23. Ⓐ Ⓑ Ⓒ Ⓓ   36. Ⓐ Ⓑ Ⓒ Ⓓ   49. Ⓐ Ⓑ Ⓒ Ⓓ
11. Ⓐ Ⓑ Ⓒ Ⓓ   24. Ⓐ Ⓑ Ⓒ Ⓓ   37. Ⓐ Ⓑ Ⓒ Ⓓ   50. Ⓐ Ⓑ Ⓒ Ⓓ
12. Ⓐ Ⓑ Ⓒ Ⓓ   25. Ⓐ Ⓑ Ⓒ Ⓓ   38. Ⓐ Ⓑ Ⓒ Ⓓ   51. Ⓐ Ⓑ Ⓒ Ⓓ
13. Ⓐ Ⓑ Ⓒ Ⓓ   26. Ⓐ Ⓑ Ⓒ Ⓓ   39. Ⓐ Ⓑ Ⓒ Ⓓ   52. Ⓐ Ⓑ Ⓒ Ⓓ

Writing and Language Test

1. Ⓐ Ⓑ Ⓒ Ⓓ   12. Ⓐ Ⓑ Ⓒ Ⓓ   23. Ⓐ Ⓑ Ⓒ Ⓓ   34. Ⓐ Ⓑ Ⓒ Ⓓ
2. Ⓐ Ⓑ Ⓒ Ⓓ   13. Ⓐ Ⓑ Ⓒ Ⓓ   24. Ⓐ Ⓑ Ⓒ Ⓓ   35. Ⓐ Ⓑ Ⓒ Ⓓ
3. Ⓐ Ⓑ Ⓒ Ⓓ   14. Ⓐ Ⓑ Ⓒ Ⓓ   25. Ⓐ Ⓑ Ⓒ Ⓓ   36. Ⓐ Ⓑ Ⓒ Ⓓ
4. Ⓐ Ⓑ Ⓒ Ⓓ   15. Ⓐ Ⓑ Ⓒ Ⓓ   26. Ⓐ Ⓑ Ⓒ Ⓓ   37. Ⓐ Ⓑ Ⓒ Ⓓ
5. Ⓐ Ⓑ Ⓒ Ⓓ   16. Ⓐ Ⓑ Ⓒ Ⓓ   27. Ⓐ Ⓑ Ⓒ Ⓓ   38. Ⓐ Ⓑ Ⓒ Ⓓ
6. Ⓐ Ⓑ Ⓒ Ⓓ   17. Ⓐ Ⓑ Ⓒ Ⓓ   28. Ⓐ Ⓑ Ⓒ Ⓓ   39. Ⓐ Ⓑ Ⓒ Ⓓ
7. Ⓐ Ⓑ Ⓒ Ⓓ   18. Ⓐ Ⓑ Ⓒ Ⓓ   29. Ⓐ Ⓑ Ⓒ Ⓓ   40. Ⓐ Ⓑ Ⓒ Ⓓ
8. Ⓐ Ⓑ Ⓒ Ⓓ   19. Ⓐ Ⓑ Ⓒ Ⓓ   30. Ⓐ Ⓑ Ⓒ Ⓓ   41. Ⓐ Ⓑ Ⓒ Ⓓ
9. Ⓐ Ⓑ Ⓒ Ⓓ   20. Ⓐ Ⓑ Ⓒ Ⓓ   31. Ⓐ Ⓑ Ⓒ Ⓓ   42. Ⓐ Ⓑ Ⓒ Ⓓ
10. Ⓐ Ⓑ Ⓒ Ⓓ   21. Ⓐ Ⓑ Ⓒ Ⓓ   32. Ⓐ Ⓑ Ⓒ Ⓓ   43. Ⓐ Ⓑ Ⓒ Ⓓ
11. Ⓐ Ⓑ Ⓒ Ⓓ   22. Ⓐ Ⓑ Ⓒ Ⓓ   33. Ⓐ Ⓑ Ⓒ Ⓓ   44. Ⓐ Ⓑ Ⓒ Ⓓ

Math Test—No Calculator

1. Ⓐ Ⓑ Ⓒ Ⓓ   5. Ⓐ Ⓑ Ⓒ Ⓓ   9. Ⓐ Ⓑ Ⓒ Ⓓ   13. Ⓐ Ⓑ Ⓒ Ⓓ
2. Ⓐ Ⓑ Ⓒ Ⓓ   6. Ⓐ Ⓑ Ⓒ Ⓓ   10. Ⓐ Ⓑ Ⓒ Ⓓ   14. Ⓐ Ⓑ Ⓒ Ⓓ
3. Ⓐ Ⓑ Ⓒ Ⓓ   7. Ⓐ Ⓑ Ⓒ Ⓓ   11. Ⓐ Ⓑ Ⓒ Ⓓ   15. Ⓐ Ⓑ Ⓒ Ⓓ
4. Ⓐ Ⓑ Ⓒ Ⓓ   8. Ⓐ Ⓑ Ⓒ Ⓓ   12. Ⓐ Ⓑ Ⓒ Ⓓ

16.
17.
18.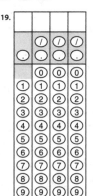
19.
20.

Math Test—Calculator

1. Ⓐ Ⓑ Ⓒ Ⓓ
2. Ⓐ Ⓑ Ⓒ Ⓓ
3. Ⓐ Ⓑ Ⓒ Ⓓ
4. Ⓐ Ⓑ Ⓒ Ⓓ
5. Ⓐ Ⓑ Ⓒ Ⓓ
6. Ⓐ Ⓑ Ⓒ Ⓓ
7. Ⓐ Ⓑ Ⓒ Ⓓ
8. Ⓐ Ⓑ Ⓒ Ⓓ

9. Ⓐ Ⓑ Ⓒ Ⓓ
10. Ⓐ Ⓑ Ⓒ Ⓓ
11. Ⓐ Ⓑ Ⓒ Ⓓ
12. Ⓐ Ⓑ Ⓒ Ⓓ
13. Ⓐ Ⓑ Ⓒ Ⓓ
14. Ⓐ Ⓑ Ⓒ Ⓓ
15. Ⓐ Ⓑ Ⓒ Ⓓ
16. Ⓐ Ⓑ Ⓒ Ⓓ

17. Ⓐ Ⓑ Ⓒ Ⓓ
18. Ⓐ Ⓑ Ⓒ Ⓓ
19. Ⓐ Ⓑ Ⓒ Ⓓ
20. Ⓐ Ⓑ Ⓒ Ⓓ
21. Ⓐ Ⓑ Ⓒ Ⓓ
22. Ⓐ Ⓑ Ⓒ Ⓓ
23. Ⓐ Ⓑ Ⓒ Ⓓ

24. Ⓐ Ⓑ Ⓒ Ⓓ
25. Ⓐ Ⓑ Ⓒ Ⓓ
26. Ⓐ Ⓑ Ⓒ Ⓓ
27. Ⓐ Ⓑ Ⓒ Ⓓ
28. Ⓐ Ⓑ Ⓒ Ⓓ
29. Ⓐ Ⓑ Ⓒ Ⓓ
30. Ⓐ Ⓑ Ⓒ Ⓓ

31.
32.
33.
34.
35.
36.
37.
38.

Reading Test

Directions: Below you will see either a passage or pair of passages. After the passage or passages there will be several questions. After you read each passage or pair of passages, please select the option that best answers each question based on anything stated or implied in the passages or the graphics that accompany them.

Questions 1–10 are based on the following passage.

This passage is adapted from Jack London's *The Call of the Wild*, originally published in 1903. Buck is a dog and John Thornton is his owner.

One night Buck sprang from sleep with a start, eager-eyed, nostrils quivering and scenting, his mane bristling in recurrent waves. From the forest came the call (or one note of it, for the call was many noted), distinct and definite as never before,—a long-drawn howl, like, yet
5 unlike, any noise made by a husky dog. And he knew it, in the old familiar way, as a sound heard before. He sprang through the sleeping camp and in swift silence dashed through the woods. As he drew closer to the cry he went more slowly, with caution in every movement, till he came to an open place among the trees, and looking out saw, erect on
10 haunches, with nose pointed to the sky, a long, lean, timber wolf.
Buck did not attack, but circled him about and hedged him in with friendly advances. The wolf was suspicious and afraid; for Buck made three of him in weight, while his head barely reached Buck's shoulder. Watching his chance, he darted away. Time and again he was cornered,
15 and the thing repeated, though he was in poor condition, or Buck could not so easily have overtaken him. He would run till Buck's head was even with his flank, when he would whirl around at bay, only to dash away again at the first opportunity.
But in the end Buck's pertinacity was rewarded; for the wolf, finding
20 that no harm was intended, finally sniffed noses with him. Then they

became friendly, and played about in the nervous, half-coy way with which fierce beasts belie their fierceness. After some time of this the wolf started off at an easy lope in a manner that plainly showed he was going somewhere. He made it clear to Buck that he was to come, and
25 they ran side by side through the somber twilight, straight up the creek bed, into the gorge from which it issued, and across the bleak divide where it took its rise.

On the opposite slope of the watershed they came down into a level country where were great stretches of forest and many streams, and
30 through these great stretches they ran steadily, hour after hour, the sun rising higher and the day growing warmer. Buck was wildly glad. He knew he was at last answering the call, running by the side of his wood brother toward the place from where the call surely came. Old memories were coming upon him fast, and he was stirring to them as
35 of old he stirred to the realities of which they were the shadows. He had done this thing before, somewhere in that other and dimly remembered world, and he was doing it again, now, running free in the open, the unpacked earth underfoot, the wide sky overhead.

They stopped by a running stream to drink, and, stopping, Buck
40 remembered John Thornton. He sat down. The wolf started on toward the place from where the call surely came, then returned to him, sniffing noses and making actions as though to encourage him. But Buck turned about and started slowly on the back track. For the better part of an hour the wild brother ran by his side, whining softly. Then
45 he sat down, pointed his nose upward, and howled. It was a mournful howl, and as Buck held steadily on his way he heard it grow faint and fainter until it was lost in the distance.

John Thornton was eating dinner when Buck dashed into camp and sprang upon him in a frenzy of affection, overturning him, scrambling
50 upon him, licking his face, biting his hand—"playing the general tom-fool," as John Thornton characterized it, the while he shook Buck back and forth and cursed him lovingly.

For two days and nights Buck never left camp, never let Thornton
out of his sight. He followed him about at his work, watched him
55 while he ate, saw him into his blankets at night and out of them in the
morning. But after two days the call in the forest began to sound more
imperiously than ever. Buck's restlessness came back on him, and he
was haunted by recollections of the wild brother, and of the smiling
land beyond the divide and the run side by side through the wide forest
60 stretches. Once again he took to wandering in the woods, but the wild
brother came no more; and though he listened through long vigils, the
mournful howl was never raised.

1. The main goal of the passage is

   A. to advocate how much dogs really love their owners.
   B. to convey a dog's dilemma between his inherent wildness and the
      love for his owner.
   C. to anthropomorphize a dog, showing that humans really have an
      inherent wildness.
   D. to explore the relationship of brothers through the eyes of a dog.

2. Which choice provides the best evidence for the answer to the
    preceding question?

   A. lines 11–12 ("Buck…advances")
   B. lines 48–52 ("John…lovingly")
   C. lines 53–57 ("For…ever")
   D. lines 60–62 ("Once…raised")

3. As used in line 19, *pertinacity* most nearly means

   A. persistence.
   B. courage.
   C. brashness.
   D. cleverness.

4. The author's use of the phrase "smiling land" in lines 58–59 is primarily meant to

   A. describe the curved shape that the land makes between mountains.
   B. describe the sunniness of the land beyond the forest.
   C. echo the feelings of happiness Buck had while running in the forest.
   D. indicate a mock smile as the "call" out to the wilderness taunts Buck.

5. The passage strongly suggests that "the call" that Buck answers is actually

   A. the need to run off his restless energy.
   B. the pull of the wild animal nature within him.
   C. the strong ties that a dog feels for its owner.
   D. the pained whelp of a wounded wolf.

6. Which choice provides the best evidence for the answer to the preceding question?

   A. lines 7–10 ("As...wolf")
   B. lines 14–16 ("Time...him")
   C. lines 31–33 ("Buck...came")
   D. lines 39–40 ("They...down")

7. As used in line 57, *imperiously* most nearly means

   A. dimly.
   B. annoyingly.
   C. mysteriously.
   D. urgently.

8. Which comparison of a dog and a wolf is supported by the passage?

   A. The timber wolf is much larger and fiercer than the average dog.
   B. A dog shares similar behavioral traits with the wolf, when it comes to showing aggression and friendliness.
   C. Though the timber wolf and the dog share the same genus, a dog is as physically different from a wolf as a domesticated cat is from a tiger.
   D. Wolves run at a much faster pace than dogs.

9. The author includes a quote from John Thornton describing Buck's frenzy in returning to camp as "playing the general tom-fool" primarily to

   A. anthropomorphize the dog as a being that understands language.
   B. underscore the description of Buck's frenzy from multiple perspectives.
   C. portray the affection that Thornton reflects back to his dog.
   D. juxtapose Thornton's words with the wolf's howl.

10. Which of the following describes what Buck desires most as evidenced by the final sentence of the passage, "Once again . . ."?

    A. A sense of belonging among wild creatures
    B. The joy of running freely in the woods
    C. To know if his "wild brother" survived his trip
    D. The wandering and the waiting rather than the actual journey

Questions 11–21 are based on the following passage.

This passage is adapted from the Environmental Health Perspective's article from April 2015: "Warming Trend: How Climate Shapes Vibrio Ecology."

Victims can contract cholera by drinking contaminated water, a fact famously demonstrated by Dr. John Snow during an 1854–1855 epidemic in London. With the rise of sewage treatment and water purification plants during the twentieth century, cholera epidemics
5   vanished from the developed world. But outbreaks continue in places where safe drinking water is unavailable, or when disaster overwhelms sanitation systems.

V. cholerae thrive in a commensal relationship with copepods, tiny planktonic crustaceans that drift with the tides and serve as the
10   bacterium's normal host organism. Rita Colwell of the University of Maryland first demonstrated this relationship in the early 1980s. She and her colleagues created monoclonal antibodies specific for *V. cholerae* that were tagged with a fluorescent molecule. Under the microscope, the

copepods lit up, their bodies outlined in bright dots that signaled the
15 presence of hitchhiking vibrios.

Colwell and many other researchers have delved into the world of
V. cholerae, discovering its ability to latch onto the chitin in the
exoskeletons of copepods, to survive for long periods in a dormant state
when copepod populations plummet, and to use chemical signals to
20 communicate and cooperate while infecting a human gut.

Researchers are tracking environmental factors that influence the
abundance of copepods. Satellite data on chlorophyll concentrations
in the Bay of Bengal revealed that cholera outbreaks in Kolkata, India,
and Matlab, Bangladesh—coastal communities where the disease is
25 endemic—were preceded by phytoplankton blooms. Given
V. cholerae's intimate relationship with copepods, this makes sense.
A phytoplankton bloom means more food for copepods and other
zooplankton; thus, as their copepod hosts become abundant, so do
vibrios.

30 In Bangladesh there are two predictable peaks of infection. The first
comes during March and April, a dry time, when the three major rivers
that feed the Bengal Delta—the Ganges, the Brahmaputra, and the
Meghna—have low flow conditions. This spring outbreak strikes only
within 200–300 kilometers of the coast, where bay water from the
35 Bengal Delta pushes upstream, carrying abundant zooplankton and
V. cholerae into ponds used by local people for domestic water.

The second cholera peak occurs in autumn, generally in September or
October, after monsoon rains have boosted river flows. The river waters
rush downstream, loaded with nutrients that fuel phytoplankton
40 blooms. As plankton-rich waters flood the delta, many people are
exposed to high concentrations of vibrio bacteria. (A colonized copepod
may carry up to 10,000 vibrios.)

In an effort to prevent cholera infections, Colwell and her colleagues
taught women in Matlab to filter untreated household water through a
45 folded cloth before using it. An old sari folded into four layers creates a
mesh fine enough to capture copepods and particulates, removing 99%

of the attached cholera bacteria in the process. Colwell documented that the local incidence of cholera in Matlab dropped by 48% over a three-year study period, and follow-up five years later showed the villagers
50   continued to use this simple technique.

Since the 1960s, Earth's oceans have absorbed an estimated 90% of the excess heat generated by anthropogenic greenhouse gas emissions. Sea surface temperatures are rising, with significant impacts on phytoplankton populations. Phytoplankton abundance has declined in
55   the tropics in recent decades as water temperatures increase—and less phytoplankton should mean fewer copepods and fewer *V. cholerae*, says Shafiqul Islam of Tufts University. But that shift may be countered by a trend toward more extreme drought in dry seasons and heavier rains during the monsoon, as predicted by the Intergovernmental Panel on
60   Climate Change. "If drought and rainfall become more extreme, cholera will also intensify," Islam says.

11. What is the main purpose of the first paragraph of the passage?

   A. To demonstrate that the causes of cholera are simple and well understood
   B. To credit the original scientist who discovered cholera
   C. To highlight the severity of the issue of cholera today
   D. To introduce the need for present-day cholera research

12. As used in line 8, *commensal* most nearly means

   A. emerging.
   B. proportional.
   C. symbiotic.
   D. competitive.

13. The main rhetorical effect of the description of the final sentence of paragraph 2 ("Under the microscope . . .") is to

   A. provide a vivid visual image to counterbalance scientific jargon.
   B. emphasize the importance of light in microscopic experiments.

C. use metaphor to portray the intensity of the scientific finding.
D. downplay the seriousness of the outbreak in the Bengal Delta.

14. Which advantageous characteristic most helps *V. cholerae* survive when copepod populations are in decline?

   A. The ability to go into a dormant state for long periods of time
   B. The ability to latch onto chitin found in the exoskeletons of many crustaceans
   C. The ability to develop antibodies that exhibit efflorescence
   D. The ability to use chemical signals for communication

15. Which choice provides the best evidence for the answer to the preceding question?

   A. lines 8–10 ("*V. cholerae*...organism")
   B. lines 11–13 ("She...molecule")
   C. lines 16–20 ("Colwell...gut")
   D. lines 21–25 ("Researchers...blooms")

16. As used in line 25, *endemic* most nearly means

   A. widespread.
   B. native.
   C. severe.
   D. exotic.

17. Which of the following best characterizes the relationship between the prevalence of *V. cholerae* in the Bengal Delta and global climate change?

   A. Global climate change creates hotter temperatures in which *V. cholerae* is more likely to flourish in the Bengal Delta.
   B. Runoff from melting polar icecaps causes an increase in flooding in the Bengal Delta, allowing *V. cholerae* to flourish in local drinking water.
   C. Phytoplankton blooms have declined with increasing ocean temperatures caused by global climate change, leading to fewer copepods and a containment of *V. cholerae* outbreaks in the Bengal Delta.

D. Global climate change creates more extreme weather patterns, leading to more intense drought and monsoon seasons in the Bengal Delta, which in turn leads to more intense outbreaks of *V. cholerae*.

18. Which choice provides the best evidence for the answer to the preceding question?

    A. lines 21–25 ("Researchers...blooms")
    B. lines 40–41 ("As...bacteria")
    C. lines 54–57 ("Phytoplankton...University")
    D. lines 57–61 ("But...intensify")

19. Based on the passage, which choice best describes the relationship between Colwell's and Islam's work?

    A. Colwell's research predicts Islam's conclusions.
    B. Colwell's research builds on Islam's conclusions.
    C. Islam's work builds on Colwell's findings.
    D. Islam's work contradicts Colwell's findings.

20. Which choice is the best hypothesis of Colwell's "experiment" in Matlab described in paragraph 7?

    A. If people drink water infested with copepods, they will contract cholera.
    B. If people learn to use a simple filtration system, cholera infection will be prevented.
    C. If copepods are removed from drinking water, it will still contain trace amounts of *V. cholerae*.
    D. If women are the primary water gatherers for a household, they should be taught how to treat household water.

21. What is the most lasting measure of success of Colwell's "experiment" discussed in the preceding question?

    A. The filtration system removes 99 percent of copepod-attached cholera bacteria in water.

B. Over the three-year study, incidence of cholera in Matlab dropped by 48 percent.
C. A five-year follow-up showed that the simple technique for filtration was still in use.
D. The creation of monoclonal antibodies specific for *V. cholerae* were tagged with a fluorescent molecule.

Questions 22–31 are based on the following passage.

This passage is adapted from an article by the National Park Service titled "Bull River Prehistoric Upland Hunting Site."

With more than 6 million acres of unspoiled wilderness, Denali's landscapes encompass an untold wealth of archaeological sites that have remained intact, largely because they are protected from such disturbances as development. In 2006, the park initiated a four-year
5 survey to learn more about known and potential archaeological sites in Denali. Brian Wygal, then an archaeology graduate student at the University of Nevada, Reno, was hired as an archaeologist to conduct the survey. During the 2007 field season, Wygal and several field assistants made an important discovery in a remote upland setting at a
10 site named Bull River.

Using meticulous excavation techniques, the field team unearthed stone tools. Once discarded at the site by prehistoric hunters, over time these artifacts were buried as fine silts and soils accumulated. The site—with its artifacts and their context—was preserved for millennia.
15 Now the artifacts were again being held by human hands.

Among the artifacts discarded thousands of years ago at the Bull River site were fragments of stone spear points used for hunting upland wild game, a scraping tool, and flint-knapped debitage. The stone artifacts recovered so far indicate that prehistoric people were
20 mining river cobbles and crafting tools from them. Because of the alpine setting, Wygal speculates that the prehistoric activities took

place during the late summer or early fall and were likely part of a wider seasonal subsistence strategy. Alongside the tool fragments and debitage, the field crew found charcoal—possibly remnants of a small
25 campfire. Before collecting the artifacts and charcoal, the archaeologists documented and mapped each find. Like forensic investigators, archaeologists rely on the precise mapping of trace evidence to infer and reconstruct past human activities.

To estimate the age of organic remains from archaeological sites (e.g.,
30 charcoal, wooden tools, bones), archaeologists often use radiocarbon dating. The carbon (C) in a woody branch, for example, used as ancient firewood began to decay radioactively when the plant died—at most a few years before the branch was burned in a campfire. Thus, the technique of radiocarbon dating fragments of charcoal provides a reliable age estimate
35 for the charcoal and, by inference, estimates (1) the age of artifacts found in close proximity to the charcoal, and (2) the time period when prehistoric peoples may have used the site.

At the Bull River site, archaeologists quickly wrapped exposed charcoal fragments in aluminum foil, sealed them in an artifact bag,
40 and carefully documented the precise location of discovery. Four charcoal fragments were radiocarbon dated to between 12,180 and 12,460 years ago. This charcoal is compelling evidence to suggest that prehistoric hunters inhabited the uplands of Denali at the very end of the last Ice Age, a time of drastic global warming and environmental
45 change.

Why are these finds important? Worldwide, archaeologists continue to seek and accumulate physical evidence associated with the prehistoric peoples who successfully migrated and inhabited "new" continents during the last Ice Age. Perhaps the most contentious
50 debate surrounds the nature and timing of the initial peopling of the Americas.

Denali is located in the eastern part of Beringia, the extensive land "bridge" that once linked Alaska with eastern Siberia. During the end of the last Ice Age, rapid melting of massive glacial ice sheets in the

55 Northern Hemisphere released a substantial volume of fresh water into the oceans, causing sea level to rise. As a result, the Bering Land Bridge disappeared—flooded beneath the present-day Bering and Chukchi Seas—but not before a variety of plants, animals (e.g., woolly mammoth), and Paleolithic hunters had migrated across Beringia into Alaska.

60   Learning about the tools and travels of the ancient people of Beringia is essential to testing hypotheses about how humans colonized the Americas. Consequently, Alaska and Siberia (the eastern and western remnants of Beringia) are the focus of intense scientific inquiry. Alaska has emerged as an essential landscape in understanding this chapter in

65 human prehistory, primarily because the Bering Land Bridge was one of the most likely migration routes for the earliest Americans.

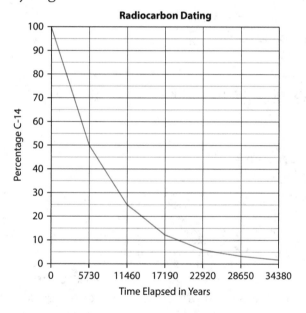

22. As used in line 49, *contentious* most nearly means

    A. overflowing.
    B. satisfying.
    C. contained.
    D. controversial.

23. Over the course of the passage, the main focus of the discussion shifts from

    A. the findings of an archaeological site to the issue of global warming.
    B. the findings of an archaeological site to the dangerous conditions of the Ice Age.
    C. the findings of an archaeological site to its implications for the settlement of the American continent.
    D. the findings of an archaeological site to its importance as a bridge between continents.

24. As used in line 18, *debitage* most nearly means

    A. debris.
    B. deficits.
    C. metal sculpting tools.
    D. charcoal.

25. The artifacts found at the Bull River site were most likely used by early people for

    A. mining.
    B. tracking seasons.
    C. crafting.
    D. hunting.

26. The passage strongly suggests that the importance of the archaeological find at Bull River is that

    A. it demonstrates the effects on a population undergoing global climate change, which affects and will continue to affect our society presently.
    B. it helps provide more evidence about the nature and timing of the settlement of the American continent.
    C. objects once held by prehistoric people can once again be held by modern archaeologists.
    D. it promotes the necessity of keeping land as natural wilderness, unspoiled by modern society's developments and cities.

27. Which choice provides the best evidence for the answer to the preceding question?

   A. lines 1–4 ("With...development")
   B. line 15 ("Now...hands")
   C. lines 42–45 ("This...change")
   D. lines 46–51 ("Worldwide...Americas")

28. Based on the passage, which choice best explains the use of the charcoal for radiocarbon dating and its relationship to the stone artifacts found at Bull River?

   A. The carbon 14 contained in the stone artifacts contains the same percentage of carbon 14 as the charcoal.
   B. Prehistoric people most likely used the stone artifacts for cooking, and the charcoal was from wood for a fire.
   C. The charcoal was found near the artifacts and is most likely from the same time period as the artifacts.
   D. The charcoal was most likely from a fire that prehistoric people used to make the tools.

29. Which choice provides the best evidence for the answer to the preceding question?

   A. lines 26–28 ("Like...activities")
   B. lines 31–33 ("The...campfire")
   C. lines 33–37 ("Thus...site")
   D. lines 38–42 ("At...ago")

30. Using the chart, and the information in the passage, which of the following is the closest percentage of carbon 14 found in the artifacts at Bull River?

   A. 7
   B. 23
   C. 29
   D. 57

31. Which claim about carbon dating is supported by the graph?

    A. The smaller the percentage of carbon 14 that an artifact contains, the less precisely we can pinpoint its age.
    B. Certain organisms can absorb the carbon 14 of their surroundings, appearing older than they actually are.
    C. Magnetic fields account for much of the disruption in radioactive carbon dating.
    D. An artifact that is relatively new, less than a decade old, cannot be dated based on percentage of carbon 14.

Questions 32–41 are based on the following passage.

The following passage is adapted from the U.S. Geological Survey's "North American Breeding Bird Survey."

During the 1960s, Chandler Robbins and his associates at the Migratory Bird Population Station (now the Patuxent Environmental Science Center) in Laurel, Maryland, developed the concept of a continental monitoring program for all breeding birds. The roadside
5 survey methodology was field tested during 1965, and the North American Breeding Bird Survey (BBS) was formally launched in 1966 when approximately 600 surveys were conducted in the United States and Canada east of the Mississippi River. The survey spread to the Great Plains states and prairie provinces in 1967. By 1968, approximately
10 2,000 routes were established across southern Canada and the contiguous 48 states, with more than 1,000 routes surveyed annually.
   The BBS was bolstered as more birders became aware of the program. During the 1980s, the BBS expanded into the Yukon and Northwest Territories of Canada, and Alaska. Additional routes have been added
15 in a number of states, so by 1994, there are approximately 3,700 active BBS routes across the continental United States and Canada, of which nearly 2,900 are surveyed annually.

Breeding Bird Surveys are conducted during the peak of the nesting season, primarily during June, although surveys in desert regions and
20 some southern states are conducted in May. Each route is 24.5 miles long, with a total of fifty stops located at 0.5-mile intervals along the route.

A three-minute point count is conducted at each stop, during which the observer records all birds heard or seen within 0.25 mile of the stop.
25 The BBS was designed to provide a continent-wide perspective of population changes. To achieve this perspective, the routes are randomly located in order to sample habitats that are representative of the entire region. Other requirements, such as consistent methodology and observer expertise, visiting the same stops each year, and
30 conducting surveys under suitable weather conditions, are needed to produce comparable data over time. A large sample of routes is needed to average local variations and reduce the effects of sampling error.

Route density varies considerably across the continent, reflecting regional densities of skilled birders. The greatest densities are in
35 the New England and Mid-Atlantic states, while densities are lower elsewhere.

Once the data are recorded in the field, it is sent to the BBS office at Patuxent, where it is computerized. Data are recorded at each stop, and then totaled over the entire 50-stop route.
40 The BBS data are very challenging to analyze. The survey produces an index of relative abundance rather than a complete count of breeding bird populations. The data analyses assume that fluctuations in these indices of abundance are representative of the population as a whole.

Despite its complicated analyses, the BBS has proven to be a very
45 valuable source of information on bird population trends. The following examples provide an indication of the types of analyses that can be performed on these data.

BBS data can be used to produce continental relative abundance maps. When viewed at continental or regional scales, these maps
50 provide a reasonably good indication of the relative abundances of

species that are well sampled by the BBS. They should be viewed
with some caution, however. Where species approach the edges of
their ranges, they tend to be rare, locally distributed, and therefore
poorly represented along BBS routes. The procedures used to produce
55 these maps also tend to distort the edges of the ranges. Hence, BBS
abundance maps provide only an approximation of range edges. The
map presented is an example of a BBS relative abundance map, for the
Bobolink.

Analyzing population changes on survey routes is probably the most
60 effective use of BBS data, but these data do not provide an explanation
for the causes of population trends. To evaluate population changes
over time, BBS indices from individual routes are combined to obtain
regional and continental estimates of trends. Although some species
have consistent trends throughout the history of the BBS, most do not.

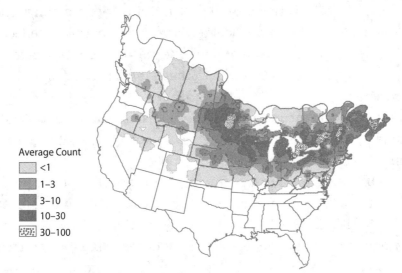

Average Count
<1
1–3
3–10
10–30
30–100

32. The main purpose of the first two paragraphs is to

A. present the historical struggle of how the BBS program came to
   relevance.
B. explain the science behind survey maps and present their relevance.

C. offer an interpretive context in order to introduce the complicated data of survey maps.
D. offer historical background of the program and show the scope of its present range.

33. As used in line 12, *bolstered* most nearly means

A. strengthened.
B. determined.
C. tempered.
D. renowned.

34. According to the passage, which choice might cause a sampling error for this project?

A. Severe climate change, which may alter the peak nesting season
B. Glitches in the computerization of the collected information
C. Varying weather conditions from year to year
D. Construction of roadways that may alter population trends

35. Which choice provides the best evidence for the answer to the preceding question?

A. lines 28–32 ("Other...error")
B. lines 37–39 ("Once...route")
C. lines 52–55 ("Where...ranges")
D. lines 61–64 ("To...not")

36. What is most salient implication of the statement "Route density varies considerably across the continent, reflecting regional densities of skilled birders"?

A. The survey conductors acknowledge a bias toward experienced birders.
B. The survey conductors acknowledge a variation in data collection due to the variable skills of data collectors.
C. Bird routes are sometimes cyclical, which accounts for much of the route densities in certain areas of the country.
D. Skilled birders tend to live where more birds are, accounting for greater route densities in the BBS.

37. Which choice presents the main purpose of the BBS?

    A. To track various bird populations across the United States and
       Canada
    B. To explain causes that affect bird population trends
    C. To explore how climate change affects bird routes across the United
       States and Canada
    D. To keep track of bird breeds that may become endangered

38. Which choice provides the best evidence for the answer to the
    preceding question?

    A. lines 12–14 ("The...Alaska")
    B. lines 23–24 ("A three...stop")
    C. lines 40–42 ("The...populations")
    D. lines 59–61 ("Analyzing...trends")

39. As used in line 41, *abundance* most nearly means

    A. an approximation.
    B. a plentiful amount.
    C. integrity.
    D. affluence.

40. Which of the following statements is supported by the graph and the
    passage?

    A. The biggest cluster densities of Bobolinks are found in the
       northeastern part of the United States.
    B. There has been a reduction in the continental population of the
       Bobolinks since 1965.
    C. Disease has caused a reduced bird population surrounding the
       Great Lakes region of the United States.
    D. The map of the Bobolink population directly correlates to weather
       patterns.

41. What does the map indicate about the survey of relative abundance in Texas?

   A. There are no birds in the southernmost states in the United States, including Texas.

   B. The white space in Texas demonstrates a sampling error for Bobolinks.

   C. Bobolinks fly north during the summer months when the surveys are conducted.

   D. There were no Bobolinks recorded in the state of Texas.

Questions 42–52 are based on the following passages.

Passage 1 is an excerpt from President Dwight D. Eisenhower's farewell address, televised on January 17, 1961. Passage 2 is an excerpt from President George Washington's farewell address, published September 19, 1796.

Passage 1

A vital element in keeping the peace is our military establishment. Our arms must be mighty, ready for instant action, so that no potential aggressor may be tempted to risk his own destruction.

Our military organization today bears little resemblance to that
5 known by any of my predecessors in peacetime, or indeed by the fighting men of World War II or Korea.

Until the latest of our world conflicts, the United States had no armaments industry. American makers of plowshares could, with time and as required, make swords as well. But now we can no longer risk
10 emergency improvisation of national defense; we have been compelled to create a permanent armaments industry of vast proportions. Added to this, three and a half million men and women are directly engaged in the defense establishment. We annually spend on military security more than the net income of all United States corporations.
15   This conjunction of an immense military establishment and a large arms industry is new in the American experience. The total

influence—economic, political, even spiritual—is felt in every city,
every State house, every office of the Federal government. We recognize
the imperative need for this development. Yet we must not fail to
20 comprehend its grave implications. Our toil, resources and livelihood
are all involved; so is the very structure of our society.

   In the councils of government, we must guard against the acquisition
of unwarranted influence, whether sought or unsought, by the military-
industrial complex. The potential for the disastrous rise of misplaced
25 power exists and will persist.

   We must never let the weight of this combination endanger our
liberties or democratic processes. We should take nothing for granted.
Only an alert and knowledgeable citizenry can compel the proper
meshing of the huge industrial and military machinery of defense
30 with our peaceful methods and goals, so that security and liberty may
prosper together.

Passage 2

   Observe good faith and justice towards all Nations; cultivate peace
and harmony with all. Religion and Morality enjoin this conduct; and
can it be, that good policy does not equally enjoin it? It will be worthy
of a free, enlightened, and, at no distant period, a great Nation, to
5 give to mankind the magnanimous and too novel example of a people
always guided by an exalted justice and benevolence. Who can doubt,
that, in the course of time and things, the fruits of such a plan would
richly repay any temporary advantages, which might be lost by a steady
adherence to it? Can it be, that Providence has not connected the
10 permanent felicity of a Nation with its Virtue? The experiment, at least,
is recommended by every sentiment which ennobles human nature.
Alas! is it rendered impossible by its vices?

   In the execution of such a plan, nothing is more essential, than
that permanent, inveterate antipathies against particular Nations,

15 and passionate attachments for others, should be excluded; and that,
    in place of them, just and amicable feelings towards all should be
    cultivated. The Nation, which indulges towards another an habitual
    hatred, or an habitual fondness, is in some degree a slave. It is a slave
    to its animosity or to its affection, either of which is sufficient to lead
20 it astray from its duty and its interest. Antipathy in one nation against
    another disposes each more readily to offer insult and injury, to lay
    hold of slight causes of umbrage, and to be haughty and intractable,
    when accidental or trifling occasions of dispute occur. Hence frequent
    collisions, obstinate, envenomed, and bloody contests. The Nation,
25 prompted by ill-will and resentment, sometimes impels to war
    the Government, contrary to the best calculations of policy. The
    Government sometimes participates in the national propensity, and
    adopts through passion what reason would reject; at other times, it
    makes the animosity of the nation subservient to projects of hostility
30 instigated by pride, ambition, and other sinister and pernicious motives.
    The peace often, sometimes perhaps the liberty, of Nations has been the
    victim.

42. Over the course of passage 1, the focus of the discussion shifts from

    A. reservations about the use of military force to a growing
       appreciation of the U.S. military's capabilities.
    B. an emphasis on the need for military readiness to reservations
       about the industry that enables that readiness.
    C. a declaration of the need for peace in our time to a warning of
       what may disrupt peace in the future.
    D. ambivalence on the power of the military to a recognition of the
       true power of the armaments industry.

43. As used in line 20 of passage 1, *grave* most nearly means

    A. interment.
    B. dishonest.
    C. aggressive.
    D. serious.

44. Which of the following is the best explication of the term "military-industrial complex" in lines 23–24 from passage 1?

    A. The interconnection of the military and an entire industry devoted to supporting military action
    B. The stockpile of war weapons used for purposes of intimidation and as a deterrent from war
    C. The psychological weight of owning a large stockpile of weapons felt by every town and citizen
    D. The mass production by the government of weapons, stockpiled for purposes of military preparedness

45. Which of the following is the best characterization of the "experiment" referred to in paragraph 1 of passage 2?

    A. That a government should maintain neutrality with all nations
    B. That morality guide government so it may be an example of benevolence in the world
    C. That a government ruled by people should also be ruled by human nature
    D. That religion should dictate government policies to create a moral world

46. As used in line 27 of passage 2, *propensity* most nearly means

    A. weightiness.
    B. sympathy.
    C. inclination.
    D. intolerance.

47. What is the most significant similarity between the two passages?

    A. Both passages provide advice for future presidents.
    B. Both passages were written by former military commanders.
    C. Both passages warn against an apathetic citizenry.
    D. Both passages advocate for peace and warn against what may disrupt peace.

48. Which choice best characterizes the relationship between Eisenhower's and Washington's warnings to the nation regarding the use of military force?

    A. Both warn that a government should use military force only when necessary.
    B. Eisenhower warns against the influence of an industry, while Washington warns against the influence of emotion.
    C. The warnings are identical—that the government should be wary of outside influences.
    D. Eisenhower warns against a future threat, while Washington warns against a present threat.

49. Which choice provides the best evidence for the answer to the preceding question?

    A. lines 4–5 of passage 1 ("Our...peacetime") and lines 23–24 of passage 2 ("Hence...contests")
    B. lines 15–16 of passage 1 ("This...experience") and lines 17–18 of passage 2 ("The Nation...slave")
    C. lines 22–24 of passage 1 ("In...complex") and lines 24–26 of passage 2 ("The Nation...policy")
    D. lines 24–25 of passage 1 ("The potential...persist") and lines 10–12 of passage 2 ("The experiment...vices")

50. Which of the following is the best characterization of differences between the methods for fostering peace as outlined in passage 1 and passage 2?

    A. Passage 1 advocates peace through a fear of the destruction of war, while passage 2 advocates that a nation act in accordance with justice and benevolence.
    B. Passage 1 suggests peace stems from the pre-established order of government, while passage 2 suggests that peace comes from the will of the people.
    C. Passage 1 advocates peace through smart diplomacy, while passage 2 advocates a naive and vague adherence to morality.
    D. Passage 1 suggests peace comes from defying malicious influences of industry, while passage 2 suggests peace comes from defying human nature.

51. Which choice provides the best evidence for the answer to the preceding question?

   A. Lines 1–3 of passage 1 ("A vital...destruction") and lines 1–2 of passage 2 ("Observe...all")
   B. Lines 8–9 of passage 1 ("American...well") and lines 3–6 of passage 2 ("It will...benevolence")
   C. Lines 24–25 of passage 1 ("The potential...persist") and lines 26–28 of passage 2 ("The Government...reject")
   D. Lines 28–31 of passage 1 ("Only...together") and lines 17–18 of passage 2 ("The Nation...slave")

52. Which of the following best describes the stance of each passage?

   A. Washington had the mind of a military man; Eisenhower had the mind of a businessman.
   B. Eisenhower was an idealist; Washington was a pragmatist.
   C. Eisenhower was a keen observer of history; Washington possessed the keen ability of foresight.
   D. Washington was an idealist; Eisenhower was a pragmatist.

END OF SECTION

Writing and Language Test

Directions: Several questions follow each passage below. Some questions might ask you to improve the passage by revising or editing it. There may be a table, graph, or other graphic that goes along with a passage or question. For some questions, you will be asked to consider an underlined portion of a passage. Still other questions will ask you to consider the passage as a whole. Read each passage. For each question, **find the number in the passage that corresponds to the question number** and decide which answer best improves the passage or makes it grammatically correct. Sometimes "NO CHANGE" will be an answer choice. If making no change is the best option, choose this answer.

Questions 1–11 are based on the following passage.

Zoning in Oak Hills

The Oak Hills neighborhood in Capitol City has seen some recent controversy over whether the city should rezone the neighborhood to accommodate population expansion. The biggest source of debate is Prince Boulevard, one of the neighborhood's busiest sections and a main artery for traffic and commerce. It is currently home to a mix of businesses [1] (storage facilities, fast food restaurants, auto repair stores, and grocery stores) that have changed very little since the 1980s. Prince Boulevard is currently zoned for commercial [2] use, meaning that new residential buildings over a certain height are not allowed under city law. [3]

One neighborhood group, the Oak Hills Community Board, [4] OHCB, is seeking to have most of the neighborhood—including Prince Boulevard—rezoned by Capitol City to allow more residential buildings. [5] This would help accommodate the large numbers of people who are moving to Oak Hills. The OHCB believes that rezoning will give the community a voice in any new development, and allow them to advocate for new, affordable housing.

[6] <u>Here is an additional note.</u> A complication is that Oak Hills has recently caught the eye of real estate developers, who see the neighborhood as a hot location for building [7] <u>its</u> large, upscale condominiums. [8] <u>Because Oak Hills has a diverse population, a location close to McDonald Park, easy accessing to public transportation for people commuting to downtown Capitol City.</u> Another local group, Not In My Backyard (NIMBY), is concerned that rezoning Oak Hills, especially the Prince Boulevard area, will open the door to these developers and [9] <u>to displace</u> longtime, lower-income residents. "We need community improvements, not luxury skyscrapers and overpriced coffee chains," NIMBY activist Mary Anne Phillips told the *Capitol City Chronicle* in March.

The community remains divided over the direction the neighborhood should take. A *Chronicle* poll of Oak Hills residents shows that [10] <u>the support for rezoning is running slightly ahead of the support for leaving the zoning as is, which is behind</u>. As a result, Community Board meetings have become lively affairs, with shouting matches frequently erupting between board members and the public.

As the OHCB continues to hear community input, members believe that the best way to maintain a voice in the process is to be involved. Community Board Chairman Marco Hendrix told NIMBY protesters at the April 13 meeting that "change is coming whether we like it or not, and I want to make sure that Oak Hills residents have a say in shaping those changes." Hendrix then referred to the census population data that showed Oak Hills's population steadily growing.

[11] The Community Board has set a deadline of May 14 for written feedback from the community, and will vote at the May 20 meeting on whether to send the final zoning request to the city planning department.

1. The writer is considering deleting the underlined phrase. Should the phrase be kept or deleted?

    A. Kept, because it provides essential detail related to the main point of the paragraph
    B. Kept, because the reader needs to know what businesses are on Prince Boulevard
    C. Deleted, because it provides unnecessary detail in the introductory paragraph
    D. Deleted, because it does not provide context on what Prince Boulevard is

2.

    A. NO CHANGE
    B. use meaning
    C. use. Meaning
    D. use; meaning

3. Which sentence is the topic sentence of the first paragraph?

    A. The Oak Hills neighborhood in Capitol City has seen some recent controversy over whether the city should rezone the neighborhood to accommodate population expansion.
    B. Prince Boulevard is currently zoned for commercial use, meaning that new residential buildings over a certain height are not allowed under city law.
    C. The biggest source of debate is Prince Boulevard, one of the neighborhood's busiest sections and a main artery for traffic and commerce.
    D. None of these is a topic sentence.

4.

    A. NO CHANGE
    B. (OHCB)
    C. —OHCB—
    D. ; OHCB

5. Which of the following sentences would provide appropriate context details for the underlined sentence?

   A. The median home price in Oak Hills in 2014 was $132,000.
   B. More than 65 people attended the last Community Board meeting.
   C. 135 households live on the street adjacent to McDonald Park.
   D. In the 2010 census, Oak Hills had 5,000 more residents than it did in the 2000 census.

6. The writer is considering revising the beginning of this paragraph. What would be a more effective transition from the second paragraph to the third?

   A. NO CHANGE
   B. However, the OHCB isn't the only group with plans for Oak Hills.
   C. Also, a complication is that Oak Hills has recently caught the eye of real estate developers . . .
   D. In conclusion, a complication is that Oak Hills has recently caught the eye of real estate developers . . .

7.

   A. NO CHANGE
   B. our
   C. his
   D. their

8. How should the underlined sentence fragment be revised?

   A. NO CHANGE
   B. Oak Hills is an appealing location for developers and new residents because it has a diverse population, a location close to McDonald Park, and easy access to public transportation for people commuting to downtown Capitol City.
   C. Because Oak Hills is appealing it has a diverse population, a location close to McDonald Park, and easy access to public transportation for people commuting to downtown Capitol City.

D. But Oak Hills has a diverse population, a location close to McDonald Park, and easy access to public transportation for people commuting to downtown Capitol City.

9.

A. NO CHANGE
B. have displaced
C. displace
D. displacing

10.

A. NO CHANGE
B. the support for rezoning is running slightly ahead of the support for leaving the zoning as is.
C. the support for rezoning is winning and running slightly ahead of the support for leaving the zoning as is.
D. there are more people who support rezoning than people who support leaving the zoning as is.

11. Which of the following would be an effective transition to begin the concluding paragraph?

A. With the community still divided on the zoning issue,
B. Prince Boulevard needs to be rezoned.
C. NIMBY activists are leading the way.
D. Additionally, the Community Board has set a deadline.

Questions 12–22 are based on the following passage.

The Plutonian Saga

In 1930, American astronomer Clyde Tombaugh discovered a previously unknown planet in the far reaches of our solar system. Named Pluto after the Roman god of the Underworld, [12] this planet was the tenth largest object orbiting the Sun, and was made up primarily of rock and ice. For approximately 76 years, Pluto was included in the group of nine planets in our solar system—that is, until the [13] IAU updated the definition of a major planet. Because Pluto didn't meet those criteria, it was reclassified as a "dwarf planet," and not considered to be on the same level as Earth, Venus, Saturn, etc. Since that decision was handed down, there has continued to be debate on the topic. Now, a growing number of scientists agree: Pluto should be reinstated as a major planet.

In 2006, the IAU set the official definition for a major planet as follows:

1. The object must orbit around the Sun.

2. The object must be spherical (round).

3. It must have [14] "cleared the neighborhood" around its orbit.

Pluto meets requirements #1 and #2, but the IAU determined that it did not meet #3, because there are other "dwarf planets" orbiting near it, and it also overlaps the planet Neptune's orbit of the Sun. [15]

However, public and scientific opinion [16] support increasingly relaxing this definition of a planet. At a 2014 astronomy meeting and forum hosted by the Harvard-Smithsonian Center, scientists on both sides debated Pluto's status as a planet. While some members of the IAU supported Pluto's downgrade, others disagreed. In fact, [17] Owen Gingerich argued that the definition of a planet has evolved over time to mean "the smallest spherical lump of matter that formed around stars." Under this broader definition, Pluto is a planet and should be identified as one.

Another point of controversy: if [18] Pluto was reinstated, the relaxed definition of a "planet" opens the door to other dwarf planets being included as well. The IAU argued at the time that there could be as many as 100 newly reclassified planets, or "too many" for basic astronomy lessons in schools and in popular culture. Such an arbitrary factor should not necessarily change 76 years of history. Would historians decide that the [19] battle of Gettysburg wasn't really a battle, because it makes Civil War history too long? [20] Get real people!

After the Harvard-Smithsonian debate, the group took an informal vote among its members: [21] Pluto's planethood won. This poll was nonbinding, but it showed that many scientists support revisiting the definition. At the very least, the IAU should open up their definition for more than just casual debate, and consider revising what a planet is—or is not. [22]

12. The writer is considering revising or deleting these details about Pluto. Which would be the most effective way to use these context details?

    A. NO CHANGE
    B. Delete them.
    C. Move Pluto's makeup and orbit information to the second paragraph to add context to the planet requirements.
    D. Add more physical details about Pluto.

13. What information should the writer add to explain who/what the IAU is?

    A. NO CHANGE
    B. A line from the IAU's mission statement
    C. The full name of International Astronomical Union
    D. The name of the person in charge of the IAU

14. How should the writer revise the underlined text for clarity?

    A. NO CHANGE
    B. It must have "cleared the neighborhood" around its orbit, meaning it cannot be surrounded by similar objects.
    C. It must have "cleared out the neighborhood that was around its orbit."
    D. It must have cleared its orbit.

15. What additional information would be most effective at the end of this paragraph?

    A. A graphic depicting Pluto and Neptune's overlapping orbit

    B. A photo of Pluto

    C. A listing of every dwarf planet

    D. Biographical details about the scientist who discovered Pluto

16.

    A. NO CHANGE

    B. support, increasingly

    C. increasingly support

    D. support increasing

17.

    A. NO CHANGE

    B. Owen Gingerich, a member of the original IAU planet definition committee, argued

    C. he argued

    D. Owen Gingerich, he argued

18.

    A. NO CHANGE

    B. Pluto be reinstated

    C. Pluto are reinstated

    D. Pluto is reinstated

19.

    A. NO CHANGE

    B. Battle Of Gettysburg

    C. battle of gettysburg

    D. Battle of Gettysburg

20. How should the writer revise the underlined sentence to be consistent with the passage's tone?

    A. NO CHANGE
    B. Delete it.
    C. Get real, people!
    D. Move it to the beginning of the paragraph.

21.

    A. NO CHANGE
    B. Plutos planethood
    C. Plutos' planethood
    D. Plutoes' planethood

22. Which of the following best summarizes the writer's thesis?

    A. The IAU should consider reversing their decision to downgrade Pluto as a major planet.
    B. The IAU is a corrupt organization.
    C. Neptune's status as a planet should also be revised.
    D. Pluto is big enough to be considered a planet.

Questions 23–33 are based on the following passage.

Jefferson and Adams: Friends and Foes

As two of the "Founding Fathers" of the United States, [23] <u>Thomas Jefferson and J. Adams</u> are often grouped together in American history. First as revolutionaries, and then as statesmen and Presidents, the two men were a major part of America's early successes. They also had a complicated [24] <u>personal friendship: that spanned</u> much of their adult lives.

Before and during the Revolutionary War, both Jefferson and Adams worked together toward a common goal: freeing America from the taxes and control of the British government. Both were instrumental in creating the Declaration of Independence (which Jefferson wrote and Adams pushed the Continental Congress to approve). [25] <u>After the war was over and the independent U.S. government was being created away from Britain's control,</u> both Adams and Jefferson were heavily involved in forming the democratic republic that we still know today. Under first president George Washington, Adams served as vice president and Jefferson served as secretary of state. And when Adams became the second U.S. president, Jefferson served as his vice president.

[26] <u>Adams and Jefferson were also friends.</u> They frequently wrote letters to one another, and sang each other's praises in letters to others. In one letter to Jefferson, Adams wrote that "intimate correspondence with you . . . is one of the most agreeable events in my life."

However, their friendship began to deteriorate, mostly due to political differences. [27] <u>Like, Adams and his Federalist Party</u> believed that the United States would be strongest with a centralized federal government, while Jefferson and his Democratic-Republican Party believed that the best course would be to have federal government support the individual states' rights to make decisions. This came to a head in the 1800 election, when Jefferson defeated Adams after a [28] <u>campaign of brutal, mean, slanderous attacks from both sides</u>. By the time Jefferson took office in 1801, the men were no longer speaking or writing to one another.

[29] <u>In 1811, the chilly relationship began to thaw. When mutual friends of Jefferson and Adams worked to open up communication between the two.</u> They resumed writing letters, discussing philosophy, politics, and many other topics. This renewed friendship continued for the rest of their lives.

In an eerie coincidence, those lives ended on the same day. [30] <u>On July 4 1826 which was also the 50th anniversary of the signing of the Declaration of Independence,</u> [31] <u>Thomas Jefferson passed away at the age of 83. Later that day, John Adams died,</u> mistakenly believing that his friend and former opponent had outlived him. [32] <u>Thomas Jefferson survives were among his last words.</u> [33]

23.

A. NO CHANGE
B. T. Jefferson and John Adams
C. Thomas Jefferson and John Adams
D. Jefferson and Adams

24.

A. NO CHANGE
B. personal friendship that spanned
C. personal: friendship that spanned
D. personal friendship, that spanned

25.

A. NO CHANGE
B. After the war was over and the independent U.S. government was being created separate from Britain's control
C. After the war was over and the independent U.S. government was being created under Britain's control
D. After the war was over and the independent U.S. government was being created

26. What would be the most effective transition at the start of this paragraph?

A. In addition to their close political ties,
B. Moreover,
C. Anyway,
D. This is interesting,

27.

A. NO CHANGE
B. Likewise,
C. For example,
D. Did you know that

28.

A. NO CHANGE
B. campaign of crazy, brutal, mean, slanderous attacks from
   both sides
C. campaign from both sides
D. campaign of slanderous attacks from both sides

29.

A. NO CHANGE
B. In 1811, the chilly relationship began to thaw! When mutual friends
   of Jefferson and Adams worked to open up communication
   between the two.
C. In 1811, the chilly relationship began to thaw: When mutual friends
   of Jefferson and Adams worked to open up communication
   between the two.
D. In 1811, the chilly relationship began to thaw when mutual friends
   of Jefferson and Adams worked to open up communication
   between the two.

30.

A. NO CHANGE
B. On July 4, 1826; which was also the 50th anniversary of the
   signing of the Declaration of Independence,
C. On July 4, 1826 (which was also the 50th anniversary of the
   signing of the Declaration of Independence),
D. On July 4 1826 (which was also the 50th anniversary of the signing
   of the Declaration of Independence),

31.

A. NO CHANGE
B. Thomas Jefferson passed away at the age of 83. Later that day,
   John Adams too,
C. Thomas Jefferson passed away at the age of 83. Later that day,
   John Adams died at the age of 90,

D. Thomas Jefferson passed away. Later that day, John Adams died at the age of 90.

32.

    A. NO CHANGE
    B. "Thomas Jefferson survives" were among his last words.
    C. Thomas Jefferson survives!, were among his last words.
    D. "Thomas Jefferson survives"—were among his last words.

33. Which of the following would be an effective concluding sentence for this passage?

    A. In death, as in American history, the two statesmen are connected forever.
    B. In conclusion, Thomas Jefferson and John Adams were a study of contrasts.
    C. In conclusion, Thomas Jefferson was a better president than John Adams.
    D. John Adams will forever be remembered as the second president of the United States.

Questions 34–44 are based on the following passage.

Water Works

    [34] More than any other resource, water is essential worldwide—for wildlife as well as humans. Fresh water makes up only about 3 percent of the world's water, and only 1 percent is readily available to humans. As the world's population grows and regions experience shortages, water conservation has become an urgent need—and a fast-growing career path for those seeking a [35] green environmentally conscious job.

    [36] Water conservation involves water use [37] in home, industries, agricultural, and commercial areas. In the sciences (typically at

the bachelor's degree level or higher), there are professionals like microbiologists and chemists, who analyze water quality and contamination. Hydrologists [38] <u>study</u> water sources and movement, particularly as they relate to geology and the environment. Water conservationists advise communities on water quality, and work to prevent contamination, while environmental scientists study how to prevent natural pollution of water sources. [39] <u>In the engineering (which also typically requires a bachelor's degree or higher) field,</u> engineers work with scientists to develop strategies and technical solutions for conserving water.

Even more hands-on are water conservation professionals who work in the agriculture, mining, construction, and grounds management industries. They are on the front lines of managing water use, and are frequently the first professionals affected by water shortages or flooding. Ten states suffered shortages or droughts in 2014. These jobs may not require advanced degrees like the science and engineering occupations, but frequently call for special certification and training. [40]

In addition to research and physical management, [41] <u>water conservation also requires significant planning as communities grow and change. A large part of the field is found in city and regional planning offices.</u> Urban and regional planners develop strategies and solutions on the local level, and work in state, local, and federal governments.

According to the U.S. Bureau of Labor Statistics, salaries in water conservation–related fields correspond with the level of education required for each occupation. While statistics are not yet available for specific water conservation occupations, analysis of related fields shows that regardless of education level, water conservation–related jobs had annual median wages close to (or above) the U.S. median annual wage of $34,750. [42]

Although these jobs have existed for many years, water conservation [43] <u>is only now starting to been</u> considered a collective industry in itself. That may change as the focus on environmental concerns and renewable living continues to grow, and [44] <u>these fields attracts</u> more college graduates.

34. Considering the supporting information given in this passage, how should the writer streamline this first sentence?

    A. NO CHANGE
    B. More than any other resource, water is essential worldwide.
    C. Water is an essential resource for animals and plant life.
    D. Water is an element.

35.

    A. NO CHANGE
    B. an environment conscious job
    C. a job
    D. an environmentally conscious job

36. Which of the following would make a good introductory sentence for the second paragraph?

    A. Occupations in water conservation can take many different forms, since water conservation
    B. Water, water everywhere. Water conservation
    C. The best way to save water is to start in your own home. Water conservation
    D. Occupations in water conservation:

37.

    A. NO CHANGE
    B. in houses, industries, agricultures, and commercial areas
    C. in many areas
    D. in residential, industrial, agricultural, and commercial areas

38.

    A. NO CHANGE
    B. studies
    C. studied
    D. studying

39.

    A. NO CHANGE
    B. In the engineering—which also typically requires a bachelor's degree or higher—field,
    C. In the engineering field (which also typically requires a bachelor's degree or higher),
    D. In the engineering field; which also typically requires a bachelor's degree or higher;

40. How should this paragraph be revised for focus on the main topic?

    A. Delete "These jobs may not require advanced degrees like the science and engineering occupations, but frequently call for special certification and training."
    B. Delete "Ten states suffered shortages or droughts in 2014."
    C. Add more industries that may employ water conservation professionals.
    D. Delete the entire paragraph.

41. How should the writer revise the flow of these two sentences?

    A. NO CHANGE
    B. water conservation also requires significant planning as communities grow and change. As such, a large part of the field is found in city and regional planning offices.
    C. water conservation also requires significant planning as communities grow and change. Regardless, a large part of the field is found in city and regional planning offices.
    D. water conservation also requires significant planning as communities grow and change, and a large part of the field is found in city and regional planning offices.

42. How could the writer most effectively resolve the conflicting information given in this paragraph?

   A. Delete "regardless of education level," and add additional supporting evidence for why the labor statistics are interpreted that way.
   B. Remove all mention of education level.
   C. Delete "According to the U.S. Bureau of Labor Statistics."
   D. Disregard and leave it as is.

43.

   A. NO CHANGE
   B. is only now started
   C. is only now starting to be
   D. only now was

44.

   A. NO CHANGE
   B. these fields have attracted
   C. these fields attracting
   D. these fields attract

END OF SECTION

Math Test–No Calculator

Directions: For questions 1–15 below, solve each problem, choose the best answer from the choices provided, then fill in the corresponding circle on your answer sheet. For questions 16–20, first solve the problem and then fill in your answer on the grid according to the directions provided before question 16. Your test booklet may be used for scratch work.

Notes:

1. You may **not** use a calculator.

2. You may assume all variables and expressions used represent real numbers unless stated otherwise.

3. You may assume figures are drawn to scale, unless noted otherwise.

4. You may assume all figures lie in a plane unless otherwise noted.

5. The domain of a given function f is the set of all real numbers x for which $f(x)$ is a real number, unless otherwise noted.

Reference:

    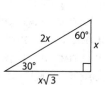

$A = \pi r^2$
$C = 2\pi r$

$A = \frac{1}{2} bh$

$c^2 = a^2 + b^2$

$A = lw$

Special Right Triangles

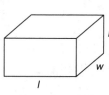 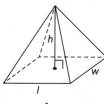

$V = lwh$

$V = \frac{1}{3}\pi r^2 h$

$V = \frac{1}{3} lwh$

$V = \pi r^2 h$

$V = \frac{4}{3}\pi r^3$

1. $$3m - 6n = -18$$
$$-\frac{2}{3}m + kn = 4$$

In the system of equations above, k is a constant. If the system has infinitely many solutions, then what is the value of k?

A. $-\frac{1}{6}$

B. $-\frac{2}{9}$

C. $\frac{2}{3}$

D. $\frac{4}{3}$

2. Oliver's garden covers 850 square feet and typically yields x pounds of tomatoes each growing season. In the equation below, what does the variable y represent?

$$y = 10\left(\frac{x}{850}\right)$$

A. The typical yield, per square foot, in 10 growing seasons
B. The typical yield, per square foot, in a single growing season
C. The yield required, per square foot, to have a total yield of 10 pounds for a single growing season
D. The yield required, per square foot, to have a total yield of 85 pounds in 10 growing seasons

3. For an angle β, $\sin\beta > 0$ and $\cos\beta < 0$. Which inequality must be true for an angle $\alpha = \pi + \beta$?

A. $0 < \alpha < \dfrac{\pi}{2}$

B. $\dfrac{\pi}{2} < \alpha < \pi$

C. $\pi < \alpha < \dfrac{3\pi}{2}$

D. $\dfrac{3\pi}{2} < \alpha < 2\pi$

4. At how many points do the graphs of $y = -3$ and $y = x^2 - 4x + 1$ intersect in the xy-plane?

A. None
B. One
C. Two
D. Three

5. $\dfrac{1}{x-1} + \dfrac{1}{x+2} = \dfrac{m-2}{x(x-1)(x+2)}$

Which of the following is equivalent to m?

A. $2x^2 - 1$
B. $2x^2 + 5x$
C. $2x^2 + x + 2$
D. $2x^2 + 3x + 2$

6. A polynomial has zeros of 2, 0, $\dfrac{1}{2}$, and $\dfrac{5}{3}$. If the polynomial can be written as $(x - a)(6x^3 - 13x^2 + 5x)$, then what is the value of a?

   A. 0

   B. 2

   C. $\dfrac{1}{2}$

   D. $\dfrac{5}{3}$

7. Anahar is studying the growth of a small company over the last five years. In the first year, the company had total sales of \$16,850.62. In each subsequent year, the sales increased by 50% over the preceding year. If this pattern continues, then which of the following represents the total sales, T, in three more years?

   A. $T = 16850.62\left(\dfrac{9}{2}\right)^3$

   B. $T = 16850.62\left(\dfrac{5}{2}\right)^3$

   C. $T = 16850.62\left(\dfrac{3}{2}\right)^7$

   D. $T = 16850.62\left(\dfrac{1}{2}\right)^7$

8. Suppose $p = 3x^2 - 5x + 1$ and $q = 16x^2 + 3x - 2$. Which expression represents $2p - q$ in terms of x?

   A. $-10x^2 - 7x$

   B. $-10x^2 - 13x + 4$

   C. $-10x^2 - 2x - 1$

   D. $-10x^2 - 8x + 4$

9. The graph of the equation $y = -3x + \dfrac{1}{2}$ is shifted three units to the left. What is the y-intercept of the resulting graph?

A. $-\dfrac{17}{2}$

B. $-\dfrac{5}{2}$

C. $\dfrac{7}{2}$

D. $\dfrac{19}{2}$

10.

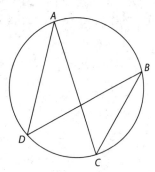

In the circle above, $m\angle A = \left(\dfrac{x}{2} + 1\right)^\circ$ and $m\angle B = \left(\dfrac{y}{5}\right)^\circ$ for nonzero numbers x and y. Which of the following represents y in terms of x?

A. $5x + 1$

C. $\dfrac{5x}{2} + 5$

B. $5x + 10$

D. $\dfrac{5x}{4} + \dfrac{5}{2}$

11. If $f(x) = \dfrac{x + 4}{2} + x$, which expression is equivalent to $f\left(\dfrac{x}{2}\right)$?

A. $x + 2$

B. $\dfrac{3x}{4} + 2$

C. $\dfrac{x}{2} + 1$

D. $\dfrac{x}{4} + 2$

12. If $a^{-\frac{1}{2}} = x^{-2}$ where $a > 0$ and $x > 0$, which of the following gives a in terms of x?

   A. x

   B. x^4

   C. $\dfrac{1}{x}$

   D. $\dfrac{1}{x^4}$

13. If $\dfrac{x}{3} - \dfrac{1}{6} = \dfrac{3x}{2}$, then what is the value of $7x$?

   A. -3

   B. -1

   C. $-\dfrac{1}{7}$

   D. $-\dfrac{1}{6}$

14. $-3x + 8y = 4$
    $-2x + 7y = 1$

   Given the system of equations above, what is the value of the difference $x - y$?

   A. -5
   B. -4
   C. -3
   D. -1

15. A gift box must have a minimum volume of 180 cubic inches. If the height of the box is h inches, the width is w inches, and the length is 14 inches, then which inequality describes all possible values of w in terms of h?

    A. $w \leq 180h$

    B. $w \leq \dfrac{90h}{7}$

    C. $w \geq \dfrac{180}{h}$

    D. $w \geq \dfrac{90}{7h}$

Directions: Solve problems 16–20 below, then enter your answer in the grid. Instructions for gridding in your response are provided below.

1. You may write your answer in the boxes at the top of the columns. This is not required, but it may help you fill in the circles accurately. The circles are filled in according to instructions to be counted as correct.

2. Fill in only one circle per column.

3. None of the questions has a negative answer.

4. If a problem has more than one possible correct answer, grid in only one answer.

5. Mixed numbers such as $5\dfrac{1}{2}$ must be gridded as 5.5 or 11/2. (If it is entered into the grid, it will be interpreted as $\dfrac{51}{2}$ not 5 1/2.)

6. Round or cut off any decimal answer that will not fit the grid, but fill the whole grid.

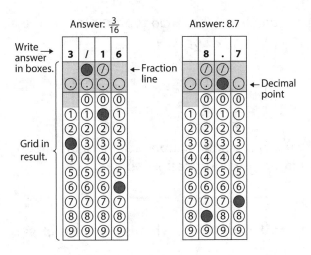

Answer: $\frac{3}{16}$

Write answer in boxes.

← Fraction line

Grid in result.

Answer: 8.7

← Decimal point

Acceptable ways to grid $\frac{1}{3}$ are:

Answer: 509 - either position is correct

NOTE: You may start your answers in any column, space permitting. Columns you don't need to use should be left blank.

16. What is the diameter of the circle represented by the equation
$x^2 + y^2 + 4x - 10y + 20 = 0$?

_____

17. $-12 \leq \dfrac{x}{2} + 1 \leq -\dfrac{x}{5} + 2$

Suppose that x is a whole number such that the inequality above is true. What is the greatest possible value of x?

_____

18. If $2y^2 - 5y = 3$ and $y > 1$, what is the value of y?

_____

19. The graph of the line $\dfrac{1}{4}x - 2y = 10$ is shifted up three units and to the left one unit. If the resulting line is represented by the equation $y = mx + b$, then what is the value of m?

_____

20. If $\sqrt{m^2 + 2m} = 2\sqrt{2}$ and $m > 0$, what is the value of m?

_____

END OF SECTION

Math Test—Calculator

Directions: Solve the problems that follow. For questions 1–30, select the best answer option and then fill in the circle on your answer sheet that corresponds to that option. For questions 31–38, grid in your response on the answer sheet. Instructions for gridding in answers appear before question 31 on how to enter your answers in the grid. Your test booklet may be used for scratch work.

Questions 1 and 2 each refer to the following information.

A survey is conducted to determine the highest education level completed and the status (part-time or full-time) of a randomly selected sample of employed individuals. The results of this survey are shown below.

	Some high school	Completed high school	Some college	Completed a two- or four-year college degree
Employed Part-Time	22	18	6	8
Employed Full-Time	28	31	25	30

1. Which education level has the highest percentage of individuals employed part-time?

    A. Some high school
    B. Completed high school
    C. Some college
    D. Completed a two- or four-year college degree

2. Of those who are employed part-time, what percentage completed a two- or four-year college degree? Round your answer to the nearest tenth of a percent.

    A. 4.8%
    B. 14.8%

C. 21.1%
D. 32.1%

3. In order to better understand the student population, a state education board asked a random sample of college students in the state whether or not they regularly visit their college's academic assistance or tutoring center. In a random sample of 1,790 college students, 820 reported that they did, and the margin of error on this estimate is 4.6%. Which of the following is not likely to be the proportion of all college students in the state who regularly visit their college's academic assistance or tutoring center?

A. 0.415
B. 0.420
C. 0.458
D. 0.514

4. The table below describes the distribution of values in a data set.

Value	Count
0 to 10	15
10 to 20	8
20 to 30	2
30 to 40	6

If the median of this data set is M, then which of the following must be true?

A. $M < 10$
B. $10 \leq M < 20$
C. $20 \leq M < 30$
D. $30 \leq M < 40$

5. As part of an experiment, a student must add 2 ml of solution to a beaker every 15 minutes. If the initial amount of solution in the beaker was 110 ml, then which of the following represents the amount of solution after x hours?

A. $110 + 30x$
B. $110 + 2x$
C. $110 + 8x$
D. $115x$

6. A shipment consists of a total of 18 portable hard drives and keyboards. Each hard drive weighs 1.6 pounds, while each keyboard weighs 2.1 pounds. The shipment weighs a total of 33.8 pounds. What is the ratio of portable hard drives to keyboards in this shipment?

A. 1:2
B. 2:7
C. 3:8
D. 4:5

7. If $4(x + 2) = 2x + 3$, then what is the value of $12x$?

A. −30
B. −10
C. −6
D. −2

8. If $-\dfrac{1}{2}x + 1 < 2$, then which of the following is a possible value of $x + 3$?

A. −1
B. 0
C. 1
D. 2

9. The value of y increases by $\dfrac{3}{4}$ units for every one-unit increase in the value of x. Further, when $x = -1$, $y = -\dfrac{1}{4}$. Given this information, which of the following equations must be true?

    A. $3x - 4y = -2$
    B. $3x - 4y = 4$
    C. $4x - 4y = -3$
    D. $4x - 4y = -5$

Questions 10 and 11 each refer to the following information.

An online electronics retailer offers a 15% discount on all items as well as a flat $5 discount on any order over $100. The $5 discount is applied after the 15% discount. Further, all shipping is free and tax is calculated after the discounts are applied with the rate being based on the state in which the customer lives.

10. Amanda lives in a state with 4.1% sales tax. She places an order from this website and is charged a total of $251.67. To the nearest cent, what was her order total before any tax or discounts were applied?

    A. $214.57
    B. $241.76
    C. $257.97
    D. $290.30

11. Suppose that x represents an order total, in dollars, before any discounts or taxes are applied. If $x < 100$, then which of the following represents the order total after discounts and a tax of y%?

    A. $\dfrac{y}{100}(0.85x)$

    B. $\dfrac{y}{100}(0.85x - 5)$

C. $\left(1 + \dfrac{y}{100}\right)(0.85x)$

D. $\left(1 + \dfrac{y}{100}\right)(0.85x - 5)$

12. The graph of each equation below is a parabola. Which shows the location of the y-intercept as a term or coefficient of the equation?

A. $y = 3x^2 - x + 3$

B. $y = (2x - 5)(x + 4)$

C. $y = -x(x - 3)$

D. $y = -2(x + 1)^2 - 8$

13. Suppose that $\sqrt{2x + 2y} = a^2 - 3$. Which of the following is an expression for $\sqrt{x + y}$ in terms of a?

A. $\dfrac{1}{2}(a^2 - 3)$

B. $\dfrac{1}{2}(a^2 - 3)^2$

C. $\dfrac{1}{\sqrt{2}}(a^2 - 3)$

D. $\dfrac{1}{\sqrt{2}}(a^2 - 3)^2$

The following information is used to answer questions 14 and 15.

The scatterplot below shows data collected on the velocity (in feet per second) of the Columbia River in Washington State at various depths, measured in feet. The line of best fit is also shown.

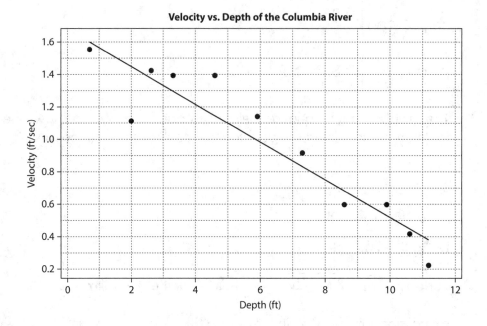

14. How many of the observed velocities were more than 0.1 foot per second higher than the predicted velocity?

A. None
B. One
C. Two
D. Three

15. Which of the following best interprets the slope of the line of best fit in this setting?

A. The predicted decrease in the velocity for a one-foot increase in depth
B. The predicted depth where the velocity of the river is 0 feet per second
C. The predicted velocity on the surface of the river (a depth of 0 feet)
D. The predicted decrease in depth for a one-foot-per-second increase in velocity

16.

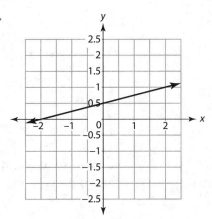

The plot above shows the graph of a line defined by the equation $y = mx + b$. Which of the following is the slope of the line $y = m(x - 2) + b$?

A. $-\dfrac{7}{4}$

B. $\dfrac{1}{4}$

C. $\dfrac{1}{2}$

D. $\dfrac{9}{4}$

17. $T_C = \dfrac{5}{9}(T_F - 32)$

$T_K = T_C + 273.15$

The formulas above are used to convert a temperature in degrees Fahrenheit (T_F) to a temperature in degrees Celsius (T_C) and a temperature in degrees Celsius to a temperature in degrees Kelvin (T_K). Which of the following is a formula for converting a temperature measured in Kelvin to Fahrenheit?

A. $T_F = \dfrac{9}{5}T_K - 459.67$

B. $T_F = \dfrac{9}{5}T_K - 255.37$

C. $T_F = \dfrac{9}{5}T_K - 241.15$

D. $T_F = \dfrac{9}{5}T_K - 133.97$

18. The ratio of x to y is 4:5 and the ratio of y to z is 1:3, where x, y, and z are real numbers. Which of the following shows the value of z in terms of x?

A. $\dfrac{4}{15}x$

B. $\dfrac{5}{12}x$

C. $\dfrac{4}{5}x$

D. $\dfrac{5}{3}x$

19.

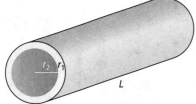

The figure above shows a section of home piping with a length of L inches, an outer radius of r_1 inches, and an inner radius of r_2 inches. If the surface area of a cylinder with radius r and height h is $2\pi rh + 2\pi r^2$, then which of the following represents the surface area of this section of pipe?

A. $2\pi L(r_1 + r_2) + 2\pi\left(r_1^2 + r_2^2\right)$

B. $2\pi L(r_1 + r_2) + 2\pi\left(r_1^2 - r_2^2\right)$

C. $2\pi L(r_1 - r_2) + 2\pi\left(r_1^2 + r_2^2\right)$

D. $2\pi L(r_1 - r_2) + 2\pi(r_1^2 - r_2^2)$

20. The value of an investment V, t years after it was made, is modeled by the equation $V = 400(1.06)^t$. What does the value 400 represent in this model?

    A. The yearly increase in value of the initial investment
    B. The initial amount that was invested in year zero
    C. The value of the investment one year after it was made
    D. The value of a regular deposit made into the investment

21. What is the value of a, where $\dfrac{3}{4}(x - 1) = \dfrac{1}{2}(ax + 2)$ has no solution?

    A. $\dfrac{3}{4}$

    B. $\dfrac{5}{4}$

    C. $\dfrac{3}{2}$

    D. $\dfrac{7}{2}$

22.

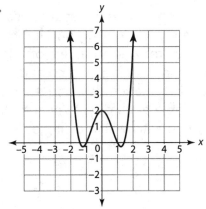

The plot above shows the graph of a polynomial function $p(x)$. Suppose that $q(x) = -p(x)$. How many solutions are there to the equation $p(x) = q(x)$?

A. One
B. Two
C. Three
D. Four

23. A nutritionist designs a study in order to understand the effects of a particular diet on inflammation as determined by blood testing. He selects a random sample of 350 individuals aged 18–34 and has each adhere to the diet for eight weeks. At the conclusion of the study, a blood test is used to detect their level of inflammation and this is then compared with the mean level for a healthy individual. Which of the following issues may prevent the nutritionist from claiming that the diet reduces inflammation in individuals from this age range?

A. Some individuals sampled may have had high or low initial levels of inflammation as compared to the mean for a healthy individual.
B. The sample size is too small to reach any general conclusions.
C. The study length is only eight weeks, which is not sufficient time for a diet change to affect levels of inflammation markers in the blood.
D. The age range is small and therefore the results cannot be applied to the general population.

24. For a particular company, the manufacture of coffee tables requires 3 labor hours of assembly and 2 labor hours of painting and finishing, while the manufacture of dining tables requires 4 labor hours of assembly and 4 labor hours of painting and finishing. The company has 16 labor hours of assembly time available each day and 12 labor hours of painting and finishing time available each day. Which of the following is an order that the company can fulfill within a single day?

A. 6 dining tables and 0 coffee tables
B. 3 dining tables and 1 coffee table
C. 2 dining tables and 3 coffee tables
D. 2 dining tables and 2 coffee tables

25.

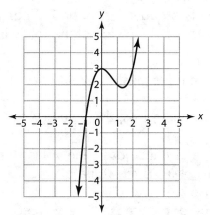

The plot above shows the graph of a function $f(x)$. For which of the following values of x is it true that $f(x) \leq f(x + 1)$?

A. $-1 < x < \infty$

B. $0 < x < 1$

C. $0 < x < 3$

D. $2 < x < \infty$

26. The value of the variable k depends on the value of the variable x. For x-values of 0, 1, and 2, the value of k is 4, 16, and 28, respectively. Given this information, which model best represents the relationship between the value of k and the value of x?

A. $k = 4(4)^x$

B. $k = 12^x + 4$

C. $k = 4x + 4$

D. $k = 12x + 4$

27. If $a = -3i + 1$ and $b = -i + 2$, then what is the product ab?

A. $-7i - 1$

B. $-7i + 5$

C. $-i - 1$

D. $-i + 5$

28. Suppose that the relationship between two quantities, m and n, can be modeled by the equation $-3m + 4n = -1$. Which of the following statements must be true?

   A. For all values of n, as the value of n increases, the value of m decreases.
   B. For all values of n, as the value of n increases, the value of m increases.
   C. For positive values of n, as the value of n increases, the value of m increases, while for negative values of n, as the value of n increases, the value of m decreases.
   D. For positive values of n, as the value of n increases, the value of m decreases, while for negative values of n, as the value of n increases, the value of m increases.

29. $$PEG_{adj} = \frac{P \div EPS}{g + d}$$

   The adjusted PEG ratio is a method of evaluating the value of stocks that pay regular dividends to shareholders. In the formula above, P represents the current price of a single share of the stock, EPS represents the most recent earnings per share, g represents the predicted growth rate, and d represents the dividend yield. Which of the following correctly represents the EPS in terms of the other quantities?

   A. $EPS = \dfrac{1}{P \times PEG_{adj}(g + d)}$

   B. $EPS = \dfrac{g + d}{P \times PEG_{adj}}$

   C. $EPS = \dfrac{P}{PEG_{adj}(g + d)}$

   D. $EPS = \dfrac{P \times PEG_{adj}}{g + d}$

30. Consider the function $f(x) = (x - 4)^2 + k$ where $k < 0$. How many real solutions does the equation $f(x) = 0$ have?

    A. None
    B. One
    C. Two
    D. More than two

Directions: Solve problems 31–38 below, then enter your answer in the grid. Instructions for gridding in your response are provided below.

1. You may write your answer in the boxes at the top of the columns. This is not required, but it may help you fill in the circles accurately. The circles are filled in according to instructions to be counted as correct.

2. Fill in only one circle per column.

3. None of the questions has a negative answer.

4. If a problem has more than one possible correct answer, grid in only one answer.

5. Mixed numbers such as $5\frac{1}{2}$ must be gridded as 5.5 or 11/2. (If it is entered into the grid, it will be interpreted as $\frac{51}{2}$ not 5 1/2.)

6. Round or cut off any decimal answer that will not fit the grid, but fill the whole grid.

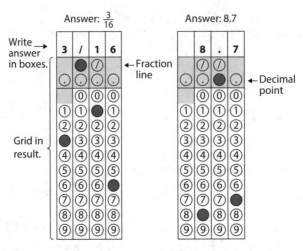

Answer: $\frac{3}{16}$ Answer: 8.7

Write answer in boxes. →   ← Fraction line   ← Decimal point

Grid in result.

Acceptable ways to grid $\frac{1}{3}$ are:

Answer: 509 - either position is correct

NOTE: You may start your answers in any column, space permitting. Columns you don't need to use should be left blank.

31.

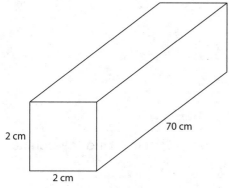

2 cm

70 cm

2 cm

Note: Figure not drawn to scale.

The figure above shows the dimensions of a solid piece of aluminum. Given that the density of aluminum is 2.7 g/cm^3, what is the weight of the represented piece, in pounds? Note that 1 pound is equivalent to approximately 453.6 grams. Round your answer to one decimal place.

32. The population of a small town has increased by 3.5% every year for the last five years. If the population this year was 14,780, then to the nearest whole number, what was the population two years ago?

33. A polynomial has four linear factors and two negative real zeros, −7 and −4. If the polynomial's graph is symmetric about the y-axis, then what is the value of the greatest zero of this polynomial?

34.

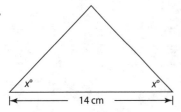

Note: Figure not drawn to scale.

The area of the triangle pictured above is 21 cm³. Find the perimeter, to the nearest tenth of a centimeter.

_____

35. A daycare center's policy requires that for every hour spent on recreational activities in a week, at least two hours must be spent on educational activities. If the center sets aside a total of 12 hours for recreational and educational activities, then what is the maximum number of hours in a week that can be spent on recreational activities?

_____

36.

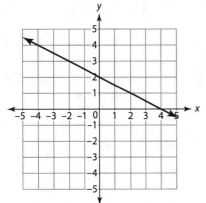

The plot above shows the graph of a linear function $f(x) = mx + b$. What is the greatest whole number value of x where the value of $f(x)$ is positive?

_____

37. The distance between the Earth and the sun is 92,960,000 miles, while the distance between Mercury and the sun is 35,980,000 miles. Given that the speed of light is approximately 186,280 miles per second, how many more minutes does it take light from the sun to reach the Earth than it takes light from the sun to reach Mercury? Round your answer to the nearest tenth of a minute.

38.

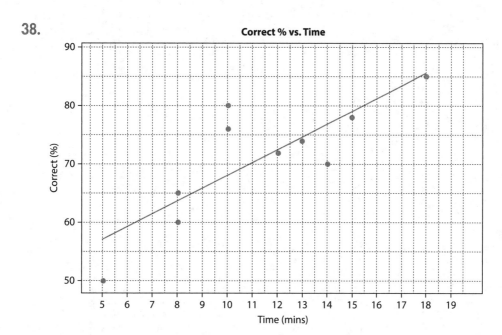

In a psychological study, participants studied an image until they felt they had memorized it, and their time was measured in minutes. Then they answered questions about the image from their memory alone. The percentage of questions that the participant answered correctly was then recorded. This data, along with the line of best fit, is shown above. To the nearest whole number, what is the predicted percentage of correct answers for an individual who studied the image for 10 minutes?

END OF SECTION

SAT Practice Test 2

Practice Test Answer Sheet

Reading Test

1. (A)(B)(C)(D)	14. (A)(B)(C)(D)	27. (A)(B)(C)(D)	40. (A)(B)(C)(D)
2. (A)(B)(C)(D)	15. (A)(B)(C)(D)	28. (A)(B)(C)(D)	41. (A)(B)(C)(D)
3. (A)(B)(C)(D)	16. (A)(B)(C)(D)	29. (A)(B)(C)(D)	42. (A)(B)(C)(D)
4. (A)(B)(C)(D)	17. (A)(B)(C)(D)	30. (A)(B)(C)(D)	43. (A)(B)(C)(D)
5. (A)(B)(C)(D)	18. (A)(B)(C)(D)	31. (A)(B)(C)(D)	44. (A)(B)(C)(D)
6. (A)(B)(C)(D)	19. (A)(B)(C)(D)	32. (A)(B)(C)(D)	45. (A)(B)(C)(D)
7. (A)(B)(C)(D)	20. (A)(B)(C)(D)	33. (A)(B)(C)(D)	46. (A)(B)(C)(D)
8. (A)(B)(C)(D)	21. (A)(B)(C)(D)	34. (A)(B)(C)(D)	47. (A)(B)(C)(D)
9. (A)(B)(C)(D)	22. (A)(B)(C)(D)	35. (A)(B)(C)(D)	48. (A)(B)(C)(D)
10. (A)(B)(C)(D)	23. (A)(B)(C)(D)	36. (A)(B)(C)(D)	49. (A)(B)(C)(D)
11. (A)(B)(C)(D)	24. (A)(B)(C)(D)	37. (A)(B)(C)(D)	50. (A)(B)(C)(D)
12. (A)(B)(C)(D)	25. (A)(B)(C)(D)	38. (A)(B)(C)(D)	51. (A)(B)(C)(D)
13. (A)(B)(C)(D)	26. (A)(B)(C)(D)	39. (A)(B)(C)(D)	52. (A)(B)(C)(D)

Writing and Language Test

1. (A)(B)(C)(D)	12. (A)(B)(C)(D)	23. (A)(B)(C)(D)	34. (A)(B)(C)(D)
2. (A)(B)(C)(D)	13. (A)(B)(C)(D)	24. (A)(B)(C)(D)	35. (A)(B)(C)(D)
3. (A)(B)(C)(D)	14. (A)(B)(C)(D)	25. (A)(B)(C)(D)	36. (A)(B)(C)(D)
4. (A)(B)(C)(D)	15. (A)(B)(C)(D)	26. (A)(B)(C)(D)	37. (A)(B)(C)(D)
5. (A)(B)(C)(D)	16. (A)(B)(C)(D)	27. (A)(B)(C)(D)	38. (A)(B)(C)(D)
6. (A)(B)(C)(D)	17. (A)(B)(C)(D)	28. (A)(B)(C)(D)	39. (A)(B)(C)(D)
7. (A)(B)(C)(D)	18. (A)(B)(C)(D)	29. (A)(B)(C)(D)	40. (A)(B)(C)(D)
8. (A)(B)(C)(D)	19. (A)(B)(C)(D)	30. (A)(B)(C)(D)	41. (A)(B)(C)(D)
9. (A)(B)(C)(D)	20. (A)(B)(C)(D)	31. (A)(B)(C)(D)	42. (A)(B)(C)(D)
10. (A)(B)(C)(D)	21. (A)(B)(C)(D)	32. (A)(B)(C)(D)	43. (A)(B)(C)(D)
11. (A)(B)(C)(D)	22. (A)(B)(C)(D)	33. (A)(B)(C)(D)	44. (A)(B)(C)(D)

Math Test—No Calculator

1. (A)(B)(C)(D)	5. (A)(B)(C)(D)	9. (A)(B)(C)(D)	13. (A)(B)(C)(D)
2. (A)(B)(C)(D)	6. (A)(B)(C)(D)	10. (A)(B)(C)(D)	14. (A)(B)(C)(D)
3. (A)(B)(C)(D)	7. (A)(B)(C)(D)	11. (A)(B)(C)(D)	15. (A)(B)(C)(D)
4. (A)(B)(C)(D)	8. (A)(B)(C)(D)	12. (A)(B)(C)(D)	

16.   17.   18.   19.   20.

(grid-in answer bubbles numbered 0–9 with fraction and decimal rows for each)

Math Test—Calculator

1. (A) (B) (C) (D)
2. (A) (B) (C) (D)
3. (A) (B) (C) (D)
4. (A) (B) (C) (D)
5. (A) (B) (C) (D)
6. (A) (B) (C) (D)
7. (A) (B) (C) (D)
8. (A) (B) (C) (D)

9. (A) (B) (C) (D)
10. (A) (B) (C) (D)
11. (A) (B) (C) (D)
12. (A) (B) (C) (D)
13. (A) (B) (C) (D)
14. (A) (B) (C) (D)
15. (A) (B) (C) (D)
16. (A) (B) (C) (D)

17. (A) (B) (C) (D)
18. (A) (B) (C) (D)
19. (A) (B) (C) (D)
20. (A) (B) (C) (D)
21. (A) (B) (C) (D)
22. (A) (B) (C) (D)
23. (A) (B) (C) (D)

24. (A) (B) (C) (D)
25. (A) (B) (C) (D)
26. (A) (B) (C) (D)
27. (A) (B) (C) (D)
28. (A) (B) (C) (D)
29. (A) (B) (C) (D)
30. (A) (B) (C) (D)

31.
32.
33.
34.
35.
36.
37.
38.

Reading Test

Directions: Below you will see either a passage or pair of passages. After the passage or passages there will be several questions. After you read each passage or pair of passages, please select the option that best answers each question based on anything stated or implied in the passages or the graphics that accompany them.

Questions 1–10 are based on the following passage.

The following passage is excerpted from Nathaniel Hawthorne's *The Scarlet Letter*, published in 1850.

Walking in the shadow of a dream, as it were, and perhaps actually under the influence of a species of somnambulism, Mr. Dimmesdale reached the spot where, now so long since, Hester Prynne had lived through her first hours of public ignominy. The same platform or
5   scaffold, black and weather-stained with the storm or sunshine of seven long years, and foot-worn, too, with the tread of many culprits who had since ascended it, remained standing beneath the balcony of the meeting-house. The minister went up the steps.
It was an obscure night in early May. An unvaried pall of cloud
10 muffled the whole expanse of sky from zenith to horizon. If the same multitude which had stood as eye-witnesses while Hester Prynne sustained her punishment could now have been summoned forth, they would have discerned no face above the platform nor hardly the outline of a human shape, in the dark grey of the midnight. But the town was all
15 asleep. There was no peril of discovery. The minister might stand there, if it so pleased him, until morning should redden in the east, without other risk than that the dank and chill night air would creep into his frame, and stiffen his joints with rheumatism, and clog his throat with catarrh and cough; thereby defrauding the expectant audience of to-morrow's
20 prayer and sermon. No eye could see him, save that ever-wakeful one

which had seen him in his closet, wielding the bloody scourge. Why, then, had he come hither? Was it but the mockery of penitence? A mockery, indeed, but in which his soul trifled with itself! A mockery at which angels blushed and wept, while fiends rejoiced with jeering 25 laughter! He had been driven hither by the impulse of that Remorse which dogged him everywhere, and whose own sister and closely linked companion was that Cowardice which invariably drew him back, with her tremulous gripe, just when the other impulse had hurried him to the verge of a disclosure. Poor, miserable man! what right had infirmity like 30 his to burden itself with crime? Crime is for the iron-nerved, who have their choice either to endure it, or, if it press too hard, to exert their fierce and savage strength for a good purpose, and fling it off at once! This feeble and most sensitive of spirits could do neither, yet continually did one thing or another, which intertwined, in the same inextricable knot, 35 the agony of heaven-defying guilt and vain repentance.

And thus, while standing on the scaffold, in this vain show of expiation, Mr. Dimmesdale was overcome with a great horror of mind, as if the universe were gazing at a scarlet token on his naked breast, right over his heart. On that spot, in very truth, there was, and there 40 had long been, the gnawing and poisonous tooth of bodily pain. Without any effort of his will, or power to restrain himself, he shrieked aloud: an outcry that went pealing through the night, and was beaten back from one house to another, and reverberated from the hills in the background; as if a company of devils, detecting so much misery and terror in it, had 45 made a plaything of the sound, and were bandying it to and fro.

"It is done!" muttered the minister, covering his face with his hands. "The whole town will awake and hurry forth, and find me here!"

But it was not so. The shriek had perhaps sounded with a far greater power, to his own startled ears, than it actually possessed. The town did 50 not awake; or, if it did, the drowsy slumberers mistook the cry either for something frightful in a dream, or for the noise of witches, whose voices, at that period, were often heard to pass over the settlements or lonely cottages, as they rode with Satan through the air.

1. As used in line 2, *somnambulism* most nearly means

   A. a type of alcoholic drink.
   B. sleepwalking.
   C. a seventeenth-century mythical creature.
   D. guilt.

2. The passage most strongly suggests that Dimmesdale is drawn to the scaffold because

   A. he wants to walk through his memory of Hester Prynne there.
   B. he feels guilty.
   C. he cannot sleep.
   D. it is a good vantage point to survey the town in the dark.

3. Which choice provides the best evidence for the answer to the preceding question?

   A. lines 1–4 ("Walking…ignominy")
   B. lines 10–14 ("If…midnight")
   C. lines 15–20 ("The minister…sermon")
   D. lines 25–29 ("He…disclosure")

4. What is the best explanation of the relationship between Remorse and Cowardice as outlined in the passage?

   A. They both stem from mockery.
   B. They are linked, yet competing, impulses.
   C. They are opposites.
   D. They are synonyms.

5. In context of the passage, the phrase "ever-wakeful one" (line 20) refers to

   A. his own eye.
   B. the eye of God.
   C. the mind's eye.
   D. the moon.

6. Dimmesdale screams primarily because

   A. he thinks he has seen a witch.
   B. he wants to wake up the town.
   C. he has a pain in his chest.
   D. he is overcome by the agony of his guilt.

7. Which choice best explains Dimmesdale's declaration: "The whole town will awake and hurry forth, and find me here!"?

   A. He will be exposed in front of the whole town for his strange nighttime activities.
   B. The town will wake up, distracting him from the prison of his mind.
   C. The town will find him on the scaffold and he will have to explain his guilt.
   D. He will finally get the attention from the whole town he desperately desires.

8. As used in line 35, *vain* most nearly means

   A. proud.
   B. supplicant.
   C. immovable.
   D. hollow.

9. Which choice best describes Dimmesdale's character?

   A. Fierce and savage
   B. Impulsive and disrespectful
   C. Fiendish and miserable
   D. Weak and sensitive

10. Which choice provides the best evidence for the answer to the preceding question?

    A. lines 22–25 ("Was...laughter")
    B. lines 25–29 ("the impulse...disclosure")
    C. lines 30–32 ("Crime...once")
    D. lines 32–35 ("This...repentance")

Questions 11–21 are based on the following passage.

The following passage is adapted from Environmental Health Perspective's article titled "Sources of Marine Plastic Pollution," written by John H. Tibbets in April 2015.

A working group of researchers recently estimated that just
20 countries, out of a total of 192 with coastlines, are responsible
for 83 percent of the plastic debris put into the world's oceans.
Lead author Jenna R. Jambeck, an environmental engineer at the
5 University of Georgia, and her colleagues estimated that, all together,
these 192 countries produce some 275 million metric tons of plastic
waste each year. Of that volume, about 4.8–12.7 million metric tons
of mismanaged plastic waste are thought to have entered the ocean
in 2010.
10 "That is the same as five five-gallon bags filled with mixed plastic
on every foot of coastline around the world," says Jambeck. Without
improvements to waste management infrastructure, and assuming
a business-as-usual projection of increasing coastal populations,
economic growth, and use of plastics, the authors predict this volume of
15 plastic debris could more than double by 2025.
The United States makes a significant contribution to marine plastic
pollution, but it's only twentieth on the list of coastal nations that
produce the most plastic waste from land. The top spots are filled by a
number of rapidly developing countries with expanding populations
20 near coastlines and poor systems of waste management, including
China, Indonesia, and the Philippines.
One of the major drivers of this trend in developing countries is
the very rapid growth of "megacities," defined as urban areas with
populations exceeding 10 million. More than 70 percent of megacity
25 growth is said to occur outside the formal planning process, and nearly
a third of the urban population in developing countries lives in slums

or informal settlements that lack city services, including solid-waste disposal.

According to Jambeck and colleagues, a nation's population density within 50 kilometers of the coast is the primary determinant of its land-based contribution to marine pollution. For instance, about 74 percent of Indonesia's population and 83 percent of the Philippines' population live in coastal regions. The second determinant is how much waste overall a coastal nation produces on a per-capita basis. At 2.58 kilograms per person per day, the United States produces far greater volumes of waste per capita than any other nation on the top-20 list except Sri Lanka, and more than twice as much as China.

The third determinant is how much of a country's waste, including plastic material, is mismanaged. The United States does well on that score. "U.S. mismanaged waste is only due to litter," says Jambeck. "We have a waste-management infrastructure that allows everyone an opportunity to throw something away properly." China's coastal population is about 2.5 times as large as that of the United States but is estimated to produce more than 30 times more mismanaged plastic waste.

The geographies of countries play an important part in their contribution to marine debris. Among the top 20 ocean polluters are Sri Lanka, an island nation; archipelago countries, such as the Philippines and Indonesia; and countries with long coastlines, such as China and Vietnam.

"This study [by Jambeck et al.] provides a first cut at how you could focus efforts in places around the world and then build some strategies to stem that flow of plastics," says George H. Leonard, chief scientist of Ocean Conservancy, an advocacy organization based in Washington, DC. "Marine debris is a global problem, but this study shows that you can work on a smaller suite of geographies [and] that you could solve a big part of the problem at the global level." The key, he says, is to improve waste management in a relatively small number of countries.

Rank	Country	Percentage of waste that is mismanaged	Quantity of mismanaged plastic waste (MMT/year)	Percentage of global mismanaged plastic waste	Quantity of plastic marine debris (MMT/Year)
1	China	76	8.82	27.7	1.32–3.53
2	Indonesia	83	3.22	10.1	0.48–1.29
3	Philippines	83	1.88	5.9	0.28–0.75
4	Vietnam	88	1.83	5.8	0.28–0.73
5	Sri Lanka	84	1.59	5.0	0.24–0.64
6	Thailand	75	1.03	3.2	0.15–0.41
7	Egypt	69	0.97	3.0	0.15–0.39
8	Malaysia	57	0.94	2.9	0.14–0.37
9	Nigeria	83	0.85	2.7	0.13–0.34
10	Bangladesh	89	0.79	2.5	0.12–0.31
11	South Africa	56	0.63	2.0	0.09–0.25
12	India	87	0.60	1.9	0.09–0.24
13	Algeria	60	0.52	1.6	0.08–0.21
14	Turkey	18	0.49	1.5	0.07–019
15	Pakistan	88	0.48	1.5	0.07–019
16	Brazil	11	0.47	1.5	0.07–019
17	Burma	89	0.46	1.4	0.07–018
18	Morocco	68	0.31	1.0	0.05–0.12
19	North Korea	90	0.30	1.0	0.05–0.12
20	United States	2	0.28	0.9	0.04–0.11

MMT = million metric tons
Adapted from Jambeck et al. (2015)

11. The author includes Jambeck's description, "five five-gallon bags filled with mixed plastic on every foot of coastline around the world" primarily to

   A. indicate the difficulty of what recapturing marine plastic waste would entail.
   B. create a visual image to better capture the scale of the problem of marine plastic debris.
   C. demonstrate the relationship between coastal polluters and marine plastic.
   D. emphasize the importance of awareness in the issue of marine plastic debris.

12. As used in line 30, *determinant* most nearly means

   A. resolution.
   B. hindrance.
   C. factor.
   D. purpose.

13. The main purpose of the study described in the passage is to

   A. estimate how many metric tons of plastic will accumulate in the ocean by 2025.
   B. prove the correlation between a country's waste production and its contribution to marine plastics.
   C. improve efficiency in waste-management infrastructure across the world.
   D. discover the source and factors by which plastic accumulates in the ocean.

14. Which choice provides the best evidence for the answer to the preceding question?

   A. lines 5–9 ("all...2010")
   B. lines 11–15 ("Without...2025")
   C. lines 29–31 ("According...pollution")
   D. lines 24–28 ("More...disposal")

15. According to the passage, "megacities" in developing nations are relevant to the issue of ocean plastic because

   A. the culture of a megacity leads people to create more plastic waste.
   B. megacities are models for how to efficiently manage plastic waste.
   C. the rapid population growth of megacities without the proper infrastructure leads to more mismanaged waste.
   D. coastal city dwellers are more likely to use the ocean for trash disposal.

16. What solution to the problem of marine plastic is suggested by the passage?

   A. Keeping population densities inland, more than 50 km from coastlines
   B. Halting the production of nonbiodegradable plastics
   C. Creating global environmental guidelines for capturing mismanaged waste
   D. Improving waste management infrastructure in developing nations

17. Which choice provides the best evidence for the answer to the preceding question?

    A. lines 24–28 ("More...disposal")
    B. lines 29–31 ("According...pollution")
    C. lines 46–50 ("The geographies...Vietnam")
    D. lines 55–58 ("Marine...countries")

18. As used in line 53, *stem* most nearly means

    A. to create an offshoot.
    B. to dam up.
    C. to progress upon.
    D. to handle frugally.

19. Using the information in the chart, which choice best explains the relationship between the "quantity of mismanaged plastic waste" and the "quantity of plastic marine debris"?

    A. It's an inverse relationship—as the quantity of a country's mismanaged plastic increases, its quantity of plastic marine debris decreases.
    B. It's a direct correlation—the greater the quantity of a country's mismanaged plastic, the greater the quantity of its plastic marine debris.
    C. It's not a direct correlation because other factors like size of the country and number of coastal cities affect the numbers.
    D. Although the numbers appear to line up, it is impossible to determine a correlation between the two.

20. Using information from the passage and the chart, which choice is the most logical conclusion to make about Brazil's quantity of plastic marine debris?

    A. Brazil's large coastline and abundance of coastal cities is likely to blame for its quantity of plastic marine debris.
    B. Brazil's large production of manufactured plastics likely increases its quantity of plastic marine debris.
    C. Brazil's poor waste management infrastructure likely increases its quantity of plastic marine debris.
    D. Brazil's environmental policies have little effect on the country's quantity of plastic marine debris.

21. Which claim about the ranking system of a country's contribution to marine plastic debris is supported by the graph?

    A. The greater the percentage of a country's mismanaged waste, the higher is its ranking.
    B. The system ranks Asian countries highest, calling into question the study's methodologies.
    C. The system ranks countries higher according to their percentage of global mismanaged plastic waste.
    D. The system ranks developing nations highest, calling into question the true purpose of the study.

Questions 22–31 are based on the following passage.

The following passage is adapted from Theodore Roosevelt's essay "The Bison or American Buffalo," originally published in 1893.

When we became a nation in 1776, the buffaloes, the first animals to vanish when the wilderness is settled, roved to the crests of the mountains which mark the western boundaries of Pennsylvania, Virginia, and the Carolinas. They were plentiful in what are now the
5 States of Ohio, Kentucky, and Tennessee. But by the beginning of the present century they had been driven beyond the Mississippi; and for the next eighty years they formed one of the most distinctive and characteristic features of existence on the great plains. Their numbers were countless—incredible. In vast herds of hundreds of thousands
10 of individuals, they roamed from the Saskatchewan to the Rio Grande and westward to the Rocky Mountains. They furnished all the means of livelihood to the tribes of Horse Indians, and to the curious population of French Metis, on the Red River, as well as to those dauntless and archtypical wanderers, the white hunters and trappers. Their numbers
15 slowly diminished, but the decrease was very gradual until after the Civil War. They were not destroyed by the settlers, but by the railways and the skin hunters.

After the ending of the Civil War, the work of constructing trans-continental railway lines was pushed forward with the utmost vigor.
20   These supplied cheap and indispensable, but hitherto wholly lacking, means of transportation to the hunters; and at the same time the demand for buffalo robes and hides became very great, while the enormous numbers of the beasts, and the comparative ease with which they were slaughtered, attracted throngs of adventurers. The result was
25   such a slaughter of big game as the world had never before seen; never before were so many large animals of one species destroyed in so short a time. Several million buffaloes were slain. In fifteen years from the time the destruction fairly began the great herds were exterminated. In all probability there are not now, all told, five hundred head of
30   wild buffaloes on the American continent; and no herd of a hundred individuals has been in existence since 1884.

The first great break followed the building of the Union Pacific Railway. All the buffaloes of the middle region were then destroyed, and the others were split into two vast sets of herds, the northern and the
35   southern. The latter were destroyed first, about 1878; the former not until 1883. My own chief experience with buffaloes was obtained in the latter year, among small bands and scattered individuals, near my ranch on the Little Missouri; two of my kinsmen were more fortunate, and took part in the chase of these lordly beasts when the herds still
40   darkened the prairie as far as the eye could see.

During the first two months of 1877, my brother Elliott, then a lad not seventeen years old, made a buffalo-hunt toward the edge of the Staked Plains in Northern Texas. He was thus in at the death of the southern herds; for all, save a few scattering bands, were destroyed
45   within two years of this time. He was with my cousin, John Roosevelt, and they went out on the range with six other adventurers.

One morning my cousin and brother had been left in camp as guards. They were sitting idly warming themselves in the first sunbeams, when their attention was sharply drawn to four buffaloes that were coming
50   to the pool to drink. As soon as they turned, my brother and cousin ran

for their rifles, but before they got back the buffaloes had crossed the bluff crest. Climbing after them, they struck a steady trot, following the animals by sight until they passed over a knoll, and but a few hundred yards from the edge, in a slight hollow, they saw the four buffaloes just

55 entering a herd of fifty or sixty that were scattered out grazing. After a whispered consultation, the two hunters crept back, and made a long circle that brought them well to leeward of the herd, in line with a slight rise in the ground. They then crawled up to this rise and, peering through the tufts of tall, rank grass, saw the unconscious beasts a

60 hundred and twenty-five or fifty yards away. They fired together, each mortally wounding his animal, and then, rushing in as the herd halted in confusion, and following them as they ran, impeded by numbers, hurry, and panic, they eventually got three more.

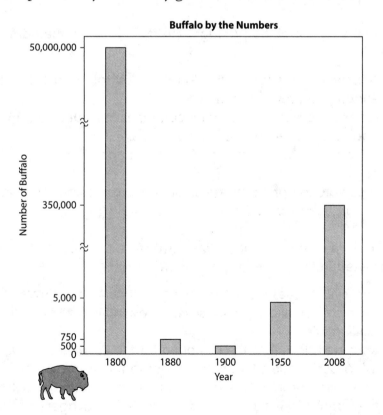

Buffalo by the Numbers

22. The description in the first paragraph indicates that what Roosevelt values most about the buffalo is that

    A. they were a distinctive feature of the American landscape.
    B. they were plentiful.
    C. they were useful to tribes and early settlers.
    D. they were wanderers, much like the early settlers of the Great Plains.

23. Which choice provides the best evidence for the answer to the preceding question?

    A. lines 7–11 ("for…Mountains")
    B. lines 11–14 ("They…trappers")
    C. lines 14–17 ("Their…hunters")
    D. lines 32–35 ("The first…southern")

24. Over the course of the passage, the main focus of the narrative shifts from

    A. a lament on the loss of the American Buffalo to a call to save the endangered few that remain.
    B. a nostalgic story of the American landscape at its birth to a screed against the overdevelopment of lands.
    C. a history of the decimation of the American Buffalo to a hunting narrative.
    D. a celebration of the progress of transcontinental transportation to one traveler's story.

25. What is the main tension in the narrative suggested by the shift discussed in the preceding question?

    A. Roosevelt argues that an abundance of hunters destroyed the buffalo population, yet Roosevelt revels in his brother's adventurous hunting tale.
    B. Roosevelt describes the nostalgia for the American landscape of 1776 but counters that with the desire for progress.
    C. Roosevelt describes the beauty in the abundance of buffalo on the Great Plains but counters that with the savagery of the buffalo hunters.

     D. Roosevelt advocates a transcontinental railway, but regrets that it was actually used by buffalo hunters.

26. As used in line 20, *indispensable* most nearly means

    A. deficient.
    B. necessary.
    C. unforgivable.
    D. frivolous.

27. Which choice best characterizes Roosevelt's views on buffalo hunting in its heyday?

    A. It is an immoral practice that should have been banned.
    B. It is a nefarious means of acquiring cash.
    C. It is an adventure.
    D. It is a great challenge for the skilled hunter.

28. Which choice provides the best evidence for the answer to the preceding question?

    A. lines 11–14 ("They…trappers")
    B. lines 16–17 ("They…hunters")
    C. lines 18–21 ("After…hunters")
    D. lines 38–40 ("two…see")

29. As used in line 59, *unconscious* most nearly means

    A. sleeping.
    B. undone.
    C. unaware.
    D. imaginary.

30. After becoming president in 1901, Theodore Roosevelt strove to protect wildlife and conserved approximately 230,000,000 acres of public land. It can thus reasonably be inferred from the graph that

    A. the actions of Roosevelt's presidency had little effect on the buffalo population.

B. Theodore Roosevelt took the reins of his presidency at the height of the buffalo population.

C. the actions of Roosevelt's presidency paved the way for the resurgence of the buffalo population.

D. Theodore Roosevelt's advocacy of a transcontinental railway must have hurt the buffalo population.

31. According to the graph, which choice is true of the resurgence of the American buffalo?

A. The buffalo population in 2008 had reached nearly half of the peak population of 1800.

B. The number of buffalo rose significantly from 1950 to 2008.

C. The rise of the buffalo population was sharper than its decline.

D. After over a century since its decimation, the buffalo population in 2008 was still dwindling.

Questions 32–41 are based on the following passage.

This passage is modified from a U.S. Geological Survey and National Parks Service's article titled "Steam Explosions, Earthquakes, and Volcanic Eruptions—What's in Yellowstone's Future?"

The Yellowstone region has produced three exceedingly large volcanic eruptions in the past 2.1 million years. In each of these cataclysmic events, enormous volumes of magma erupted at the surface and into the atmosphere as mixtures of red-hot pumice, volcanic ash (small,
5 jagged fragments of volcanic glass and rock), and gas that spread as pyroclastic ("fire-broken") flows in all directions. Rapid withdrawal of such large volumes of magma from the subsurface then caused the ground to collapse, swallowing overlying mountains and creating broad cauldron-shaped volcanic depressions called "calderas."
10   The first of these caldera-forming eruptions 2.1 million years ago created a widespread volcanic deposit known as the Huckleberry Ridge Tuff, an outcrop of which can be viewed at Golden Gate, south

of Mammoth Hot Springs. This titanic event, one of the five largest individual volcanic eruptions known anywhere on the Earth, formed a
15   caldera more than 60 miles (100 km) across.

A similar, smaller but still huge eruption occurred 1.3 million years ago. This eruption formed the Henrys Fork Caldera, located in the area of Island Park, west of Yellowstone National Park, and produced another widespread volcanic deposit called the Mesa Falls Tuff.

20   The region's most recent caldera-forming eruption 640,000 years ago created the 35-mile-wide, 50-mile-long (55 by 80 km) Yellowstone Caldera. Pyroclastic flows from this eruption left thick volcanic deposits known as the Lava Creek Tuff, which can be seen in the south-facing cliffs east of Madison, where they form the north wall of the caldera.
25   Huge volumes of volcanic ash were blasted high into the atmosphere, and deposits of this ash can still be found in places as distant from Yellowstone as Iowa, Louisiana, and California.

Each of Yellowstone's explosive caldera-forming eruptions occurred when large volumes of "rhyolitic" magma accumulated at shallow levels
30   in the Earth's crust, as little as 3 miles (5 km) below the surface. This highly viscous magma, charged with dissolved gas, then moved upward, stressing the crust and generating earthquakes. As the magma neared the surface and pressure decreased, the expanding gas caused violent explosions. Eruptions of rhyolite have been responsible for forming
35   many of the world's calderas, such as those at Katmai National Park, Alaska, which formed in an eruption in 1912, and at Long Valley, California.

If another large caldera-forming eruption were to occur at Yellowstone, its effects would be worldwide. Thick ash deposits would
40   bury vast areas of the United States, and injection of huge volumes of volcanic gases into the atmosphere could drastically affect global climate. Fortunately, the Yellowstone volcanic system shows no signs that it is headed toward such an eruption.

More likely in Yellowstone than a large explosive caldera-forming
45   eruption is eruption of a lava flow, which would be far less devastating.

Since Yellowstone's last caldera-forming eruption 640,000 years ago, about 30 eruptions of rhyolitic lava flows have nearly filled the Yellowstone Caldera. Other flows of rhyolite and basalt (a more fluid variety of lava) also have been extruded outside the caldera. Each day,
50 visitors to the park drive and hike across the lavas that fill the caldera, most of which were erupted since 160,000 years ago, some as recently as about 70,000 years ago. These extensive rhyolite lavas are very large and thick, and some cover as much as 130 square miles (340 square km), twice the area of Washington, D.C. During eruption, these flows
55 oozed slowly over the surface, moving at most a few hundred feet per day for several months to several years, destroying everything in their paths. Today, most of the landforms within the Yellowstone Caldera reflect the shapes of these young lava flows.

32. As used in line 2, *cataclysmic* most nearly means

  A. cyclic.
  B. biblical.
  C. tragic.
  D. earth-shattering.

33. What claim about calderas is supported by the passage?

  A. The oldest caldera of the Yellowstone region mentioned in the passage is also the largest.
  B. The youngest caldera of the Yellowstone region mentioned in the passage is also the smallest.
  C. The youngest caldera of the Yellowstone region mentioned in the passage is also the largest.
  D. The oldest caldera of the Yellowstone region mentioned in the passage is also the smallest.

34. Which choice provides the best evidence for the answer to the preceding question?

  A. lines 10–15 ("The first…across")
  B. lines 16–19 ("A similar…Tuff")

C. lines 20–22 ("The region's...Caldera")
D. lines 49–54 ("Each...km")

35. According to the passage, what is mainly responsible for the caldera-forming eruptions?

    A. The accumulation of magma near the earth's crust
    B. A buildup of dissolved gases in the earth's inner core
    C. Mounting pyroclastic flows from the earth's outer core
    D. The interaction of rhyolite and basalt in the earth's mantle

36. Which choice provides the best evidence for the answer to the preceding question?

    A. lines 6–9 ("Rapid...calderas")
    B. lines 20–23 ("The region's...Tuff")
    C. lines 22–25 ("Pyroclastic...atmosphere")
    D. lines 28–30 ("Each...surface")

37. As used in line 32, *stressing* most nearly means

    A. signifying.
    B. coercing.
    C. unsettling.
    D. exposing.

38. The passage strongly suggests that most of the landforms at Yellowstone Park were shaped by

    A. the Henrys Fork Caldera.
    B. volcanic ash deposits.
    C. the Lava Creek Tuff.
    D. lava flows.

39. The passage strongly suggests that if another large caldera-forming eruption were to occur at Yellowstone

    A. it would be contained to the area surrounding Yellowstone.
    B. it would have worldwide consequences including drastic climate change.

C. the ash deposits would be the most devastating to the global climate.
D. the eruption would destroy much of the United States, but the rest of the world would be fine.

40. The main rhetorical effect of discussing the possibility of another large caldera-forming eruption is to

A. produce alarm so a reader may take the warning seriously.
B. contextualize the magnitude of a cataclysmic eruption.
C. produce a vivid image for the reader.
D. exaggerate the effects of previous cataclysmic eruptions.

41. The use of the phrase "young lava flows" in the final sentence is primarily meant to

A. emphasize that 70,000 years is relatively young for lava flows.
B. indicate that new lava flows occur in Yellowstone every day.
C. describe the vigor of the lava flows.
D. convey irony because the lava flows are many thousands of years old.

Questions 42–52 are based on the following passages.

Passage 1 is an excerpt from the Declaration of Independence written by Thomas Jefferson in 1776. Passage 2 is an excerpt of President John F. Kennedy's inaugural address delivered in 1961.

Passage 1

... When in the Course of human events, it becomes necessary for one people to dissolve the political bands which have connected them with another, and to assume, among the Powers of the earth, the separate and equal station to which the Laws of Nature and of Nature's
5 God entitle them, a decent respect to the opinions of mankind requires that they should declare the causes which impel them to the separation.

We hold these truths to be self-evident, that all men are created equal, that they are endowed by their Creator with certain unalienable Rights, that among these are Life, Liberty, and the pursuit of

10 Happiness—That to secure these rights, Governments are instituted among Men, deriving their just powers from the consent of the governed,—That whenever any Form of Government becomes destructive of these ends, it is the Right of the People to alter or to abolish it, and to institute new Government, laying its foundation on

15 such principles and organizing its powers in such form, as to them shall seem most likely to effect their Safety and Happiness. Prudence, indeed, will dictate that Governments long established should not be changed for light and transient causes; and accordingly all experience hath shown, that mankind are more disposed to suffer, while evils are

20 sufferable, than to right themselves by abolishing the forms to which they are accustomed. But when a long train of abuses and usurpations, pursuing invariably the same Object evinces a design to reduce them under absolute Despotism, it is their right, it is their duty, to throw off such Government, and to provide new Guards for their future

25 security.—Such has been the patient sufferance of these Colonies; and such is now the necessity which constrains them to alter their former Systems of Government. The history of the present King of Great Britain is a history of repeated injuries and usurpations, all having in direct object the establishment of an absolute Tyranny over these

30 States.

Passage 2

... We observe today not a victory of party but a celebration of freedom, symbolizing an end as well as a beginning, signifying renewal as well as change. For I have sworn before you and Almighty God the same solemn oath our forebears prescribed nearly a century and three-

5 quarters ago.

The world is very different now. For man holds in his mortal hands the power to abolish all forms of human poverty and all forms of human life. And yet the same revolutionary beliefs for which our forebears fought are still at issue around the globe—the belief that the rights of man come not from the generosity of the state but from the hand of God.

We dare not forget today that we are the heirs of that first revolution. Let the word go forth from this time and place, to friend and foe alike, that the torch has been passed to a new generation of Americans, born in this century, tempered by war, disciplined by a hard and bitter peace, proud of our ancient heritage, and unwilling to witness or permit the slow undoing of those human rights to which this nation has always been committed, and to which we are committed today at home and around the world.

Let every nation know, whether it wishes us well or ill, that we shall pay any price, bear any burden, meet any hardship, support any friend, oppose any foe to assure the survival and the success of liberty.

This much we pledge—and more.

To those old allies whose cultural and spiritual origins we share, we pledge the loyalty of faithful friends. United there is little we cannot do in a host of cooperative ventures. Divided there is little we can do; for we dare not meet a powerful challenge at odds and split asunder.

To those new states whom we welcome to the ranks of the free, we pledge our word that one form of colonial control shall not have passed away merely to be replaced by a far more iron tyranny. We shall not always expect to find them supporting our view. But we shall always hope to find them strongly supporting their own freedom; and to remember that, in the past, those who foolishly sought power by riding the back of the tiger ended up inside.

42. The main goal of passage 1 is

    A. to define the concept of just government.
    B. to philosophize about the powers that rule people.
    C. to explain the reasons for establishing a new government.
    D. to detail the principles on which governments are founded.

43. Which choice provides the best evidence for the answer to the preceding question?

    A. lines 5–6 ("a decent...separation")
    B. lines 7–10 ("We...Happiness")
    C. lines 10–12 ("Governments...governed")
    D. lines 27–30 ("The history...States")

44. As used in line 18 of passage 1, *transient* most nearly means

    A. uncompromising.
    B. fleeting.
    C. wandering.
    D. harmless.

45. Which choice best characterizes the tone of passage 2?

    A. Sarcastic
    B. Somber
    C. Commanding
    D. Exuberant

46. According to the discussion in passage 2, which choice does Kennedy value most as leader of the free world?

    A. Pragmatism
    B. Loyalty
    C. Liberty
    D. Security

47. As used in line 29 of passage 2, *colonial* most nearly means

    A. hive-minded.
    B. Puritan.
    C. dictatorial.
    D. quaint.

48. What is the best explanation of the metaphor in the final sentence of passage 2?

    A. It shows how allies of tyrants may find themselves ruled by those tyrants.
    B. It shows how people who abuse power also feed power.
    C. It describes how countries join to become a superpower.
    D. It describes how tyrannical countries become overthrown.

49. According to passage 2, which choice highlights an important difference between the world of Thomas Jefferson and the world that John F. Kennedy oversaw as president?

    A. While Jefferson's America had to overthrow its tyrants, Kennedy's America, as a superpower, had to be careful of becoming a tyrant to the world.
    B. The world of America in 1961 has increased technology, including the atomic bomb, able to affect the lives of every person on the planet.
    C. In 1961, there were no concerns about revolution in America or around the world.
    D. Jefferson's America was based on the idea that people's rights are endowed by their creator, while Kennedy asserts it comes from the hand of God.

50. Which choice provides the best evidence for the answer to the preceding question?

    A. lines 6–8 ("The world...life")
    B. lines 8–11 ("And yet...God")
    C. line 12 ("We...revolution")
    D. lines 28–30 ("To...tyranny")

51. Which choice best characterizes the relationship between the two documents?

    A. Passage 2 builds on the concepts of passage 1.
    B. Passage 1 anticipates the issues of passage 2.
    C. Passage 2 dissects the arguments of passage 1.
    D. Passage 1 contradicts the arguments of passage 2.

52. Which choice best describes the stances of each passage?

    A. Kennedy asserts power as a ruler; Jefferson asserts power as a sufferer of tyranny.
    B. Kennedy speaks as a neutral observer; Jefferson speaks as an active participant.
    C. Jefferson builds on historical principles; Kennedy tears down historical precedents.
    D. Jefferson opportunistically seeks power; Kennedy sets forth idealistic principles.

END OF SECTION

Writing and Language Test

Directions: Several questions follow each passage below. Some questions might ask you to improve the passage by revising or editing it. There may be a table, graph, or other graphic that goes along with a passage or question. For some questions, you will be asked to consider an underlined portion of a passage. Still other questions will ask you to consider the passage as a whole. Read each passage. For each question, **find the number in the passage that corresponds to the question number** and decide which answer best improves the passage or makes it grammatically correct. Sometimes "NO CHANGE" will be an answer choice. If making no change is the best option, choose this answer.

Questions 1–11 are based on the following passage.

The "I" of the Storm

[1] If you asked me if I think giving hurricanes and tropical storms regular human names would be especially controversial, I would say no. [2] But since domestic and international weather organizations adopted the practice in the 1950s, there has been no shortage of policy revisions and controversy.

Starting in 1953, storms in the United States were assigned [3] women names. By 1979, both male and female names were used for storms all over the country after public debate suggested that using only female names for severe weather events was unfair. [4] A list of names for each country's storms; one name per year for each letter of the alphabet; is maintained by the World Meteorological Organization, and recycled on a six-year rotation. However, if there is a storm that becomes especially deadly or destructive, that name is "retired" and taken out of the rotation.

New names are only added to the list as older names are retired from use. The replacements are voted on by the WMO's Hurricane

Committee, and adopted internationally. One example of this process in action was Hurricane Sandy in 2012, which caused at least 233 deaths in eight countries and resulted in more than $68 billion dollars in damage. The WMO quickly voted to remove "Sandy" from the list and [5] will replace it with "Sara" in 2018 when the 2012 storm name list is used again.

[6] The policy of naming tropical storms and hurricanes initially began as a way of helping the National Oceanic and Atmospheric Administration (NOAA) [7] to tracking and recording storm data on the [8] West Coast of the united states. [9] Weather scientists in the United States had experienced challenges with the existing system, which involved tracking storms by the year and the order in which they appeared. There would sometimes be confusion if two different storms appeared in entirely different regions around the same time, causing communication and record-keeping problems. [10] Having recognized these challenges, the decision was made to give each storm a distinct, easily assigned name to smooth the process. Now people in California would no longer risk getting mistaken tropical storm advisories for a hurricane approaching Florida that happened to have been identified at the same time. [11]

1. How should the writer revise this sentence to match the tone of the rest of the passage?

   A. NO CHANGE
   B. You might not expect naming hurricanes to be a complicated issue, but the process that has evolved for it over the past 70 years has been complex.
   C. Do you share a name with a hurricane? You might!
   D. This is how we name storms in the United States.

2.

    A. NO CHANGE
    B. Right, but
    C. Yet,
    D. Since

3.

    A. NO CHANGE
    B. lady names
    C. female names
    D. male names

4.

    A. NO CHANGE
    B. A list of names for each country's storms . . . one name per year for each letter of the alphabet . . .
    C. A list of names for each country's storms. One name per year for each letter of the alphabet,
    D. A list of names for each country's storms (one name per year for each letter of the alphabet)

5.

    A. NO CHANGE
    B. will be replaced
    C. were replacing it
    D. will replace them

6. Where should the writer place this paragraph (currently paragraph 4) to make sure the entire passage flows well?

    A. Delete it altogether.
    B. Place it before paragraph 2 ("Starting in 1953 . . .")
    C. Place it before paragraph 3 ("No names . . .")
    D. Leave it where it is.

7.

    A. NO CHANGE
    B. to track and recording
    C. to track and record
    D. for tracking and recording

8.

    A. NO CHANGE
    B. West coast of the United states
    C. west coast of the united states
    D. west coast of the United States

9. Which of the following would be a transition word (or phrase) the writer could use in this sentence?

    A. Previously, weather scientists in the United States
    B. In the future, weather scientists in the United States
    C. Maybe, weather scientists in the United States
    D. Now we know, weather scientists in the United States

10.

    A. NO CHANGE
    B. These challenges made the decision
    C. Despite the challenges, the various weather agencies decided
    D. Having recognized these challenges, the various weather agencies decided

11. What would be a concise topic sentence to summarize the passage?

    A. The process for naming storms has changed greatly in the twenty-first century.
    B. The process for naming storms is complicated and has evolved over time.
    C. Storms should not be named after people.
    D. Hurricane Sandy was a difficult and costly storm.

Questions 12–22 are based on the following passage.

In the past, people who commuted to work on bikes were often a very tiny minority. [12] <u>Fitness fanatics, environmentalists, or just plain people who did not want to drive for one reason or another.</u> As more and more cities have adopted "bike share" programs, where members can rent a bicycle at one place and return it at another, the way we look at commuting choice has changed. Accordingly, there should be a bike sharing program in every city in the United States.

[13] <u>Bike sharing programs has seen</u> a sharp [14] <u>uptick</u> in use in the cities where they've been adopted and encouraged by local governments. According to Metrobike.net, the number of programs worldwide increased more than 800 percent between 2007 and 2012, from 62 programs to 497.

Global Bike Share Programs

[15] <u>Europe has been the biggest adopter, with Asia and North America following.</u> In the United States, bike sharing programs exist mostly in large cities like Washington, D.C., Indianapolis, Chicago, and Boston. [16] <u>These cities are so diverse in geography and location that they underscore how universal the need is for these programs.</u>

The environmental benefits of bike sharing need to be considered by city governments as well. In large cities with public transportation systems, a commuter bicycling to work is a commuter who is not using buses and trains that contribute to poor air quality. In smaller cities where driving is the norm, [17] bicyclists use less fuel and creating less air pollution than drivers. Bicyclists also [18] cause significantly and considerably less damage to roadways than cars and trucks, saving resources on expensive construction.

[19] Implementing bike sharing programs is often expensive, and requires that cities add special lanes for safety. Safety is one of the top concerns when thinking about implementing a bike sharing program, because mixing bicyclists and motorists on the road can often have dangerous consequences.

Bike sharing programs also benefit members personally. Membership is less expensive than commuting by [20] Car, Bus, or Train, and can save the rider from parking issues, overcrowded trains, and heavy traffic. Being able to pick up a bike at point A and [21] than return it securely to point B for the next user also means that the rider does not have to worry about theft or vandalism. There are health benefits as well, since biking provides strong aerobic exercise. A commuter who bikes to work or school at least a few times a week has made a commitment to her health. [22]

12. How should the writer revise this underlined text?

    A. NO CHANGE
    B. Delete the sentence.
    C. They were often seen as fitness fanatics, rabid environmentalists, or merely people who did not want to drive.
    D. We were often seen as fitness fanatics, environmentalists, or merely people who did not want to drive.

13.

    A. NO CHANGE
    B. Bike sharing programs has seen
    C. Bike sharing programs will have seen
    D. Bike sharing programs have seen

14. Based on the context, what does the underlined word *uptick* mean?

    A. Decrease
    B. Increase
    C. Market
    D. Description

15. What would be the most effective way to support the underlined text?

    A. Delete it from the passage.
    B. Include a graph showing the population of the U.S. cities that have bike sharing programs.
    C. Include a graph showing the number of bike sharing programs in different regions of the world.
    D. Add historical details about the first bike sharing program in Germany.

16. Which of the following would be a good supporting point for the underlined sentence?

    A. For example, Miami's population and geography are much different than San Francisco's, but both cities have created thriving bike share programs.
    B. People are different wherever you go, so everyone should be accommodated.
    C. Because this has worked in Europe, it will definitely work here in the United States.
    D. This just goes to show, American cities are very diverse.

17.

    A. NO CHANGE
    B. bicyclists use less fuel and create less air pollution
    C. bicyclists use less fuel and air pollution
    D. bicyclists are using less fuel and create less air pollution

18.

    A. NO CHANGE
    B. cause significantly, considerably
    C. are causing significantly and considerably
    D. cause significantly

19. What should the writer do with this underlined paragraph?

    A. Add a graph about bicyclist injuries.
    B. Add statistics on start-up costs for bike sharing programs.
    C. Delete it from the passage.
    D. Make it the closing paragraph.

20.

    A. NO CHANGE
    B. car, bus, or train
    C. car; bus; or train
    D. Car; bus; or Train

21.

    A. NO CHANGE
    B. whereas
    C. then
    D. when

22. Which of the following would make the most effective conclusion to the passage?

    A. Because we now know that bike sharing programs provide so many potential benefits to riders and cities, they should be welcomed as an alternative to the public and private transportation we've always known.
    B. The facts are clear on this issue: cities in the United States should ban commuting by car.
    C. Now that the world has gotten on board with bike sharing programs, it is time for every city in the United States to follow suit.
    D. Because bicycling is a safer way of driving to work or school, it should become our top priority in public transportation.

Questions 23–33 are based on the following passage.

[23] In the *New York Times* in 1992: author Robert Coover write a piece titled "The End of Books," in which he mused about whether print books as we knew them could survive "video transmissions, cellular phones, fax machines, computer networks, and in particular out in the humming digitalized precincts of avant-garde computer hackers, cyberpunks and hyperspace freaks." More than 20 years later, the answer to that is [24] YES. While there may not be as many brick-and-mortar bookstores around as there were in 1992, there is no shortage of [25] hardcovers, paperbacks, textbooks, at all. But the industry has expanded to include digital books as well, and to create a separate and evolving career path in publishing.

In the [26] 1990's and early 2000's, publishing professionals who worked on digital products like ebooks and website content were called "desktop publishers." In this specific role, a person would gather text and/or art, [27] format it, and finalize files. Desktop publishers have become a bit of an endangered species, as companies diversify these jobs among a number of professionals like graphic artists, web designers, and content editors who all work together to create pieces of the final product. [28] The statistics predict that as software improves, the [29] only desktop publisher role will continue to decline at least 5 percent between 2012 and 2022, while graphic designers and editors are likely to grow at least 5 to 10 percent.

[30] Traditional book publishers have seen ebook sales grow slightly over the past 10 years, and they have grown their digital publishing programs accordingly. An editor works with the content to make sure that there are no print-only [31] references (for example "turn to page 23" might be accurate in a print book but would mystify a reader who doesn't have page numbers visible on his reading device). Graphic artists redesign the cover and the book's interior as necessary to make sure the book looks as good on a tablet or smartphone screen as it does on the page. And a digital developer works with the file "under the hood"

to make sure that the ebook is readable on the many different devices used by the public. All of these careers are likely to continue growing between 5 and 10 percent by 2022, per the U.S. Bureau of Labor Statistics.

[32] These digital publishing programs are small compared to their print counterparts. In 2013, ebook sales were only 27 percent of overall book sales, according to publishing industry group Digital Book World. However, the growth of this field shows that while there's no [33] imminent threat to print books, there is plenty of career opportunity to be seized.

23.

A. NO CHANGE
B. In the *New York Times* in 1992; author Robert Coover
C. In the *New York Times* in 1992, author Robert Coover
D. In the *New York Times* in 1992 (author Robert Coover)

24.

A. NO CHANGE
B. "YES."
C. yes.
D. "yes."

25.

A. NO CHANGE
B. hardcovers/paperbacks/textbooks at all.
C. hardcovers; paperbacks; textbooks; at all.
D. hardcovers, paperbacks, and textbooks at all.

26.

A. NO CHANGE
B. nineteen-nineties and early two-thousands
C. 1990s and early 2000s
D. Nineteen-Nineties and early Two-Thousands

27. What kind of detail(s) should the writer add to support this underlined point?

    A. Naming a few different types of software used by desktop publishers or methods for formatting
    B. Outlining the differences between ebooks and websites
    C. None. The writer should delete this sentence altogether.
    D. Including the salary of a desktop publisher in 1998

28. How should the writer edit this sentence for clarity?

    A. The statistics predict that as software becomes more sophisticated and accessible to the average person,
    B. The U.S. Bureau of Labor and Statistics predicts that as software becomes more sophisticated and accessible to the average person,
    C. Statistics say that publishing software is improving,
    D. Software will continue to improve, which means that in the eyes of the U.S. Bureau of Labor Statistics,

29.

    A. NO CHANGE
    B. every
    C. specific
    D. all

30. How should the writer revise the underlined text based on this chart?

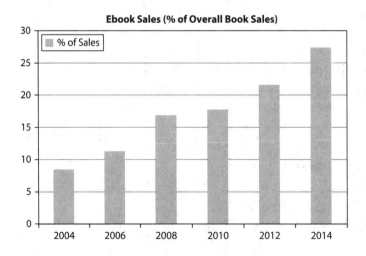

Ebook Sales (% of Overall Book Sales)

A. NO CHANGE
B. Traditional book publishers have seen ebook sales more than triple over the past 10 years
C. Traditional book publishers have seen ebook sales decline over the past 10 years
D. There is not enough data to make conclusions about traditional publishers' ebook sales

31.

A. NO CHANGE
B. references, for example, "turn to page 23" might be accurate in a print book but would mystify a reader who doesn't have page numbers visible on his reading device.
C. references. For example, ("turn to page 23") might be accurate in a print book but would mystify a reader who doesn't have page numbers visible on his reading device.
D. references. For example, "turn to page 23" might be accurate in a print book but would mystify a reader who doesn't have page numbers visible on his reading device.

32. How could the writer combine the underlined sentences?

A. These digital publishing programs are small compared to their print counterparts: in 2013, ebook sales were only 27 percent of overall book sales,
B. These digital publishing programs are small compared to their print counterparts. . . . In 2013, ebook sales were only 27 percent of overall book sales,
C. These digital publishing programs are small compared to their print counterparts, therefore, in 2014, ebook sales were only 27 percent of overall book sales,
D. These digital publishing programs are small compared to their print counterparts because in 2013, ebook sales were only 27 percent of overall book sales,

33.

A. NO CHANGE
B. eminent
C. delayed
D. big

Questions 34–44 are based on the following passage.

I Am Malala

[34] <u>Sometimes the strongest voices come from the least likely of sources.</u>

Malala Yousafzai was born in 1997, in northwestern Pakistan. Early on, [35] <u>her school owner and education activist father</u> taught her the value of education. Young Malala was interested in becoming a doctor or possibly a politician when she grew up, and knew that education [36] <u>would have key to her future goals</u>. Unfortunately, this contrasted with the growing political power of the [37] <u>Taliban</u> in her region of Pakistan, and their increasing bans on women's activities in the country.

By the time Malala was 11, the Taliban had barred women from shopping in public or attending school, in addition to broader cultural bans on music and television. Discontent to have her education and future ripped away from her, Malala began speaking out against these drastic limitations. [38] *How dare the Taliban take away my basic right to education?* she asked the audience in a public press club meeting, before revealing that she would continue her education any way possible, including sneaking textbooks in her clothing. This outspoken activist was a mere 12 years old.

Shortly after Malala began speaking out about the [39] <u>draconian</u> boundaries placed on young girls by the Taliban, she was recruited by the British Broadcasting Corporation (BBC) to be an anonymous blogger, a schoolgirl's voice among the growing chaos in Pakistan as the Taliban struggled for control of the region. She became less anonymous as she kept speaking out, and appeared in a documentary about Pakistani education. Her growing public profile put her in danger from the [40] <u>Taliban . . . threats and harassment</u> that culminated in a horrific 2012 assassination attempt where Malala and two other schoolgirls were shot on a bus by a masked gunman. All three survived, but the attack generated immediate outrage, sympathy, and support from around the world.

[41] <u>Malala continued her activism</u>—and now she had a global platform. Under the motto "I am Malala," the United Nations passed a resolution [42] <u>calling on Pakistan to establish educational rights for all its children, and for outlawing discrimination against women and girls</u>. Later, in 2013, Malala addressed the U.N. General Assembly directly, and met with various world leaders to discuss her message of equality and education. Malala's book, also called *I Am Malala*, was published in October of that year. The book was an instant bestseller, and has been translated into dozens of languages worldwide.

Even as the awards and support [43] <u>will have poured in</u> for Malala's brave fight against a brutal system, perhaps the most important award was yet to come. In 2014, 17-year-old Malala Yousafzai won the Nobel Peace Prize, making her the youngest Nobel laureate in the history of the awards. [44] <u>For many that kind of recognition is the capstone to decades of activism,</u> but for Malala it was likely a launching pad for what comes next in the struggle for worldwide equality.

34. What should the writer do with this brief introductory statement?

    A. Delete it from the passage.
    B. Move it to the very end.
    C. Add more details about unlikely voices.
    D. Include a personal anecdote.

35.

A. NO CHANGE
B. her school owner, and education activist father
C. her father, a school owner and education activist,
D. her school owner and education activist

36.

A. NO CHANGE
B. would be key to her future goals
C. would have been key to her future goals
D. are key to her future goals

37. Which parenthetical description would be most effective for the underlined text?

A. (a fundamentalist military group)
B. (in Pakistan)
C. (at the time)
D. (the political leaders)

38.

A. NO CHANGE
B. "How dare the Taliban take away my basic right to education?"
C. HOW DARE THE TALIBAN TAKE AWAY MY BASIC RIGHT TO EDUCATION?
D. How dare the Taliban take away my basic right to education?

39. Based on the context, what does *draconian* mean?

A. Severe
B. Necessary
C. Pointless
D. Immoral

40.

    A. NO CHANGE
    B. Taliban, threats and harassment
    C. Taliban. Threats and harassment
    D. Taliban. She was the target of threats and harassment

41. Which of the following would be an effective transitional phrase for the underlined text?

    A. Anyway,
    B. That said,
    C. After her recovery,
    D. At least

42.

    A. NO CHANGE
    B. calling on Pakistan for establishing educational rights for all its children, and for outlawing discrimination against women and girls.
    C. calling on Pakistan establishing educational rights for all its children, and outlawing discrimination against women and girls.
    D. calling on Pakistan to establish educational rights for all its children and to outlaw discrimination against women and girls.

43.

    A. NO CHANGE
    B. have poured in
    C. will pour in
    D. were poured in

44. Which of the following revisions would best complement the underlined text?

    A. For many, like fellow Nobel winners Dr. Martin Luther King Jr. or Mother Theresa, that kind of recognition is the capstone to decades of activism,
    B. For many, that kind of recognition is the capstone to a long life of activism,
    C. Most Nobel laureates are elderly,
    D. The Nobel Prize is enough of an accomplishment in and of itself,

END OF SECTION

Math Test—No Calculator

Directions: For questions 1–15 below, solve each problem, choose the best answer from the choices provided, then fill in the corresponding circle on your answer sheet. For questions 16–20, first solve the problem and then fill in your answer on the grid according to the directions provided before question 16. Your test booklet may be used for scratch work.

Notes:

1. You may **not** use a calculator.

2. You may assume all variables and expressions used represent real numbers unless stated otherwise.

3. You may assume figures are drawn to scale, unless noted otherwise.

4. You may assume all figures lie in a plane unless otherwise noted.

5. The domain of a given function f is the set of all real numbers x for which $f(x)$ is a real number, unless otherwise noted.

Reference:

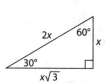

$A = \pi r^2$
$C = 2\pi r$

$A = \frac{1}{2}bh$

$c^2 = a^2 + b^2$

$A = lw$

Special Right Triangles

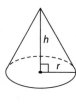
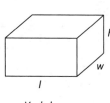
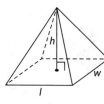
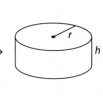

$V = lwh$

$V = \frac{1}{3}\pi r^2 h$

$V = \frac{1}{3}lwh$

$V = \pi r^2 h$

$V = \frac{4}{3}\pi r^3$

1.

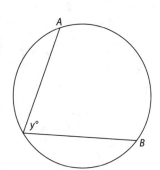

In the circle above, $m\overset{\frown}{AB} = (4x - 3)°$. What is the value of x in terms of y?

A. $x = \dfrac{y + 3}{4}$

B. $x = \dfrac{2y + 3}{4}$

C. $x = \dfrac{y + 3}{8}$

D. $x = \dfrac{y + 6}{8}$

2. Suppose that x, y, and z are nonzero constants. If $z = \dfrac{(8x^{-2}y)^{-1}}{y^2}$, then which of the following is equivalent to $\sqrt[3]{z}$?

A. $\dfrac{-2\sqrt[3]{x^2}}{y}$

B. $\dfrac{\sqrt[3]{x^2}}{2y}$

C. $\dfrac{2}{y\sqrt[3]{x^2}}$

D. $\dfrac{1}{2y\sqrt[3]{x^2}}$

3. The length of a rectangle is three units shorter than twice the width. Let w represent the width of this rectangle, A its area, and P its perimeter. Which of the following shows $A - P$ in terms of w?

A. $2w^2 - 9w + 6$
B. $2w^2 - 12w + 6$
C. $2w^2 - 3w - 3$
D. $2w^2 - 8w - 3$

4. At how many points in the xy-plane do the graphs of $y = 3x$ and $y = x^2 + 1$ intersect?

A. None
B. One
C. Two
D. Three

5. As part of a charity event, Darlene must raise a total of at least $500. If each of her x acquaintances and y friends donated an equal amount, A, then which of the following inequalities must be true for Darlene to meet her quota?

A. $x + y \geq A$

B. $A(x + y) \geq 500$

C. $\dfrac{x + y}{500} \geq A$

D. $\dfrac{A}{x + y} \geq 500$

6. The graph of a polynomial crosses the x-axis at the points $\left(-\dfrac{1}{2}, 0\right)$, $(1, 0)$, and $(4a, 0)$, where a is a nonzero constant. If the polynomial can be written as $p(x) = (2x^2 - 5x - 3)(x - 1)$, then what is the value of a?

A. -1

B. $-\dfrac{1}{4}$

C. $\dfrac{3}{4}$

D. 3

7. Kaitlyn earns \$14 an hour and is saving money to purchase a new vehicle. Suppose that she plans to save a total of D dollars for this purchase. If Kaitlyn works h hours each week and has weekly expenses of \$$y$, then what does x represent in the equation below?

$$x = \dfrac{D}{14h - y}$$

A. The number of hours she would have to work to save for the vehicle after considering other expenses

B. The number of hours she would have to work to save for the vehicle if she had no other expenses

C. The remaining amount she must save after working one week and paying one week's expenses

D. The remaining amount she must save after working one week if she had no other expenses

8. $2x + 4y = 2$

    $6x - y = -\dfrac{15}{4}$

    Given the system of equations above, what is the value of $\dfrac{1}{2}y$?

    A. $-\dfrac{27}{8}$

    B. $-\dfrac{1}{4}$

    C. $\dfrac{3}{8}$

    D. $\dfrac{31}{4}$

9. The graph of the line $y = -\dfrac{3}{4}x + \dfrac{1}{4}$ is shifted three units to the left and four units up. What is the x-coordinate of the point at which the resulting graph intersects the line $y = 8$?

    A. $-\dfrac{25}{3}$

    B. -8

    C. $-\dfrac{7}{3}$

    D. -2

10. Each of the following represents a circle in the xy-plane. Which circle has a center in Quadrant II?

    A. $(x - 1)^2 + (y - 4)^2 = 3$
    B. $(x + 5)^2 + (y + 9)^2 = 4$
    C. $(x - 3)^2 + (y + 1)^2 = 10$
    D. $(x + 4)^2 + (y - 5)^2 = 16$

11. If $\dfrac{ax + 4}{2} = 5$, then what is the value of $2ax$?

    A. 2
    B. 12
    C. 20
    D. 28

12. How many real-valued solutions does the equation

    $\sqrt{3x + 4} = 2x - 4$ have?

    A. One
    B. None
    C. Two
    D. More than two

13. If $f(x) = 2x^2 - 4x + 1$, then which expression is equivalent to $f(k + 1)$?

    A. $2k^2 - 1$
    B. $2k^2 + 3$
    C. $2k^2 - 4k + 4$
    D. $2k^2 - 4x + 3$

14. The graph of a linear function passes through the points (x, y) and $(x + 1, y + 4)$. Which of the following could be the equation for this function?

    A. $x + y = 4$
    B. $3x + 12y = 6$
    C. $8x - 2y = 1$
    D. $x + 2y = 8$

15. Which of the following is equivalent to $\dfrac{\pi}{4}$ radians?

    A. 30°
    B. 45°
    C. 90°
    D. 120°

Directions: Solve problems 16–20 below, then enter your answer in the grid. Instructions for gridding in your response are provided below.

1. You may write your answer in the boxes at the top of the columns. This is not required, but it may help you fill in the circles accurately. The circles are filled in according to instructions to be counted as correct.

2. Fill in only one circle per column.

3. None of the questions has a negative answer.

4. If a problem has more than one possible correct answer, grid in only one answer.

5. Mixed numbers such as $5\frac{1}{2}$ must be gridded as 5.5 or 11/2. (If it is entered into the grid, it will be interpreted as $\frac{51}{2}$ not 5 1/2.)

6. Round or cut off any decimal answer that will not fit the grid, but fill the whole grid.

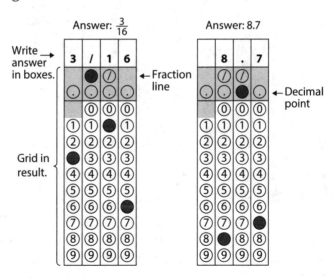

Acceptable ways to grid $\frac{1}{3}$ are:

Answer: 509 - either position is correct

NOTE: You may start your answers in any column, space permitting. Columns you don't need to use should be left blank.

16. Let n represent a whole number. If $m = 8$ and $2m - 5n < 7$, what is the least possible value of n?

17. The system of equations below has infinitely many solutions. What is the value of k?

$$3x - 4y = 8$$

$$2x - \frac{8}{3}y = k$$

18. The equation $x^2 - 4x - 23 = 0$ has two solutions, one of which is of the form $2 - 3\sqrt{a}$. What is the value of a?

_____

19. When dividing $3x^3 + 4x^2 + 2x + 1$ by $x + 2$, the result can be written as $3x^2 - 2x + 6 - \dfrac{r}{x + 2}$. What is the value of r?

_____

20. What is the solution to the equation $\dfrac{1}{x} + \dfrac{1}{2x} = \dfrac{3}{2}$?

_____

END OF SECTION

Math Test–Calculator

Directions: Solve the problems that follow. For questions 1–30, select the best answer option then fill in the circle on your answer sheet that corresponds to that option. For questions 31–38, grid in your response on the answer sheet. Instructions for gridding in answers appear before question 31 on how to enter your answers in the grid. Your test booklet may be used for scratch work.

1. A total of 32 students are taking a Spanish class. In this class, the ratio of students who have studied Spanish before to those who have not is 3:5. How many fewer students have studied Spanish than haven't?

   A. 3
   B. 8
   C. 12
   D. 20

2.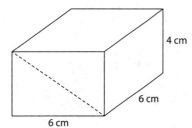

   The rectangular prism above is sliced completely through the labeled diagonal to form two right triangular prisms. To the nearest tenth of a cubic centimeter, what is the volume of one of these prisms?

   A. 72.0
   B. 519.2
   C. 144.0
   D. 1038.4

3. For each hat it sells, a small shop earns a revenue of $18. Suppose that the shop has fixed monthly costs of $6,500 as well as a cost of $10 for each hat. If profit is the difference between revenue and cost, which of the following equations represents the monthly profit P when selling x hats each month?

A. $P = 18(x - 6,500)$
B. $P = 10x - 6,500$
C. $P = 8x - 6,500$
D. $P = 10(x - 6,500)$

4. For which of the following data sets would an exponential model best represent the relationship between x and y?

A.
x	−4	−3	−2	−1
y	−8	−6	−4	−2

B.
x	1	2	3	4
y	4	7	10	13

C.
x	−4	−3	−2	−1
y	16	9	4	1

D.
x	1	2	3	4
y	2	4	8	16

5.

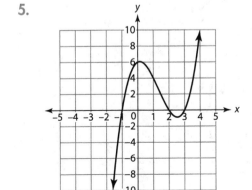

Based on the graph of f(x) above, for which of the following is it true that f(x) > 0 for all x in the given range?

A. $-6 < x < \infty$

B. $-\infty < x < -1$

C. $-1 < x < 2$

D. $-\infty < x < 6$

6. The yearly sales, over the past two years, of a particular brand of cell phone are best modeled by $S(t) = 18500(0.98)^t$ where t is the number of years elapsed (0, 1, 2, etc.). Which statement must be true?

A. Sales have fallen by 98% each year.
B. Sales have fallen by 2% each year.
C. Sales have increased by 2% each year.
D. Sales have increased by 98% each year.

7. If $-\dfrac{2}{5}(x + 5) = 3$, then what is the value of $-2x$?

A. 3
B. 7
C. 15
D. 25

8. $3y - 2x \geq 3$
$\qquad x > 5$

Suppose that (x, y) is in the solution set for the system of inequalities above. What must be true about the values of x and y?

A. $x < 0$ and $y < 0$

B. $x < 0$ and $y > 0$

C. $x > 0$ and $y < 0$

D. $x > 0$ and $y > 0$

9. Find $2x - y$ if $x = 1 - 3i$ and $y = 4 + 2i$.

    A. $-2 - i$

    B. $-2 - 4i$

    C. $-2 - 5i$

    D. $-2 - 8i$

Use the following information to answer questions 10 and 11.

A survey was conducted of full-time employed individuals who work in the downtown area of a large city but live in the suburbs. Each employee was asked to use a GPS device to record the time spent commuting to and from work on a randomly selected day of the week. The data for 10 of the surveyed employees is shown below.

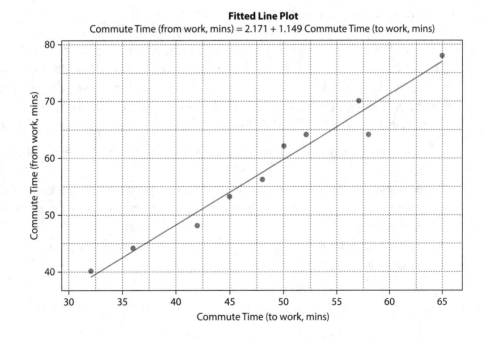

Fitted Line Plot

Commute Time (from work, mins) = 2.171 + 1.149 Commute Time (to work, mins)

10. For how many of the employees shown does the linear model predict a longer commute home than was actually observed?

    A. None
    B. One
    C. Four
    D. Six

11. Which of the following best interprets the slope of the line of best fit?

    A. For each additional minute spent commuting to work, the predicted time spent commuting from work increases by 2.171 minutes.
    B. The predicted commute from work is 2.171 minutes for someone who has a 0-minute commute to work.
    C. For each additional minute spent commuting to work, the predicted time spent commuting from work increases by 1.149 minutes.
    D. The predicted commute from work is 1.149 minutes for someone who has a 0-minute commute to work.

12. A student is comparing the per-game attendance records at two different major league baseball stadiums. The mean attendance per game for each park is approximately the same. However, the standard deviation for the first park is 1,280.6, while the standard deviation for the second park is 2,320.9. Which of the following statements is true?

    A. The attendance per game is more variable for the first park than for the second.
    B. The attendance per game is about the same at each park.
    C. The attendance per game is more variable for the second park than for the first.
    D. A different calculation should be made in order to compare variabilities.

13. The value of a real number z depends on the value of a real number w. When $w = 2$, $z = \dfrac{7}{4}$, and when the value of w increases by 4 units, the value of z increases by 2. Based on this information, which of the following equations must be true?

    A. $4z - 2w = -9$
    B. $4z - 16w = -25$
    C. $4z - 16w = 7$
    D. $4z - 2w = 3$

14. Which of the following shows the slope of the line in the xy-plane defined by the equation as a coefficient or constant of the equation?

    A. $x = -\dfrac{1}{4}y + 2$

    B. $y = -\dfrac{2}{3}x - 5$

    C. $4y = -2x + 1$
    D. $3x + 5y = 5$

15. In the first two weeks a contest is open, entries are received at a rate of x entries each day and then in the third week, a total of 23 more entries are received. Which of the following expressions shows the total number of entries received in the first three weeks of the contest?

    A. $23x$
    B. $37x$
    C. $14x + 23$
    D. $23x + 14$

16. Szymon finds that he can complete 5 homework problems every 15 minutes, while Christine finds she can complete 8 every 40 minutes. Let x and y represent the number of homework problems that Szymon and Christine can complete in one hour respectively. Which of the following is equivalent to $x:y$?

    A. 5:3
    B. 5:1
    C. 5:8
    D. 5:16

17 Which of the following is equivalent to $(x + x^2)\left(x - \dfrac{1}{x}\right)$?

    A. $x^2 - x$

    B. $x^2 - \dfrac{1}{x^3}$

    C. $x^2 - x - 1$
    D. $x^3 + x^2 - x - 1$

Use the following information for questions 18 and 19.

A survey of individuals who utilized monthly storage units was conducted to compare how long they had rented storage space and the size of the storage unit. The data from this survey is shown below.

Size of unit	Length of Time Storage Has Been Leased			
	Less than three months	Three to six months	More than six months to less than one year	One year or more
5′ × 10′	152	84	70	72
10′ × 10′	80	64	60	68
10′ × 15′	65	196	88	64

18. For surveyed individuals, what was the most common length of time that storage units were leased?

    A. Three to six months
    B. Less than three months
    C. More than six months to less than one year
    D. One year or more

19. To the nearest tenth of a percent, what percentage of units rented for one year or more were $10' \times 10'$?

    A. 6.4%
    B. 19.2%
    C. 25.6%
    D. 33.3%

20. $$\frac{1}{R_T} = \frac{1}{R_1} + \frac{1}{R_2}$$

    In a parallel circuit, the total resistance R_T can be found using the above formula, where R_1 is the resistance of the first resistor in the circuit and R_2 is the resistance of the second. Which of the following shows R_1 in terms of the other values?

    A. $R_1 = \dfrac{1}{R_2 + R_T}$

    B. $R_1 = \dfrac{R_T R_2}{R_2 - R_T}$

    C. $R_1 = \dfrac{R_T - R_2}{2}$

    D. $R_1 = \dfrac{R_2(R_T - 1)}{1 - R_T}$

21. The value of m is 8% of the value of n, and the value of n is 315% of the value of p. To the nearest tenth of a percent, what percentage of m is p?

    A. 25.2%
    B. 30.7%
    C. 323.0%
    D. 396.8%

22. A psychologist would like to conduct a survey to better understand what percentage of young adults who use social media websites have had a disagreement with a family member through one of these websites in the last year. Which of the following groups should he use to select his sample?

    A. Young adults in general
    B. Young adults who use social media websites
    C. Young adults who have had disagreements with family members in the last year
    D. Young adults who have had disagreements with family members through a social media website in the last year

23. The function $f(x) = \dfrac{2}{3}x + b$ represents a line in the xy-plane. In terms of b, what is the y-intercept of the function $f\left(\dfrac{1}{2}x\right)$?

    A. b

    B. $\dfrac{1}{2}b$

    C. $\dfrac{1}{3}b$

    D. $\dfrac{2}{3}b$

24. The venue for a wedding requires that there be no more than 85 guests in the main building at any one time due to fire codes. Suppose that a wedding includes a bride, a groom, an officiant, and m guests, each of whom brings one additional person. Which of the following best describes the restrictions on the value of m?

    A. $m \leq 41$

    B. $m \leq \dfrac{85}{2}$

    C. $m \leq 81$

    D. $m \leq 84$

25. Each year, Richard's job pays a bonus based on the number of sales he made, s, and a fixed amount based on a review of his performance. This year, his bonus can be found using the formula $B = 0.05s + k$ for a positive integer k. What does the value k represent in this formula?

    A. The number of sales he made this year
    B. The fixed portion of his bonus
    C. The total value of the bonus this year
    D. The portion of sales for which he receives a bonus

26. Scientists selecting a region of the southern Pacific Ocean to sample from find that only 42% of locations pass the requirements. After this initial screen, 4 more locations are determined to be viable, giving a total of 67 potential locations for sampling. How many locations were initially considered?

    A. 150
    B. 159
    C. 168
    D. 170

27. For what value of k does the equation $\dfrac{x}{4} + k = \dfrac{1}{4}(x + 3) + 1$ have infinitely many solutions?

    A. 4

    B. $\dfrac{3}{4}$

    C. 1

    D. $\dfrac{7}{4}$

28. Suppose $-r + 2s \geq \dfrac{1}{2} + s$. If $s = -1$, then which of the following is the maximum value of $2r + 4$?

    A. $\dfrac{1}{2}$

    B. 1

    C. 2

    D. $\dfrac{5}{2}$

29. A news reporter hypothesizes that the mean amount of time the typical American spends reading the news each day is less than 25 minutes. She conducts a survey of a randomly selected group of Americans and finds that for this sample, the mean time spent reading the news is 19.7 minutes. If the margin of error of her estimate is 8 minutes, then which of the following statements is true?

    A. The sample suggests that the reporter's hypothesis may be correct since $19.7 < 25$.
    B. The sample suggests that the reporter's hypothesis may be correct since only values of 25 or less are reasonable possible values for the true population mean.
    C. The sample suggests that the reporter's hypothesis may not be correct since some reasonable estimates for the true population mean are greater than 25.
    D. The sample suggests that the reporter's hypothesis may not be correct since $25 \neq 19.7$.

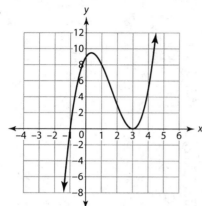

30.

The figure above shows the graph of a polynomial function $p(x)$. Which of the following must be a factor of $p(x)$?

A. x
B. $x - 3$
C. $x - 1$
D. $x - 9$

Directions: Solve problems 31–38 below, then enter your answer in the grid. Instructions for gridding in your response are provided below.

1. You may write your answer in the boxes at the top of the columns. This is not required, but it may help you fill in the circles accurately. The circles are filled in according to instructions to be counted as correct.

2. Fill in only one circle per column.

3. None of the questions has a negative answer.

4. If a problem has more than one possible correct answer, grid in only one answer.

5. Mixed numbers such as $5\frac{1}{2}$ must be gridded as 5.5 or 11/2. (If it is entered into the grid, it will be interpreted as $\frac{51}{2}$ not 5 1/2.)

6. Round or cut off any decimal answer that will not fit the grid, but fill the whole grid.

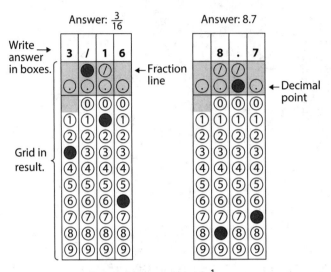

Answer: $\frac{3}{16}$

Write answer in boxes.

Grid in result.

←Fraction line

Answer: 8.7

←Decimal point

Acceptable ways to grid $\frac{1}{3}$ are:

Answer: 509 - either position is correct

NOTE: You may start your answers in any column, space permitting. Columns you don't need to use should be left blank.

31. The volume of a sphere is 28 cubic meters. To the nearest tenth of a meter, what is the radius of this sphere?

_____

32. The depth of water can be measured using a unit called a fathom, which is equivalent to approximately 1.8 meters. Suppose that an unmanned submarine is lowered to a depth of 12 fathoms at a rate of $\frac{1}{2}$ meters per second. To the nearest second, how long will it take for the submarine to reach this depth?

_____

33. If the mean of the data set x, 5, 1, 5, 9 is 6.4, then what is the value of x?

_____

34. Two items are purchased for a total of $8.61 after a sales tax of 7% has been added. If the lower-priced item is not purchased, the after-tax total is only $5.24. What is the pretax cost of the higher-priced item, to the nearest cent?

_____

35. A quadratic function reaches a minimum value when $x = 2$ and crosses the x-axis at the points (1, 0) and (3, 0). What is the minimum value of this function?

_____

Use the following graph of a polynomial $p(x)$ to answer questions 36 and 37.

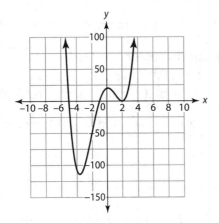

36. If $x > 0$, what is the solution to the equation $p(x - 2) = 20$?

_____

37. What is the greatest value of a for which $p(a) = 0$?

_____

38. According to the most recent data, the population density of New York City is 27,012 people per square mile, whereas the population density of Manila is 42,857 people per square kilometer. If 1 mile is approximately 1.6 kilometers, then how many times as dense is Manila as New York City? Round your answer to the nearest tenth.

_____

END OF SECTION

PRACTICE TESTS ANSWER KEYS

SAT Practice Test 1
Answer Key

Reading Test

1. Choice **B** is correct. The passage describes the dog's desire to run free with his "wood brother," the wolf, but also portrays the dog's reluctance to go too far and the happiness he has at the sight of his owner.

2. Choice **C** is correct. The answer to the preceding question deals with the dog's dilemma, and this evidence portrays the conflict of the dog, who at first keeps a careful watch on his owner and then shifts back to the desire to be out in the wilderness.

3. Choice **A** is correct. *Pertinacity* means "persistence," and in context this choice makes the most sense. The paragraph that precedes the use of the word describes Buck's repeated attempts to befriend a wolf that continually runs away from him. His repeated tries show persistence more than any other answer choice.

4. Choice **C** is correct. The smiling land is meant to describe the perspective of the dog and the happiness he associates with the land.

5. Choice **B** is correct. The main tension of the passage is the dilemma the dog feels between his happiness with John Thornton and his desire to run free in the wild with his "wood brother"—the "call" as the passage describes it.

6. Choice **C** is correct. This quote directly speaks to the nature of the "call" that the passage continually discusses, and portrays the dog as happy being a wild animal beside his "wood brother," the wolf.

7. Choice **D** is correct. *Imperiously* means "urgently." In context, it describes the "call" that the passage refers to several times—a call that intrigues Buck. The restlessness described in the following sentence that results from this call, makes most sense if the call is urgent.

8. Choice **B** is correct. The passage portrays a similarity in the wildness of the dog and his "wood brother," the wolf, especially in their initial responses to each other, which eventually become friendly. This answer choice is the main one that discusses a similarity rather than a difference. The main difference the passage advocates is not one of a physical nature (as the rest of the answer choices portray), but one within the "mind" of the dog.

9. Choice **B** is correct. The situation portrays the relationship between the dog and the owner. The story is narrated primarily through the dog's perspective, and quoting Thornton shows his perspective.

10. Choice **A** is correct. Buck is not happy simply running freely on his own, suggesting the "call" is more closely tied to companionship than simply being wild.

11. Choice **D** is correct. The first paragraph operates as an introduction and explains that while most people may think cholera is a thing of the past, there are still outbreaks, which is why the rest of the passage and the discussion of cholera research is relevant.

12. Choice **C** is correct. *Symbiotic* is a synonym of *commensal* that describes an interconnected relationship between organisms that benefits one species without harming the other. This is the nature of the relationship described in the passage—that one organism is a "host" to the other.

13. Choice **A** is correct. The passage author provides a vivid description of the scientific finding for the purpose of providing interest and a visual image for a nonscientist reader. This counterbalances the scientific language like "monoclonal antibodies" within this paragraph.

14. Choice **A** is correct. The passage pinpoints the ability to go into a dormant state for long periods as what helps vibrios survive when their main host organism is in decline.

15. Choice **C** is correct. This quote specifically mentions what happens when "copepod populations plummet," pinpointing the ability to go dormant for long periods of time as what helps *V. cholerae* survive.

16. Choice **B** is correct. *Endemic* means "native" (not to be confused with *epidemic*, which means "widespread"). In context, the adjective describes a location, specifically coastal communities, so native makes the most sense because it is a quality specific to location.

17. Choice **D** is correct. The passage suggests that the intensity of *V. cholerae* outbreaks correlates with the intensity of drought and monsoon seasons, which increases with global climate change.

18. Choice **D** is correct. The passage suggests that climate change could reduce the number of cholera outbreaks through warming ocean temperatures or alternately intensify outbreaks as monsoon and drought seasons intensify. This answer choice most directly pinpoints the correlation between cholera and climate change in a location where outbreaks are tied to drought and monsoon seasons.

19. Choice **C** is correct. Colwell demonstrated the relationship between *V. cholerae* and copepods. Islam's area of expertise relates to climate change and cholera, which builds on the knowledge of *V. cholerae*'s relationship to copepods that feed off phytoplankton, which thrive or decline with the changes in weather.

20. Choice **B** is correct. Colwell's aim was to prevent cholera infections in Matlab. The possible solution was to teach people in Matlab how to use a simple filtration system, which resulted in a reduction in the incidence of cholera in the area.

21. Choice **C** is correct. If the purpose of the experiment was to prevent cholera infections by teaching people a simple filtration technique, the lasting effect is the practical application of the solution—the fact that the technique was still in use beyond the study.

22. Choice **D** is correct. The word *contentious* often applies to an argument or a controversy. In context, it describes a debate among archaeologists who may have opposing theories for the timing and nature of the settlement of the American continent.

23. Choice **C** is correct. The importance of the findings at the site at Bull River is that the artifacts give insight into the nature and timing of the settlement of the Americas by prehistoric people.

24. Choice **A** is correct. *Debitage* means "stony debris." The fragments of stone tools are accompanied by "flint-knapped" debitage, so in context the most likely thing for the stone tools to be surrounded by is the debris that was scraped off the stones that were used to make them.

25. Choice **D** is correct. The passage states that early people were "mining river cobbles and crafting tools" in order to hunt wild game.

26. Choice **B** is correct. The artifacts provide information about early inhabitants of the Americas, providing insight into some of their activities, and the time frame in which they inhabited the site at Bull River. Together with findings at other archaeological sites, this can help provide a bigger picture of settlement of the Americas.

27. Choice **D** is correct. The preceding answer's correct choice has to do with the importance of the find at Bull River, which helps provide insight into the lives, movements, and timing of the settling of the early Americas. This answer pinpoints the importance of the find—that it can provide more evidence in this "contentious debate."

28. Choice **C** is correct. The passage details two inferences from carbon dating the charcoal—that it is likely that the artifacts found nearby are from the same time period, which in turn, indicates a time that prehistoric people may have used the site.

29. Choice **C** is correct. The preceding question asks the relationship between the charcoal and the artifacts for the purposes of carbon dating. This answer explains two inferences that can be made based on the location of the charcoal and the artifacts.

30. Choice **B** is correct. Following the curve on the graph, it is clear that the percentage of carbon 14 is 25 after 11,460 years. The more time elapses, the smaller the percentage of carbon 14 there is, so the date range on the graph for the artifacts (which were dated to between 12,180 and 12,460 years ago according to the passage) would be slightly less than 25.

31. Choice **A** is correct. The graph does not account for disruptions (choice C) or specify a difference for different types of organisms (choice B) but simply portrays the numeric percentage of C-14 versus time elapsed in a specimen. As the percentage of carbon decreases, the graph flattens exponentially, and therefore a smaller percentage of carbon correlates to a wider range of time.

32. Choice **D** is correct. The first two paragraphs provide an overview of the program, discussing its growth over time to its present-day scope.

33. Choice **A** is correct. *Bolstered* means "strengthened" or "supported." In context, it is most likely that the program was strengthened as more birders participated in the program.

34. Choice **C** is correct. The passage emphasizes the consistency of the conditions in which the information is collected as important to reduce sampling error. The weather is one factor that the passage suggests in addition to collecting data at a consistent location, and maintaining data collectors of a certain expertise.

35. Choice **A** is correct. This quote pinpoints the issue of "sampling error" and its possible causes.

36. Choice **B** is correct. The statement ties the data collected to the skills of the birders who collect the data, suggesting certain regional clusters may result from particularly skilled birders.

37. Choice **A** is correct. The maps of relative abundance and BBS data do not explain causes of trends in bird populations (choices B & C) but simply track them. The passage does not indicate whether or not this information is used to track endangered species (choice D).

38. Choice **D** is correct. This is the only answer that speaks to the true purpose of the data collected, specifically pinpointing its "most effective use."

39. Choice **B** is correct. *Abundance* means "a plentiful amount." In context, the sentence explains that the survey cannot account for every bird, but instead creates an "index of relative abundance," meaning it collects a large enough amount of data to extrapolate to the bird population as a whole.

40. Choice **A** is correct. The map shows an average count of Bobolinks in regions across the United States, with the highest density in the northeastern quarter of the country indicated by the darker shades and speckled sections that correlate to higher bird numbers. This information is also stated in the passage.

41. Choice **D** is correct. The map shows white space in the southernmost states because there were no Bobolinks recorded in the region at the time of the survey. Given the limited information, this is either because there are no survey routes conducted in this region or there are no Bobolinks recorded by birders in this area.

42. Choice **B** is correct. The passage discusses the creation of a new armaments industry, first focusing on its necessity and then moving on to possible complications of the existence of such an industry.

43. Choice **D** is correct. *Grave* means "serious." The next passage sentence details the "grave implications," basically saying that "toil, resources and livelihood" are at stake, even "the very structure of our society." These implications lead to only one answer choice that makes sense in context: serious.

44. Choice **A** is correct. The crux of the issue discussed in passage 1 is the issues of power that emerge when a large industry is created to support military action. The military and the industry become inherently tied, with the possible interest/ability to influence the government to go to war.

45. Choice **B** is correct. The first paragraph entertains the possibility that the morality of a nation can foster peace throughout the world. The tenets of such an experiment would be the "steady adherence" to "justice and benevolence," and the results of such an experiment would be peace.

46. Choice **C** is correct. *Propensity* means "inclination." In context, the sentence describes the government's being swayed by the passions and emotions of individuals. The nation, as a collection of people, is inclined to be moved by passions, but Washington warns that the government should be ruled by best policy and not this inclination.

47. Choice **D** is correct. The main focus of both presidential farewell addresses concerns peace, though they speak from two entirely different historical contexts.

48. Choice **B** is correct. Both former presidents make a warning about what may unduly influence a war. The important difference is the nature of that influence.

49. Choice **C** is correct. The answer to the preceding question deals with each passage's warning against war due to two very different influences. The first quote demonstrates Eisenhower's warning against the armaments industry's influence, and the second quote demonstrates Washington's warning against emotional influences.

50. Choice **A** is correct. The opening paragraph of passage 1 makes a clear case that peace comes from intimidating possible threats to peace through military might, while the opening paragraph of passage 2 suggests "good faith and justice towards all nations" will cultivate peace.

51. Choice **A** is correct. Both quotes pinpoint an explanation for how to cultivate peace, which lies in the beginning of each passage.

52. Choice **D** is correct. The first paragraph of passage 2 is highly idealistic, and Washington advocates peace simply: "amicable feelings towards all should be cultivated." Eisenhower, in passage 1, on the other hand, focuses on preparing for possible outcomes, evidenced by his insistence on the need for military readiness but also his ability to foresee the possible issue that an industry devoted to creating military weapons might advocate their use.

Writing and Language Test

1. Choice **C** is correct. The reader doesn't necessarily need to know what kind of businesses are on Prince Boulevard, just that the street is zoned for commercial use.

2. Choice **A** is correct. The comma separates the independent clause ("Prince Boulevard is currently zoned for commercial use") from the dependent, explanatory clause ("meaning that new residential buildings over a certain height . . .").

3. Choice **A** is correct. The rest of the passage talks about the disagreement in the community about whether the neighborhood should be rezoned.

4. Choice **B** is correct. OHCB is an abbreviation for Oak Hills Community Board that will be used throughout the passage, and it should be set off by parentheses.

5. Choice **D** is correct. The underlined sentence refers to population data, so any supporting sentence added here should include population data.

6. Choice **B** is correct. This answer tells the reader that the passage is moving from the OHCB's perspective to the next perspective.

7. Choice **D** is correct. The object of the sentence is "developers," so the correct pronoun for agreement is *their*.

8. Choice **B** is correct. This choice revises the sentence so that it also has an independent clause ("Oak Hills is an appealing location for developers and new residents") in addition to the dependent clause ("because . . ."), which completes the thought.

9. Choice **C** is correct. The underlined text has equal weight to "open the door" in the previous part of the sentence, and should be parallel. *Open* is singular and present tense, so the form of the verb *displace* should be as well.

10. Choice **D** is correct. This is the most concise way to state the poll information, while the other options are excessively wordy or contain redundancies.

11. Choice **A** is correct. This transition phrase wraps up the writer's point about the different perspectives in the neighborhood, and moves into the concluding point that the Community Board will be finalizing its recommendation.

12. Choice **C** is correct. The details about Pluto would be more effective when the writer discusses whether or not Pluto meets planetary requirements, rather than in the middle of the introductory paragraph.

13. Choice **C** is correct. Abbreviations should be spelled out on the first use of an organization's name so that the reader knows what the abbreviation refers to throughout the passage.

14. Choice **B** is correct. It explains what the specific phrase "cleared the neighborhood" means.

15. Choice **A** is correct. The other choices are not directly related to the planet definition laid out in this paragraph, so the graphic illustrating point #3 would be the most effective use of additional information.

16. Choice **C** is correct. In the original sentence, the modifier *increasingly* is misplaced.

17. Choice **B** is correct. This choice explains who Owen Gingerich is (and why his perspective is related to the passage), and correctly punctuates the subordinate clause.

18. Choice **D** is correct. The writer is talking about a future event ("if"), so the verb tense should agree with that. Choice D also has the correct subject-verb agreement, since Pluto is one planet and needs a singular verb to reflect that.

19. Choice **D** is correct. The writer is talking about a specific battle in a specific place, so both "Battle" and "Gettysburg" should be capitalized. However, the preposition *of*, which connects the two proper nouns, should not be capitalized.

20. Choice **B** is correct. The exclamation is out of place with the explanatory details and the calm argument the writer is creating for why Pluto's status should be revisited.

21. Choice **A** is correct. The singular possessive *Pluto* should end with a simple apostrophe and *s*.

22. Choice **A** is correct. The writer gives information throughout that shows that the 2006 definition of a planet is problematic when it comes to Pluto.

23. Choice **C** is correct. The first time names are used in a piece of writing, the writer should use the full name before later abbreviating letters or using just the last name.

24. Choice **B** is correct. No additional punctuation is needed, because the sentence is one complete clause.

25. Choice **D** is correct. The word *independent* already tells the reader that the U.S. government was no longer being controlled by Britain, so the extra phrase at the end ("away from Britain's control") is redundant.

26. Choice **A** is correct. This transitional phrase leads the reader from Jefferson and Adams's political relationship toward details about their personal friendship.

27. Choice **C** is correct. The transitional phrase tells the reader that the writer will be giving context for the preceding statement. *Like* is often a casual, conversational transition that is out of place with the tone and syntax of the passage.

28. Choice **D** is correct. The adjective *slanderous* already tells the reader that something is false and/or malicious, so the extra adjectives are redundant.

29. Choice **D** is correct. "When mutual friends of Jefferson and Adams" is an adverbial phrase that modifies the verb *thaw*. As a standalone phrase, it's a fragment, and should be included in the sentence containing the verb it modifies. No additional punctuation is necessary.

30. Choice **C** is correct. There should be a comma separating the day from the year in the date, with the descriptive phrase set in parentheses.

31. Choice **C** is correct. Because the age is included for Jefferson, it should be included for Adams as well to keep the sentence parallel. (Alternatively, it could be taken out for both.)

32. Choice **B** is correct. The phrase "Thomas Jefferson survives" is a direct quote, and so it needs quotation marks. Because it is used as a predicate, no additional punctuation is necessary.

33. Choice **A** is correct. This choice mentions the connection between the two men, which is the main theme of the passage.

34. Choice **B** is correct. The passage deals mostly with water conservation occupations that deal with human use. There's no supporting information about wildlife or careers related to that.

35. Choice **D** is correct. Having both "green" and "environmentally conscious" is redundant, and eliminating one of them streamlines the sentence.

36. Choice **A** is correct. This sentence offers a transition from the first paragraph and lets the reader know that the next paragraph will begin talking about the different occupations related to the field.

37. Choice **D** is correct. Adjusting the adjectives to be parallel and equal makes the sentence clearer and stronger.

38. Choice **A** is correct. The plural *hydrologists* needs a plural verb to agree.

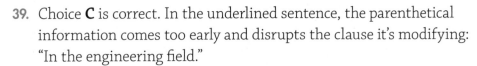

39. Choice **C** is correct. In the underlined sentence, the parenthetical information comes too early and disrupts the clause it's modifying: "In the engineering field."

40. Choice **B** is correct. This detail is unnecessary to the main topics of both the paragraph (physical water conservation occupations) and the overall passage (career paths that relate to water conservation), and should be deleted.

41. Choice **B** is correct. Connecting the sentences runs the risk of creating a run-on sentence. By adding the transitional phrase *as such*, the writer helps improve the flow from one sentence to the next.

42. Choice **A** is correct. The writer starts the paragraph by suggesting that the labor statistics support the idea that higher degrees mean higher salaries. In the second sentence of that paragraph, the writer also says that the salary information is "regardless of education level." Assuming the writer wants to keep his main statement, "regardless of education level" should be deleted, and any additional supporting information should be included (if possible).

43. Choice **C** is correct. The word *now* tells the reader that the sentence should be present tense, so "starting to be" is the best choice.

44. Choice **D** is correct. *Fields* is plural and present tense, and so the related verb must agree with that.

Math Test—No Calculator

1. **D**

In order for the system to have infinitely many solutions, the two

equations must be multiples of each other. Since $\dfrac{-\dfrac{2}{3}}{3} = -\dfrac{2}{3} \times \dfrac{1}{3} = -\dfrac{2}{9}$,

k must equal $-6 \times -\dfrac{2}{9} = \dfrac{12}{9} = \dfrac{4}{3}$.

2. **A**

The yield per square foot would be $\dfrac{x}{850}$. Multiplying this by 10 gives the yield per square foot over 10 growing seasons.

3. **D**

For $\sin\beta > 0$ and $\cos\beta < 0$ to be true, β must be in the second quadrant. That is, it must be that $\dfrac{\pi}{2} < \beta < \pi$. Given that $\alpha = \pi + \beta$,

$\dfrac{\pi}{2} + \pi < \alpha < \pi + \pi$ or $\dfrac{3\pi}{2} < \alpha < 2\pi$.

4. **B**

Setting the two equations equal, $-3 = x^2 - 4x + 1$ or $x^2 - 4x + 4 = 0$. This equation has one solution since $x^2 - 4x + 4 = (x - 2)^2$.

5. **C**

The denominators in this equation can be cleared by multiplying both sides by $x(x - 1)(x + 2)$. Doing this results in the equation $x(x + 2) + x(x - 1) = m - 2$. Simplifying the left-hand side: $2x^2 + x = m - 2$. Thus, $m = 2x^2 + x + 2$.

6. **B**

The factor $6x^3 - 13x^2 + 5x$ can be written as

$x(6x^2 - 13x + 5) = x(2x - 1)(3x - 5)$. This accounts for the zeros of

$0, \dfrac{1}{2}$, and $\dfrac{5}{3}$. The remaining factor, $x - a$ must account for the zero of 2.

Thus, $a = 2$.

7. **C**

Since the sales are increasing by 50% each year so far, the sale in one year

can be found by multiplying the preceding year's sales by 1.5 or $\dfrac{3}{2}$. This

growth is represented by an exponential model of the form $T = a\left(\dfrac{3}{2}\right)^x$

where x is the number of years since the first year and a is the sales
in the initial year. Since $x = 0$ for the first year, and it has been
five years, the sales in three more years will be (if the pattern

continues) $T = 16850.62\left(\dfrac{3}{2}\right)^7$.

8. **B**

$$\begin{aligned}
2p - q &= 2(3x^2 - 5x + 1) \\
&\quad - (16x^2 + 3x - 2) \\
&= 6x^2 - 10x + 2 - 16x^2 - 3x + 2 \\
&= -10x^2 - 13x + 4
\end{aligned}$$

9. **A**

The equation of the resulting line would be $y = -3(x + 3) + \dfrac{1}{2} =$

$-3x - 9 + \dfrac{1}{2} = -3x - \dfrac{17}{2}$. This is in the form $y = mx + b$ where b is

the y-intercept.

10. **C**

Both of the given angles are subtended by the same arc, so their measures must be equal. If $\dfrac{x}{2}+1=\dfrac{y}{5}$, then $y=5\left(\dfrac{x}{2}+1\right)=\dfrac{5x}{2}+5$.

11. **B**

$$f\left(\frac{x}{2}\right)=\frac{\dfrac{x}{2}+4}{2}+\frac{x}{2}=\frac{\dfrac{x}{2}+4+x}{2}$$

$$=\frac{\dfrac{3x+8}{2}}{2}=\frac{3x+8}{4}=\frac{3x}{4}+2$$

12. **B**

The given equation can be written as $\dfrac{1}{\sqrt{a}}=\dfrac{1}{x^2}$. Cross multiplying, $x^2=\sqrt{a}$. Finally, squaring both sides yields $x^4=a$.

13. **B**

Multiplying both sides of the equation by 6 yields the equation $2x-1=9x$. Subtracting $2x$ from both sides shows that $-1=7x$.

14. **C**

Multiplying the first equation by 2 and the second by -3 yields the equations $\begin{array}{l}-6x+16y=8\\6x-21y=-3\end{array}$. Adding these equations, we have $-5y=5$ or $y=-1$. Substituting this into the first equation, $-3x+8(-1)=4$ or $-3x=12$. This shows that $x=-4$. Finally, $x-y=-4-(-1)=-3$.

15. **D**

If the volume must be at least 180 cubic inches, then $V=LWH\geq180$. Using the given values, this means that $14hw\geq180$. Solving for w, $w\geq\dfrac{180}{14h}=\dfrac{90}{7h}$.

16. 6

Completing the square gives the equivalent equation
$(x + 2)^2 + (y - 5)^2 = 9$, where the radius is $\sqrt{9} = 3$. Thus, the diameter
is 6.

17. 1

Multiplying all parts of the inequality by 10 gives the equivalent
inequality $-120 \leq 5x + 10 \leq -2x + 20$. Since we are looking for the
greatest possible value, assuming $x > 0$, we can write that $7x \leq 10$ or
$x \leq \dfrac{10}{7}$. If x is a whole number, the greatest it can be is 1 since $\dfrac{10}{7}$ is
greater than 1 but less than 2.

18. 3

Subtracting 3 from both sides of the equation, $2y^2 - 5y - 3 = 0$ or
$(2y + 1)(y - 3) = 0$. The roots of this equation are $-\dfrac{1}{2}$ and 3. Since
$y > 1$, the value of y must be 3.

19. $\dfrac{1}{8}$

The slope of the line is not changed by the stated transformations. Thus,
writing the line in the form $y = mx + b$ will reveal the correct slope.
$$-2y = 10 - \frac{1}{4}x \Rightarrow y = -5 + \frac{1}{8}x$$

20. 2

Squaring both sides of the equation, $m^2 + 2m = 4(2)$ or
$m^2 + 2m - 8 = 0$. Using factoring, this can be written as
$(m + 4)(m - 2) = 0$. The roots of this equation are -4 and 2. Since m is
positive, its value must be 2.

Math Test—Calculator

1. **A**

   For those who completed some high school, a percentage of $100 \times 22/(22 + 28)$ or 44% are employed part-time.

2. **B**

   A total of $22 + 18 + 6 + 8 = 54$ of those surveyed are employed part-time, and of those, 8 have completed a two- or four-year college degree. This gives a percentage of $100 \times 8/54 = 14.8\%$.

3. **D**

   The sample proportion is 820/1790 or about 0.4581. Using the margin of error, it is reasonably likely that the population proportion is between $0.4581 - 0.046 = 0.4121$ and $0.4581 + 0.046 = 0.5041$. Any value outside of this range is unlikely to be the value of the true proportion.

4. **B**

   There are a total of $15 + 8 + 2 + 6 = 31$ values in the data set. This means that the median is the sixteenth value.

5. **C**

   There are 60 minutes in an hour, so the student is adding 2 ml of solution to the beaker every $\dfrac{15}{60} = \dfrac{1}{4}$ hour. That is, 4 times an hour. This means after 1 hour that the student will add 8 ml. Since the initial amount was 110 ml, the total after x hours is $8x + 110$.

6. **D**

   If H is the number of hard drives and K is the number of keyboards, then $H + K = 18$ and $1.6H + 2.1K = 33.8$. Solving this system of equations, $K = 8$ and $H = 10$. The ratio $H{:}K$ is thus 8:10 or 4:5.

7. **A**

Distributing the 4 on the left-hand side gives the equation $4x + 8 = 2x + 3$, which is equivalent to $2x + 8 = 3$ or $2x = -5$. Multiplying both sides by 6, $12x = -30$.

8. **D**

Multiplying both sides by -2, $x - 2 > -4$. Adding 5 to both sides, $x + 3 > 1$. Only D has a value that follows this requirement.

9. **A**

If the value of y increases by $\dfrac{3}{4}$ units for every one-unit increase in the value of x, then a linear equation with a slope of $\dfrac{3}{4}$ models the relationship between x and y. If $y = \dfrac{3}{4}x + b$ and when $x = -1$, $y = -\dfrac{1}{4}$, then $-\dfrac{1}{4} = \dfrac{3}{4}(-1) + b$ or $b = \dfrac{1}{2}$. The equation $y = \dfrac{3}{4}x + \dfrac{1}{2}$ is equivalent to the equation $3x - 4y = -2$.

10. **D**

If the original order total is T, then $1.041(0.85T - 5) = 251.67$. The \$5 discount is applied since an after-tax total of 251.67 was certainly more than \$100 before taxes. Solving this linear equation yields $T = 290.30$.

11. **C**

A 15% discount means that the person will pay 85% of the total, or $0.85x$. The \$5 discount is not applied to this since $x < 100$, but the tax is applied to this total. The total after a tax of $y\%$ is found by multiplying the total by $1 + \dfrac{y}{100}$.

12. **A**

The y-intercept is the value of y when $x = 0$. Only the equation in choice A shows this value as a term of the equation (the last term).

13. C

$$\sqrt{2x + 2y} = a^2 - 3 \Rightarrow \sqrt{2(x + y)}$$
$$= a^2 - 3 \Rightarrow \sqrt{2}\sqrt{x + y}$$
$$= a^2 - 3 \Rightarrow \sqrt{x + y} = \frac{a^2 - 3}{\sqrt{2}}$$

14. C

A predicted value is along the line, while an observed value is represented by a point on the scatterplot. There are two points that are more than 0.1 unit above the line of best fit.

15. A

In general, slope is interpreted as the change in the dependent variable for a one-unit increase in the independent variable.

16. B

The slope of the new equation will be exactly the same as the original since this is just a translation. Using the x- and y-intercepts, the slope is $m = \dfrac{0.5 - 0}{0 - (-2)} = \dfrac{1}{4}$.

17. A

Solving for T_F in the first equation yields $T_F = \dfrac{9}{5}T_C + 32$, and solving for T_C in the second yields $T_C = T_K - 273.15$. Substituting:

$$T_F = \frac{9}{5}(T_K - 273.15) + 32 \text{ or } T_F = \frac{9}{5}T_K - 459.67.$$

18. A

Given the information about the ratios, we can write $4x = 5y$ and $y = 3z$. Using the first equation, $y = \dfrac{4}{5}x$. Now using the second equation, $\dfrac{4}{5}x = 3z$ or $z = \dfrac{4}{15}x$.

19. **B**

The surface area will include the outside of the pipe, the inside of the pipe, and the ring on the top and bottom of the pipe. This can be found by adding the two terms from $2\pi rh$ (for the inside and outside of the pipe) and then subtracting the two terms that represent the circles at the ends of the pipe (leaving only the ring). This gives $2\pi r_1 h + 2\pi r_1^2 + 2\pi r_2 h - 2\pi r_2^2 = 2\pi L(r_1 + r_2) + 2\pi L(r_1^2 - r_2^2)$.

20. **B**

In an exponential model $a(b)^x$, a represents the initial value.

21. **C**

For this equation to have no solution, the two x terms on opposite sides of the equal sign must have the same coefficient. Distributing on both sides, this equation is $\frac{3}{4}x - \frac{3}{4} = \frac{a}{2}x + 2$ so $\frac{3}{4} = \frac{a}{2}$. Therefore, $a = \frac{3}{2}$.

22. **D**

The negative of the polynomial will have the same graph, but reflected across the x-axis. Any values along the x-axis will remain the same, so these four values will be shared by the two graphs and thus be solutions to the equation $p(x) = q(x)$.

23. **A**

Statement C may or may not be true, but if it were, there would be larger issues than just generalizing the study results. Statement B is not true as this is a large sample, and statement D is not relevant since the nutritionist is only hoping to apply the results to this age range. However, statement A notes an important error in the study. Instead of comparing the individuals' final levels of inflammation with their initial levels, the study compares their final levels with the typical level. Individuals may have high variation in these values, and that would likely affect the data and not allow a conclusion to be made.

24. D

If C represents the number of coffee tables and D the number of dining tables, then the inequalities are $3C + 4D \leq 16$ and $2C + 4D \leq 12$. Of the given choices, only $C = 2$ and $D = 2$ satisfies *both* inequalities.

25. D

The inequality is true if for all the given x-values, the function is increasing. That is, if for all the given x-values, the graph of the function is rising from left to right.

26. D

The values of k increase by a constant amount (12 units) for each one-unit increase in x. This means that a linear model best represents this relationship and that the slope of the model would be 12.

27. A

$$(-3i + 1)(-i + 2) = 3i^2 - 6i - i + 2$$
$$= -3 - 7i + 2 = -7i - 1$$

28. B

Solving for m yields the equation $m = \dfrac{4}{3}n + \dfrac{1}{3}$. This is a linear equation with a positive slope. So, as the value of one variable increases, so does the value of the other. Since this is linear, this is true over the entire domain.

29. C

$$\text{PEG}_{\text{adj}} = \frac{P \div \text{EPS}}{g + d} \Rightarrow \text{PEG}_{\text{adj}}(g + d)$$

$$= \frac{P}{\text{EPS}} \Rightarrow \text{EPS}(\text{PEG}_{\text{adj}}(g + d))$$

$$= P \Rightarrow \text{EPS} = \frac{P}{\text{PEG}_{\text{adj}}(g + d)}$$

30. **C**

Without k, $(x - 4)^2$ has one real zero: 4. If k is negative, then it will shift the graph of this equation down k units. The graph of $(x - 4)^2$ is a parabola opening up, so shifting it down will cause it to cross the x-axis at two points, meaning that $f(x) = (x - 4)^2 + k$ will have two real zeros.

31. **1.7**

The volume of the piece of aluminum is $2 \times 2 \times 70 = 280$ cm^3. Using the density, this means that it weighs 280 cm$^3 \times 2.7$ g/cm$^3 = 756$ g;

$$756 \text{ g} \left(\frac{1 \text{ lb}}{453.6 \text{ g}} \right) \approx 1.7 \text{ lb.}$$

32. **13797**

If x is the population two years ago, then $14780 = 1.035^2 x$

and $x = \dfrac{14780}{1.035^2} \approx 13797$.

33. **7**

If the graph is symmetric about the y-axis, then the graph will cross the x-axis at points on the positive side of the x-axis that are the same distance from the origin as the points -7 and -4. That is, it will also have zeros 4 and 7. Thus, the greatest zero of the polynomial is 7.

34. **29.2**

Using the area formula, $\frac{1}{2}(14)h = 21$, where h is the height. Solving this equation, $h = 3$. Since the angles on both the left and right have the same measure, this is an isosceles triangle, so the two opposite sides have the same length. That length can be found with the Pythagorean theorem using the height and $\frac{1}{2} x$ the base. That is, if the side length is L, then $h^2 + 7^2 = L^2$, or, since $h = 3$, $L^2 = 3^2 + 7^2 = 58$ and $L = \sqrt{58} \approx 7.6$. Thus, the perimeter is approximately $14 + 7.6 + 7.6 = 29.2$ cm.

35. **4**

If the number of hours spent on recreational activities is R and the number of hours spent on educational activities is E, then $E \geq 2R$ or $R \leq \dfrac{1}{2}E$. Thus, the maximum amount of time that can be spent on recreational activities is $\dfrac{1}{2}E$. If there are 12 hours set aside each week, then this means that $\dfrac{1}{2}E + E = 12$ or $E = 8$. Thus, at most, half this time, or 4 hours, can be spent on recreational activities.

36. **3**

The value of $f(x)$ is positive for all x-values where the graph is above the x-axis. This is true for all x-values less than 4 (the value of $f(x)$ at 4 is zero). Thus, the greatest whole number where $f(x) > 0$ is 3.

37. **5.1**

The difference between the times is $\dfrac{92960000}{186280} - \dfrac{35980000}{186280} \approx$ 305.9 seconds or $\dfrac{305.9}{60} \approx 5.1$ minutes.

38. **68**

Using the line of best fit, when the time is 10 minutes, the line is closest to 68%.

SAT Practice Test 2
Answer Key

Reading Test

1. Choice **B** is correct. *Somnambulism* means "sleepwalking." In context of the sentence, somnambulism follows "walking in the shadow of a dream." The second half of the sentence must relate to the disorientation of waking up from a dream. The key lies in the word *actually*, so the author suggests that Dimmesdale may "actually" still be sleeping.

2. Choice **B** is correct. The main focus of the passage is to portray Dimmesdale wrestling with his guilt. He stands on the scaffold because that is where a guilty person receives punishment.

3. Choice **D** is correct. The quote specifically states that "he had been driven hither" and targets remorse as his reason.

4. Choice **B** is correct. Dimmesdale is full of remorse for a crime he committed, yet he is too cowardly to confess and alleviate his guilt.

5. Choice **B** is correct. Dimmesdale is a minister. The passage evokes religious imagery in angels, devils, and Satan. The guilt the minister feels is compounded by the idea that he is being watched and judged by God.

6. Choice **D** is correct. The passage describes Dimmesdale's being seized by a "horror of mind" in which he imagines the universe staring at the spot over his heart. The mental anguish causes him to scream.

7. Choice **C** is correct. The character's main dilemma is that he feels guilt, but is too cowardly to confess his crime. If he had to explain his actions to the whole town for why he was screaming in the middle of the night on the scaffold, he might overcome his cowardice to actually confess.

8. Choice **D** is correct. *Vain* in this context means "hollow"—the "vain show" is like an empty gesture. *Vain* can also mean "proud." However, plagued by guilt, Dimmesdale stands on the scaffold where criminals might normally be punished, but does so in the dark in front of no one, not actually receiving judgment. It helps to know that *expiation* also means "atonement," so his "vain show" is just an ineffectual attempt to make amends for his crime.

9. Choice **D** is correct. The passage describes Dimmesdale as a "feeble and sensitive spirit," which is why he is not suited to crime.

10. Choice **D** is correct. The answer to the preceding question is "weak and sensitive," and this quote uses a synonym for *weak* as well as *sensitive* to describe Dimmesdale in this situation.

11. Choice **B** is correct. Marine plastic in the study is measured in "million metric tons," which sounds like a large quantity, but the scale is probably not well understood by the average reader. Describing what it would look like and how much of the plastic would cover the coast helps a reader visualize the amount.

12. Choice **C** is correct. *Determinant* means "factor." The study lists factors that affect a nation's contribution to marine plastic.

13. Choice **D** is correct. The study attempts to locate which countries are the biggest contributors to marine plastic (the source) and what factors cause that contribution.

14. Choice **D** is correct. While the study also calculates the amount of plastic in the ocean, finding the source of that plastic is its main purpose, and this quote directly pinpoints that purpose, citing the "primary determinant" of a country's contribution to marine plastic.

15. Choice **C** is correct. The mismanaged plastic waste for the rapidly growing megacity population contributes to more marine plastic debris.

16. Choice **D** is correct. The passage targets how much coastline a country has, how close population centers are to the coast, how much waste the country produces per capita, and how much of that waste is mismanaged. Logically, you can't uproot whole cities, or change the shape of a country, so the solution would have to target waste and waste management. The passage mentions waste-management infrastructure several times as a target for improving the marine plastic issue.

17. Choice **D** is correct. This quote imagines how the study might be used to create a solution, and specifically mentions improving waste management in a few countries (the proposed solution from the preceding question).

18. Choice **B** is correct. *Stem* in this usage means "to stop the flow of" or "to dam up," which makes sense in context since the desire is to reduce the amount of plastics.

19. Choice **B** is correct. Simply looking at the numbers on the chart, the values in the indicated columns both decrease from 1 to 20. Choice C may be tempting because the other factors listed are mentioned in the passage, but while country size and number of coastal cities would affect the numbers, they would not change the direct correlation between the amounts of mismanaged plastic waste and plastic marine debris. Those other factors would simply make both numbers higher or lower.

20. Choice **A** is correct. The passage lists three determinants for a country's contribution to plastic marine debris: large cities within 50 km of the coast, how much waste the country produces per capita, and how much of that waste is mismanaged. Most of the other countries listed have a high percentage of mismanaged waste, but Brazil's is the second lowest. So either of the other two determinants is likely to blame for Brazil's inclusion in the top 20 contributors to plastic marine debris.

21. Choice **C** is correct. This is the only choice that is definitively true. Countries are ranked by their contribution to marine plastic debris.

22. Choice **A** is correct. Beginning with the first sentence, Roosevelt makes the connection between the buffalo and the history of the United States, detailing where they roamed and describing the landscape full of buffalo.

23. Choice **A** is correct. The quote highlights the buffalo as "one of the most distinctive and characteristic features of existence on the great plains," which is strong evidence for the preceding question.

24. Choice **C** is correct. The passage begins by discussing the history of the buffalo and their decimation, then shifts to discuss a hunting tale of President Roosevelt's brother.

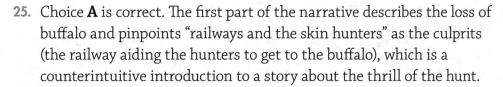

25. Choice **A** is correct. The first part of the narrative describes the loss of buffalo and pinpoints "railways and the skin hunters" as the culprits (the railway aiding the hunters to get to the buffalo), which is a counterintuitive introduction to a story about the thrill of the hunt.

26. Choice **B** is correct. *Indispensable* means "necessary." In context, it describes transportation that had previously been lacking for hunters. Logically, if the transportation was lacking, it is probably something that is needed.

27. Choice **C** is correct. Roosevelt doesn't go so far as to state or imply that buffalo hunting is immoral or nefarious (choices A or B) but reserves judgment. He, in fact, describes his brother and cousin as "fortunate" and even calls buffalo hunters "adventurers" several times. And when the buffalo were plentiful, hunting them was not a great challenge (choice D).

28. Choice **D** is correct. This quote describes the chase, the "lordly beasts," and the prairie with a certain amount of fondness, and describes his brother, the buffalo hunter, as "fortunate" to be able to get to chase the plentiful buffalo.

29. Choice **C** is correct. *Unconscious* usually would mean "sleeping," but in context it is clear that the herd of buffalo is grazing. If the "beasts" are not conscious, they are not aware of what is about to happen.

30. Choice **C** is correct. According to the graph, the low point of the buffalo population is about 500, which coincides with the beginning of Roosevelt's presidency, and the numbers have improved drastically from there.

31. Choice **B** is correct. It's important to note the numbers on the *y*-axis do not go up at regular intervals as in most graphs. The number of buffalo rises from 500 to 5,000 to 350,000, which is a rapid rise as time goes on, but nowhere near the 50,000,000 at the height of the population according to the graph.

32. Choice **D** is correct. *Cataclysmic* describes a violent change, often used in a more metaphorical sense, but in context a volcanic eruption actually can break the earth.

33. Choice **A** is correct. The passage discusses three large volcanic eruptions. The first and oldest mentioned formed a caldera 60 miles across. The second does not mention a specific size but is described as smaller. The third eruption mentioned is 35 miles wide and 50 miles long. Choice A is the only choice that definitely lines up with the facts discussed in the passage.

34. Choice **A** is correct. It mentions the oldest eruption as one of the five largest on the earth, which supports the preceding question's answer.

35. Choice **A** is correct. The answer choices span different layers of the earth outlined in earth science, but the passage only mentions the earth's crust when it explains what is responsible for the eruptions.

36. Choice **D** is correct. The quote pinpoints the passage's discussion of the earth's crust and what causes the caldera-forming eruptions.

37. Choice **C** is correct. *Stressing* in this context means to "disturb" or to "subject to pressure." While *coercing* (choice B) means pressuring, it is often used in the context of intimidation. The earth's crust when facing pressure cannot be intimidated but can be unsettled, which would occur during an earthquake.

38. Choice **D** is correct. The final paragraph mentions the park specifically, and the final sentence of the passage discusses the more recent lava flows and the landforms they created.

39. Choice **B** is correct. The passage suggests that the effects of another eruption would be worldwide. Ash would cover the United States, but volcanic gases would change the global climate.

40. Choice **B** is correct. The passage discusses how another event is unlikely but imagines the effects of a cataclysmic eruption today anyway, which helps the reader grasp the scope of previous eruptions.

41. Choice **A** is correct. The age of the lava flow is relatively young compared to the age of the earth and various other formations. While it sounds funny that something at least 70,000 years old is "young," the passage deals with a subject that spans an enormous amount of time.

42. Choice **C** is correct. The passage, in fact, does all of the above, but the main goal is to declare independence from Great Britain.

43. Choice **A** is correct. This quote offers proof that the main goal of the passage is "to explain the reasons for establishing a new government," which is another way of saying, "they should declare the causes which impel them to the separation." It operates as a thesis while the other quotes offer evidence and declarations that support this thesis.

44. Choice **B** is correct. *Transient* means "fleeting" or "temporary." A fleeting issue is not likely to result in the overthrow of a "long established" government because the government has endured a long time, whereas the issue will go away quickly.

45. Choice **C** is correct. Kennedy addresses the world as a new commander-in-chief, so it is likely he would strike a commanding tone.

46. Choice **C** is correct. Kennedy states, "Let every nation know, whether it wishes us well or ill, that we shall pay any price, bear any burden, meet any hardship, support any friend, oppose any foe to assure the survival and the success of liberty." This quote demonstrates how highly Kennedy values liberty in his inaugural address.

47. Choice **C** is correct. *Colonial* refers to a colony, generally a territory beholden to a ruling power of a far-off country. In context, "colonial control" is compared to an "iron tyranny"—one being a more harsh form of the other. Considering the root words—*dictator* or *tyrant*—*dictatorial* is the closest in meaning.

48. Choice **A** is correct. In the context of the passage, Kennedy addresses nations that have newly become free of colonial control. It is a warning not to forget what tyranny can do. To paraphrase the metaphor, those who go along for the ride, allying themselves with the powerful, may be devoured by that power.

49. Choice **B** is correct. In the second paragraph, Kennedy discusses a major difference in the world from the time of the revolution, specifically citing man's ability to abolish "all forms of poverty and all forms of human life."

50. Choice **A** is correct. This quote specifically states, "The world is very different now," which introduces the information that answers the preceding question.

51. Choice **A** is correct. Kennedy's inaugural address appears to reference the "Declaration of Independence" directly. He also states, "We dare not forget today that we are the heirs of that first revolution."

52. Choice **A** is correct. The basic nature of an inaugural address is one in which a new president takes the reins of his government. The basic nature of the "Declaration of Independence" was to throw off the power of the British government. Both passages assert their own power in two very different contexts.

Writing and Language Test

1. Choice **B** is correct. The rest of the passage is informative but not so casual, so this option provides the best and smoothest opening sentence.

2. Choice **D** is correct. Try to avoid starting sentences with a coordinating conjunction (*and, but, for, nor, or, so, yet*) in formal writing.

3. Choice **C** is correct. You should be looking for an adjective to describe the names, whereas the underlined *women* is a noun.

4. Choice **D** is correct. The descriptive clause "one name per year for each letter of the alphabet" needs to be set off as separate from the list it describes, and a parenthetical clause is a good way to do that.

5. Choice **A** is correct. This phrase correctly shows the future tense and ensures that the pronoun (*it*) agrees with the verb.

6. Choice **B** is correct. This paragraph gives background on why the weather services would need names, so it would be logical to place it before the specific details about the process for naming storms.

7. Choice **C** is correct. Both verbs should be infinitive and parallel.

8. Choice **D** is correct. "West coast" is used as an adjective phrase and is not a proper noun here, so it should not be capitalized. *United States* is a proper noun because it's a country, and should be capitalized.

9. Choice **A** is correct. The writer is trying to convey how and why the weather scientists had experienced challenges in the past, so using *previously* tells the reader that the events happened before.

10. Choice **D** is correct. The phrase "having recognized these challenges" is a dependent clause because it's incomplete—the reader does not know yet who recognized the challenges. The next part of the sentence should tell you the subject, and fill in that blank. In this case, "the decision" is not accurate, so choice D fixes the dangling modifier and provides the reader with the correct subject of the sentence.

11. Choice **B** is correct. The passage discusses how the process came to be in the 1950s and how it has changed up until the current day.

12. Choice **C** is correct. This sentence clarifies that the writer is talking about how bicyclists used to be perceived. Also, there is no indication that the writer is talking about himself, so *they* is a better pronoun choice.

13. Choice **D** is correct. The past perfect verb (in this case a variation on *to have*) should agree with the plural noun *programs*.

14. Choice **B** is correct. In the next sentence, the writer mentions how the number of bike sharing programs has grown.

15. Choice **C** is correct. Providing some actual numbers would show the reader how popular bike sharing programs have become in various parts of the world.

16. Choice **A** is correct. This gives the reader an example of different cities that have successfully created bike sharing programs, while contrasting the two. The writer could also add additional details about Miami and San Francisco's programs to further illustrate the point.

17. Choice **B** is correct. The verbs should be parallel and agree with the plural noun *bicyclists*, so *use* and *create* are the right choices here.

18. Choice **D** is correct. *Significantly* and *considerably* both mean "to a large extent," so keeping both in the sentence is redundant.

19. Choice **C** is correct. These points are negative and do not fit with the writer's argument that cities should adopt bike sharing programs. He is offering a counterargument, which in this case weakens the main point of the passage.

20. Choice **B** is correct. The punctuation is correct, but *car*, *bus*, and *train* are common nouns and should not be capitalized.

21. Choice **C** is correct. The writer is talking about steps in a process. *Then* conveys the next step in a process, while *than* is a word that compares one thing with the next.

22. Choice **A** is correct. This sentence includes and summarizes the writer's overall point about bike sharing programs' offering more to cities and riders than previously thought.

23. Choice **C** is correct. "In the New York Times in 1992" is not an independent clause and it's not prompting a list of items to follow, so the punctuation here should be a comma.

24. Choice **D** is correct. The quotation marks indicate that this is a response to the question asked, but it's not a full sentence or thought, so it does not need to be capitalized.

25. Choice **D** is correct. Single items in a list should be separated by commas, with the final list item preceded by *and*. "At all" is not part of the list, but rather an additional clause that modifies *shortage*.

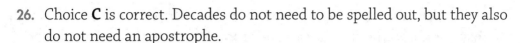

26. Choice **C** is correct. Decades do not need to be spelled out, but they also do not need an apostrophe.

27. Choice **A** is correct. The phrase "format it" is vague, so the writer could improve the paragraph by fleshing out what desktop publishers did day-to-day and providing more detail on how they formatted files.

28. Choice **B** is correct. This indicates where the statistics are coming from and helps explain why desktop publishers' skills are becoming less relevant.

29. Choice **C** is correct. The writer is trying to say that the desktop publisher alone is less in demand, so *specific* is the only one of the choices that supports that context.

30. Choice **B** is correct. If you look at the progression of the sales over the years of the graph, you can see that the sales have clearly increased from about 7 percent to about 27 percent between 2004 and 2014.

31. Choice **D** is correct. The easiest way to avoid a run-on sentence in this case is to split up the two ideas and contain the example in its own sentence.

32. Choice **A** is correct. The first sentence acts as an introductory clause for the second sentence, so you can join them using a colon.

33. Choice **A** is correct. *Imminent* means "immediate," and the writer is discussing the current state of publishing.

34. Choice **A** is correct. This sentence tells the reader nothing about the narrative that will follow, and it does not give any context for what an "unlikely" source is, or what a "strong" voice is. It would be best to remove it from the narrative.

35. Choice **C** is correct. The writer should clarify that Malala's father is both a school owner and an education activist by setting it off as a clause.

36. Choice **B** is correct. The word *future* tells you that the sentence is looking ahead, so the verb *to be* should be in the future tense.

37. Choice **A** is correct. This provides additional information to a reader who may not know who the Taliban are. From the rest of the paragraph, the reader already knows that they are in Pakistan, approximately when this was taking place, and that the Taliban held political control at the time.

38. Choice **B** is correct. This is presented as a direct quote, so the only formatting necessary is to add quotation marks around the sentence.

39. Choice **A** is correct. Earlier in the passage, the writer referred to the limitations as "drastic," and has also described the extreme nature of the bans.

40. Choice **D** is correct. The underlined text is missing content that clarifies how Malala was in danger.

41. Choice **C** is correct. This narrative follows Malala on a timeline, and "after her recovery" lets the reader know when Malala resumed her activism.

42. Choice **D** is correct. The infinitive "to establish" is correct, and changing "for outlawing" makes the two clauses parallel.

43. Choice **B** is correct. The writer is describing events that had already happened, which means that the writer should use past tense to describe the awards and support in comparison to the award that came next (the Nobel Prize).

44. Choice **A** is correct. By including other famous Nobel winners, the writer helps put Malala in the context of other advocates for global change.

Math Test—No Calculator

1. **D**

   The measure of the inscribed angle y is half the measure of the arc it intercepts. Therefore, $4x - 3 = \dfrac{y}{2}$. Adding 3 to both sides and then dividing both sides by 4 yields $x = \dfrac{y}{8} + \dfrac{3}{4} = \dfrac{y+6}{8}$.

2. **B**

   Applying the rules of exponents: $z = \dfrac{(8x^{-2}y)^{-1}}{y^2} = \dfrac{1}{y^2(8x^{-2}y)} = \dfrac{x^2}{8y^3}$.

   Thus, $\sqrt[3]{z} = \sqrt[3]{\dfrac{x^2}{8y^3}} = \dfrac{\sqrt[3]{x^2}}{\sqrt[3]{8y^3}} = \dfrac{\sqrt[3]{x^2}}{2y}$.

3. **A**

   The area of the rectangle is $A = w(2w - 3) = 2w^2 - 3w$, while the perimeter is $P = 2w + 2(2w - 3) = 2w + 4w - 6 = 6w - 6$. Thus, $A - P = 2w^2 - 3w - (6w - 6) = 2w^2 - 9w + 6$.

4. **C**

   Setting the two equations equal results in $3x = x^2 + 1$ or $0 = x^2 - 3x + 1$. Using the quadratic formula, $x = \dfrac{3 \pm \sqrt{9 - 4(1)(1)}}{2} = \dfrac{3 \pm \sqrt{5}}{2}$. This shows that there are two x-values that make this equation true, meaning the graphs cross at two points.

5. **B**

   Each of her x friends and y acquaintances donated A dollars. This gives a total of $Ax + Ay$ or $A(x + y)$ donated. This must be at least 500, so $A(x + y) \geq 500$.

6. **C**

$2x^2 - 5x - 3 = (2x + 1)(x - 3)$, which has roots $-\dfrac{1}{2}$ and 3. Since $x - 1$ accounts for the root of 1 (x-intercept of $(1, 0)$), it must be that $4a = 3$ or $a = \dfrac{3}{4}$.

7. **A**

In the denominator of the fraction, we find $14h - y$. This is the amount of money she earns after h hours, minus her expenses. The amount she wants to save, D, is divided by this amount. Therefore, x must be the number of hours she would have to work to save enough for the vehicle, after considering expenses.

8. **C**

Multiplying the first equation by -3 and adding it to the second results in the equation $-13y = -\dfrac{39}{4}$, which means $y = \dfrac{3}{4}$. Thus, $\dfrac{1}{2}y = \dfrac{3}{8}$.

9. **A**

The line after the described transformations will have the equation $y = -\dfrac{3}{4}(x + 3) + 4 = -\dfrac{3}{4}x - \dfrac{9}{4} + 4 = -\dfrac{3}{4}x + \dfrac{7}{4}$. Setting this equal to 8 and solving for x gives $x = -\dfrac{25}{3}$.

10. **D**

In the second quadrant, values of y are positive and values of x are negative. The center of the circle defined by $(x + 4)^2 + (y - 5)^2 = 16$ is at $(-4, 5)$ which satisfies these requirements.

11. **B**

Multiplying both sides of the equation by 4 yields $2ax + 8 = 20$. Thus $2ax = 20 - 8 = 12$.

12. **A**

Squaring both sides of the equation yields $3x + 4 = 4x^2 - 16x + 16$ or $0 = 4x^2 - 19x + 12$. Since $4x^2 - 19x + 12 = (4x - 3)(x - 4)$, this equation has solutions $x = \dfrac{3}{4}$ and $x = 4$. However, the first solution is extraneous.

13. **A**

$$f(k + 1) = 2(k + 1)^2 - 4(k + 1) + 1 = 2(k^2 + 2k + 1) - 4k - 4 + 1$$
$$= 2k^2 + 4k + 2 - 4k - 3 = 2k^2 - 1$$

14. **C**

Given the information, we can determine that increasing x by 1 unit increases y by 4 units. This means the slope of the line is 4. Solving each equation for y, only the equation in choice C represents a line with slope 4.

15. **B**

$$\frac{\pi}{4}\left(\frac{180°}{\pi}\right) = 45°$$

16. **2**

If $m = 8$, then $16 - 5n < 7$, which is equivalent to $-5n < -9$ or $n > \dfrac{9}{5}$.

Since $\dfrac{9}{5} < \dfrac{10}{5} = 2$ and n is a whole number, the minimum value of n is 2.

17. $\dfrac{16}{3}$

To have infinite solutions, the two equations must be multiples. To get the second equation from the first, the 3 in $3x$ must be multiplied by something to get 2. Let this value be a. Then $3a = 2$, so $a = \dfrac{2}{3}$. Multiplying 8 by this value gives $k = \dfrac{16}{3}$.

18. 3

Using the quadratic formula,

$$x = \frac{4 \pm \sqrt{16 - 4(1)(-23)}}{2} = \frac{4 \pm \sqrt{108}}{2} = \frac{4 \pm 6\sqrt{3}}{2} = 2 \pm 3\sqrt{3}$$

19. 11

Long division shows that the remainder here is -11, so $r = 11$.

20. 1

Multiplying both sides of the equation by $2x$ yields $2 + 1 = 3x$. Thus, $x = 1$.

Math Test–Calculator

1. B

Let x represent the number of students who have taken Spanish before, and let y represent the number who haven't. We know that $x + y = 32$ and $\dfrac{x}{y} = \dfrac{3}{5}$ or $5x = 3y$. Solving for x, $x = \dfrac{3}{5}y$ so $\dfrac{3}{5}y + y = 32$. Solving this for y, $y = 20$. Since the total is 32, $x = 12$ and the difference is 8.

2. A

Slicing along this diagonal will result in a prism with exactly half the volume of the original. The original prism has a volume of $6(6)(4) = 144$ cubic centimeters. Half of this is 72.

3. C

If the shop sells x hats each month, then its revenue will be $18x$ and the cost will be $10x + 6500$. Thus, the profit will be $18x - (10x + 6500) = 8x - 6500$.

4. D

Linear growth will be represented by y values that increase by the same amount (adding), while exponential growth will show an increase in y values by the same multiple. This can be seen in the last table.

5. C

For all values in this range, the graph is above the x-axis.

6. B

If you test values in the formula, you will see that each time, you are multiplying by 0.98 one or more times. You can think of this as the value being multiplied keeping only 98% of its value each time.

7. D

Multiplying both sides of the equation by 5 yields $-2x - 10 = 15$. Thus, $-2x = 25$.

8. D

Solving the first inequality for y: $3y \geq 3 + 2x \Rightarrow y \geq 1 + \dfrac{2}{3}x$. This is a region above a line with positive slope that goes through the point $(0, 1)$. Furthermore, the region $x > 5$ is all of the xy-plane to the right of $x = 5$. Thus, the overlap of the two regions, which is the solution set, will be in the first quadrant.

9. D

$$2(1 - 3i) - (4 + 2i) = 2 - 6i - 4 - 2i = -2 - 8i$$

10. C

Points as described are those below the line of best fit.

11. C

In general, when the slope is written in this form, it is interpreted as the change in y for a one-unit increase in x.

12. **C**

A higher standard deviation generally means higher variability (as long as the means are reasonably close).

13. **D**

If the value of z increases by 2 units whenever the value of w increases 4 units, then the equation relating them is linear with slope $\dfrac{2}{4} = \dfrac{1}{2}$. This means $z = \dfrac{1}{2}w + b$ for some number b. Using the fact that when $w = 2$,

$z = \dfrac{7}{4} : \dfrac{7}{4} = \dfrac{1}{2}(2) + b$ so $b = \dfrac{7}{4} - 1 = \dfrac{3}{4}$. The equation $z = \dfrac{1}{2}w + \dfrac{3}{4}$ is equivalent to $4z = 2w + 3$ or $4z - 2w = 3$.

14. **B**

Only this equation is in $y = mx + b$ form.

15. **C**

There are 14 days in two weeks, so in the first two weeks a total of $14x$ entries are received. Add 23 more and you have $14x + 23$.

16. **A**

For Szymon, $\dfrac{5 \text{ problems}}{15 \text{ mins}} \left(\dfrac{60 \text{ mins}}{1 \text{ hour}} \right) = \dfrac{20 \text{ problems}}{1 \text{ hour}}$, so he can do 20 problems in 1 hour. For Christine, $\dfrac{8 \text{ problems}}{40 \text{ mins}} \left(\dfrac{60 \text{ mins}}{1 \text{ hour}} \right) = \dfrac{12 \text{ problems}}{1 \text{ hour}}$, so she can do 12 problems in 1 hour. The ratio 20:12 is equivalent to 5:3.

17. **D**

Using FOIL:
$$(x + x^2)\left(x - \frac{1}{x}\right) = x^2 - x\left(\frac{1}{x}\right) + x^3 - x^2\left(\frac{1}{x}\right)$$
$$= x^2 - 1 + x^3 - x = x^3 + x^2 - x - 1$$

18. **A**

Finding the totals for each of the columns shows that the greatest total is from the second column.

19. **D**

The total number of units rented for one year or more is $72 + 68 + 64 = 204$. Of these, 68 were $10' \times 10'$, so the percentage is $\frac{68}{204} \times 100\% \approx 33.3\%$.

20. **B**

Multiplying both sides of the equation by $R_T R_1 R_2$ gives $R_1 R_2 = R_T R_2 + R_1 R_T$. Collecting like terms and factoring out the variable of interest yields $R_1(R_2 - R_T) = R_T R_2$. Finally, dividing gives $R_1 = \frac{R_T R_2}{R_2 - R_T}$.

21. **D**

We can write that $m = 0.08n$ and $n = 3.15p$. Substituting, $m = 0.08(3.15p) = 0.252p$, meaning m is 25.2% of p. But the question asks "What percentage of m is p?" Solving for p, $p = \frac{1}{0.252}m \approx 3.968m$. Thus, p is 396.8% of m.

22. **B**

To be valid, the sample must be from the population of interest. Further, specifically selecting those who have had disagreements through the websites would not let the psychologist determine the percentage he is interested in.

23. **A**

$$f\left(\frac{1}{2}x\right) = \frac{2}{3}\left(\frac{1}{2}x\right) + b,$$ so the y-intercept is unchanged.

24. **A**

Since we know for sure that 3 people will be there besides the guests, we know that at most, the number of other people attending can be $85 - 3 = 82$. Since each guest will bring one person, there will be a total $2m$ additional people. Therefore, $2m \leq 82$ or $m \leq 41$.

25. **B**

The value of k is not dependent on s, so it must be the fixed portion of the bonus.

26. **A**

Let x be the initial number considered. Using the given information, $0.42x + 4 = 67$, or $x = 150$.

27. **D**

Since $\dfrac{x}{4} + k = \dfrac{1}{4}(x + 3) + 1$ is equivalent to $\dfrac{x}{4} + k = \dfrac{1}{4}x + \dfrac{3}{4} + 1$ or $\dfrac{x}{4} + k = \dfrac{1}{4}x + \dfrac{7}{4}$, it must be that $k = \dfrac{7}{4}$ as that would be the only way that both sides of the equation will be identical.

28. **B**

If $s = -1$, then $-r - 2 = -(r + 2) \geq \dfrac{1}{2} - 1 = -\dfrac{1}{2}$. That is, $r + 2 \leq \dfrac{1}{2}$.

Multiplying both sides by 2, $2r + 4 \leq 1$.

29. **C**

Adding and subtracting the margin of error gives the reasonable range of values for the true mean. Since $19.7 + 8 = 27.7$, it is reasonable that the true mean is greater than 25. This means the reporter may be incorrect.

30. **B**

The graph has x-intercepts -1 and 3, giving linear factors $(x + 1)$ and $(x - 3)$.

31. **1.9**

Using the formula for the volume of a sphere $V = \frac{4}{3}\pi r^3$, $28 = \frac{4}{3}\pi r^3$.

Therefore, $r^3 = 28\left(\dfrac{3}{4\pi}\right) \approx 6.6845$ and $r \approx \sqrt[3]{6.6845} = 1.88$.

32. **43.2**

The depth is equivalent to 12 fathoms $\left(\dfrac{1.8 \text{ meters}}{1 \text{ fathom}}\right) = 21.6$ meters.

At the given rate, the time to get to this depth would be

21.6 meters $\left(\dfrac{1 \text{ second}}{\frac{1}{2} \text{ meter}}\right) = 43.2$ seconds.

33. **12**

$\dfrac{x + 5 + 1 + 5 + 9}{5} = 6.4$ is equivalent to $\dfrac{x + 20}{5} = 6.4$ or $x + 20 = 32$,

so $x = 12$.

34. **$3.15**

Let the lower-priced item be x and the higher-priced item be y. We know that $1.07(x + y) = 8.61$ and that $1.07y = 5.24$. Solving for y, y is approximately 4.90. Substituting into the original equation: $1.07(x + 4.90) = 8.61$. Solving for x, x is approximately equal to 3.15.

35. **−1**

The described function is $f(x) = (x - 1)(x - 3) = x^2 - 4x + 3$ and $f(2) = 2^2 - 4(2) + 3 = 4 - 8 + 3 = -1$.

36. **2**

    The graph of $p(x - 2)$ will be the same graph shifted to the right 2 units. Since the y-intercept of $p(x)$ is 20, shifting the graph to the right 2 units will place the point $(0, 20)$ at $(2, 20)$ so the solution will be $x = 2$.

37. **2**

    Values of a for which this is true will be where the graph crosses or touches the x-axis. The greatest such value is 2.

38. **4.1**

    If 1 mile is about 1.6 kilometers, then 1 square mile is about $1.6 \times 1.6 = 2.56$ square kilometers. Therefore, New York City's density can be written as $\dfrac{27012 \text{ people}}{2.56 \text{ sq km}} = \dfrac{10551.5625 \text{ people}}{1 \text{ sq km}}$. Thus, Manila is about $42857 \div 10551.5625 \approx 4.06$ times as dense as New York City.

EXERCISE ANSWER KEY

Answer Key

1

Reading for Information and Ideas

EXERCISE 1–1

1. B
2. A

EXERCISE 1–2

1. C
2. D
3. B

EXERCISE 1–3

1. D
2. B

EXERCISE 1–4

1. C
2. B
3. A
4. D

EXERCISE 1–5

1. **A**
2. **D**

EXERCISE 1–6

1. **C**
2. **B**

EXERCISE 1–7

1. **B**
2. **C**
3. **A**

EXERCISE 1–8

1. **D**
2. **C**
3. **D**
4. **B**

Reading for Rhetoric

EXERCISE 2–1

1. **D**
2. **B**
3. **B**

EXERCISE 2–2

1. A
2. C
3. D
4. B
5. A

EXERCISE 2–3

1. D
2. A

EXERCISE 2–4

1. C
2. D
3. C

EXERCISE 2–5

1. D
2. A
3. D

EXERCISE 2–6

1. C
2. A
3. B

EXERCISE 2–7

1. B
2. A
3. C

Reading for Synthesis

EXERCISE 3–1

1. D
2. B
3. D
4. C
5. B
6. A
7. B
8. A
9. C
10. D
11. C
12. A
13. B

EXERCISE 3–2

1. A
2. B
3. D
4. A
5. C
6. D
7. B

Writing: Standard English Conventions

EXERCISE 4–1

1. C
2. D
3. D
4. D
5. A
6. C
7. B
8. A
9. D
10. D
11. B
12. C

EXERCISE 4–2

1. D
2. C
3. D
4. A
5. C
6. A

EXERCISE 4–3

1. B
2. A
3. B
4. A

EXERCISE 4–4

1. A
2. D
3. C
4. A
5. B
6. B

EXERCISE 4–5

1. B
2. A
3. C

4. C

5. A

6. D

7. D

8. C

EXERCISE 4–6

1. C

2. A

3. D

4. B

EXERCISE 4–7

1. A

2. B

3. C

4. B

5. D

Writing: Expression of Ideas

EXERCISE 5–1

1. C

2. D

3. D

4. A

5. C

6. A

7. D

8. B

9. C

EXERCISE 5-2

1. C

2. A

3. A

4. C

5. B

EXERCISE 5-3

1. B

2. C

3. D

4. D

5. A

6. C

7. B

8. A

9. B

10. C

11. A

12. D

Working with Expressions

EXERCISE 6-1

1. $8x^8y^8$

2. $\dfrac{2n}{m}$

3. $-\dfrac{x^3}{y}$

4. $\dfrac{y^3}{8x^2}$

5. $\dfrac{3y^2}{x^4}$

EXERCISE 6-2

1. $8x^5y$

2. $3x^2y^2\sqrt[3]{2xy^2}$

3. $\dfrac{x^3}{4}\sqrt{\dfrac{6}{y}}$

4. $\dfrac{1}{2x\sqrt[3]{2x^2y^2z}}$

5. $2\sqrt{\dfrac{6x}{y}}$

EXERCISE 6-3

1. $x^2 - 4$

2. $-2^4 + x^2 - 3x - 7$

3. $4x^3 - 2x^2 + 2x$

4. $2x^2 + 14x - 10$

5. $x^5 + x^4 - x^3 - 6$

EXERCISE 6-4

1. $x^2 + 7x - 18$

2. $3x^2 - 21x + 30$

3. $\dfrac{1}{4}x^2 + \dfrac{1}{2}x - 12$

4. $-10x^4 + 18x^2 + 4$

5. $3x^4 + 2x^3 - x^2$

EXERCISE 6-5

1. $2x^3 - 9x^2 - 7x + 10$

2. $3x^3 + 5x^2 + 5x + 2$

3. $-3x^4 + 14x^3 - 9x^2 + 14x + 4$

4. $x^4 + 10x^3 + 25x^2 - 1$

5. $-8x^4 + 18x^3 - 47x^2 + 36x - 35$

EXERCISE 6-6

1. $\dfrac{4}{3}x^3 - x + \dfrac{1}{3}$

2. $-\dfrac{1}{2}x^2 + \dfrac{3}{2}x - 2$

3. $3x - 1$

4. $x - 1 + \dfrac{3}{2x + 1}$

5. $4x^2 + 3x + 4 + \dfrac{3}{x - 1}$

EXERCISE 6–7

1. $\dfrac{2x^2 - 3}{x^4}$

2. $\dfrac{13x + 7}{x^2 + 3x - 4}$

3. $\dfrac{x^2 + x + 1}{x^2 + x}$

4. $\dfrac{-x^2 - 12x + 5}{(x - 3)(x + 2)^2}$

5. $\dfrac{3x^2 + 7x}{x^2 - 4}$

EXERCISE 6–8

1. $\dfrac{4}{x^2 - x - 6}$

2. $\dfrac{5x - 15}{x + 3}$

3. $\dfrac{x^2 - 6x + 5}{x + 5}$

4. $\dfrac{3x}{x + 5}$

5. $20x + 4$

EXERCISE 6–9

1. $\dfrac{1}{x^2 + 4x + 4}$

2. $\dfrac{x^2 + 5x + 6}{2x^3}$

3. $x^3 - 5x^2 - 9x + 45$

4. $\dfrac{6}{5}$

5. $\dfrac{14x + 7}{9x + 54}$

Solving Equations and Inequalities

EXERCISE 7–1

1. $x = \dfrac{1}{4}$

2. $x = -\dfrac{3}{5}$

3. $x = 1$

4. $x = \dfrac{2}{5}$

5. $x = 36$

EXERCISE 7–2

1. infinitely many solutions
2. no solution
3. no solution
4. $a = -2$
5. $a = 4$

EXERCISE 7–3

1. $m = 2 - \dfrac{n}{2}$

2. $a = \dfrac{-x - 3}{2}$

3. $y = \dfrac{9}{2} - x$

4. $h = \dfrac{V}{\ell W}$

5. $b = \dfrac{2A}{h}$

EXERCISE 7–4

1. $x > 3$

2. $x \geq -\dfrac{19}{7}$

3. $x > \dfrac{6}{5}$

4. $x \geq -\dfrac{11}{4}$

5. $x < \dfrac{4}{7}$

EXERCISE 7–5

1. $n = \dfrac{3m + 2}{4}$

2. $m \geq 2800$

3. $h = \dfrac{8000}{x}$

4. 15 pounds

5. $s \leq \dfrac{b}{2}$

EXERCISE 7–6

1. $x = \dfrac{1}{2}$ and $y = 4$

2. $x = 0$ and $y = 2$

3. $x = -3$ and $y = 7$

4. $x = 2$ and $y = 4$

5. $x = -1$ and $y = \dfrac{1}{4}$

EXERCISE 7–7

1. no solution

2. infinitely many solutions

3. infinitely many solutions

4. $a = -\dfrac{1}{4}$

5. $a = \dfrac{21}{2}$

EXERCISE 7–8

1. $x = \pm 3\sqrt{5}$
2. $x = \pm 1$
3. $x = \pm \dfrac{1}{\sqrt{2}}$
4. $x = 1 \pm \sqrt{3}$
5. $x = -7, -3$

EXERCISE 7–9

1. $x = -2, 1$
2. $x = -5, -4$
3. $x = 3$
4. $x = -4, \dfrac{9}{2}$
5. $x = -\dfrac{4}{3}, -\dfrac{1}{3}$

EXERCISE 7–10

1. $x = 1 \pm 3\sqrt{2}$
2. $x = 3 \pm \sqrt{2}$
3. $x = \dfrac{2 \pm \sqrt{5}}{3}$
4. $x = \dfrac{1 \pm \sqrt{3}}{2}$
5. $x = \dfrac{5 \pm 4\sqrt{2}}{2}$

EXERCISE 7-11

1. $x = 150$
2. $x = 12$
3. $x = -1$
4. $x = -\dfrac{7}{5}$
5. $x = \dfrac{1}{128}$

EXERCISE 7-12

1. $x = \dfrac{4}{15}$
2. $x = 2$
3. $x = 13$
4. $x = \dfrac{1}{2}$
5. $x = -1, \dfrac{1}{3}$

8

Functions and Graphs

EXERCISE 8-1

1. 9
2. $-\dfrac{3}{17}$
3. $12x^2 - 8x + 2$

4. $\dfrac{x-4}{x+3}$

5. $-\dfrac{x}{2} + \dfrac{x^2}{4}$

EXERCISE 8–2

1. slope: $-\dfrac{3}{5}$

   x-int: $-\dfrac{1}{3}$

   y-int: $-\dfrac{1}{5}$

2. slope: $\dfrac{1}{2}$

   x-int: -3

   y-int: $\dfrac{3}{2}$

3. $y = 3x + 3$

4. $y = -\dfrac{1}{2}x + \dfrac{5}{2}$

5. $y = 2x + 2$

EXERCISE 8–3

1. $\dfrac{15}{8}$

2. none

3. $(0, 1)$

4. $(-4, 0)$ and $\left(\dfrac{1}{2}, 0\right)$

5. $(-2, 0)$

EXERCISE 8–4

1. $x = 1, x = 0$, or $x = -4$
2. $-\dfrac{3}{2}$
3. $(x + 3)(x - 1)(x - 3)$
4. $(0, -6)$
5. $(x - 3)(x - 1)(x + 2)$

EXERCISE 8–5

1. $-\dfrac{7}{3}$
2. -4 and 4
3. $f(x) + 5$ has no real zeros; $f(x + 5)$ has two real zeros
4. $p(x - 4)$ is increasing for all values of $x < 3$, $4 < x < 5$, and $x > 6$
5. -7 and -1

EXERCISE 8–6

1. $\left(\dfrac{1}{2}, 1\right)$
2. $(3, 9)$ and $(-1, 1)$
3. $\left(\dfrac{23}{17}, \dfrac{26}{17}\right)$
4. They never intersect./They are parallel.
5. three

EXERCISE 8–7

1.

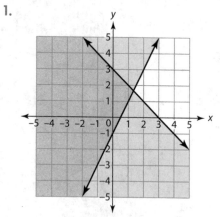

2.

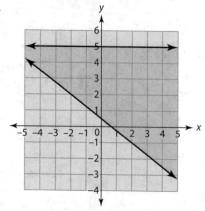

3.

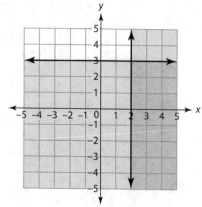

4.

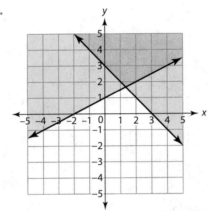

5.

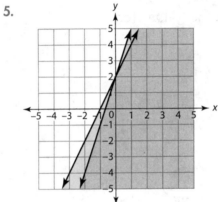

Ratios, Rates, Proportions, and Percentages

EXERCISE 9–1

1. Six are red

2. 3:5

3. 431:312

4. $\frac{1}{2}$ cup of sugar and $1\frac{1}{2}$ cups of flour

5. 4:9

EXERCISE 9–2

1. 9.1 minutes

2. $0.21

3. 270 min

4. Store A has the better deal at $0.33 per apple.

5. Noah ran faster at a rate of 4.66 minutes per kilometer.

EXERCISE 9–3

1. 3 eggs

2. 102 bricks

3. 20.32 centimeters

4. $x = 2$

5. The width is $5\frac{1}{3}$ inches, so the perimeter is $26\frac{2}{3}$ inches.

EXERCISE 9–4

1. $x = \dfrac{37}{3}$

2. $15.12

3. 14.3%

4. $(1.06)^3 = x$

5. $k = 75.6$

10
Statistics

EXERCISE 10–1

1. mean: 57.375; median: 59; mode: 60

2. $x = 6$

3. 170 lbs.

4. 25

5. 15

EXERCISE 10–2

1. The median will be the average of the 29th and 30th entry, so it will be greater than 200.

2. 7

3. the second class's scores

EXERCISE 10–3

1. about 21°F

2. negative linear

3. about $19–$20

4. three

5. Larger homes will have overall higher costs regardless of the temperature; only homes of one particular type should be studied at one time.

EXERCISE 10-4

1. three

2. about 5,000

3. For each additional customer that checks in during a shift, the total amount of tips the employee receives increases by about $2.51.

4. If no customers check in during an employee's shift, the predicted total amount of tips is about $0.86. This doesn't quite make sense in the situation since tips are from customers.

5. $13.42

EXERCISE 10-5

1. C

2. The range would be from 6,360 − 5,640, which is 720.

Additional Topics

EXERCISE 11-1

1. $x = 20$

2. $x = \dfrac{72 + k}{2}$

3. 32.7°, 49.1°, 98.2°

4. $x = 130$

5. $y = 25$

EXERCISE 11–2

1. $\sqrt{29}$

2. $6\sqrt{2}$

3. $m = \sqrt{100 - n^2}$

4. $\sin x = \dfrac{12}{13}$ $\cos x = \dfrac{5}{13}$ $\tan x = \dfrac{12}{5}$

   $\csc x = \dfrac{13}{12}$ $\sec x = \dfrac{13}{5}$ $\cot x = \dfrac{5}{12}$

5. $\cos B = \dfrac{4}{5}$

EXERCISE 11–3

1. $\dfrac{16\pi}{9}$ rad

2. $15°$

3. $x = \dfrac{5\pi}{18}$

4. negative

5. $x = \dfrac{\pi}{2}$ and $y = \pi$

EXERCISE 11–4

1. 3π

2. 6π

3. $x = 67.5$

4. $y = 33.25$

5. $y = \dfrac{x - 1}{2}$

EXERCISE 11–5

1. center: $(5, 2)$; radius: $3\sqrt{2}$
2. center $(0, -3)$; radius: $\sqrt{10}$
3. $x^2 - 4x + y^2 - 8y + 14 = 0$
4. center $(-1, -5)$; radius: $2\sqrt{2}$
5. center $(2, 1)$; radius 1

EXERCISE 11–6

1. $2 + 6i$
2. $2 - 4i$
3. 1
4. $-1 + 3i$
5. $7i$
6. 5
7. $32 + 16i$
8. $3i$
9. $2 - i$
10. $-\dfrac{1}{5} - \dfrac{3}{5}i$

NOTES

NOTES

NOTES

NOTES

NOTES

NOTES

NOTES

NOTES

NOTES

NOTES